THE LEGEND OF ZELDA

Phantom Hourglass

Prima Official Game Guide

Written by:
Stephen Stratton
Fletcher Black

Prima Games
A Division of Random House, Inc.
3000 Lava Ridge Court, Suite 100
Roseville, CA 95661
www.primagames.com

Product Manager: Mario De Govia
Editor: Brooke N. Hall
Manufacturing: Suzanne Goodwin
Design & Layout: Calibre Grafix

TM & © 2007 Nintendo. All Rights Reserved.

Acknowledgements:

Steve would like to thank all the good people at Nintendo for their incredible help and support, without which this guide would not have been possible: Damon Baker, Seth McMahill, Yugo Sato, Michael Leslie, Brian Van Buren, Tim Vodder, and Angel Lopez. Thanks also to the Prima wonder crew for keeping me on task throughout this project: Mario De Govia, Brooke Hall, and Sara Wilson. Big ups to Calibre Grafix for working its uncanny design magic, and of course, to my fellow esteemed author, Mr. Fletcher Black, for all his tireless efforts (and for listening to my near-tireless ranting). Extra special thanks to my best girl Julie for sticking beside me through another crazy Zelda project. I love you, babykins!

Important:

ISBN: 978-0-7615-5647-3
Library of Congress Catalog Card Number: 2007
Printed in the United States of America

07 08 09 10 LL 10 9 8 7 6 5 4 3 2 1

Author Bios

Stephen Stratton has worked on more than 30 projects in his five years of writing strategy guides for Prima. His repertoire of mastered games includes *Counter-Strike: Condition Zero*, *Rome: Total War*, *Mercenaries: Playground of Destruction*, *The Legend of Zelda: The Wind Waker*, *Super Mario Sunshine*, *Hitman: Contracts*, and *Splinter Cell: Chaos Theory*.

Steve is a lifelong video gamer who attended the Rochester Institute of Technology in Rochester, NY. In addition to his Prima Games guides, he also held a staff position with Computec Media and managed the strategy section of their incite.com video game website.

We want to hear from you! E-mail comments and feedback to sstratton@primagames.com.

Fletcher Black has been playing video games since his parents first set an Atari 2600 down on the orange shag carpet of their suburban paradise. While peers declared their desire to be firefighters or astronauts, Fletcher set his sights on all things pixilated. Similarly, Fletcher earned a journalism degree from the University of Oregon, but while the other students wanted to expose political corruption or corporate scandal, Fletcher sought to reveal greater truths, such as how to beat Bowser, find all the pieces of the Tri-Force, and collect every single Pokémon. When not waist-deep in a video game, Fletcher enjoys writing, movies, travel, and shepherding his animal army. His Prima guides include *FEAR*, *Perfect Dark Zero*, *Ghost Recon Advanced Warfighter*, and *Heroes of Might and Magic V*.

We want to hear from you! E-mail comments and feedback to fblack@primagames.com.

Contents

Introduction

The Legends of Zelda

The Legend of Zelda,
1987 (NES)

Many consider the original *Legend of Zelda*, released for the 8-bit Nintendo Entertainment System in July 1987, to be the title that took videogames to a new level. It was the first non-linear adventure game, meaning that gamers weren't led by the nose to the next objective. They could spend hours exploring the Overworld if they wanted to, and continually discover new and unexpected things.

The *Legend of Zelda* established most of the major game elements that have since appeared in every *Zelda* game to date. It featured Link, the boy hero dressed in green; Zelda, the imperiled Princess of Hyrule; and Ganon, the monstrous archenemy who tried to bring darkness to Hyrule. Link's main objective was to assemble the eight shards of Zelda's Triforce of Wisdom and defeat Ganon in his Death Mountain liar.

Best of all, when you finished the game, you could play through a wholly different second version, in which the placement of the dungeons had been switched around. You could also jump straight into the second version of the quest by entering "ZELDA" as your name.

The Adventure of Link,
1988 (NES)

The only *Legend of Zelda* game not to have the word "Zelda" in the title, *The Adventure of Link* was a dramatic departure from the original game. Although there was a top-down Overworld perspective in the game, most of the action took place in a side-scrolling platform perspective.

Many of the original game's elements were retained for the sequel, however. Link quested through dungeons in search of piece of an artifact of great power (shards of a Magic Crystal, rather than pieces of the Triforce of Wisdom), all to save Princess Zelda, who was put into an enchanted sleep. Instead of Ganon, Link fights his own shadow at the game's climax!

While some of the *Adventure of Link*'s innovations were discarded (such as Link's ability to earn experience points and raise his skill level), some remain, including the ability to learn new sword techniques.

The Legend of Zelda:
A Link to the Past,
1992 (SNES)

Link's third adventure, *A Link to the Past* was his first adventure on the Super Nintendo Entertainment System. Released in April 1992, *A Link to the Past* was a return to the original game's top-down, dungeon-crawling, Overworld-exploring formula. During his

quest, Link gathered magic amulets and crystals to rescue Zelda, free Hyrule, and stop the evil plans of Ganon and his accomplice, Agahnim.

> *A Link to the Past* was the first *Zelda* game to imply that each game featured a different Link. It was described as a prequel to the original *Legend of Zelda*, taking place long before the events of the first game.

A Link to the Past drew inspiration from the original *Legend of Zelda*, but thanks to the power of the 16-bit SNES, it had twice as much of everything: more detailed graphics, more dungeons, more enemies and bosses, more items—even two Overworlds that Link could warp between!

A Link to the Past was one of the Super Nintendo's most popular games, and it is remembered as one of the greatest *Zelda* games ever created. Its timeless appeal was proved by its successful re-release as a Game Boy Advance game in December 2002, *The Legend of Zelda: A Link to the Past/Four Swords*.

The Legend of Zelda: Link's Awakening,
1993 (Game Boy)

Link's Awakening was Link's first adventure on the original Game Boy, and it proved that the grand adventure of the *Zelda* series worked perfectly on the small black-and-white screen of the Game Boy. Shipwrecked on Koholint Island, Link recovered the eight Instruments of the Sirens to awaken the Wind Fish and return to the land of Hyrule.

When the Game Boy made way for the Game Boy Color, *Link's Awakening* was re-released in December 1998 as the full-color *Link's Awakening DX*, with an additional hidden dungeon.

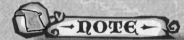

> The Picto Box/Nintendo Gallery sidequest of *The Wind Waker* was inspired by a similar photo-taking sidequest in *Link's Awakening*, in which there were 12 photo opportunities. After you took a photo in *Link's Awakening*, you could print it with a Game Boy Printer!

The Legend of Zelda: Ocarina of Time, 1998 (N64)

After alternating between two-dimensional perspectives for four adventures, Link broke into the third dimension in November 1998 with *Ocarina of Time*. The first *Zelda* game for the 64-bit Nintendo 64, *Ocarina of Time* brought the lush landscapes of Hyrule to life in an epic quest for the power of the Seven Sages of Hyrule.

The storyline of *Ocarina of Time* was divided between two time periods—one featured Link as a boy, the other, set seven years later, featured Link as a young man. It had all the action and adventure of the previous *Zelda* games, but many gamers loved *Ocarina* for the detail it brought to Link, Zelda, and Ganon, and the kingdom of Hyrule and all its major races.

Ocarina of Time introduced several new gameplay mechanics into the *Zelda* franchise, including Z-targeting, playing notes on an instrument, wearing masks, and sidequests for hundreds of hidden items! As the first 3-D *Zelda* game, *Ocarina* has become the standard against which all other 3-D adventure games are judged.

NOTE

Ocarina of Time featured two eras, but it was neither the first nor the only *Zelda* game to use the "two worlds" concept. *A Link to the Past* had a Light World and a Dark World that Link could warp between with the Magic Mirror, and *The Wind Waker* and the original *Legend of Zelda* could be played through a second time for a different gameplay experience.

The Legend of Zelda: Majora's Mask, 2000 (N64)

A sequel to *Ocarina of Time*, *Majora's Mask* found Link in a parallel version of Hyrule called Termina, into which the moon was going to crash within 72 hours! Fortunately, Link retained his time-warping talents from *Ocarina* (and learned a few new ones) that allowed him to travel through time to save the day. By the end of the game, Link had recovered his horse, Epona, and his Ocarina of Time from the Skull Kid, who had misused the Majora's Mask's power to pull the moon from its orbit.

Majora's Mask was the first (and only so far) *Zelda* game to set time limits on Link's quest. Much of the Overworld exploration of earlier *Zelda* titles became a different sort of exploration in *Majora's Mask*. Every area in the game changed from the beginning of the 72-hour deadline to the end, with different people to talk to and different sidequests to explore.

The Legend of Zelda: Oracle of Seasons/Oracle of Ages, 2001 (Game Boy Color)

Oracle of Seasons and *Oracle of Ages*, two Game Boy Color Games, took the "two worlds" concept to a new level. Both were released on May 14, 2001. In *Ages*, Link found himself in the distant land of Labrynnia, where he had to defeat Veran, the Sorceress of Shadows, by recovering the eight Essences of Time. In *Seasons*, Link's adventure took place in Holodrum, where he had to defeat the power-hungry general Onox by collecting the eight Essences of Nature.

The games were complete adventures individually, but players also could link up the games and transfer secret items and information between them to unlock new items, abilities, and a hidden ending featuring Ganon!

The Legend of Zelda: A Link to the Past/Four Swords, 2002 (Game Boy Advance)

The first *Zelda* game for the Game Boy Advance, *A Link to the Past/Four Swords* was a pixel-perfect translation of the SNES classic to Nintendo's latest portable console. It also included *Four Swords*, the first multiplayer *Zelda* game. Two to four players could link up their Game Boy Advances, cooperating and competing across four worlds to rescue Zelda from the clutches of Vaati, the Wind Sorcerer.

As a bonus, performing certain feats in *Four Swords* unlocked hidden sidequests in *A Link to the Past*, such as a scavenger hunt and the Palace of the Four Swords. Similarly, achieving certain goals in *A Link to the Past* gave a *Four Swords* player new abilities, such as the power to fire magical blasts from his or her sword!

The Legend of Zelda: The Wind Waker, 2003 (GameCube)

Carrying the *Zelda* franchise to new heights, *The Wind Waker* shocked fans with its beautiful-yet-controversial cell-shaded graphics, and with its dramatic departure from the Overworld norm. Set at least 100 years after the conclusion of *Ocarina of Time*, the Overworld is completely flooded in *The Wind Waker*, transforming the entire land of Hyrule into a gigantic ocean! Instead of traversing a vast land on foot or with the aid of Link's trusty steed, Epona, players ventured between 49 individual islands via a small sailboat, the King of Red Lions, in their quest to rescue Link's sister and save the land from the clutches of Ganon once more.

The combination of its whimsical graphical style and watery Overworld antics threw many fans for a loop, but those who gave *The Wind Waker* a chance found that it was indeed worthy of the critical acclaim it received. Refining the control scheme of its 3-D predecessors, *The Wind Waker*'s combat system was second to none, allowing Link to roll circles around his enemies, attacking them from all sides with the timely press of a button. The enemies themselves were a treat for franchise fans to encounter, as many were brilliantly imagined evolutions of classic franchise foes, including Octoroks, Darknuts, and Wizzrobes.

As the first GameCube *Zelda*, expectations were high for *The Wind Waker*. After its release, many fans pined for a more realistic graphical style, while others begged for more cell-shaded genius. With the releases of *Twilight Princess* and now *Phantom Hourglass*, both wishes have at last been fulfilled!

The Legend of Zelda: Four Swords Adventure,
2004 (GameCube)

Taking full advantage of the connectivity between the Game Boy Advance and GameCube, *The Legend of Zelda: Four Swords Adventure* provided one of the GameCube's most unique gameplay experiences. Up to four players could connect their GBAs to a GameCube, each assuming the role of one of four different-colored Links. Similar in many ways to the *Four Swords* portion of *A Link to the Past/Four Swords* on the GBA—but larger in every detail—players worked together to solve brain-teasing puzzles and defeat imaginative foes as they ventured deep into danger-filled dungeons.

Although the GBA-to-GameCube connectivity wasn't required to play *The Legend of Zelda: Four Swords Adventure*, the game was meant to be enjoyed that way. When linked up, the action seamlessly shifted from the TV display to a player's GBA screen each time they entered a house or delved into an underground cavern. Similarly, all text-based messages and dialogs with non-player characters occurred on the GBA screen, leaving the TV display clear and the action uninterrupted. The many ways in which the game utilized this unique connectivity were truly impressive, making *The Legend of Zelda: Four Swords Adventure* a testament to the gaming goodness that can be achieved when handhelds and consoles are linked together.

The Legend of Zelda: The Minish Cap,
2005 (Game Boy Advance)

Borrowing from the innovative gameplay mechanics and robust graphical style displayed in the *Four Swords* portion of the GBA's *A Link to the Past/Four Swords* outing, *The Minish Cap* pushed the boundaries of Nintendo's previous handheld to astonishing heights. Featuring the same fundamental gameplay of its 2-D predecessors, *The Minish Cap* piled on the mind-bending puzzles and top-down, dungeon-delving fun that series fans have come to love.

The chief villain from the GBA's *Four Swords* adventure, Vaati, made his evil return in *The Minish Cap* when he cursed Princess Zelda and turned her to stone! Aided by a comical talking cap that shrank Link down to itty-bitty proportions, the boy hero set out to search for four sacred elements that could help him break Zelda's curse and punish the wicked Vaati. Link got additional help in his quest by the Minish, a race of miniature beings with whom Link could interact whenever he shrank down to his tiny size and explored his surroundings in a whole new way.

The Legend of Zelda: Twilight Princess,
2006 (GameCube, Wii)

Unquestionably the most ambitious and profound *Zelda* title ever imagined, *Twilight Princess* finally gave hardcore *Zelda* fans the epic adventure they'd been dreaming of since the GameCube's debut. Boasting hyper-realistic graphics, a massive Overworld, nine labyrinthine dungeons, and a host of hard-to-find collectibles, *Twilight Princess* simply piled on the gameplay. Its incredible production value and rich plotline satisfied even the hungriest of *Zelda* series fans. You might still be playing it now!

The Legend of Zelda: Phantom Hourglass,
2007 (DS)

We could try to sum up the wonder of *Phantom Hourglass* in a couple of paragraphs, but we've got the rest of this guide to cover it in glorious detail! In short, this is the game that *Zelda* fans have been waiting for ever since they beat *The Wind Waker* for the tenth time. It's huge, it's innovative, and it's amazing! We hope you enjoy playing it as much as we enjoyed crafting its guide!

How to Use this Book

Thank you for purchasing Prima's Official Game Guide to *The Legend of Zelda: Phantom Hourglass*. We've spared no effort in cramming this guide full of vital tips and strategy to help you get the most out of your time in Link's world. This information will be of little use if you can't find what you're looking for, of course, so let's go over here what you'll discover in each major section of this guide.

Training

Phantom Hourglass features a stylus-based control scheme, and this new method of controlling Link takes a bit of getting used to! When you grow accustomed to using the stylus, though, we think you'll agree that it's the best way to adventure on the DS. Before you unfurl the sails and launch into the world of *Phantom Hourglass*, make sure to flip through our detailed training section. Here we discuss the ins and outs of the controls, along with all the major actions and interactions Link can perform.

Items

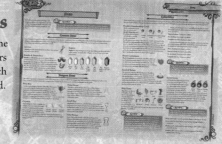

As you might expect, Link discovers a wide variety of wondrous and unique items as he explores his vast new world. Some items are common and found regularly, while others are unique and vital to the young hero's progress. This section of the guide details each and every special item and tool that Link can find.

Friends and Fiends

The Great Sea is populated by an assortment of extraordinary beings. Many of these beings are simple folk going about their daily lives, while others are willing to aid Link in his heroic quest. Also, there are those villainous monsters that yearn to stop the young hero dead in his tracks! Here we provide descriptions and information on every character and hostile entity Link encounters.

Walkthrough

The vast majority of this sizable tome is devoted to the walkthrough: a step-by-step guide through Link's first-ever adventure on the DS! Our walkthrough is geared toward providing you with a complete journey through Link's epic quest to save Tetra, showing you all the tips and tricks you need to prevail over even the most challenging of obstacles. Because so much of what can be seen and done in Link's world is purely optional, we've implemented a number of **Missing Links** sidebars to show you the best times to complete all sidequests and obtain every beneficial collectible. The (sometimes sizable) Missing Links sidebars inform you when optional tasks become available to you, while at the same time keeping these elective activities separate from the critical path. Adventurers who aren't interested in pursuing such optional ventures can simply ignore the sidebars until they feel up to a bit of ancillary exploring!

Multiplayer

Did we mention *Phantom Hourglass* contains one of the richest and most addictive multiplayer experiences you'll enjoy on the DS? In **Battle Mode**, two players can compete via the Nintendo Wi-Fi Connection, facing off in one of eight unique mazes and battling for supremacy over a collection of Force Gems. One player controls a trio of freaky Phantoms, while the other scurries around the maze as Link, carting heavy Force Gems back to a base. It's a wild game that offers hours of laughs and challenging entertainment, and our in-depth Multiplayer section offers you unbeatable tips and tactics for every board.

The Legendary Checklist

With an entire ocean to explore and nearly 20 islands to visit, there's plenty to see and do all across the Great Sea! It's easy to become lost if you aren't keeping track, so be sure to make good use of the many handy checklists at the back of the guide. Each time you accomplish a task, earn a reward, or find an important item, mark it off in the appropriate checklist. Check off everything in each of these lists and consider yourself an ace adventurer!

Training

Setting Sail

Before you unfurl the sails and launch into the world of *Phantom Hourglass*, make sure you know all the tips and tactics that will keep Link's journey on course. Whether it's reading sea charts while riding the chop of the ocean or diving beneath the crust to explore a creepy dungeon, this guide gives you the full scoop on everything a budding hero needs to survive the wrath of the Ghost Ship.

Getting Started

When you begin the game, you must create a new save file. There are two save slots on the DS card, allowing either two different players to test their mettle in *Phantom Hourglass* or one player to copy saves at pivotal points in the game. (Maybe you want to replay a particularly awesome boss battle.)

The first thing you must do is choose a name for your adventurer. You don't always have to go with Link. You can name the hero anything you wish. The save file then shows the current status of the hero, such as the number of hearts you have recovered and how many spirits have joined your party.

After you select your save file, you can choose either **Adventure** or **Battle**. The first option, Adventure, is the single-player quest to rescue Tetra from the spectral Ghost Ship. Battle takes you to the multiplayer game that pits one hero against three dastardly Phantoms. (For more information on the multiplayer game, please check out the Multiplayer chapter near the end of this guide.)

After you meet the festive Freedle on Mercay Island, Tag Mode becomes a third option. This mode allows you to see if any friends have sent you cool treasures or ship parts on the Nintendo Wi-Fi Connection.

Game Screen

On Land

When you hit the high seas in search of adventure, you had better make good use of all the available information onscreen. Whether you are on land or exploring the briny blue, the Touch Screen displays loads of useful stuff.

1. **Hearts**—These hearts measure your vitality. You can find additional heart containers on your quest. If these hearts empty, Link falls.

2. **Rupees**—How many Rupees you currently possess.

3. **Spirit**—This is the spirit currently guiding Link. You can change powered-up spirits at the Collection Menu. The only way to determine which spirit is guiding Link is by the color of the spirit icon on the screen—red, blue, or yellow.

4. **Item**—This is your currently selected special item, such as Bombs or the Boomerang.

5. **Menu**—This button brings up a bar with options such as Collection menu or game save.

At Sea

1. **Hull**—These hearts measure the integrity of your vessel. You start with four. The more matching ship parts you assemble, the more hearts you can earn. When these hearts are empty, the ship sinks and your game is over.

2. **Rupees**—The amount of Rupees you currently possess.

3. **Engine Control**—Tapping this gauge starts and stops your engine. This is useful if you need to brake to deal with an enemy or take a peek around.

4. **Menu**—This reveals options such as Collection menu, Salvage, and Fishing.

5. **Route**—Need to chart a new course across the waves? Tap this to bring up the sea chart and draw a new course.

Collection Menu

Collection Menu

Link accumulates dozens of special items, goodies, and treasures during his adventure on the high seas and in the darkest dungeons. Keep track of these treasures via the Collection menu, a useful catalog of your accomplishments. You can bring up the Collection menu via the menu bar on either land or sea.

The Collection menu occupies both screens of the Nintendo DS. You can actually tap on entries to see exactly what you have collected, such as Spirit Gems, Phantom Hourglass, Sand of Hours, and letters. If you want to touch items on the top screen, use the Swap icon in the lower right corner of the screen to flip the contents of the Collection menu. This is a great tool for tracking your progress, especially the Spirit Gem collection. (Those three colorful spheres are Spirit Gems.) When you get ten of a specific Spirit Gem, you can unlock some really cool powers.

From the Collection menu, you can scroll to the left to check out your fishing accomplishments. (This opens up after you get the Fishing Rod.) To the right, you can inspect your collection of treasures like Zora Scales and Goron Amber, as well as your catalog of found ship parts.

Treasure Screen   *Ship Parts Screen*

Map Screens

The world of *Phantom Hourglass* is enormous, filled with more than a dozen islands and miles upon miles of rocky seas. Fortunately, you have several in-game maps to help you navigate. These maps show you a general overview of your current location, such as a dungeon floor or a quadrant of the sea. The maps in this guide are augmented with additional, life-saving information, such as every single treasure chest and special feature.

The touch-screen functionality of the Nintendo DS allows you to interact with the onscreen maps, though, offering you a great way to take notes and make special marks, such as puzzle solutions or treasure chests you cannot quite reach at that point in your adventure. Jot them down and return later.

There are three types of maps in *Phantom Hourglass*: Overworld maps, dungeon maps, and sea charts. The way you read and interact with each onscreen map is different, so make sure you know the basics before heading out.

Overworld Maps

When you are exploring an island, you view the Overworld map on the top screen of the Nintendo DS. The Overworld map shows special locations, such as huts and houses, dungeon doors, and cave openings. The tiny Link head on the map indicates your current position.

~NOTE~

Each Overworld map has a harbor icon. It looks like a boat. Whenever you want to shove off to the sea, return to the harbor. It's the only place you can transition between land and sea.

When you want to make notes on the map, tap the Menu tab and choose Map. This moves the map to the bottom screen on the Nintendo DS. You can now draw notes directly on the map. If you want to erase a note (maybe you found the noted chest or solved a tricky puzzle that required written hints), tap the eraser on the left side of the map and then wipe away the unneeded text or drawing.

What kind of notes should you be taking while adventuring? Note down anything that you have to come back to get! With so many chests and interactive objects, it's easy to forget locations. So use this guide and the Touch Screen to make sure you never miss things like:

- Treasure chests
- Switches
- Bomb cracks
- Wooden pegs
- Puzzle solutions
- Secret paths

Dungeon Maps

Inside a dungeon, you see a map of the current floor on the top screen of the Nintendo DS. The map shows the available exits. In the special Temple of the Ocean King dungeon, the map shows the location of enemies like the Phantoms. (Other dungeon maps, like the one for the Temple of Courage, do not show enemy locations. You'll have to let us point those bad guys out for you!) The dungeon maps don't show the location of switches and traps, so you may want to scribble those in as you explore the dungeon.

To make notes on a dungeon map, use the Menu tab. Choose the Map option to pull the dungeon map down to the lower screen. You can make and delete notes on the dungeon map the same way you do on an Overworld map. However, unlike an Overworld map, you can tap on the Floor label (on the left) to see the dungeon's different floors.

~NOTE~

You can only look at maps of the floors you have visited. After you visit a floor for the first time, you can always view the map.

Sea Charts

The open sea is vast—you definitely need a map to negotiate the currents and sail to your desired destination. The Great Sea is so large it takes four different sea charts to map the entire thing. You cannot sail to all four quadrants at first. You must recover the quadrant's corresponding sea chart from the Temple of the Ocean King to visit that particular part of the sea. Whether you are on land or sea, you can tap on the Sea Chart icon in the Menu to view the entire visible sea. Then, tap on a specific quadrant to get a closer look.

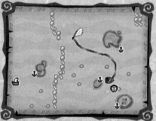

To sail to a specific location, such as an island or a sunken treasure, you draw on a sea chart. When in your ship, choose the Route tab to bring up the interactive sea chart. Using the stylus, draw a line from your boat to your desired stop. When you lift the stylus, you are asked if you want to set sail. If you made a mistake, decline and draw a new course. To start pushing across the waves to your destination, agree to the course. The map shuffles to the top screen and you can watch your boat's progress as it sails along the line you drew. Just don't watch it too closely—you'll miss sea monsters and pirates that try to intercept your vessel.

Link's Moves and Abilities

The Legend of Zelda: Phantom Hourglass may have several features that connect it to other games in The Legend of Zelda series, such as The Wind Waker, but there's one particular facet that completely sets it apart: its revolutionary controls. You have never interacted with Zelda game like this. Instead of moving Link with a traditional directional pad or control, you direct the hero via the Touch Screen. No more pressing a button to lunge forward with a sword attack. Now you tap or draw short lines to engage the enemy. It's totally different—but within minutes, you will be well on your way to legendary hero status.

Basic Moves on Land

Movement

To make Link move, you move the stylus across the Nintendo DS Touch Screen. Dragging the stylus just ahead of the hero makes him move at a more measured pace. Quickly moving the stylus out ahead of the hero initiates a sprint. Practice this technique on the starting island, Mercay Island. Various situations call for all sorts of movement speeds. Need to carefully negotiate a narrow bridge? Gingerly and deliberately drag the stylus right in front of Link, carefully directing him across the screen. Need to dodge an enemy's blow? Place the stylus a good distance from Link and start drawing his course well ahead. Link springs into motion, running toward the spot where you have the stylus.

NOTE

Link can also perform a little somersault maneuver if you draw tiny circles at the edge of the screen. Link tucks and rolls in the direction of your circle. Somersault into trees to shake loose goodies, like Rupees.

CAUTION

Link cannot swim, so be careful near the edges of islands. If Link topples into the drink, he loses half a heart.

Combat

After Link discovers his first sword, the Oshus Sword, he can draw on enemies in battle. There are four different ways you can attack an enemy. Each attack has its benefits and shortcomings. You do not need to unlock any of the four techniques—you can use them as soon as you get your hands on the Oshus Sword.

- **Thrust:** Quickly draw a short line from Link to an enemy to make the hero lunge forward and stab with his sword. This is a stronger attack than a basic stab, but keep in mind, while lunging, you can be attacked from the sides.

- **Targeted Attack:** Tap a nearby enemy to make Link make a fast stab. This is a great way to quickly target an enemy as it gets close, but it is not Link's strongest attack.

- **Side Slash:** Draw a short line that divides Link from a nearby enemy. Link swipes at the enemy with his sword. This is a good attack, but you leave yourself open while drawing the line.

- **Spin Attack**: Draw a quick circle around Link to make him spin on his heels with the sword outstretched. Any enemy within range (the range is noted by a green blur along the path of the sword) is hit. if you ever find yourself surrounded, this is a great attack. However, if you try to use the spin attack more than three times in rapid succession, Link gets dizzy and must take a small breather. During his rest, you are completely vulnerable to attack.

As you quest, you discover which attacks are best against Link's different enemies. Smaller foes, like Red ChuChus, can be dispatched with a quick stab. But against tougher monsters, like Zora Warriors, you may find stronger attacks like the lunge are better suited.

Did we say *four* attack techniques? Well, Link actually has five, but you must complete a small quest to unlock the final power. However, you don't need to use a different stylus motion to unleash it.

Items

In addition to his sword and shield, Link also has a variety of special items he uses during his adventure, such as a Boomerang or Bombs. If you're a *Legend of Zelda* fan, you surely have experience with many of these items, but controlling them with the Nintendo DS Touch Screen is very different from using a traditional controller.

To select an item, tap the Menu tab and choose the Item tab. This brings up a bar along the bottom of the screen. Tap the item you want to equip. The selected item then appears in the upper-right corner of the lower screen. Tap the onscreen item icon to use the item or put it away.

You can use the L and R buttons to equip the currently selected item. The item can be easily unequipped in any instance by clicking L or R again.

Boomerang

One of the first items you discover is the Boomerang. This handy item doubles as both a weapon and a retrieval device. If you throw the boomerang at a pot, it shatters it and brings back the enclosed pick-up, like a heart or rupee. As a weapon, the Boomerang can be thrown to stun or dispatch an enemy depending on the strength of the target. You can also activate orbs and torches by hitting them with the Boomerang.

To throw the Boomerang, draw a line from Link to the target. You can arc the Boomerang around the screen—this is how you throw the Boomerang behind an enemy and hit it in the back. (It's an effective technique against enemies with armor.) You can

target multiple objects, too, by drawing a line from Link to the various targets. Maybe you need to hit for orbs to open a door? Draw the line around the room, touching each orb.

Be economical with your Boomerang throws. Don't draw lengthy lines between targets unless absolutely necessary, as the Boomerang can only go so far.

Bombs

As soon as you get bombs, you can use them offensively or to blow open Bomb cracks. Tapping the equipped Bomb icon raises a Bomb over Link's head. To throw a Bomb, tap the target destination. Link cannot heave a Bomb across the entire screen. He can only throw it a short distance. Once it's been thrown, the timer starts. You only have a few seconds to get away. When you see a Bomb turn red, you know it's about to explode. If it blows up next to you, you lose half a heart.

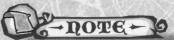

Not every Bomb spot is marked with a crack. Look for discoloration or a break in scenery patterns as a hint.

You can only carry as many Bombs as your Bomb Bag allows. The maximum is 30. To conserve Bombs, look for bomb flowers. Tap a bomb flower to pick the explosive and then throw it like a regular Bomb.

Bow and Arrows

After you pick up the Bow, you can shoot Arrows over great distances. Arrows can be used to attack enemies from safety or target their weak spots, such as their faces or symbols on their backs. You can also use Arrows to trigger switches. Look for eye symbols on the walls of dungeons and caves. Fire an Arrow when the eye is open (some of them blink from time to time) and you'll see different effects like materializing treasure chests or mysteriously appearing bridges.

To use the Bow, equip it and then tap on your target. Link automatically knocks an Arrow and sends it flying. Until you tap the Bow icon in the upper right corner again to deselect it, every time you tap somewhere on the screen, Link shoots an arrow in that direction.

Grappling Hook

When you're first starting out, you notice wooden pegs sticking out of the ground. There is little you can do with them at first, save for jumping on them and balancing just for fun. However, after you acquire the Grappling Hook, you can use these pegs to cross gaps and access previously unreachable areas.

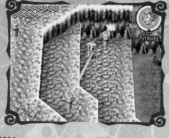

With the Grappling Hook equipped, tap a peg to throw the tool and zip over to it. You can also create a tightrope between two pegs by equipping the Grappling Hook and then drawing a line from one peg to the other. Link can then cross the gap by walking along the taut rope. The next time you use the Grappling Hook, though, the previous tightrope disappears. With the Grappling Hook, you can also fashion a slingshot out of two pegs. Draw a tightrope between two pegs and then stand next to the middle of the rope. Move Link against the rope, drawing the stylus across the screen. Link puts his back against the rope and makes the rope taut. When you release, Link flies up and across the screen.

The Grappling Hook can latch onto more than just pegs. See a treasure chest across the water? Hit it with the Grappling Hook and Link is pulled right to it. You can also use the Grappling Hook to grab loose items and pull them back toward you.

Shovel

After you discover the Shovel, you can dig up patches of earth. This is a great way to scrape Rupees out of the soil—you never know what you'll pull out of the ground by just randomly shoveling. However, there are special digging spots that contain valuable treasure, such as big Rupees or treasure maps. These special patches are often marked by slight discolorations in the soil. There also are unmarked spots, though, so you must find clues that tell you just where to dig.

Bombchus

These cute little bombs actually scurry across the ground before exploding. When you discover the Bombchu, you can attack enemies or activate switches from a huge distance. Bombchus are also small enough to sneak through tiny openings you sometimes spot in walls.

To use a Bombchu, select the item and then draw its path on the map that appears on the bottom screen. When you lift the stylus after drawing the path, the Bombchu starts following your instructions. You can watch the Bombchu on the bottom screen, but this leaves you open to attack. After releasing the Bombchu, tap the bottom screen to return the focus to Link. While the Bombchu is running, you can move Link again.

NOTE

After drawing the path for the Bombchu, you are asked if you want to release it or redraw the path. If you made a mistake, just redraw the path for no penalty.

Hammer

The final item you discover on your adventure, the Hammer, is a hoot to use. When selected via the Item tab, the cursor turns into a small Hammer icon. You can then tap enemies or objects. Instead of Link using the Hammer, though, your spirit actually hoists the mallet and brings it crashing down. This is a great way to flatten enemies from a distance. If you want to increase the power of the Hammer strike, hold the stylus on the place, enemy, or object you want to hit. When you release, the Hammer comes thundering down.

NOTE

There are rusty switches that cannot be triggered by stepping on them. These switches can only be activated with a strong Hammer strike.

At-Sea Moves

Sailing

When it's time to raise anchor and set out across the ocean with the waves lapping against your bow, the controls change drastically. As mentioned in the sea chart description, you actually plot a course by drawing a line on the chart itself. While the ship is cutting through the water, you only control the engine. Tapping the Engine icon on the screen's right side brings the ship to a full stop or sends it lurching forward.

You can control the camera by dragging the stylus across the screen. Rotating the camera is important—enemies in the ocean attack from all sides. Linebeck calls out when an enemy is close, but you must then move the camera to bear down on your foe. When an enemy is spotted, though, a tiny skull appears on the map so you know which way to spin the camera.

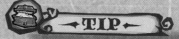

TIP

Always rotate the camera while sailing—you never know what you might see! You could get an early heads-up on a field of exploding barrels floating just off the stern. Or you might even spot a super-secret uncharted island....

You can even make your ship jump by tapping the arrow at the center of the screen's bottom edge. This is how you avoid taking damage from water-bound enemies in your path.

Cannon

After you buy the cannon from Eddo, you can finally defend yourself as you sail the Great Sea. The cannon doesn't need to be equipped or upgraded—once it's installed, you can always count on it. To use the cannon against an enemy, all you need to do is tap the enemy with the stylus. The cannon pops out of the cargo hold and fires off a powerful shot.

Some enemies can be dispatched with just a single cannonball. However, others, like pirates, require multiple hits. When going up against stronger enemies, repeatedly tap them to lay down a volley of cannonballs.

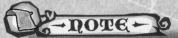

NOTE

The cannon is sometimes used for more than just blasting your way through enemies. While sailing, you may catch sight of golden frog hopping out of the ocean. Maybe a cannonball will get its attention?

Salvage

Not only does Eddo sell you a cannon for defending yourself, but he also invented a salvage arm for pulling sunken treasure out of the ocean. After it is bought and installed, the salvage arm can be used at sea by tapping the Menu tab and then selecting Salvage. This brings the ship to a full stop. The salvage arm then rises from the hold and a claw is lowered beneath the waves.

Once the salvage arm has been deployed, you must control the claw's descent and ascent. The controls for the claw are placed at the bottom of the screen. Using the stylus, slide the claw left and right to avoid the Octomines and pick up Rupees floating in bubbles. Move the little lever on the control panel up and down to speed and slow the claw. Speeding up the claw is a good way to avoid moving Octomines that suddenly float into the claw's path. Slowing the claw helps you make measured movements, such as carefully sliding between Octomines or avoiding the rocky contours of the seafloor.

You must direct the claw right to the sunken treasure. After you grab the treasure, you must hoist it back out of the water. As you pull the treasure back out, follow a different path to scoop up more rupees.

The salvage arm is not invincible. It can take only five hits from Octomines or crashes against rock walls. If you break it, you cannot salvage any more sunken treasure until you seek port at Mercay Island and pay the fellow at the Shipyard to repair it.

TIP

It's cheaper to repair the salvage arm before it's completely broken. If you've exhausted all five hits, the repair bill is a steep 100 Rupees.

NOTE

Only drop the salvage arm over sunken treasure spots marked with red Xs. These spots are called out every time you recover a treasure map or sometimes after you defeat a flag-bearing pirate ship. If you drop the claw into the water randomly, all you get are a bunch of Octomines.

Fishing

As soon as you earn the Fishing Rod from Bannan island, you can start your side career as a professional angler. Pulling healthy catches from the deep impresses the man who gives you the Fishing Rod, so keep returning to his house and show him any new fish you reel in. There are six types of fish in the ocean, from the tiny Skippyjack to the lovely leviathan, the Neptoona.

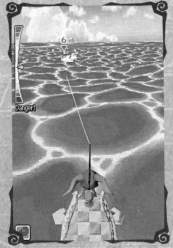

When you want to go fishing, direct your boat over a fish shadow on the sea chart. Select the Fish button from the Menu tab . The ship stops and you automatically cast your lure into the water. When the fish bites, you must quickly drag the stylus down the screen to hook your catch.

The real fight begins once you have the fish on the line. Reel in the fish by drawing circles onscreen, just as if you were reeling in a real fish. You also must manage line tautness. A meter on the screen's left side shows the status of the line—if the fish is pulling hard and pushing the meter into the red danger zone, hold the stylus down at the bottom of the screen to raise the meter from red to green. When you tucker the fish out a little and the meter rises back into the green, start reeling again. Eventually, you'll have that fish in your boat and added to your Collection menu.

Nice catch!

→ NOTE ←

Rarer, larger fish put up incredible fights. If you find yourself struggling with a catch, chances are you have a real monster on the other end of the line.

→ TIP ←

When pulling against a fighting fish, drag the stylus down the side of the screen opposite the fish. This helps put the tautness meter back in the green.

Interactive Objects

As you explore the world, you interact with a host of objects, such as doors and switches. Many of these objects are quite familiar to *Legend of Zelda* fans. (Everybody knows you slash through grass to discover hidden Rupees and hearts, right?) Some objects require further explanation.

Common Interactions

Cutting grass reveals hidden Rupees and hearts.

Lift pots, rocks, or barrels to throw them at enemies or break them apart. You can also strike pots to shatter them and reveal hidden goodies.

Just tap a treasure chest to make Link open it and claim the prize inside.

Tap a movable object like a block to make Link grab it. Then tap the arrow indicating the direction you wish to push or pull it.

Crystal orbs are often connected to puzzles or hazards. For example, striking an orb can lower spikes or make an invisible treasure chest appear.

Walk over floor switches to trigger them.

Tap on people to initiate a conversation.

Tap on wall maps to read the inscriptions and then copy them to your own maps and charts.

Locked Doors

Throughout your dungeon exploration, you stumble across locked doors that halt your progress. You must find small keys to open these doors. Small keys are sometimes dropped by enemies or stashed inside treasure chests. After you retrieve a small key, you can open a locked door. However, small keys can only be used once—so as soon as you unlock a door, the key is lost forever.

Boss Key blocks are tougher obstacles that lock you out of boss monster lairs. These require special Boss Keys that are typically hidden deep inside a dungeon. When you do uncover the Boss Key, you discover that it's rather heftier than a small key. You must carry the Boss Key overhead  as you traverse the dungeon to the Boss Key block. While holding the key, you cannot attack or defend yourself. If you encounter an enemy, drag a fast line away from Link to drop the Boss Key. Now you can fight. When the battle is over, tap the Boss Key to pick it up again and resume your travel to the Boss Key block.

Prima Official Game Guide

Training

Introduction ~ Training ~ Items ~ Friends & Fiends ~ Walkthrough ~ Multiplayer ~ Checklist

Boing Statues

Those strange, one-eyed statues you see around all the islands not only see everything, but they also are quite the little chatterboxes. When you hit the statue with your sword, the wobbly statue starts talking. Some of these statues reveal clues about the area, others offer pieces of puzzle solutions. Always hit these statues because the information they provide is usually helpful.

TIP

In most dungeons, you can find a statue on each floor that tells you how many treasure chests are still on the floor. This information isn't free, though. These statues charge Rupees for their secrets—so if you pony up for the goods, make sure you write down the hidden chest locations. Of course, we call out every single treasure chest on the maps in this guide, so feel free to save your Rupees....

Gust Geysers

Gust geysers are columns of wind that erupt from the ground. Some of these geysers are plugged up by soil, so you must use the Shovel to dig out the blockage. You also find some geysers that activate when a switch is triggered. You can use these gust geysers to float up to a high ledge. Sometimes, you may even be called to throw a Bomb in the geyser to blast some stones blocking your path before riding the geyser yourself.

Force Gems

Force Gems are triangular jewels that must be used to unlock secret doors. When you spy a triangle of Force Gems laid out on the floor of a dungeon, you must accumulate three errant Force gems and place them on the triangle-shaped pedestals to open the door. Force Gems are heavy—they really slow you down. Much like a Boss Key, you cannot defend yourself while holding a Force Gem, so you must drop it if you need to engage in a little swashbuckling.

Blue Light

When you reach certain milestones inside a dungeon, such as the room just before the boss lair, you uncover blue circles of light. These circles are warps that take you back to the dungeon entrance. When you warp to the starting point, another blue light is waiting to send you back to the bottom of the dungeon. Use these blue lights to go shopping for useful potions or replenish spent items (like Bombs or Arrows) before going into battle against a fearsome boss monster.

Mailboxes

Almost every island has a bright red mailbox. When you have mail waiting for you, the mailbox bounces back and forth, almost like it's waving hello. Tap on the mailbox and the mailman flutters in to deliver your special letter. Some letters are just cordial greetings or notes containing useful quest information, but some island citizens send you presents to show gratitude.

NOTE

You encounter lots of island- and dungeon-specific objects during your travels. For these special objects, often found only once or twice (like a Tongue Statue), we provide exact instructions for interaction right at the point of your first encounter in the walkthrough.

Items

Link discovers all manner of unique and wondrous items as he explores his vast new world. This chapter details each and every special item and tool the young hero can find.

NOTE

Refer to the Legendary Checklist portion of this guide for handy checklists of all items and collectibles in *Phantom Hourglass*. Use them to keep track of everything you've found, and to quickly locate goodies you may have missed!

Common Items

Some items are found all over the place. Link commonly discovers such items when smashing pots, rocks, and barrels, and when cutting down tall grass, somersaulting into certain trees, digging about with the Shovel, and slaying evil monsters. He can also purchase common items from shops and vendors he meets in his travels.

Arrows

Arrows provide ammunition for the Bow. You can't use one without the other!

Bombs & Bombchus

Bombs and **Bombchus** are quite unique. They're considered quest items when you first obtain them in their respective dungeons. Thereafter, you commonly find Bombs and Bombchus while breaking pots and the like. You can also buy these items from shops. In this fashion, Bombs and Bombchus are considered both common items and quest items—and they're great fun to use!

Rupees

Rupees are big, shiny pieces of currency. Link keeps them safe in his wallet, and he can hold **a lot** of Rupees in there! Here's what each one's worth:

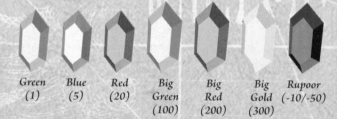

| Green (1) | Blue (5) | Red (20) | Big Green (100) | Big Red (200) | Big Gold (300) | Rupoor (-10/-50) |

Dungeon Items

The following items are primarily found within dungeons, dark places filled with danger that Link must brave to bring peace to his world. Any temple or structure that's more complex than a simple house or cavern is considered a dungeon in this guide.

Boss Key

Nearly every dungeon features a **Boss Key**. These giant items are too big for Link to stash in his pack, so he must carry them overhead instead! Bring a dungeon's Boss Key to its Boss Key block and then tap the block to make Link heave the key into it, thereby removing the obstacle. If danger lurks nearby, tap the Touch Screen to make Link set down or toss a Boss Key so that he may draw his sword.

Crystals

Some dungeons feature **crystals** of a certain shape that must be brought to same-shaped pedestals to open new pathways, reveal vital chests, or create other such changes in the environment. Link interacts with these items just like Boss Keys: He must carry crystals overhead and transport them to their appropriate pedestal.

Round Crystal   Square Crystal   Triangle Crystal

Force Gems

Two floors of the Temple of the Ocean King feature a number of **Force Gems** that must be found and then brought to special pedestals on the same floor. Link must carry these items overhead just like crystals and Boss Keys. When all Force Gems have been placed on the pedestals, a new path opens.

Red Pot

Red pots are exclusively found within the Temple of the Ocean King. Smashing a red pot spills a safe zone on the floor of the dungeon. Link can step into this small safe zone to avoid the Phantoms just like the permanent safe zones on each dungeon level. These red pots can be carried around the dungeon (even between floors) and smashed wherever a temporary safe zone is needed.

Small Key

Small keys are common and exist within most dungeons. Link stores these items on his person and uses them to open locked doors within the dungeon; simply tap a locked door to open it. Any small keys Link has are shown at the lower-right corner of the Map screen.

Time Bonus

Time is life in the Temple of the Ocean King. If the Phantom Hourglass runs out of sand, Link is in trouble! Fortunately, the young hero can acquire **time bonuses** by smashing yellow pots he finds within the temple. Each one restores either 15 or 30 seconds' worth of sand to the Phantom Hourglass, prolonging its protective effects.

Collectibles

Some items Link can acquire are not at all mandatory to completing his quest. Obtaining these collectible items is beneficial, though: Many increase Link's abilities, making him more powerful and combat less dicey. We highly recommend going out of your way for these goodies!

Beedle's Membership Cards

While cruising the ocean blue, set a course for **Beedle's Shop Ship** and board the vessel to speak with Beedle, a friendly traveling merchant.

Freebie Card   Compliment Card   Complimentary Card

Beedle's prices seem steep at first, but he rewards customer loyalty through his unique **membership program**. Every 100 Rupees you spend at Beedle's earns you 1 membership point, and you get special prizes for reaching certain membership milestones, including big discounts and special **cards** that Beedle mails you! Spend lots of cash at Beedle's Shop Ship to collect all three of his membership cards, then visit Beedle to use them and see what happens!

Heart Containers

Heart Containers are precious collectibles. Each one you find permanently extends Link's heart meter by one full heart! You're always rewarded with a Heart Container each time you slay a dungeon's powerful boss monster. Others are more difficult to find!

Sand of Hours

The mystical sand that fills the Phantom Hourglass is called the **Sand of Hours**. Two minutes' worth of this special sand is automatically acquired each time you defeat a dungeon's cruel boss, but you can find an additional five minutes' worth of sand by hauling up five specific sunken treasures from the seafloor! See the Legendary Checklist portion of this guide for details.

Ship Parts

Ship Parts are special collectibles. Find these items and then visit the Shipyard at Mercay Island to install them onto Linebeck's ship. Customizing the craft

Prow   Anchor   Hull   Cannon
Handrail   Bridge   Chimney   Wheel

in this manner adds a personal flair and can also increase the vessel's defensive capabilities!

NOTE

Ship parts are always found at random. Whenever you visit a shop, open a treasure chest, or receive a ship part as a reward, you never know which part you'll get! For this reason, the walkthrough and checklists never mention you receiving specific ship parts—they simply tell you where random ship parts can be found.

All ship parts belong to one of nine different sets. Sets are made up of eight parts of a kind. Combine parts to extend the craft's heart meter as follows:

Three of a Kind: One heart is added.

Six of a Kind: Two hearts are added.

Complete Set: Three hearts are added.

If you're extremely lucky, you may stumble across very rare ship parts made of pure gold. These parts belong to an exceptional set that grants the following benefits when installed:

Three of a Kind: One heart is added.

Four of a Kind: Two hearts are added.

Six of a Kind: Three hearts are added.

Complete Set: Four hearts are added.

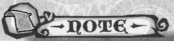
NOTE

Ship parts can also be sold to the Treasure Teller at Mercay Island for Rupees. See the Legendary Checklist for their values. Consider selling your duplicate ship parts for extra cash.

Spirit Gems

Link finds these glittering gemstones in the most unusual places. Many are well-hidden and must be sought. Each **Sprit Gem** holds a fraction of the power that once belonged to the Spirits of Power, Wisdom,

Power Gem   Wisdom Gem   Courage Gem

and Courage. These noble spirits lost their power when evil seized control of the land. By collecting the Spirit Gems and then visiting the sacred spring at Spirit Island, Link can restore power to the spirit fairies, unlocking their true potential. The Spirits of Power, Wisdom, and Courage then assist Link in a variety of ways, as indicated by the following list.

NOTE

After powering up a spirit fairy, you must equip her at the Collection menu to gain her benefits. Only one spirit can be equipped at a time.

Power (10): Link's sword is coated in flames, increasing its damage.

Power (20): The flames burn hotter and the damage it deals is increased.

Wisdom (10): Link's shield becomes stronger, able to deflect more powerful attacks.

Wisdom (20): Link becomes covered in a powerful shield that greatly reduces damage.

Courage (10): Link's sword emits a short shockwave when used, increasing its attack range.

Courage (20): The shockwave is greatly enhanced, striking everything that stands before Link.

Treasure Maps

Link can seek out 31 different **treasure maps** as he explores his world. Each of these maps points to a sunken treasure lying somewhere at the bottom of the Great Sea. With the aid of the Salvage Arm, Link can sail to these sunken treasure locations and then haul up the loot! Common prizes include random, usually rare ship parts, and Sand of Hours.

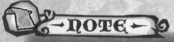

→NOTE→

It seems odd that there are 31 maps, but this becomes clear when you factor in the thirty-second sunken chest: a mandatory find that contains the Sun Key!

Treasures

Treasures are trinkets and baubles that Link finds in many places during his travels. Some are more rare than others, and each of these little beauties can be sold to the Treasure Teller at Mercay Island for easy profit. Their Rupee values are shown above.

Pink Coral (50)   Pearl Necklace (150)   Dark Pearl Loop (800)   Zora Scale (150)

Goron Amber (800)   Ruto Crown (150)   Helmaroc Plume (50)   Regal Ring (1,500)

You'll find treasures inside certain treasure chests and on sale at many shops. Like ship parts, the treasures you find are completely random. You never know which ones you'll encounter!

→NOTE→

As you can see, the Treasure Teller pays high price for the Regal Ring—but you can find an even better rate! Visit the Ho Hos aboard their Traveler's Ship at the southeast quadrant and sell off your Regal Rings for top Rupee.

Quest Items

Link finds the following items over the course of his adventure. Most are gained through completing deeds of valor or careful exploration, while others can simply be purchased from shops. Nearly all of these items must be acquired for Link to complete his quest and bring peace to the land and peoples living near the Great Sea.

Aquanine

Where to Get: Temple of Ice

How to Get: Defeat dungeon boss Gleeok, Two-Headed Dragon

Use: One of three pure metals needed to forge the Phantom Sword

Azurine

Where to Get: Mutoh's Temple

How to Get: Defeat dungeon boss Eox, Ancient Stone Soldier

Use: One of three pure metals needed to forge the Phantom Sword

Big Catch Lure

Where to Get: Bannan Island: Old Wayfarer's Hut

How to Get: Catch the Loovar fish and show it to the Old Wayfarer

Use: Makes it easier to land the Rusty Swordfish and allows you to catch the legendary fish, Neptoona

Bomb Bag #1

Where to Get: Bannan Island: Cannon Game

How to Get: Set the high score on Salvatore's Cannon Game

Use: Increases Bomb capacity to 20 Bombs

Bomb Bag #2

Where to Get: Beedle's Shop Ship (after obtaining Sea Chart #3)

How to Get: Buy for 1,000 Rupees (nonmember cost)

Use: Increases Bomb capacity to 30 Bombs

Bombchu Bag #1

Where to Get: Goron Island Shop

How to Get: Buy for 1,000 Rupees

Use: Increases Bombchu capacity to 20 Bombchus

Bombchu Bag #2

Where to Get: Dee Ess Island: Goron Game

How to Get: Set a new record time at the Goron Game

Use: Increases Bombchu capacity to 30 Bombchus

Bombchus

Where to Get: Goron Temple

How to Get: Obtained while clearing the dungeon

Uses: Blowing up stuff from afar; defeating enemies from range; activating out-of-reach switches, etc.

Bombs

Where to Get: Temple of Wind

How to Get: Obtained while clearing the dungeon

Uses: Blasting through weak walls; destroying bomb blocks; harming and defeating enemies, etc.

Boomerang

Where to Get: Temple of Fire

How to Get: Obtained while clearing the dungeon

Uses: Smashing distant pots; retrieving remote items; activating out-of-reach switches; spreading fire between torches; stunning and defeating enemies from range, etc.

Bow

Where to Get: Temple of Courage

How to Get: Obtained while clearing the dungeon

Uses: Smashing distant pots; activating out-of-reach switches and eye crests; stunning and defeating enemies from range, etc.

Cannon

Where to Get: Cannon Island: Eddo's Garage

How to Get: Buy for 50 Rupees

Use: Allows you to combat enemies at sea and blast golden frogs to learn their secret symbols

Crimsonine

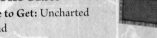

Where to Get: Goron Temple

How to Get: Defeat dungeon boss Dongorongo, Armored Lizard

Use: One of three pure metals needed to forge the Phantom Sword

Cyclone Slate

Where to Get: Uncharted Island

How to Get: Solve island's riddle; speak with Golden Chief Cylos

Use: Allows you to warp about the sea after you know the secret symbols of the golden frogs

Fishing Rod

Where to Get: Bannan Island: Old Wayfarer's Hut

How to Get: Unite the Old Wayfarer with the mermaid, Joanne

Use: Allows you to fish at special fish shadows that begin to appear about the Great Sea

Ghost Key

Where to Get: Ghost Ship

How to Get: Obtained while clearing the dungeon

Use: Like a Boss Key, it allows you to remove a block obstacle so that you may progress

Guard Notebook

Where to Get: SEQ Traveler's Ship

How to Get: Trade with a Ho Ho for the Telescope

Use: Give to Nyave aboard his SWQ Traveler's Ship to receive the Wood Heart

Hammer

Where to Get: Mutoh's Temple

How to Get: Obtained while clearing the dungeon

Uses: Smashing enemies; pounding rusty pressure switches; activating catapult floorboards, etc.

Hero's New Clothes

Where to Get: NEQ Traveler's Ship

How to Get: Speak with the Man of Smiles after defeating monsters aboard his Traveler's Ship

Use: Give to the so-called hero at the NWQ Traveler's Ship to receive the Telescope

Grappling Hook

Where to Get: Temple of Ice

How to Get: Obtained while clearing the dungeon

Use: Pulling remote items toward you; zipping over to heavier objects; stunning and defeating enemies; stretching tightropes across two pegs to cross wide gaps; propelling you onto tall ledges or across gaps when using the rope like a slingshot, etc.

Jolene's Letter

Where to Get: Any island's postbox

How to Get: Delivered after your first run-in with Jolene

Use: Give to Jolene's sister, Joanne (the mermaid) at Bannan Island to receive Wisdom Gem #9

King's Key

Where to Get: Isle of Ruins

How to Get: Visit the spirit of second knight Doylan

Use: Lowers the surrounding sea level

Oshus's Sword

Where to Get: Mercay Island: Oshus's Storehouse

How to Get: Open the chest at the rear of the storehouse

Uses: Defeating monsters; activating statues and switches; cutting tall grass and skinny trees, etc.

Phantom Hourglass

Where to Get: Temple of the Ocean King

How to Get: Revisit the Temple of the Ocean King after clearing the Temple of Fire

Use: Prevents the temple's curse from draining Link's health energy as long as sand remains in the timepiece

Phantom Sword

Where to Get: Mercay Island: Oshus's House

How to Get: Visit Oshus after you've obtained the Sword Blade from Zauz the Blacksmith

Uses: Defeating enemies, including Phantoms and their evil lord, Bellum

Prize Postcard

Where to Get: NEQ; Traveler's Ship

How to Get: Speak with the Man of Smiles after defeating monsters aboard his Traveler's Ship, and after obtaining the Hero's New Clothes and treasure map from him

Use: Mail at any island's postbox to enter a fun sweepstakes. You'll receive treasures and ship parts in the mail at random!

Purple Potion

Where to Get: Various shops

How to Get: Buy with Rupees (amount varies)

Use: Restores up to eight of Link's hearts; automatically used when Link is about to fall in battle

Quiver #1

Where to Get: Molida Island; Romanos's Hut

How to Get: Set the high score at Romanos's Shooting Range

Use: Increases arrow capacity to 30 arrows

Quiver #2

Where to Get: Molida Island Shop

How to Get: Buy for 1,000 Rupees

Use: Increases arrow capacity to 50 arrows

Red Potion

Where to Get: Various shops

How to Get: Buy with Rupees (amount varies)

Use: Restores up to six of Link's hearts when used

Regal Necklace

Where to Get: Isle of the Dead

How to Get: Pass through the Phantom Corridor

Use: Disperses the giant cyclone that blocks access to the Isle of Ruins

Salvage Arm

Where to Get: Cannon Island: Eddo's Garage

How to Get: Purchase from Eddo (amount varies)

Use: Allows you to haul up sunken treasure chests from the seafloor

Sea Chart #1

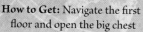

Where to Get: Temple of the Ocean King

How to Get: Navigate the first floor and open the big chest

Use: Reveals the southwest quadrant of the Great Sea

Sea Chart #2

Where to Get: Temple of the Ocean King

How to Get: Delve down to B3 and then open the big chest within the Checkpoint Chamber

Use: Reveals the northwest quadrant of the Great Sea

Sea Chart #3

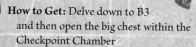

Where to Get: Temple of the Ocean King

How to Get: Delve down to B9 and then open the big chest within the Elevator Chamber

Use: Reveals the southeast quadrant of the Great Sea

Sea Chart #4

Where to Get: Temple of the Ocean King

How to Get: Delve down to B13 and then open the big chest there

Use: Reveals the northeast quadrant of the Great Sea

Shovel

Where to Get: Molida Island: Wayfarer's Hideaway #1

How to Get: Discover the Wayfarer's first hideaway and open the chest inside

Uses: Digging up soft ground to find items; digging up special mounds of soil or sand to unearth a variety of surprises; filling in shallow holes, etc.

Sun Key

Where to Get: Southwest quadrant of the sea

How to Get: Explore the Temple of the Ocean King to learn its location; haul up a sunken chest with the Salvage Arm

Use: Opens a special locked door inside a cavern at Molida Island, allowing you to explore the northern half of the island and reach the Temple of Courage

Sword Blade

Where to Get: Zauz's Island

How to Get: Give Zauz all three pure metals; defeat Jolene in duel one last time; return to Zauz

Use: Must be shown to Oshus so the Phantom Sword can be completed

Swordsman's Scroll

Where to Get: Bannan Island: Old Wayfarer's Hut

How to Get: Trade items between all four Traveler's Ships to obtain the Wood Heart; give the Wood Heart to the Old Wayfarer aboard his special Traveler's Ship; visit the Old Wayfarer at his hut at Bannan Island to receive the scroll as a reward

Use: Enables Link to perform the great spin attack, a very powerful yet exhausting maneuver

Telescope

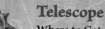

Where to Get: NWQ Traveler's Ship

How to Get: Give the Hero's New Clothes to the self-proclaimed hero aboard his Traveler's Ship

Use: Give to a Ho Ho aboard the SEQ Traveler's Ship to receive the Guard Notebook

Wood Heart

Where to Get: SEQ Traveler's Ship

How to Get: Give the Guard Notebook to Nyave aboard his Traveler's Ship

Use: Give to the Old Wayfarer aboard his special Traveler's Ship to receive the Swordsman's Scroll the next time you visit him at Bannan Island

Wooden Shield

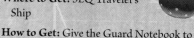

Where to Get: Mercay Island Shop

How to Get: Buy for 80 Rupees

Use: Automatically defends against light frontal attacks just by holding it

Yellow Potion

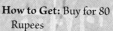

Where to Get: Goron Island Shop

How to Get: Buy for 150 Rupees

Use: Restores all of Link's hearts when used

Friends and Fiends

A wide variety of extraordinary beings inhabit the many islands of the Great Sea. Some even live in the sea itself! Many of these beings are kind-hearted, willing to aid Link in his quest to banish evil and save his lost friend. Others are villainous and cruel, yearning to stop the young hero in his tracks.

Characters

Anouki

The Anouki are very gruff and sarcastic and live upon a frigid Isle of Frost. They've always had to tread lightly in their homeland, as the dangerous and unpredictable Yook live just east of them in a horrible place called the Great Ice Field. Link finds the Anouki tribe in a state of disorder when he first visits their icy isle: A wily Yook has infiltrated the Anouki village and is posing as one of them! Naturally, the young hero tries his best to help resolve the situation.

Anouki Island Chief

The long-bearded leader of the Anouki tribe is known only as the Island Chief. This thick-skinned chieftain has seen much hardship in his time, and many of his recent burdens stem from the Yook: a nasty tribe of wicked creatures that reside in the Great Ice Field to the east. The Island Chief hopes that Link can help him settle things between the Yook and Anouki once and for all. If peace can be achieved, perhaps he'd be willing to part with his tribe's pure metal!

Aroo

A member of the easy-going Anouki tribe, Aroo finds himself skating on thin ice when he's kidnapped by one of the fearsome Yook that live alongside the Anouki at the Isle of Frost. Aroo is not only taken hostage, but also is replaced in his village by a Yook imposter! He remains in captivity deep within the Temple of Ice until Link comes to his aid.

Astrid

A sage fortune-teller, Astrid has the unique ability to see far into the future. Link comes to her aid after she is assailed by monsters, and the wise woman repays his heroism with gifts of knowledge and precious artifacts. After Link further demonstrates his valor by braving the Temple of Fire, Astrid sees immense promise in the boy and does her best to guide him along his just and noble path.

Beedle

This savvy merchant sails all across the Great Sea, peddling his wares from is world-renowned Shop Ship. Though known to drive a hard bargain, Beedle is really just a friendly guy who loves the freedom his unique lifestyle provides him. He honors loyal customers with his special membership program, giving greater and greater discounts to those who spend their hard-earned Rupees at Beedle's!

Biggoron

Noble leader of the proud Goron tribe, Biggoron has seen much in his long tenure as elder. His great size and strength are matched only by his great heart—and his vast love of Goron culture! To gain acceptance among his tribe, Link must prove that his affinity for all things Goron runs just as deeply as the gentle elder's. Only then will the lad gain the help he needs to carry out his great quest!

Ciela

A tiny fairy with a big heart, Ciela comes to Link's aid when he washes ashore at Mercay Island. After listening to his story and hearing of his friend's capture by the nefarious Ghost Ship, Ciela's natural reaction is to help Link in any way she can. Perhaps this is because she knows something of feeling scared and alone; the little fairy lost her memory long ago and was rescued by a kind old man when she found herself stranded on Mercay Island. A guiding light and clever advisor, Ciela sticks by Link through the many hardships he must face during his quest to track down the mysterious Ghost Ship.

Eddo

Small and squirrelly, Eddo is the genius inventor behind a variety of sea craft products and accessories. Some of his latest and greatest achievements are a remarkable cannon that can be mounted to the deck of any good-sized vessel and a salvage arm, which can haul up treasure from the seafloor. A true workaholic, Eddo takes his calling very seriously, often locking himself away inside his workshop so he can achieve total concentration on the task at hand.

Freedle

This free spirit has a fondness for fun! Freedle whiles away the days at Mercay Island's northeast islet, strumming a guitar and singing praises about Magic Boxes to all who'll listen. Freedle just wants folks to share the love—of treasures and ship parts, that is! Meeting Freedle for the first time unlocks Tag Mode, a special mode that allows players to share their excess collectibles with folks who connect to their DS. When everybody pitches in, no one's left out!

Fuzo

A friendly, bulging man, Fuzo lives a simple life on Cannon Island. He loves to do his master's bidding, but that isn't much of a job these days. Old Eddo has kept himself locked away inside his workroom for quite some time. Perhaps out of loneliness, Fuzo decides to help Link sneak into his master's workshop. Maybe when someone has purchased the cannon Eddo has been working on, he will finally choose to come out!

Golden Chief Cylos

Don't get the name wrong: This is Golden Chief Cylos, friend of the Ocean King! A giant golden bullfrog living on an uncharted isle, noble Cylos grants Link the ability to warp about the sea with the aid of his "gilt minions"—those little golden frogs Link encounters while sailing the ocean blue! This method of travel is only possible through the use of his Cyclone Slate, which Cylos gives to Link because he has the spirits with him and is trying to help the Ocean King, who had taken care of Cylos in the past.

Gongoron

Gongoron is Biggoron's one and only heir. Brash and immature, he doesn't warm up to Link at first. Instead, Gongoron resents the young outsider for trying to become a brother to the Goron tribe for selfish reasons. Gongoron soon learns that Link's heart is in the right place however, and the two end up relying on each other to get through a variety of harrowing trials.

Gorons

A proud and ancient race of noble beings, the Gorons make their home on a giant island at the south end of the Great Sea. These large, rotund creatures are exceptionally strong and naturally resistant to harsh climates. They're so tough that they're perfectly comfortable living amongst the cliffs of their rocky island home! Link must prove himself to this quiet tribe in order to gain their trust, for only with their aid can he banish evil from the land.

Ho Hos

A band of intrepid explorers from the far-off land of Wayaway, the Ho Hos sail about the southeast quadrant of the sea aboard their Traveler's Ship, searching for random items. These unique individuals prize nothing above that rarest of all baubles: the Regal Ring. If Link ever gets his hand on one of those precious treasures, he'd do well to pay the Ho Hos a visit!

Kayo

When hoards of monsters suddenly appeared on his volcanic island, brave Kayo wasted no time in trying to save his beloved mistress, the fortune-teller, Astrid. Unfortunately, he was unprepared for the evil that arrived, and Kayo gave his life trying to save the seer. Now he's doomed to drift as a spirit, floating near the place where he fell at a far end of the island. Kayo is an upbeat soul, however, and he always sees the upside in every situation. He doesn't mind being a ghost at all—at least he's lost a lot of weight!

Linebeck

Captain of the mighty S.S. *Linebeck* steam ship, this salty seaman is brash and bold, and he doesn't mind saying so! A real man of the sea, Linebeck enjoys sailing hither and yon in search of fortune and glory—almost as much as he enjoys downing tall glasses of dairy at the local Milk Bar! Although he claims to have braved dangers and hardships untold, Linebeck always seems to have some excuse for keeping himself well out of harm's way. While this forces Link to do most of the adventuring, the young hero wouldn't be able to get around without Linebeck's help. Together, the two make quite the pair of explorers!

Man of Smiles

A peculiar man leading a peculiar life, the Man of Smiles searches the northeastern waters of the sea for high adventure aboard his little Traveler's Ship. Unfortunately, however, adventure ends up finding *him*: A gang of monsters seizes control of his vessel! After being rescued from the beasts by Link, the Man of Smiles becomes forever grateful to the lad. He rewards Link with a special item that starts the hero on a path to unlocking a powerful new ability!

Nyave

Nyave is a loyal member of the maritime defense force. Sailing the southwest quadrant in his trusty vessel, this hard-featured soldier joined the force so he could learn to become a hero like his big bro. Unfortunately, Nyave's natural reaction when faced with danger is to play dead. This isn't exactly the type of posture that becomes a true hero!

Nyeve

Though he runs an exciting Cannon Game challenge from his little stand at Bannan Island, and always refers to himself as the "Hero," Nyeve is an extremely bored, downtrodden individual. This is most likely because his stand sees very few customers, but what can he expect? He couldn't have chosen a more remote spot to run his attraction! Link is able to cheer the man up considerably by playing—and winning at—Nyeve's Cannon Game.

Old Wayfarer

This guy lives for adventure! Having left his wife, son, and native island of Molida long ago, the man known only as the Old Wayfarer has sacrificed all in pursuit of his great dream: to venture forth into the thrilling unknown! After spending most of his adult life charting the northwestern portion of the Great Sea, the Wayfarer now seeks to settle down. Not with his family, mind you, but with a legendary creature known as the mermaid!

Oshus

A wise, kindhearted old man, Oshus has lived on Mercay Island his whole life. When Ciela washed ashore long ago, her memory gone, Oshus took her in and provided a safe environment for her to rest and recover her strength, and perhaps one day, her memory. Saddened to hear of the loss of Link's friend because of the nefarious Ghost Ship, Oshus helps Link by steering him in the direction of another person who might be of more help—and later, by showing the lad the finer points of using pointy weapons.

Postman

A hardworking fellow with a penchant for parcels, the Postman lives for special deliveries! This good-natured guy makes it his mission to mingle mail between the many islands of the Great Sea. How does he do this all by himself? He just wings it… with the wings on his back!

Romanos

This young man has a lot to be angry about when Link first meets him. His estranged father took off long ago, leaving Romanos and his mom at their island home while venturing off to explore the sea. Romanos simply can't understand such selfishness, but Link manages to help him identify with his father's feelings. After Link finds Romanos's dad's old hideaway, Romanos reads his father's journal and begins to understand what it means to have a wayfaring soul. He even decides to become an explorer himself, and opens a Shooting Range to make money for his first expedition!

Self-Proclaimed Hero

Something about this guy seems *very* familiar, but Link is too polite to say anything. This so-called hero claims to have sailed the seas aboard his **red lion ship**, battling evil and saving the world from tyranny. However, a quick bout of swordplay with the man shows his skills to be somewhat lacking! Still, Link is always happy to have a sparring partner, and the self-proclaimed hero is always up for a few dueling rounds with his favorite new "apprentice."

Shipyard Worker

This burly fellow loves getting his hands dirty, but not when it comes to fixing bridges! Ship parts are his one and only passion, and he's happy to install any part Link finds onto Linebeck's ship, free of charge. He'll even tune up a broken salvage arm should the device become damaged during an overzealous salvage op! Just don't expect him to buy any parts off you; he's already got a collection you wouldn't believe!

Tetra

A brash, pretty young girl, Tetra is leader to a hodgepodge band of pirates. She met Link while exploring the seas one day, and while sharing many adventures together, the two became the best of friends. During their travels, Tetra discovered that she is actually the princess of an ancient, ruined kingdom: She's **Princess Zelda** of the **Kingdom of Hyrule**! For this reason, Tetra was kidnapped by a dark lord, who sought the sacred power passed down to Hylian princesses. Link overcame many perils in his quest to save the girl, at last defeating the evil wizard and rescuing his friend. However, Tetra soon finds herself in grave danger again when she boldly boards a creepy Ghost Ship in search of its fabled treasure! The Ghost Ship quickly spirits the girl away, and Link must journey to rescue his friend once more.

Treasure Teller

Hold fast your valuables! The Treasure Teller makes his living buying and trading collectible commodities, including all the various treasures and ship parts Link acquires during his travels. This makes the Treasure Teller a great guy to know when you need some fast cash. If you find you're carrying around multiple identical ship parts and treasures, feel free to pawn some to the Treasure Teller and fatten your wallet for future buys.

Zauz, the Blacksmith

A monster of a man, Zauz lives a life of solitude on his own, private island. Dedicated to his craft, he whiles away the days hammering out weaponry and tools of unrivaled quality. Intense and intimidating, yet kindhearted and wise, this burly blacksmith eventually plays an important role in helping Link unlock his true destiny.

Enemies

Red ChuChu

Threat Meter

Speed: Slow

Attack Power: 1/2 heart (contact)

Defense Power: 1 hit to defeat

These are some of the most basic and harmless enemies Link encounters. They move very slowly and their only method of attack involves moving into contact with their quarry. Not the best combination! Link's fast, far-reaching targeted attack is the best way to dispatch these less-than-worthy foes until he acquires more effective tools, such as the Grappling Hook. Employ spin attacks if they take you by surprise or manage to swarm you.

Keese

Threat Meter

Speed: Fast

Attack Power: 1/2 heart (contact)

Defense Power: 1 hit to defeat

These ugly bloodsuckers can be quite a handful when they attack in groups! Their quick, unpredictable movements make them hard to track with targeted attacks, so use Link's spin attack for 360-degree mayhem instead. After Link acquires a shield, he can repel these creatures when they dive toward him. And after acquiring the Boomerang, he can easily dispatch these fluttering pests from afar!

Rope

Threat Meter

Speed: Slow, then fast!

Attack Power: 1/2 heart (contact)

Defense Power: 1 hit to defeat

Beware of these little snakes! Though they seem quite docile and harmless at first, Ropes quickly spring to life as soon as they notice Link, racing toward him in a straight line at top speed. Run circles around these enemies, keeping out of sight to prevent them from dashing toward you. Throw the Boomerang or Grappling Hook, or simply use targeted attacks to quickly dispatch unwary Ropes from the side or behind!

Rat

Threat Meter

Speed: Medium

Attack Power: 1/2 heart (contact)

Defense Power: 1 hit to defeat

These dirty vermin are nothing to fear! They don't chase after Link, but instead move about randomly in sporadic bursts of speed. Simply keep your distance, wait for a Rat to stop running, then quickly tap it for a quick, targeted attack. Presto! Items like the Boomerang and Grappling Hook also make dispatching rats a breeze.

Crow

Threat Meter

Speed: Fast

Attack Power: 1/2 heart (contact)

Defense Power: 1 hit to defeat

Look up from time to time: dangerous Crows are known to perch in tall trees. They quickly descend on unwary travelers to lighten their wallets of Rupees! Don't give these dirty birds a chance to pilfer your hard-earned cash; run straight away whenever one swoops near. Unleash a fast spin attack at just the right moment to give the Crow a powerful smack. Or just keep on running; these lazy birds only make one attack run before flying off, regardless of whether they hit you!

Octorok

Threat Meter

Speed: Slow

Attack Power: 1/2 heart (contact); 1/2 heart (rock)

Defense Power: 2 hits to defeat

These hardworking hostiles have put in appearances in nearly every major *Zelda* title, and *Phantom Hourglass* is no exception! Octoroks are classic baddies that attack by firing rocks from their oversized snouts. They're also somewhat resilient foes, requiring two normal targeted attacks to defeat (or one potent jump or spin attack). Fortunately, Link can deflect an Octorok's painful projectiles and bounce these guys around by charging them with his shield. This makes Octoroks somewhat easy to handle, provided Link doesn't show them his back!

Tektite

Threat Meter

Speed: Fast

Attack Power: 1/2 heart (contact)

Defense Power: 2 hits to defeat

Resilient and tough to predict, Tektites can be a real handful for Link. Making fast, sudden leaps, these adversaries like to pounce on their quarry, then quickly hop away to safety. Don't play their game! Stay mobile to dodge their jump attacks and wait for the Tektite to land nearby. Then be quick to show it the sharp side of Link's sword! Targeted attacks work well enough, but powerful spin attacks are the fastest ways to put an end to these threats. Be especially careful around red Tektites; they're even tougher, requiring three hits to squash!

Yellow ChuChu

Threat Meter

Speed: Slow

Attack Power: 1/2 heart (contact)

Defense Power: 1 hit to defeat

Running into one of these ChuChus can be quite the shocking experience! Keep a distance from these electrified adversaries, who can leap toward Link from range to zap him with contact damage. Don't attack a Yellow ChuChu while it's lit up either, or its radiant current will flow through Link's blade for an unpleasant jolt. Wait for their charge to dissipate instead, then be quick about tapping them to retaliate with a

targeted blow. Or simply whack them with the Boomerang or Grappling Hook from range to turn out their lights!

Green Slime

Threat Meter

Speed: Fast

Attack Power: 1/2 heart (contact)

Defense Power: 2-3 hits to defeat

These revolting piles of goo leap about with surprising speed, relentlessly chasing Link. Maybe they're attracted to his stylish green outfit? In any case, be very wary of these foes; each time you strike one, it splits into two smaller, even more annoying blobs! Tiny Green Slimes don't damage Link when they leap onto him; instead, they slow him down and prevent him from drawing his sword. Naturally, this is a terrible burden when other monsters are about! Quickly rub the stylus back and forth when hampered by bitsy slimes; this causes Link to shrug them off. Be quick to retaliate with spin attacks afterward!

Fire Bubble

Threat Meter

Speed: Normal

Attack Power: 1/2 heart (contact)

Defense Power: 1 hit to defeat

Don't lose your head when faced with these frightening foes! These flaming skulls don't actually chase after Link; they simply hover about, blindly bouncing off walls and other objects. And although Fire Bubbles are immune to Link's sword while airborne, they are vulnerable to a quick toss of his Boomerang! It's best to trace a quick zigzag pattern between Link and the Fire Bubble to ensure the Boomerang strikes its target. Once it's grounded, quickly follow up with a targeted attack to burst that Bubble once and for all!

Fire Keese

Threat Meter

Speed: Fast

Attack Power: 1/2 heart (contact)

Defense Power: 1 hit to defeat (Boomerang)

Until Link acquires more advanced items, his only option for dispatching these dangerous dive bombers is the Boomerang! Don't bother with cold hard steel; simply keep your distance, ready the Boomerang, and then trace a quick zigzag pattern between Link and the burning beastie. Fire Keese move in irregular patterns, so this is the best way to ensure that the Boomerang finds its mark! Like normal

Keese, these little fry guys are too weak to withstand even one whack from the mighty Boomerang.

Phantom

Threat Meter

Speed: Slow (patrolling); Fast (alerted)

Attack Power: 1 heart (contact)

Defense Power: Seemingly invulnerable

Whoa, look at the size of these guys! Phantoms are the guardians of the Temple of the Ocean King, and they take their job *very* seriously. These brutes are so tough, Link has no hope of defeating them in combat until he acquires the legendary **Phantom Sword!** The young hero must instead outwit Phantoms, keeping out of sight and dashing to hide at safe zones whenever he's been spotted. Phantoms pack quite a wallop when they strike Link, reducing his health energy by one full heart. Worse, each Phantom's attack drains 30 precious seconds from the Phantom Hourglass and sends Link back to the entrance of the current floor. Yikes! Red Phantoms are faster than normal, while gold ones can warp directly to Link's location. Keep a distance from these dangerous watchmen, stick close to safe zones, and monitor your map carefully.

Bee

Threat Meter

Speed: Fast

Attack Power: 1/2 heart (contact)

Defense Power: 1 hit to defeat

Be nice to Bees! These harmless buzzers don't aggressively pursue Link unless he angers them first, so why be mean to them? The only real way to tick off a Bee is to mess with its hive; this prompts a large swarm to zip out and attack! Bees can hardly be considered enemies as they really just want to be left alone. Let them go about their bizzzness, will ya!

Miniblin

Threat Meter

Speed: Fast

Attack Power: 1/2 heart (spear)

Defense Power: 2 hits to defeat

They travel in packs and attack from the back! Miniblins are easily bested in small numbers, but they can be quite a handful when they start to swarm. These little menaces love keeping *just* out of reach of Link's blade, quickly darting in to poke the young hero with their spears whenever chance permits. When faced with a group of Miniblins, it's usually best to pick one beastie and pursue it relentlessly with targeted attacks. Or whack them with the Boomerang to slow them down! Though Miniblins take two normal hits to defeat, their penchant for backpedaling often causes Link to lash out at them with double-damage jump attacks. Of course, your best option when you're being overwhelmed is the powerful spin attack. When properly timed, a spinning slash can wipe out multiple Miniblins at once!

Zora Warrior

Threat Meter

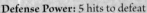

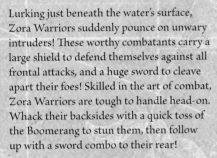

Speed: Normal

Attack Power: 1/2 heart (sword)

Defense Power: 5 hits to defeat

Lurking just beneath the water's surface, Zora Warriors suddenly pounce on unwary intruders! These worthy combatants carry a large shield to defend themselves against all frontal attacks, and a huge sword to cleave apart their foes! Skilled in the art of combat, Zora Warriors are tough to handle head-on. Whack their backsides with a quick toss of the Boomerang to stun them, then follow up with a sword combo to their rear!

Sandworm

Threat Meter

Speed: Very Fast

Attack Power: 1 heart (devour)

Defense Power: 1 Bomb to defeat

Guardians of the sacred windmills on the Isle of Gust, Sandworms are completely docile until an unwelcome visitor happens across their peaceful habitat. Owning a keen sense of hearing, even the slightest noise alerts these fearsome beasts, who burrow to the site of the disturbance with alarming speed! When they've caught up to their quarry, Sandworms burst up from the desert sands, swallowing the intruder whole! Wise travelers keep very silent when crossing into Sandworm country, walking slowly to create as little noise as possible. The craftiest wayfarers have learned to throw Bombs to distract Sandworms, potentially tricking the beasts into swallowing the explosive by mistake!

Rock ChuChu

Threat Meter

Speed: Slow

Attack Power: 1/4 heart (burst from rock); 1/2 heart (contact)

Defense Power: 1 Bomb to weaken; 1 hit to defeat

Be careful when lifting up rocks: You never know what you might find! Rock ChuChus are tough nuts to crack. They hate being hit so much that they often hide under large boulders and wait for trouble to come find them! Once exposed, a Rock ChuChu relies on its strong stone shell to protect it from Link's sword. While sword attacks can keep a Rock ChuChu at bay, the only way to remove their rocky armor is to blast it off with a Bomb! After they've been stripped of their stone coatings, Rock ChuChus are nothing more than run-of-the-mill Red ChuChus. Finish them off in the usual fashion!

Phantom Eye

Threat Meter

Speed: Normal

Attack Power: None

Defense Power: 1 hit to defeat

These hideous floating eyeballs act as sentries for those frightening Phantoms, alerting the brutes to Link's presence whenever they spy him. Phantom Eyes can't do much to defend themselves, though, and it's best to exploit this weakness without delay! Blacken their eyes with the Boomerang from afar, then dash in close to poke them shut with Link's pointy sword. Or use more advanced weaponry, such as Bombchus, to annihilate them from afar. At that point, the eyes have had it!

Moldorm

Threat Meter

Speed: Normal

Attack Power: 1/2 heart (contact)

Defense Power: 3 hits to defeat

Watch out when combating these creepy crawlers! Although slow, Moldorms are relentless and tough to handle in groups. Link's greatest advantage against them is his superior speed and mobility. The young hero must outmaneuver Moldorms so he can stick them where it hurts. One of the easiest ways to kill a Moldorm is

to strike the red area with an arrow—they die instantly. Keep away from their pincers and run circles around these dangerous foes, and hack at their vulnerable tails at every chance!

Shell Beast

Threat Meter

Speed: Slow

Attack Power: 1/2 heart (contact)

Defense Power: Invincible

For these guys, slow and steady wins the fight! Incapable of moving very quickly, Shell Beasts pursue their prey with steady determination. They damage Link if they manage to touch him, so keep these creatures at bay! Although well shielded by their thick, natural armor, Shell Beasts can be knocked about by Link's stiff sword attacks. Beat these beasts backward and try to knock them off ledges and the like—they weren't built to take a fall!

Winder

Threat Meter

Speed: Slow

Attack Power: 1/2 heart (contact)

Defense Power: Invincible

Always steer clear of Winders! These electrically charged baddies snake through halls and corridors, bouncing ever onward to zap anything in their path. Winders' current is always active, and it races up Link's sword if he tries to attack them. It's best simply to avoid these shockingly dangerous foes!

Green ChuChu

Threat Meter

Speed: Slow

Attack Power: 1/2 heart (contact)

Defense Power: 1 hit to defeat

These guys come in green, too? Wild! Whatever you do, don't take Green ChuChus lightly: They can make themselves invincible by shrinking into tiny puddles! None of Link's attacks affect a puddled Green ChuChu, so it's best to keep away and wait for it to reform once more. The moment you see the ChuChu return to its normal shape, tap it to unleash a fast targeted attack. Splat!

primagames.com

Pols Voice

Threat Meter

Speed: Normal

Attack Power: 1 (contact)

Defense Power: 1 good scream to weaken; 1 hit to defeat

When faced with one of these long-eared foes, simply holler into your DS microphone. This sonic assault forces the Pols Voice to shrink into a tiny ball! Follow up with a fast sword attack to finish the creature off in style. Make sure to deal with Pols Voices quickly; they hop about with surprising speed, yearning to crush Link under their incredible bulk!

Beamos

Threat Meter

Speed: Immobile

Attack Power: 1/2 heart (laser)

Defense Power: Invincible

These immobile stone sentries are something to be feared! A Beamos's only moving part is its laser eye, which rotates 360 degrees around the top of the statue, scanning the vicinity for intruders. When a threat is identified, a Beamos quickly fires a powerful laser from its eye, carving a line into the floor—and into anything caught standing in its path! Link can shoot out the eye of a Beamos with an arrow, making it incapable of attacking. However, if Link leaves the floor, it will be repaired when he returns.

Jolene

Threat Meter

Speed: Fast

Attack Power: 1/2 heart (sword swipe); 1 heart (dash attack)

Defense Power: Multiple hits to defeat!

This is one woman whose fury truly has no equal! Fast and accurate with her curved blade, Jolene is a very dangerous adversary. While her normal attacks are potent, she enjoys dashing forward at lightning speed to deliver an extremely punishing blow! Link must keep away from this woman's curved blade at all times and try to circle around behind her when she prepares to unleash a powerful dash! This helps Link avoid the coming blow, and also positions him to retaliate with some fancy swordplay of his own!

Poe

Threat Meter

Speed: Slow

Attack Power: 1/2 heart (fireball)

Defense Power: 1 hit to defeat

You can never be sure if a room is empty anymore! Poes are evil spirits with the frightening ability to disappear and reappear right under Link's nose. These wicked ghosts float just out of reach, often vanishing before the young hero can strike them with his blade. If a Poe gets a chance, it quickly spits out a blue fireball that cannot be blocked. Dodge these dangerous projectiles and look to retaliate with a fast attack from Link's Boomerang or Bow.

Skulltula

Threat Meter

Speed: Immobile (drop and hang)

Attack Power: 1/2 heart (contact)

Defense Power: 1 hit to defeat

These freaky creepers are nothing to fear, as long as they don't get the drop on you! Skulltulas periodically plunge down from the Ghost Ship's rafters, attempting to snare Link by surprise. However, their positions are given away by their shadows, and by the rattling sound they make just before they fall! Link does well to walk slowly when Skulltulas are about, dispatching each one after they drop in to say hello.

Reapling

Threat Meter

Speed: Normal

Attack Power: 2 hearts (scythe)

Defense Power: Invincible

The terror of the Ghost Ship and bane of all would-be heroes, Reaplings scour the lower decks of their haunted craft in search of trespassers. Similar in many ways to Phantoms, these massive wraiths are faster and more menacing by far. A Reapling's ethereal form allows it to see and travel right through solid walls; it can spy intruders from afar and quickly cross great distances. Fortunately, Reaplings still can't see or pass through safe zones! Link must keep well out of sight and stick close to safe zones so he can quickly reach cover whenever he is spotted. Risk takers don't last long when Reaplings are about!

Wizzrobe

Threat Meter

Speed: Normal

Attack Power: 15 seconds drained (scythe)

Defense Power: 1 hit to defeat

Feel a chill in the air? Better take a look behind you: A Wizzrobe may be close on your heels! These ghouls remain invisible until they slip behind Link, then they swing at him with their scythes. Each hit they score instantly drains 15 seconds from the Phantom Hourglass! Wizzrobes can pass through walls and the like to get close to Link with frightening speed. The young hero must keep tabs on them by glancing at his map, and make good use of safe zones to escape the Wizzrobes' wrath. Fortunately, each time a Wizzrobe draws near, Link has a chance to retaliate by unleashing a quick spin attack! One spinning blow from Link's sword is all it takes to wipe a Wizzrobe from existence.

Eye Brute

Threat Meter

Speed: Slow

Attack Power: 1/2 heart (contact); 1 heart (Bomb)

Defense Power: Multiple hits to defeat

What an eyesore! These big, blue, one-eyed brutes may not have much in the way of looks, but they make up for that in sheer strength. Eye Brutes like to batter Link up close and hurl Bombs at him from afar. It's tempting to try to run from such frightening creatures, but Link's best option is to simply stare these foes right in the eye. Or better yet, let lose a few arrows! Poking out an Eye Brute's one and only eye is a surefire way to calm them down. Then Link can rush forward to inflict serious damage with his trusty blade.

Blue ChuChu

Threat Meter

Speed: Normal

Attack Power: 1/2 heart (contact)

Defense Power: Stun with Boomerang; 2 hits to defeat

This most dangerous form of ChuChu is nothing to toy with! Blue ChuChus stalk after Link with surprising ferocity, leaping and bounding forward to zap the young hero with their electrified frames. As with Yellow ChuChus, Link suffers harm if he tries attacking these guys while they're powered up. Stun them with a Boomerang toss to make them safe to strike, or simply dispatch Blue ChuChus with Bombs or arrows from range.

Like Like

Threat Meter

Speed: Slow

Attack Power: 1/2 heart (devour)

Defense Power: 1 Bomb to weaken; 1 hit to defeat

Keep well away from Like Likes: They quickly suck Link up and start digesting him. Getting sucked up by a creepy Like Like is bad news because these cylindrical villains love snacking on shields! They don't do so well after munching down Bombs though, and Link can trick these hungry uglies into doing just that!

Armos

Threat Meter
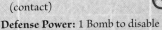

Speed: Normal

Attack Power: 1/2 heart (contact)

Defense Power: 1 Bomb to disable

Huge and intimidating, these statue-like sentries remain completely docile until an intruder draws near. As soon as it detects a trespasser, an Armos suddenly comes to life, stomping about in pursuit to eliminate the threat! While these massive beings are too sturdy to take damage from Link's sword, they're highly vulnerable to explosives. Just one blast from a Bomb shuts down an Armos for good!

Eye Slug

Threat Meter
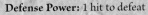

Speed: Normal

Attack Power: 1/2 heart (contact)

Defense Power: 1 hit to defeat

These slithering fiends sure look mean, but they barely register on the threat meter. Link has faced far more dangerous creatures by the time he encounters these little pests and can easily wipe them out however he chooses. The spin attack usually works quite well, as Eye Slugs tend to attack in groups and can quickly swarm Link.

Yook

Threat Meter

Speed: Slow

Attack Power: 1/2 heart (club); 1 heart (breath attack)

Defense Power: 1 Bomb to stun; 5 hits to defeat

Yook are members of a dangerous tribe of creatures that live in the Isle of Frost's eastern wastelands. Having suffered years of oppression at the hands of a rival tribe, the Yook are incredibly mean-spirited and quick to attack anything that steps foot on their turf. Their favorite method of harassment involves inhaling deeply and then roaring out a huge cone of frost, effectively turning their harsh environment against their enemies. Link can exploit this attack by tossing Bombs into a Yook's open mouth. It's the only way to close their yappers!

Stag Beetle

Threat Meter

Speed: Normal

Attack Power: 1/2 heart (contact)

Defense Power: Grappling Hook to weaken; 1 hit to defeat

These bugs mean business! Stag Beetles are incredibly tenacious, relentlessly pursuing their quarry. They attack simply by rushing forward and poking their foe with their sharp horns! Link is ill-equipped to deal with Stag Beetles until he acquires a handy new Hammer at the Isle of Frost that allows him to combat them on even terms.

Ice Bubble

Threat Meter

Speed: Normal

Attack Power: 1/2 heart & freeze (contact)

Defense Power: 1 hit to defeat

Like Fire Bubbles, these flaming skulls don't actually pursue Link; they just blindly bounce about. They're immune to Link's sword while airborne, but are easily grounded by a quick toss of his Grappling Hook or Boomerang. Use these tools to help you defeat Ice Bubbles, and don't let them get too close: They'll freeze Link for a moment if they manage to touch him!

Ice Keese

Threat Meter

Speed: Fast

Attack Power: 1/2 heart & freeze (contact)

Defense Power: 1 hit to defeat (Boomerang)

Keese seem to adapt to any climate. The ones Link encounters within the Temple of Ice have grown quite accustomed to the cold! Keep well away from Ice Keese, using the Boomerang or Grappling Hook to dispatch them from afar. Like other forms of Keese, these frigid minions are too weak to withstand even one whack!

Rupee Like

Threat Meter

Speed: Slow

Attack Power: 1/2 heart (devour); Rupees lost over time

Defense Power: 1 Bomb to weaken; 1 hit to defeat

Who knew picking up loose change could be so dangerous? Beware of innocent-looking Rupees on the ground: They might actually be monsters in disguise! Rupee Likes are similar to Like Likes, except they have a taste for Rupees instead of Wooden Shields. Rupee Likes try to suck Link up and munch away at his wallet, steadily chewing up his hard-earned Rupees. Rupee Likes are always vulnerable to Link's sword.

Stalfos

Threat Meter

Speed: Normal

Attack Power: 1/2 heart (bone); 1/2 heart (contact)

Defense Power: 2 hits to defeat

Not every fallen adventurer was a kind soul in life. Some of the bones that lie on the ground once belonged to wicked men who still seek to do evil! When Link nears a Stalfos, its lifeless bones quickly snap together, and the remade skeletal villain springs up to attack. Stalfoses are quick and agile, easily capable of jumping away from Link's blade and then hurling sharp bones at him from afar. Dispatching these monsters with steel alone is tricky: Link's Grappling Hook, Bombs, and even the Boomerang help him make short work of Stalfoses!

Shell Spinner

Threat Meter

Speed: Fast

Attack Power: 1/2 heart (contact)

Defense Power: Hammer to weaken, 1 hit to defeat

These little guys aren't too challenging, but boy are they fun to watch! Shell Spinners just love to spin and spin, bumping into walls and objects in search of something soft and heroic to slam into. They don't attack with much oomph however, and Link can easily fend them off with his shield. Unfortunately, little can be done against Shell Spinners until Link finds the Hammer. When he has the right tool, he can flip these baddies over and put an end to their antics!

Great Sea Enemies

Sea Trap

Threat Meter

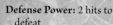

Speed: Slow

Attack Power: 1 heart (contact)

Defense Power: 2 hits to defeat

Sea Traps are the first watery ne'er-do-wells Link encounters while navigating the Great Sea. They resemble thorny tripwires stretched between a pair of ugly sea urchins. Sea Traps surface from the depths in surprise attack and then slowly move toward Link's ship, attempting to ram it. Your best option to avoid a hazardous collision with a Sea Trap is to tap the Jump Arrow at just the right moment and sail clean over it. Wahoo!

Flying Fish

Threat Meter

Speed: Normal

Attack Power: 1 heart (contact)

Defense Power: 1 hit to defeat

Flying Fish aren't really much of a threat to your vessel. After emerging from the ocean, these little guys hover in midair for a moment before diving straight at you! Tap these fish out of water the second you spot them to blast them from the sky. Fish sticks, anyone?

Eyeball Monster

Threat Meter

Speed: Normal

Attack Power: 1 heart (contact)

Defense Power: 1 hit to defeat

Some airborne entities you encounter in eastern waters of the sea are actually Eyeball Monsters that flutter high above the surface of the ocean. These fiends travel in tight packs, eager to swoop down and assault unwary wayfarers by slamming into their vessels. Fortunately, these minor threats are somewhat slow and easy to blast from the sky. Just unleash a barrage of cannonballs until you've obliterated the whole pack!

Ocean Octorok

Threat Meter

Speed: Normal

Attack Power: 1 heart (rock)

Defense Power: 1 hit to defeat

These aquatic Octoroks have adapted to life underwater. When an unsuspecting vessel happens their way, Ocean Octoroks surface to punch holes in their hull with long-range rock bombardments! It's tough targeting these nimble sea creatures, as they commonly circle around your ship. Sometimes they even dive underwater to give you the slip! Track an Ocean Octorok's movements carefully and aim just ahead of them. This gives your cannonballs time to travel through the air and strike the Ocean Octorok as it circles your craft. One hit is all it takes to sink these watery predators!

Eye Plant

Threat Meter

Speed: Immobile

Attack Power: 1 heart (contact); 1 heart (seed)

Defense Power: 2 hits to defeat

Some of the most dangerous creatures you'll encounter at sea are Eye Plants. These hideous villains resemble large eyeballs attached to tall stalks that poke up from the water when a tasty meal passes by. Eye Plants favor spitting large seeds at their prey to weaken them from afar, but they often surface directly in front of your ship, inflicting contact damage if you ram into them. It takes two direct cannon blasts to drop an Eye Plant, and their seeds can be shot down in midair as well. Blast these monsters the moment you spot them; they can inflict great damage in short order!

Mini Cyclone

Threat Meter

Speed: Slow

Attack Power: 1 heart (contact)

Defense Power: 2 hits to defeat

Mini Cyclones are tough to see, and this may be their most dangerous attribute! Keep a sharp eye out for these little devils, which can send your ship spinning if you sail into them. Being twirled by these whirlwinds drains one full heart from your ship's heart meter, so it's not a fun ride! Fortunately, dispelling Mini Cyclones is a breeze: Just lob two cannonballs at one to make it quiet down.

Cannon Boat

Threat Meter

Speed: Fast

Attack Power: 1 heart (cannon)

Defense Power: 5 hits to defeat

Sound the alarm! Cannon Boats are the terror of the high seas, firing on innocent vessels from afar the moment they spot them. Their cannons are just as powerful and accurate as Link's, and they unload their cannonballs at great speed! These mobile aggressors chase you all about, and never go down without a fight. Keep your ship sailing when facing a Cannon Boat, and just keep firing away until you sink these dangerous craft!

Jolene's Ship

Threat Meter

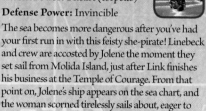

Speed: Fast

Attack Power: 1 heart (torpedo)

Defense Power: Invincible

The sea becomes more dangerous after you've had your first run in with this feisty she-pirate! Linebeck and crew are accosted by Jolene the moment they set sail from Molida Island, just after Link finishes his business at the Temple of Courage. From that point on, Jolene's ship appears on the sea chart, and the woman scorned tirelessly sails about, eager to claim vengeance against Linebeck. Don't bother battling with Jolene at sea: Either let her board Linebeck's ship and then fend her off, or bust out the Cyclone Slate and warp away from her fury!

Pirate Ship

Threat Meter

Speed: Fast

Attack Power: 1 heart (cannon)

Defense Power: 5 hits to defeat

The moment Link and company sail into the southeast quadrant's waters, they're greeted by a scary Pirate Ship! The craft is fast and fearsome: every bit as dangerous as Jolene's. These pirates will sink Linebeck's vessel if they must, but their real goal is to board the ship and take the crew for everything they're worth! Blast the Pirate Ship multiple times to sink it, or allow the scallywags to board you and then dispatch the mob of Miniblins that storms the hull. Beware of other Pirate Ships lurking amongst Cannon Boat patrols thereafter! When Link sinks a Pirate Ship, a salvage marker appears where it sank. If needed, Link can salvage for ship parts. However, once Link docks at an island or leaves the quadrant, the marker disappers.

Gyorg

Threat Meter

Speed: Fast

Attack Power: 1 heart (contact)

Defense Power: 1 hit to defeat

When the fins of these large, sharklike creatures suddenly peek up from the surface, you know you're in trouble! Gyorgs are some of the most dangerous enemies prowling the northeastern sea. They hunt in packs, often speeding past their quarry and then suddenly rounding to attack by means of a head-on collision! Blasting these fast-moving predators with the cannon is difficult—it's usually easier just to wait for a Gyorg to make its attack run, then jump of harm's way before impact!

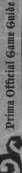

Bosses

NOTE

These are just brief glimpses at each of the terrible boss enemies Link must face at the end of dungeons. If you're stuck and not finding answers here, check the walkthrough for in-depth looks at each epic clash.

Blaaz, Master of Fire

Threat Meter

Speed: Normal

Attack Power: 1/2 heart (contact); 1/2 heart (fireball)

Defense Power: Multiple hits to defeat!

A wicked sorcerer with the power to split himself into three duplicates, Blaaz enjoys encircling and tormenting Link throughout their battle. Link must use the Boomerang to merge Blaaz's multiples together so he can assault the fiend with his righteous blade!

Cyclok, Stirrer of Winds

Threat Meter

Speed: Normal

Attack Power: 1/2 heart (contact); 1/2 heart (cyclone)

Defense Power: 1 Bomb to weaken; multiple hits to defeat!

A massive, wily Octorok with the power to summon cyclones, Cyclok enjoys flying high above Link, swooping down to batter the lad and sending whirlwinds to keep him off-balance. Link must avoid these attacks as he endeavors to blast Cyclok from the sky with Bombs. Once grounded, the fiend proves quite vulnerable to cold steel!

Crayk, Bane of Courage

Threat Meter

Speed: Normal

Attack Power: 1/4 heart per second (grab and shake); 1/2 heart (contact); 1/2 heart (Craykling)

Defense Power: Multiple hits to defeat!

This monstrous crablike baddie has the power to make itself invisible! Link faces a true test of courage in trying to best this beast: He must first blind it with a well-placed arrow, then bring the full weight of his sword to bear on its protective shell!

Diabolical Cubus Sisters

Threat Meter

Speed: Normal

Attack Power: 1/2 heart (laser); 1/2 heart (energy balls)

Defense Power: 2 hits to defeat each sister

Link believes he's saving these girls from captivity aboard the Ghost Ship, but nothing on that spectral vessel is as it appears! The Cubus sisters soon have their way with the young hero, forcing him to compete against them in a high-stakes game of dead man's volley! Link must beat the diabolical sisters at their own game if he hopes to rescue Tetra!

Dongorongo, Armored Lizard

Threat Meter

Speed: Slow

Attack Power: 1/2 heart (contact); 1/2 heart (fireball); 1 heart (charge); 1/2 heart (Eye Slugs)

Defense Power: Weaken with Bombchus; multiple hits to defeat!

This huge hulking creature would be tough for Link to handle all by himself. Fortunately, he's assisted by Gongoron, son of the Goron tribe's elder! Working together, the two brave heroes are able to topple the beast and force-feed it a very rich diet of Bombchus.

Gleeok, Two-Headed Dragon

Threat Meter

Speed: Immobile

Attack Power: 1 heart (fireball); 1 1/2 heart (snowball); 1 heart (bite); 1 heart (tidal wave)

Defense Power: Grappling Hook to weaken; multiple hits to defeat!

Beware when venturing too far out to sea: Here there be dragons! This two-headed fiend makes its home deep within the Temple of Ice, and it seems nearly impossible to harm by any normal means. Link must use his Grappling Hook in creative ways to turn the monster's attacks back on itself!

Cox, Ancient Stone Soldier

Threat Meter

Speed: Slow

Attack Power: 1 heart (fist smash/foot stomp); 1/2 heart (arrow)

Defense Power: Hammer to weaken; multiple hits to defeat!

This massive stone warrior has been making quite a ruckus within Mutoh's Temple. So much so that the former ruler of the once-mighty Cobble Kingdom finds it impossible to enjoy his eternal rest! Link must make a bit more noise while trying to batter the giant apart with the Hammer. Getting some air and smashing at the brute's weak points are the first steps to quieting the king's halls.

Evil Phantom Bellum

Threat Meter

Speed: Fast

Attack Power: 1/4 heart (ooze); 1/2 heart (ooze minion); 1/2 heart (tentacle slap); 1 heart (ram)

Defense Power: Hookshot & Bow to weaken; multiple Phantom Sword hits to defeat!

At last armed with the legendary Phantom Sword, Link has the ability to vanquish the evil that lurks deep within the Temple of the Ocean King. The final conflict puts the young hero's heart and ability to the ultimate test. Can he use all he has learned to emerge victorious over the sea's greatest nemesis?

Chapter 1

Contents

Getting Your Feet Wet: Exploring Mercay Island

Mercay Island

Temple of the
Ocean King

Milk Bar

Shop

1

2

Legend

1	Overworld Chest #1: Oshus's Sword
2	Overworld Chest #2: Treasure
	Bomb Wall

Mercay Island: Overview

During his courageous attempt at rescuing Tetra from the clutches of the fearsome Ghost Ship, Link accidentally tumbles overboard and splashes into the murky depths of the surrounding sea. Our young hero eventually awakens to find himself washed up on an unfamiliar island. What happened to that awful Ghost Ship? Where could it have taken poor Tetra? Link must get his bearings and seek out a means of getting off this strange bit of land, but it won't be easy: Mercay Island is quite large and filled with dangers of every sort. Fortunately, many kindhearted souls inhabit the island as well, and with their help, Link will soon be on his way to tracking down his lost friend.

1 Obtain Oshus's Sword

2 Journey to Mercay Island's Harbor

3 Locate Captain Linebeck

4 Find the Sea Chart & Set Sail

A Link to the Present

Items to Obtain

Big Green Rupee	Blue Rupee	Green Rupee	Oshus's Sword	Power Gem #1	Purple Potion	Red Potion	Red Rupee	Wooden Shield

Overworld Denizens

Characters — Enemies

Ciela · Farmer · Mercay Shop Mistress · Milk Bar Owner · Oshus · Shipyard Worker · Crow · Red ChuChu

Task 1: Obtain Oshus's Sword

Beached Hero

Link awakens to the sound of faint tinkling and finds himself lying face up on an sandy shore. Sitting upright, he notices a shimmering fairy fluttering about overhead. How peculiar! The fairy calls out to Link in a familiar voice, urging the lad to wake up.

The fairy introduces herself as Ciela and asks Link what happened to him. His mind reeling, the boy takes a moment to recall the events leading up to his becoming beached on the shore. Then it all comes flooding back: the Ghost Ship! Tetra! Link remembers he tried to save her, but he couldn't hang onto the haunted vessel and fell into the sea. He must have lost consciousness and washed up on this island!

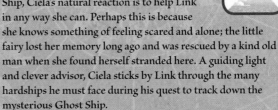

As luck would have it, Ciela informs Link that her grandpa knows something about the Ghost Ship. She urges Link to visit her grandpa, whose house isn't far. Ciela wishes she could be of more help, but reluctantly admits that she's lost her memory. She washed up on this very island herself some time ago, alone and with nowhere to turn. But good old Grandpa rescued her, and has since looked after Ciela as if she were his own.

Ciela

A tiny fairy with a big heart, Ciela comes to Link's aid when he washes ashore at Mercay Island. After listening to his story and hearing of his friend's capture by the nefarious Ghost Ship, Ciela's natural reaction is to help Link in any way she can. Perhaps this is because she knows something of feeling scared and alone; the little fairy lost her memory long ago and was rescued by a kind old man when she found herself stranded here. A guiding light and clever advisor, Ciela sticks by Link through the many hardships he must face during his quest to track down the mysterious Ghost Ship.

There's no rush to visit Grandpa, so take a moment to familiarize yourself with the unique stylus controls. Using the stylus, tap anywhere near Link to make him **slowly walk** in that direction. Tap farther away from Link to make him **dash forward** at top speed! Link never tires from running, so feel free to dash about as much as you like.

→NOTE←

During adventure sequences like this one, Ciela acts as the pointer for your stylus. Wherever you tap, that's where she flies!

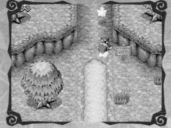

Another useful maneuver is the **somersault**. This one takes a bit of practice, and now's the time to brush up! While running about, trace tiny circles at the far edge of the screen with your stylus. This causes Link to tuck and roll, bashing into whatever may lie ahead. While this maneuver isn't used all that often, it's good to know how to perform it!

NOTE

Rolling four times in a row makes Link dizzy, and it takes him a few seconds to recover. This can be a problem if monsters are about, so watch how you roll!

CAUTION

While running about the beach, be careful not to jump into the surrounding ocean! Falling into deep water hurts Link, washing away half a heart from his heart meter. (Gulp!)

There isn't much to do near the beach, so when you feel comfortable steering Link, go north across the wooden bridge. Follow the path to the left to meet up with a nearby farmer in a red outfit. The man calls out to Link from afar, urging him to come near. Tap the farmer with the stylus to make Link bolt toward him and engage the man in friendly conversation. This is how to speak with folks you meet! The farmer advises Link to interact with other objects, like signs and barrels, by tapping them as well.

TIP

When you're not tapping with the stylus, Ciela flies out and hovers above nearby objects of interest in the environment. Whenever you notice Ciela circling over something, give it a tap and see what happens!

Two barrels stand beyond the fence just north of the farmer. Move between the fence and nearby tree to reach the barrels, then tap one to make Link lift it overhead. Quickly tap and release anywhere in the environment to make Link throw the barrel with great accuracy. Nice toss! Now tap the other barrel to pick up. This time, tap and hold to make Link walk about, carrying the barrel to a new location. Quickly tap and release to toss the second barrel as near or far as you like, smashing it to bits.

NOTE

Goodies randomly pop out of barrels you smash. If you were really lucky, a *heart* or *green Rupee* may have popped out of these!

Green Rupee
You got a **green Rupee**! It's worth one Rupee!

Heart
You got a **heart**! Each one you collect restores one heart in Link's heart meter.

See that fluffy Cucco clucking about the area? Link can lift up these little guys, too! Tap the Cucco to make Link run toward it and lift it overhead just like a barrel. Cuccos usually run away from sudden movements, so you may need to walk Link slowly toward this one before you're able to tap and lift it. You remember how to make Link walk instead of run, right? Sure you do! Just tap anywhere near him.

NOTE

Why would you want to pick up a Cucco? Their frantic wing-flapping allows Link to glide through the air when he leaps off tall ledges and the like. This can help him clear wide gaps and reach otherwise inaccessible areas. That's why!

Task 1:
Obtain Oshus's Sword

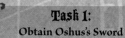

Now let's take a peek inside the farmer's house. He won't mind! Tap the darkened doorway to make Link enter the building. Link sees the farmer's wife busy with housework inside. Tap her to speak with the woman, who seems to have heard of the creepy Ghost Ship that spirited Tetra away. Well, who hasn't? The thing is kidnapping people like crazy!

> **NOTE**
>
> Did you notice the two barrels inside the farmer's house? Tap to lift each one, then toss them both to smash them in search of goodies.

A small signpost stands near the north path just east of the farmer's house. Tap the sign to read it and learn that dangerous monsters lie ahead! Fearing for Link's safety, Ciela won't let him venture any farther north; she urges Link to speak with her grandpa instead.

Continue east to discover a large rock sitting on the lawn nearby. Tap the rock to make Link lift it overhead. He's so strong! Quickly tap and release anywhere to toss the rock and smash it apart just like a barrel. Or, tap and hold to make Link carry it about. Show off!

Ciela won't allow Link to venture very far to the east, either; she insists he speak with her grandpa first. There isn't much else to do around here, so climb the nearby wooden steps to the north to reach Grandpa's house. Lift and toss the two barrels right near the house for potential items, if you like, then tap the darkened doorway to go inside.

A stooped old man with a huge red cane stands inside the house. This must be Ciela's grandpa! Tap the man with the stylus to speak with him just as you did the farmer.

Oshus the Wise

Ciela's grandpa introduces himself as Oshus. He tells Link that Ciela has already informed him of Tetra's abduction by the eerie Ghost Ship. He knows Link wants to track down the haunted vessel, but forbids him to do so. He warns the boy that pure evil fills the sails of the Ghost Ship, and that none of its victims have ever escaped its wicked grasp. Scary!

Ciela interjects on Link's behalf. They can't just leave Tetra to her fate! Something must be done to save her. Realizing there's no convincing them otherwise, Oshus reluctantly advises Link to go east and visit the island's harbor. There, an infamous sailor by the name of Linebeck should be able to tell Link more about the Ghost Ship, and perhaps even assist the lad in tracking down the foreboding craft. Oshus even points out the harbor's location on Link's map. How nice!

Thrilled that her grandpa is willing to help, Ciela asks that she be allowed to join her new friend on his journey. Seeing her excitement, and knowing how helpful Ciela can be, Oshus agrees that his little fairy ward should indeed travel along with Link to aid and advise him. The old man issues one final warning before sending them off: be careful of monsters out there!

Before leaving Oshus's house, notice the pots sitting in each corner of the room. Like rocks and barrels, Link can lift pots overhead and give them a toss, smashing them for potential rewards. Unlike rocks and barrels, Link is able to run about at full speed while carrying a pot overhead, and he can toss them into other pots to smash several at a time! Shatter these objects for goodies and then step outside.

Oshus

A wise, kindhearted old man, Oshus has lived on Mercay Island his whole life. When Ciela washed ashore long ago, her memory gone, Oshus took her in and provided a safe environment for her to rest and recover her strength, and perhaps one day, her memory. Saddened to hear of the loss of Link's friend because of the nefarious Ghost Ship, Oshus helps Link by steering him in the direction of another person who might be of more help—and later, by showing the lad the finer points of using pointy weapons.

The bridge to the east leads directly toward the harbor. Descend the wooden steps in front of Oshus's house and then turn right, moving east toward the bridge. Suddenly, the ground begins to shake with violent force. It's an earthquake! Mercay Island has been plagued with such tremors lately, and this one's done a number on the east bridge. Guess you'll have to find another way to reach the harbor!

Turn around and go west from the ruined bridge. Pay another visit to the nearby farmer, who once again calls out to Link from afar. It seems that the recent earthquake has sent several large rocks tumbling into the farmer's garden. What a pity! Help clear

away the debris by lifting the rocks and then giving them a toss to smash them to bits. Destroy all the rocks and then speak with the farmer, who rewards you with a green Rupee. Gee, thanks!

Realizing his one-Rupee reward might have been a bit on the stingy side, the farmer makes good by revealing a nifty secret: something valuable is hidden in a tree up north! The farmer points to the tree's location on your map and tells you to bash the tree really

hard when you get there. This tip won't help if you forget it though, so press Ⓑ to call up the Map menu. Then use the stylus to draw a circle or mark an X near the tree's location so you'll remember it in the future. Handy!

TIP

If your note-taking skills are a bit off, tap the Eraser icon on the left side of the Map menu and then use the eraser to clear your wayward scribbling. Then tap the Memo icon and try again!

You've done your good deed for the day; now it's time to move on and explore the northern trail. Run north along the path to reach a new section of the island that Ciela wouldn't allow you to visit before. It's easy to see why: several mean-looking monsters begin lurching toward you, intent on putting a premature stop to your adventure. Seeing that it's way too dangerous out here, Ciela urges Link to turn around and go back to safety. You'll deal with these enemies soon enough, but for now, follow Ciela's advice and make a hasty retreat.

Whew! That was close. Maybe Oshus has some advice for you.... Return to his house and speak with the old man once more. Oshus seems to know that the east bridge is out and that monsters are swarming the trail to the north. He tells Link to forget about

visiting the harbor until the bridge is fixed; the northern path is far too dangerous for such a young boy. The old man has nothing more to say on the matter, so smash the surrounding pots and then go outside.

Oshus's Storehouse

Oh, what to do? Ciela is quick to point out that if you only had a sword, you could easily deal with those pesky monsters to the north. Wait a minute, Oshus couldn't have been an old fogey his entire life, right? He must have used a sword in his youth.... Maybe he's been keeping it safe in his storehouse! Toss the barrels to the east of Oshus's house to uncover an entrance to a cavern in the cliff, then go inside.

Task 1:
Obtain Oshus's Sword

A massive door stands at the north end of the cavern. Ciela thinks she remembers Oshus storing his old sword in the chamber beyond the door, but she can't quite remember how to open the door itself. All she remembers is that Oshus used to write a number on the sign near the door, and after he did so, the door would open. Unfortunately, she can't quite recall the number—her memory is a bit hazy, after all. But Ciela does remember that Oshus said it was the same as the **number of palm trees on the beach**. What a clue!

You could exit the cavern, travel south to return to the beach, and count all the palm trees down there, but we'll make it easy for you: there are seven. Tap the sign near the door to read it, then draw the number 7 on the sign when prompted. The door slides away, revealing a secret passage!

TIP

If you make a mistake while sketching on the sign, tap the Rewrite button at the bottom-right to erase the board and try again.

Approach the chest at the far end of the storeroom and open it to claim **Oshus's Sword**. It's the perfect size! Those monsters won't stand a chance against you now!

**Overworld Chest #1:
Oshus's Sword**

Now that you've got a sword, you don't need to lift and throw those little clay pots anymore. Simply shatter them with sword strikes! Try it now: draw lines with the stylus to start slicing away, bashing apart the four pots near the chest in short order. See how easy that was? Fun and profitable: two of the pots yield sparkly blue Rupees! However, you are not guaranteed blue Rupees—pot contents are random. Exit the cavern when you're ready to move on.

Blue Rupee
You got two **blue Rupees**!
They're each worth five Rupees!

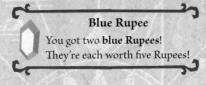

TIP

Tap the open book on the desk near the chest for a quick tip on using Oshus's Sword.

Oshus waits just outside the cavern. He must have known Link and Ciela would go after his old sword! Although disappointed in the pair at first, Oshus soon realizes that their intentions were good. He understands that Link must hurry on to save his friend; there's no time to wait around for the bridge to be repaired. Still, Oshus has no intention of letting Link leave—not without first learning the basics of swordplay, that is!

Oshus's Sword

You got **Oshus's Sword**! This razor-sharp blade was once used by Oshus to banish evil during his bygone adventuring days, but it has been gathering dust in his storehouse for quite awhile now. No more! Link makes good use of this weapon during his quest to track down the shadowy Ghost Ship. The sword can be used to smash certain objects, cut down tall grass and thin trees, and most importantly, defeat enemies! Here are some key swordplay tips and maneuvers:

Targeted Attack: Simply tap on nearby hostiles to make Link lash directly at them. If the enemy is far away, Link leaps toward them with a powerful jump attack that deals double damage!

Side Slash: Draw a horizontal line that divides Link and his target to make him swing out in a wide arc. Keep drawing lines as fast as you can to make Link swing over and over! This is a great defensive attack to employ against agile enemies that close in rapidly.

Thrust: Draw a line straight from Link's body toward your target to make Link stab straight forward. This fast attack has quite a long reach!

Spin Attack: Trace a circle around Link to make him execute a powerful spin attack! This is a great way to fend off swarming hostiles from all angles, or to quickly cut down lots of grass at once. The spin attack also deals twice as much damage as other attacks! Watch out, though: Four spin attacks in quick succession make Link dizzy!

primagames.com

When you arrive at Oshus's house, speak with the old man to begin a quick swordplay tutorial. He teaches Link the ease of the **targeted attack**, the defensive nature of the **side slash**, and the versatility of the mighty **spin attack**. Follow Oshus's instructions and destroy all four wooden targets with each of these potent maneuvers!

Oshus can teach you nothing more. You're now ready to venture out into the world and face down danger like a true hero! There's no time to waste, either; Tetra needs your help! Exit Oshus's house and make for the northern passage once more. Things will be a bit different this time!

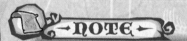

Danger lurks ahead, so now's a good time to save your game. Tap the Menu tab in the screen's lower-left corner and then tap Save to store your current progress. Remember: a wise adventurer saves often!

Task 2:
Journey to Mercay Island's Harbor

Missing Links

Slashing for Cash

Now that you've got a sword, take a moment to wreak a bit of havoc around the southern area—and to gain a bit more practice with your newfound weapon. First thing's first: you can now chop down every tall patch of grass you see to reveal hidden goodies. Like barrels, rocks, and pots, the reward you get from slicing up greenery is usually random and minor—little more than a heart or a few Rupees. Still, this is a great way to pad your wallet and locate hearts when Link's health is low!

Send Me a Sign

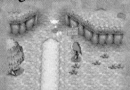

Be careful when swinging that sword around! Link's new blade can get him into a bit of trouble if he isn't careful. For starters, wooden signposts can be chopped down with a wayward slash, preventing you from reading whatever was posted on them. You'll need to exit the area and then return to reset a fallen sign and read it!

Crazed Cuccos!

Attacking Cuccos is now possible as well, but the result can be quite the harrowing experience! If you're feeling brave, corner the farmer's Cucco somewhere in his yard and then slash it repeatedly with the sword—but you might want to save your game first! Assaulted Cuccos soon become enraged, turn bright red, and quickly call for backup: a gaggle of Cuccos flies in and starts pecking away at poor Link in an effort to teach him some manners!

Each Cucco that scores a peck against Link drains a quarter heart from his heart meter, so this is no joke! Start running away as fast as you can, and don't stop until the Cucco onslaught finally subsides. Those Cuccos mean business, and they don't disband for quite a while. If the situation deteriorates, run for cover inside either the farmer's or Oshus's house. And next time, think twice before ruffling a Cucco's feathers!

Bad News for ChuChus

Proceed up the north trail and get ready to take on some monsters. Those red blobs you noticed earlier are still milling about, and they don't seem to fear Link's new blade. Silly them! Teach these guys a lesson by tapping each one with the stylus to make Link execute fast **targeted attacks**. Link automatically dashes forward and strikes each blob, dispatching each one in turn. Sweet!

Red ChuChu

Threat Meter

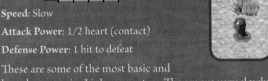

Speed: Slow

Attack Power: 1/2 heart (contact)

Defense Power: 1 hit to defeat

These are some of the most basic and harmless enemies Link encounters. They move very slowly and their only method of attack involves moving into contact with their quarry. Not the best combination! Link's fast, far-reaching targeted attack is the best way to dispatch these less-than-worthy foes, but feel free to employ spin attacks if they take you by surprise or manage to swarm you.

Slash down the surrounding grass for items and then continue north to locate an odd statue. Tap the statue with the stylus to make Link whack it with his sword; the statue then jiggles a bit and speaks! It tells Link how to perform the **somersault** maneuver by scribbling tiny circles at the edge of the screen, and hints that he should try somersaulting into the big tree nearby.

Get some room and then run toward the tree, tracing little circles at the edge of the screen to make Link tuck and roll into it. A successful somersault collision with the tree causes a **red Rupee** to fall out of its limbs! Collect this valuable prize to fatten your wallet before moving onward.

➤NOTE◄

None of the trees you've encountered up to this point have held any special prizes, so there's no need to backtrack and roll into them. But remember to roll into every big tree you encounter from this point on!

Red Rupee

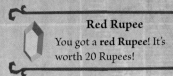

You got a **red Rupee**! It's worth 20 Rupees!

A line of skinny trees blocks your progress along the trail to the east. No need to roll into these trees; simply hack them down with your sword to clear a path. Proceed into the dark cavern beyond to get your first taste of a dungeon: a short mountain passage filled with monsters.

Mountain Passage

see maps on next page

Items to Obtain

Red Rupee · Small Key x3

Dungeon Denizens

Enemies

Keese · Rat · Red ChuChu · Rope

Mountain Passage: 1F

This forbidding passage is packed with all sorts of creepy crawlers, so keep your wits about you! Making it through this short cavern is essential: now that the east bridge is out, this is the only route toward Mercay Island's harbor. Make sure you're comfortable executing Link's various sword attacks before venturing any farther. Danger lurks ahead!

Lift and toss the rocks that block the entry tunnel to clear the way forward. Ciela points out a large locked door just beyond the rocks. You've no way to open the door just yet, so continue east along the tunnel and dispatch the four Red ChuChus that pop up from the floor in a surprise attack.

Mountain Passage: 1F

to 2nd Floor

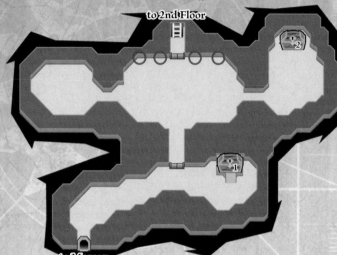

to Mercay

Legend

Dungeon Chest #1: Small Key

Dungeon Chest #2: Red Rupee

○ Lever

Mountain Passage: 2F

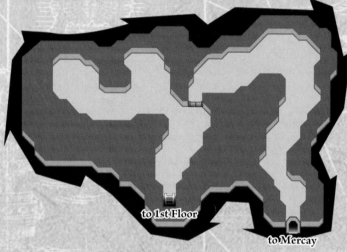

to 1st Floor

to Mercay

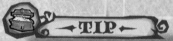

TIP

Remember, when enemies swarm in, trace a circle around Link to perform a powerful spin attack! This is a great way to fend off groups of would-be attackers.

Open the treasure chest that the ChuChus were guarding to claim a **small key**. Bet you know what this unlocks! Return to the large door you passed by a moment ago and tap it. Link uses the key to open the door and access the northern half of the cavern.

Dungeon Chest #1: Small Key

Small Key

You got a **small key**! Use it to open a door in this dungeon.

NOTE

When Link carries a small key, a small key icon appears at the Map screen's lower-right corner. Each small key can be used only once; it vanishes afterward.

Task 2:
Journey to Mercay Island's Harbor

NOTE

Whenever Link creates a change in the environment, such as using a small key to open a door in a dungeon, a special icon appears at the appropriate location on the Map screen. These icons vanish after a time, but you can always press Ⓑ to call up the Map menu and scribble in your own permanent notes!

Go north and explore the wide chamber beyond the door. Run about the room and dispatch the five Red ChuChus that pop from the floor, then examine the north wall. Another big locked door prevents you from moving any farther north, and four levers jut out from the north wall, two on either side of the door.

TIP

Smash the pots in the chamber for hearts if Link's health is low.

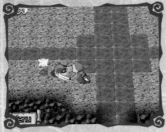

An odd stone tablet sits near the levers. Tap the stone tablet to make Link read it just like a signpost! This one warns him that the four nearby levers must be pulled in the correct order to open the locked door... or else! Good to know, but how can you be sure in which order to pull them?

Before you start yanking those levers, head west to discover another stone tablet. Tap the tablet to read it. The tablet hints that Link can grab hold of certain blocks and then shove them around. Notice the stone block that's plugging up the west passage? Tap it to make Link grab hold of it. Two arrow icons then appear at either side of the block; tap the left arrow and hold the stylus on it to make Link shove the block west, giving him access to a side chamber. Neat!

Be careful: two new enemies flutter about inside this chamber! These little fiends are called Keese, and they can be tough to handle in groups. Trace circles around Link to unleash spin attacks and wipe them both out!

Keese

Threat Meter

Speed: Fast

Attack Power: 1/2 heart (contact)

Defense Power: 1 hit to defeat

These ugly bloodsuckers can be quite a handful when they attack in groups! Their quick, unpredictable movements make them hard to track with targeted attacks, so use Link's spin attack for 360-degree mayhem instead. After Link acquires a shield, he can repel these creatures when they dive toward him. After repelling a Keese, quickly tap it to retaliate with a fast targeted attack!

When pulling the levers:
First: 2nd from the left.

After clearing out the Keese, tap the stone tablet against the north wall. The tablet provides a tip on how to pull the levers! It says to pull the **second lever from the left** first. Good to know!

TIP

Press Ⓑ to call up the Map menu, then scribble the number 1 on your map where the **second lever from the left** is located. Now you won't forget to pull that one first!

Exit the side chamber and go east. Another stone block plugs up the east passage, preventing you from exploring any farther. Wonder what's over there? Tap the block to make Link grab hold of it, then tap the right arrow and hold down the stylus to make Link shove the block eastward.

Get ready to fight: many Keese flutter about the east side chamber! The spin attack is your best maneuver here; unleash a few quick spins to wipe out the pesky batlike creatures. Remember not to spin more than three times in a row or Link becomes dizzy and vulnerable!

After you've bested the Keese, smash the pots against the east wall for hearts, then tap the stone tablet against the north wall to read it. This one provides a clue on how to correctly pull two more levers! It tells you to pull the **first lever on the left** second, and to pull the **second lever from the right** last. This must mean you need to pull the **far-right lever third**! Mark those down on your map, then open the nearby chest to claim a shiny **red Rupee**. Cha-ching!

Dungeon Chest #2: Red Rupee

Red Rupee

You got a **red Rupee**! It's worth 20 Rupees!

Time to open that north door. Move to the levers and pull them in the following order, from left to right: 2, 1, 4, 3. To pull a lever, simply tap it with the stylus, then tap the arrow icon that appears below Link to give it a good tug. Pull all four levers in the proper order to make a **small key** drop from the ceiling. You're now free to move on! Pick up the key and use it to unlock the north door.

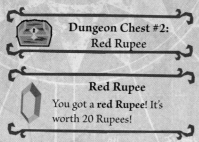

Small Key

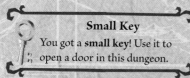

You got a **small key**! Use it to open a door in this dungeon.

If you make a mistake or pull the levers in the incorrect order, you're treated to a special fight against a number of new enemies: Ropes! These venomous snakes drop from the ceiling and slowly crawl about. When they see Link, they suddenly dart toward him with frightening speed! Keep moving and try to stay out of their line of sight, using targeted attacks to quickly defeat each one in turn.

Rope

Threat Meter

Speed: Slow, then fast!

Attack Power: 1/2 heart (contact)

Defense Power: 1 hit to defeat

Beware of these little snakes! Though they seem quite docile and harmless at first, Ropes quickly spring to life as soon as they notice Link, racing toward him in a straight line at top speed. Run circles around these enemies, keeping out of sight to prevent them from dashing toward you. Use targeted attacks to quickly dispatch unwary Ropes from the side or behind!

Mountain Passage: 2F

The stairs beyond the door lead up to the mountain passage's second floor, and there's a nasty Rat infestation up here! Play the role of the exterminator and use targeted attacks to clear the tunnel of vermin. Eliminate all the Rats in the tunnel, ignoring the locked door to the northeast for the moment.

Rat

Threat Meter

Speed: Medium

Attack Power: 1/2 heart (contact)

Defense Power: 1 hit to defeat

These dirty vermin are nothing to fear! They don't chase after Link, but instead move about randomly in sporadic bursts of speed. Simply keep your distance, wait for a Rat to stop running, then quickly tap it for a quick, targeted attack. Presto! Couldn't you just tap Rats all day?

You've probably noticed that one Rat is hard to catch. This one runs about the northwest portion of the cavern, darting out from one of the two holes in the north wall and then bolting directly toward the opposite hole. You've got to put a stop to this Rat's antics in order to nab the **small key** it carries, but it won't be easy—that's one fast Rat!

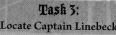

TIP

You can track the Rat's movements on your map. While the Rat itself isn't shown, the small key it carries is!

You'll need a little help in order to trap that pesky Rat. Head west to locate a moveable block, then tap it to make Link grab hold. Tap the arrow icons to shift the block, first pulling it away from the wall and then shoving it north to seal off the nearby Rat hole.

Nice work! Now the Rat can only emerge from the northeast hole. The Rat is smart enough not to peek its head out while Link stands nearby, so go east and wait near the locked door you noticed earlier. Keep an eye on your Map screen and watch for the Rat to dart out of the hole, heading toward the northwest hole.

You've blocked off the northwest hole, so the Rat can't enter and is forced to turn around. When your Map screen shows that the Rat has reached the halfway point, run westward to cut it off. Tap the Rat when it runs toward you to put a stop to its tomfoolery. Take that, Rat! Now grab the **small key** the Rat drops and use it to unlock the northeast door.

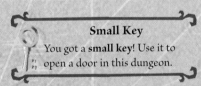

Small Key

You got a **small key**! Use it to open a door in this dungeon.

The final passage is filled with Keese and lined with rocks. Target attack each Keese to dispatch them from a distance. Or, if you're feeling lucky, lift those rocks and hurl them at your foes! Move forward and proceed through the exit door to leave this creepy passage.

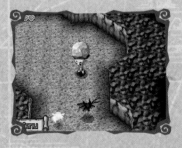

Task 3: Locate Captain Linebeck

Mercay Village & Harbor

You've risked life and limb by taking the treacherous mountain passage to make it this far, but that's all behind you now: you've finally reached Mercay Island's village and harbor! There's lots to see and do here, but don't get too carried away. Remember: you're here to speak with Captain Linebeck!

Go south from the cavern's mouth and speak with the woman in the purple dress. She welcomes you to the port village, saying that things are pretty slow right now due to rumors of the Ghost Ship's return. She goes on to say that one brave sailor has docked a ship at the harbor, however. That must be the infamous captain Linebeck!

If you like, head west to examine the ruined east bridge from the opposite side. A funny-looking worker stands near the bridge, grumbling that he has to fix it every time an earthquake shakes it loose. He wishes he could get back to fixing ships at the Shipyard near the harbor, but he doesn't want to hear Oshus's nagging about the bridge repairs. Leave the poor character to his work and go back toward town; he's got enough on his mind at the moment!

There's more to see and do around town, but for now, let's just go to the harbor and see if Linebeck's about. The harbor is marked by a ship icon on your Map screen; head southeast until you reach the port.

A man stands on the harbor, admiring a ship that's docked at the pier. Could this be that old salty dog, Captain Linebeck?

> But aren't you a tad short to be in here? Take no offense, sir.

> Linebeck just dashed out, saying he was off to the Temple of the Ocean King.

Nay! It turns out that the man isn't Linebeck at all. He's just a serious ship aficionado with an eye for seaworthy craft! The man says that the docked vessel does indeed belong to one Captain Linebeck, but he hasn't seen the good captain about. He advises Link to visit the village's Milk Bar and speak with the owner, as Captain Linebeck is known to drop anchor there from time to time.

Link isn't here for a tall glass of dairy, however. When the bartender learns that Link's actually looking for Linebeck, things change a great deal! He says the good captain was indeed enjoying a refreshing beverage here at the bar just moments ago, but then dashed off quite suddenly, saying he was headed for the Temple of the Ocean King.

The nearby Shipyard is presently closed; its operator is currently working on fixing the bridge to the west! You can't do much with the nearby postbox at the moment, either, but know that each major island on the Great Sea has one such box. How else could folks send letters to one another?

> None dare step into the Temple of the Ocean King, so put it out of your mind!

Overhearing the conversation, an old man sitting at the bar suddenly pipes up. He tells Link that the Ocean King is the just and noble ruler of all creation, and that temple standing at the island's northern tip was built in his great honor. However, the old man goes on to warn Link that a terrible curse has been laid on the temple—one that quickly sucks the souls away from all who enter. He urges the boy to stay away from that awful place!

Ignore all of these distractions for the moment and head directly for the large building at the west end of town, which houses the local Milk Bar. Tap the bartender—who's also the proprietor—to address him directly.

Northward, Ho!

The bartender has pointed out the location of the temple, the massive structure at the northern tip of the island. Smash the barrel in the Milk Bar for a potential prize, and speak with the old man again to learn that, though hazardous, the Temple of the Ocean King is rumored to house a fantastic treasure. Intriguing! Leave the bar and travel south, entering a small nearby tent to visit the town's local shop. Time to stock up on supplies!

The bartender looks up from his work and addresses Link in a friendly tone. He welcomes the lad to his fine establishment, but reluctantly says that Link's a bit too short to be visiting such a place. Perhaps when he's gone a bit further in life....

Tap the shop mistress to speak with her and begin browsing her wares. She sells a variety of exciting and useful goods. Tap each item for a closer view and a brief description, including its price. Tap the Buy button at the bottom of the screen to

Task 3:
Locate Captain Linebeck

purchase an item if you have enough Rupees, or tap the Quit button to continue browsing. You can't purchase the Bombs just yet, but you're free to buy anything else you like. Definitely buy the Wooden Shield if you can afford it, along with a Red Potion. The rest can wait, but these two items are sure to come in handy!

NOTE

What's up with the random treasure that's for sale? These items are collectible goods that can be traded for fun and profit! Treasures are always found at the same locations—for example, this shop will always have a treasure for sale—but the treasure you find is completely random each time you play! Some treasures are more rare and valuable than others, and they can be sold for great fortune. Check the Items portion of this guide for complete details!

NOTE

Potions are used to replenish Link's heart meter when he's dangerously low on health energy. Unlike many previous *Zelda* games, empty bottles are not required to carry potions in *Phantom Hourglass*. To drink a potion, tap the Items tab at the lower-right corner of the screen, then tap the potion you wish to consume.

Mercay Island Shop

Item	Cost	Description	Notes
Bombs (10)	50 Rupees	Volatile explosives	Requires a Bomb Bag to carry.
Power Gem #1	500 Rupees	Collectible item (Spirit Gem)	Used to power up the Power Spirit.
Purple Potion	150 Rupees	Recovery item	Restores up to 8 hearts; available after you purchase Wooden Shield.
Red Potion	50 Rupees	Recovery item	Restores up to 6 hearts.
Treasure	Varies	Collectible item (Treasure)	A random treasure. Collect and sell these for profit!
Wooden Shield	80 Rupees	Defensive equipment	Automatically blocks light frontal attacks.

Power Gem #1

You got a **Power Gem**! Collect these items and use them to power up the Power Spirit.

Purple Potion

You got a **Purple Potion**! Drink it to replenish up to eight hearts whenever Link's health energy is low. If Link falls in battle, this item is used automatically to bring him back!

Treasure

Random

You got a **treasure**! Collect these items and sell them to the highest bidder!

Red Potion

You got a **Red Potion**! Gulp it down to replenish up to six hearts whenever Link's health energy is low.

Wooden Shield

You got a **Wooden Shield**! This important piece of adventuring equipment lets Link block all light frontal attacks.

NOTE

There are loads of items and collectibles in *Phantom Hourglass*, and it's easy to lose track of what you've found and what there's still to get. Keep organized by making good use of the Legendary Checklists at the back of this guide. They're fantastic resources, and diligent checklist usage ensures you won't miss a thing!

Missing Links

Flight-By-Fowl

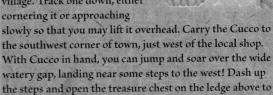

Looking for a bit of early adventure? There's a treasure chest within your grasp! All you need is a little help from one of the Cuccos milling about the village. Track one down, either cornering it or approaching slowly so that you may lift it overhead. Carry the Cucco to the southwest corner of town, just west of the local shop. With Cucco in hand, you can jump and soar over the wide watery gap, landing near some steps to the west! Dash up the steps and open the treasure chest on the ledge above to claim a random **treasure**.

Overworld Chest #2: Treasure

Treasure

Random

You got a **treasure**! Collect these items and sell them to the highest bidder!

After you've finished shopping, go north and examine the northeast-ernmost building. This is the Treasure Teller shop, but it hasn't opened for business yet. Remember its location for future reference though, and continue north when you're ready to move on.

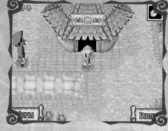

 **TIP**

Tall grass always reappears each time you exit and reenter an area. It sure grows fast! If you want to save up to buy those expensive items at the store, just keep mowing the lawn, collecting green and blue Rupees in the process.

 **NOTE**

Are you an observant adventurer? Did you notice the treasure chest on the high ledges to the north of town? You won't be able to reach it for a while, but make sure to mark its location on your map so you don't forget it!

The overgrown field to the north of town is filled with Red ChuChus. Target attack each one to defeat them with ease. Watch out for the Crow that swoops down from a big tree in the northwest; these creatures love to strike fast and steal your Rupees away!

Crow

Threat Meter

Speed: Fast

Attack Power: 1/2 heart (contact)

Defense Power: 1 hit to defeat

Look upward from time to time: dangerous Crows are known to perch in tall trees. They quickly descend on unwary travelers to lighten their wallets of Rupees! Don't give these dirty birds a chance to pilfer your hard-earned cash; run straight away whenever one swoops near. Unleash a fast spin attack at just the right moment to give the Crow a powerful smack. Or just keep on running; these lazy birds only make one attack run before flying off, regardless of whether they hit you!

Clear the lower area of the woods and then go north up the wooden steps. Check your Map screen; you're right near the tree the farmer told you to bash! Somersault into the second big tree you encounter to knock a **big green Rupee** to the ground. Score!

 **TIP**

If you were low on funds and couldn't afford the Wooden Shield and Red Potion at the shop before, now's the time to go back and buy them!

Big Green Rupee

You got a **big green Rupee**! It's worth 100 Rupees!

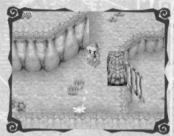

Continue exploring this upper level of the woods, slashing away patches of grass for hearts and Rupees. Ignore the two strange blocks that sit atop some nearby steps; you need Bombs to destroy these objects, and you don't have any such explosives at the moment. Proceed west, also ignoring the large crack you see in the north cliff. Again, you need Bombs to blow the crack wide open. Guess you'll have to come back here after you get some explosives!

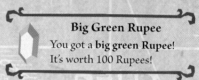 **TIP**

Mark that bomb wall on your map for future reference!

You encounter no more resistance on your way to the Temple of the Ocean King. Steel yourself for what may lie in store, then muster the courage to step inside. Linebeck must be found!

Temple of the Ocean King

Items to Obtain	Dungeon Denizens
	Characters

Sea Chart #1   Small Key

Fallen Adventurer   Linebeck

 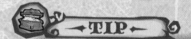  

1   2   3   4

Task 3:
Locate Captain Linebeck

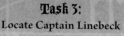

Temple of the Ocean King: Entry Hall

A once-sacred place built in devotion to the great Ocean King, this ancient temple now ruins the lives of all who dare to enter. A wicked curse has been placed on this sacred shrine; the souls of all who trespass here are quickly sucked away by some malevolent force. Could Linebeck really have come here? And if so, what has become of him? There's only one way to find out!

Entry Hall

Ocean Temple 1F

Legend

 Dungeon Chest #1:	Empty!
Dungeon Chest #2:	Sea Chart #1
Orb	

The skeletons that litter the floor of the temple's entry hall sure are creepy, but there's nothing for you to fear in this first chamber. Tap each pile of bones to summon the spirit of their former owner. It seems that these skeletons are all that remains of foolhardy adventurers who brazenly entered this temple in search of treasure. Each fallen adventurer's spirit provides you with an important clue about the dangers that lurk ahead. Pay close attention and make sure you don't share their fate!

Smash the pots that line the walls near the stairs for potential goodies, then go upstairs and check out the odd hourglass on the northern dais. Wonder what this could be? You can't do much with the hourglass, so return downstairs and pass through the lower north door to reach the temple's first floor.

Temple of the Ocean King: 1F

Link hears a voice call out to him as he enters the temple's first floor. Moving forward a few paces, he's able to make out the figure of a man in the darkness ahead. The man seems in dire straights, waving his arms and pleading for rescue. Ciela recognizes the man as Linebeck. You have found him at last!

Somehow, Linebeck has gotten himself trapped in a small chamber just north of Link's position. He boldly states that he could free himself with no problem, if only he hadn't sprained his ankle. When Link agrees to help, Linebeck orders him to do something to remove the spikes that are holding him captive in the center of the area. What a guy!

At high alert and ready for anything, Link and Ciela cautiously enter the Temple of the Ocean King. The massive entry chamber greets them with a terrible sight: dried bones and skeletal remains line the floor. Could one of these piles of bones be all that remains of Captain Linebeck? Let's hope not!

Smash the nearby pots for hearts if Link's health energy is low, then move north toward Linebeck. The man suddenly calls out, warning Link that the temple will suck the life out of him if he moves off the glowing purple sections of floor. These purple spaces are **safe zones**, where the temple's curse has no effect. Link was safe standing on the purple space on the entry landing, but he'll start losing health energy when he moves away!

→ NOTE ←

Safe zones are shown on the map. Link's map icon turns purple while he stands in a safe zone. Try to plot courses through the temple that let you leapfrog from one safe zone to the next, smashing pots for hearts when Link needs some healing.

When you're ready to go, dash to the left and head for the southwest safe zone. Good job! Linebeck shouts his encouragement from his place of confinement when you make it there. Smash the pots for hearts if need be, then get ready to dash north for the next safe zone ahead.

→ NOTE ←

The temple's curse drains 1/4 heart from Link's heart meter every two seconds. Don't linger outside those purple spaces for long!

That wasn't so bad, now, was it? The northwest safe zone features an odd crystal orb and a locked door to the north. You don't have a key to open the door, so give that crystal orb a whack with Link's sword.

Amazed that Link actually managed to save him, Linebeck wastes no time bolting for the southern safe zone. Hey, what happened to his sprained ankle? Oh well; looks like it's time to go!

Before heading south to catch up with Linebeck, dash east and move toward the northeast safe zone. There, a giant, ornate treasure chest sits on the floor! Tap the chest to open it and claim...absolutely nothing! The chest is empty! Someone must have already gotten to it.

Dungeon Chest #1: Empty!

→ TIP ←

Four pots are in the central safe zone where Linebeck was being held. Smash them for hearts if you feel the need.

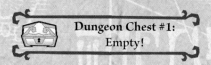

→ NOTE ←

The massive door just north of Linebeck's holding cell won't budge. It's marked with an odd design.... Maybe you'll figure out how to open it later.

Time to bail out of this creepy place! Dash south and make for the southern safe zone. Linebeck awaits you there, already exhausted from his brief sprint. What a character!

Task 4:
Find the Sea Chart & Set Sail

Task 4:
Find the Sea Chart & Set Sail

Back Into the Temple

Linebeck wastes no time in giving himself a grand introduction. Afterward, he asks Link what he's doing in such an awful place as this temple. Link explains he needs Linebeck's help—or rather, his ship—to sail the seas in search of the Ghost Ship that captured Tetra.

As luck would have it, Linebeck and Link share the same goal! Linebeck is also searching for the Ghost Ship, but not to save anyone. He's determined to claim its legendary treasure instead! This is why Linebeck was exploring the Temple of the Ocean King; rumor has it that vital clues to tracking down the Ghost Ship can be found here.

Insisting he's still suffering a serious ankle injury (despite how quickly he was running just moments ago), Linebeck tells Link to reenter the temple and seek out a clue to finding the Ghost Ship. Jostling Link silly, he drives home the importance of finding such an item. Linebeck then hands Link a small key he found inside the temple shortly before falling into captivity. The rest is up to our young hero!

Linebeck

Captain of the mighty *S.S. Linebeck* steam ship, this salty seaman is brash and bold, and he doesn't mind saying so! A real man of the sea, Linebeck enjoys sailing hither and yon in search of fortune and glory—almost as much as he enjoys downing tall glasses of dairy at the local Milk Bar! Although he claims to have braved dangers and hardships untold, Linebeck always seems to have some excuse for keeping himself well out of harm's way. While this forces Link to do most of the adventuring, the young hero wouldn't be able to get around without Linebeck's help. Together, the two make quite the pair of explorers!

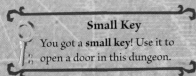

Small Key
You got a **small key**! Use it to open a door in this dungeon.

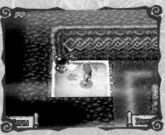

Back into the temple you go! Remember to move quickly when not on a purple safe zone to avoid suffering damage from effects of the temple's curse. All the pots in the temple have reappeared, so there are plenty of hearts for you to grab. Dash north to reach the central safe zone where Linebeck was previously held captive. From there, run north and then west, heading for the safe zone where you noticed a locked door earlier. Using the small key Linebeck gave you, open the door and explore the northern half of this floor!

NOTE

So *that's* what was in that big empty chest! Linebeck must have taken the small key from it before falling into the temple's trap. He's a crafty one!

Your next destination is the safe zone in the map's northwest corner. Run straight to it, keeping close to the west wall the whole way. This is the best way to avoid the spike trap in the northernmost corridor.

At the safe zone, you find another one of those darkened crystal orbs. Smash the pot near the orb for a heart, then whack the orb to activate it. The orb lights up!

CAUTION

The spike traps on this floor are shown as small dotted lines on your map. There's one to the northeast and another to the northwest. Beware!

Activating the orb temporarily shuts off the nearby spike trap. While the orb is lighted, a ticking sound can be heard in the distance. Time to run! Dash east past the inactive spike trap, cutting straight across the floor and heading directly toward the northeast safe zone. Keep close to the north wall the entire way for the shortest and safest route.

Watch out for the trapdoor near the northeast safe zone! Keep close to the north wall and run past the northeast spike trap to avoid being dunked into the pit and losing 1/2 heart.

Another spike trap is on the floor near the northeast safe zone, and this one's still active. You may need to stop in front of it and wait a moment for the spikes to withdraw into the floor. Bolt to the safe zone when the spikes are down, then quickly whack the crystal orb there to disable the spike trap. Well done! If you were fast enough, activating this orb should cause a large door to slide away from the north wall behind you.

NOTE

You must reach and activate the northeast orb before time runs out and the northwest orb deactivates. Both orbs must be lighted to open the north door!

With the north door open, you may now access the northernmost safe zone. Backtrack westward and head straight for it. There sits a huge treasure chest! This one isn't empty; it contains the clue you've been searching for: a **sea chart**!

Dungeon Chest #2:
Sea Chart #1

Sea Chart
You got a **sea chart**! This must be an important clue for tracking down the Ghost Ship.

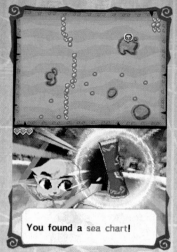

Fantastic! You've located a vital clue to tracking down that awful Ghost Ship. This old sea chart reveals the entire southwest quadrant of the Great Sea! Now you can see all the islands you'll soon be exploring. Better show this to Linebeck and see what he thinks!

NOTE

You may now access your sea chart at any time by tapping the Menu tab and then tapping the Sea Chart icon. We'll cover the usage of the sea chart shortly!

Run south and then west, leapfrogging from one safe zone to the next as you backtrack toward the southernmost safe zone. Arriving there, you find Linebeck nowhere in sight! Where has that crafty rascal gone to? Head through the south doorway to return to the temple's entry hall, then continue south to exit the temple.

The Sea Chart's Secret

Link and Ciela find Linebeck standing just outside the temple. Linebeck laughs at how long it took his "little monkey" helper to get the goods. The nerve of that guy, sending Link to retrieve the sea chart all alone. What a coward!

Looking at the sea chart, Linebeck seems thoroughly unimpressed, until he realizes its potential to net him fortune and glory! Having no further use for Link, Linebeck dashes off with his prize. Apparently his wounded ankle isn't so bad after all!

Linebeck must be headed for his ship at the harbor. You've got to catch him! Go southeast from the temple, navigating the island's northern woods once more en route to the village. Watch out for those Red ChuChus and that pesky Crow as you go!

When you arrive at town, go west to find that the shipyard worker has completed the bridge repairs. Well, it's not pretty, but it'll do! No need to cross the bridge right now; Oshus isn't at home. Turn around and head for the harbor as fast as you can!

Link finds Linebeck standing on the pier, conversing with old man Oshus. With the bridge finally fixed, Oshus decided to visit the harbor and check in on Ciela and Link. Word has already spread across the island of how Link survived the temple's wrath, and Oshus congratulates the lad on his courageous achievement.

Naturally, Linebeck pipes up to take all the credit. After all, it was he who ventured into the temple first! When Oshus mocks the arrogant captain's ineptitude, Linebeck is quick to point out his ankle injury. What a hack!

Getting back to business, Oshus asks Linebeck what he's been able to learn from the sea chart Link recovered from the temple. Frustrated, Linebeck tosses the map at the old man, saying it's next to useless.

Oshus knows there's more to the map than meets the eye, even though the haughty captain can't see it. With a twinkle in his eye, the old man tells Link that this is no ordinary chart! He asks Link to rub one section of the chart. Sure enough, some loose bits of parchment flake off, revealing a secret marker!

The marker highlights an island to the south, which Oshus identifies as the Isle of Ember. He says a far-seeing fortune teller named Astrid resides there, who should know more about the whereabouts of the Ghost Ship! Knowing her guidance will prove to be an invaluable asset, Oshus also asks Ciela to accompany Link on his journey. Perhaps seeing some of the outside world may help the little fairy recall something of her past.

Although agitated that he now has to haul two little tikes around, Linebeck is eager to get on the move. He asks Link if he's ready to head out and explore the open sea. If you haven't purchased the Wooden Shield from the shop yet, tap **Not yet** and do so—you'll need it's protection where you're going! With shield in hand, speak with Linebeck and tell him you're **Ready** to cast off.

Bring Me That Horizon

The time has finally come to explore the ocean blue! Navigating the Great Sea is quite different from exploring dry land. Link is in charge of plotting courses while Linebeck handles the engine room controls. Plotting a course is easy; simply call up your sea chart by tapping the Route tab at the screen's lower-right corner, then tap and drag the Feather Pen icon, drawing the route you wish to take.

How do you survive a Sea Trap, then? By jumping over it, of course! Whenever a Sea Trap pops up to cause you grief, tap the Jump Arrow at the bottom of the screen with your stylus to make a daring hop over the Sea Trap. If you time this just right, no collision occurs, and the Sea Trap reluctantly submerges once more.

TIP

Tap various icons on the sea chart, such as anchors, for a handy pop-up description of each one.

After plotting a course, you're asked whether you want to **Go** there, or **Cancel** and plot a new route. If you're happy with the course you've plotted, tap **Go**. The order is then sent down to Linebeck, who fires up the ship's engine. Off you go!

As soon as you start sailing along, the DS screens switch position, placing the sea chart up top and the view of Linebeck's ship down below. This enables you to tap the corners of the Touch Screen and pan your view all around the ship. It's important to keep an eye on the horizon ahead; you don't want to go crashing into anything!

NOTE

Linebeck's ship features its own health energy, shown by green hearts in the upper-left corner of the screen when sailing. Collisions at sea cause damage to the vessel, reducing its health. Keep alert, avoid hazards, and dock at a harbor to restore the ship's health energy whenever it gets low.

While sailing about, you can bring the ship to a quick halt by tapping the engine controls along the right edge of the screen. Tap the engine controls once to drop anchor, and again to resume course. You may also tap the Route tab in the lower-right corner to call up the sea chart and plot a new course whenever you like.

Finally, know that the sea features its share of dangers! While avoiding collisions with rocks and islands is important, dodging hostile sea creatures is vital as well. The only monsters you'll face on the open sea for now are Sea Traps: creepy-looking creatures that surface from the depths without warning and attempt to send you crashing into their long, thorny tripwires. These guys always appear directly in front of your vessel, so it's tough to avoid them!

Sea Trap

Threat Meter

Speed: Slow

Attack Power: 1 heart (contact)

Defense Power: 2 hits to defeat

Sea Traps are the first watery ne'er-do-wells Link encounters while navigating the Great Sea. They resemble thorny tripwires stretched between a pair of ugly sea urchins. Sea Traps surface from the depths in surprise attack and then slowly move toward Link's ship, attempting to ram it. Your best option to avoid a hazardous collision with a Sea Trap is to tap the Jump Arrow at just the right moment and sail clean over it. Wahoo!

Now that you know the basics of sailing, it's time to get a move on! Tap the Route tab to call up the sea chart, then tap and drag the Feather Pen icon, tracing a line from your current position all the way to the Isle of Ember in the southeast corner of the quadrant. Make sure to plot your course carefully so that you land at the anchor icon on the west edge of the island. Otherwise, you might go crashing into its rocky shores by accident!

Missing Links

Astrid awaits you at the Isle of Ember, but there's a whole quadrant of sea to check out if you dare. While you can't do much right now except visit a traveling merchant, it's fun to explore!

Task 4:
Find the Sea Chart & Set Sail

...continued

Beedle's Shop Ship

See that funny-looking icon of a man's face on your sea chart, the one that slowly moves about the ocean? Tap the icon to learn that this is actually a ship owned by Beedle, a traveling salesman. Plot an intercept course to Beedle's Shop Ship and hop aboard to see what he offers. Just be wary of any Sea Traps you may encounter along the way!

Beedle has a number of interesting items for sale, including Red Potions, a random Treasure, and a random ship part. You'll definitely want to purchase that Wisdom Gem off him at some point, and you can do so right now if you like! If you choose not to buy the gem, remember that it's sold here for future reference.

→NOTE←

Ship parts are expensive collectibles that you'll eventually be able to install onto Linebeck's ship when the Shipyard opens at Mercay Island. Like treasures, you can also sell ship parts to a special collector for fast cash! You'll learn all about ship parts when the Shipyard opens. For now, consider this one as an optional purchase.

Beedle's Shop Ship (SWQ)

Item	Cost	Description	Notes
Red Potion	80 Rupees	Recovery item	Restores up to 6 hearts.
Ship Part	Varies	Collectible item (Ship Part)	A random upgrade for Linebeck's ship.
Treasure	Varies	Collectible item (Treasure)	A random treasure. Collect and sell these for profit!
Wisdom Gem #1	500 Rupees	Collectible item (Spirit Gem)	Used to power up the Wisdom Spirit.

Beedle is a savvy merchant, and he shows great appreciation to his favorite customers. The first time you make a purchase from Beedle, he informs you of his special **membership program**. Every item you buy from Beedle you earn membership points, and the more Rupees you spend, the more points you earn! Though Beedle's prices seem steep at first, their cost drops dramatically as you advance along his membership system. Become a VIP member for insane bargains and huge discounts!

...continued

→NOTE←

You're awarded 1 membership point for every 100 Rupees you spend at Beedle's Shop Ship.

→NOTE←

Beedle mails you a special letter each time you advance to a new membership level. Most of these "thank you" letters include special prizes! You must reach the point in the adventure when you've received your first letter from the Postmaster before you can receive any mail from Beedle.

Beedle's Membership Program

Points	Status	Discount	Bonus Prize
0-19	Normal	None	None
20-49	Silver	10 percent off	"Thank you" letter & Freebie Card.
50-99	Gold	20 percent off	"Thank you" letter & Compliment Card.
100-199	Platinum	30 percent off	"Thank you" letter & Complimentary Card.
200+	VIP	40 percent off	"Thank you" letter.

Ship Part
Random
You got a **ship part**! Visit a Shipyard to install it onto Linebeck's ship.

Treasure
Random
You got a **treasure**! Collect these items and sell them to the highest bidder!

Wisdom Gem #1
You got a **Wisdom Gem**! Collect these items and use them to power up the Wisdom Spirit.

Beedle

This savvy merchant sails all across the Great Sea, peddling his wares from his world-renown Shop Ship. Though known to drive a hard bargain, Beedle is really just a friendly guy who loves the freedom his unique lifestyle provides him. He honors loyal customers with his special membership program, giving greater and greater discounts to those who spend their hard-earned Rupees at Beedle's!

...continued

Cannon Island

Coming ashore at Cannon Island proves a short visit, as there's little to do here at the moment. You can't access the curious Bomb Garden, and Eddo's Garage is all but closed. However, you can enjoy a quick run-in with the Postman, who sits atop a postbox near Eddo's Garage. The Postman has no mail for you, and you've nothing to send out, but it's nice to meet a friendly face!

Postman

A hardworking fellow with a penchant for parcels, the Postman lives for special deliveries! This good-natured guy makes it his mission to deliver mail to the many islands of the Great Sea. How does he do this all by himself? He just wings it...with the wings on his back!

Enter the building just beyond the postbox to visit Eddo's Garage. The owner himself isn't about, but his assistant stands just inside. Speak with the man to learn that his master is working on a new **cannon**. Interesting! The cannon isn't quite ready, so a future visit is certainly in order.

Rocky Reef

Though your sea chart shows a small gap in the rocky reef that divides the quadrant, there's actually no way of getting through. This is due to a collection of massive brown boulders that are plugging up the gap, preventing you from exploring the quadrant's western half. Oh well! Maybe if your ship had a **cannon**, you could blast a way through....

...continued

Cyclone of Doom

Be wary of venturing too far north! A giant whirlwind is up there, one that's easily capable of lifting your tiny craft into the skies. This frightful cyclone seems to seek out craft and toss them southward, preventing you from exploring very far to the north. While this whirlwind never harms your ship, being sucked up into it is quite the trying experience!

Golden Frog

Sail between the triangular-shaped rocks poking up from the sea just north of the Isle of Ember for a unique encounter. A sparkling golden frog playfully hops up from the water, seemingly enjoying itself a great deal. Who knows what this little guy is up to? Maybe you should mark its location on your sea chart for future reference! To make notes on the sea chart, tap the Menu tab, then tap the Sea Chart icon. Tap the southwest quadrant of the sea, then scribble away to your heart's content!

Tasks:
Complete!

Contents

Turning Up the Heat: Isle of Ember & Temple of Fire

Isle of Ember

Legend

3 Overworld Chest #3: Red Rupee

Temple of Fire

Astrid's House

Isle of Ember Overview

With the help of Captain Linebeck's seaworthy vessel, and with the aid of the sea chart Link so bravely recovered from the Temple of the Ocean King, our hero's quest to track down Tetra and the nefarious Ghost Ship has finally begun. His first stop is the Isle of Ember, a relatively small island dominated by a massive central volcano. It is at this remote and forbidding isle that a wise fortune-teller named Astrid is said to reside. Oshus believes Astrid knows a great deal about the Ghost Ship, and has advised Link to speak with her without delay. Though the island's volcano is inactive when Link arrives, many other dangerous creatures inhabit the land. Best to make this a short visit!

1. Find and Speak with Astrid

2. Speak with Kayo; Find the Torches

3. Enter & Clear the Temple of Fire

4. Return to Astrid; Sail to Mercay

A Link to the Present

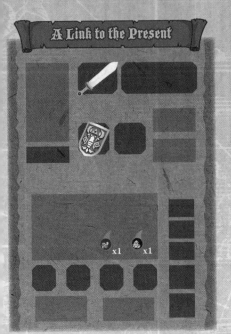

x1   x1

Items Already Acquired

Oshus's Sword | Wooden Shield | Power Gems x1 | Wisdom Gems x1

Items to Obtain

Power Gem #2 | Red Rupee x3

Overworld Denizens

Characters: Astrid, Kayo
Enemies: Octorok, Crow, Red ChuChu, Tektite, Yellow ChuChu

Task 1: Find and Speak with Astrid

The Volcano Rumbles

Link, Ciela and Linebeck disembark at the Isle of Ember, whose giant volcano rumbles quietly in the distance. Linebeck takes the opportunity to talk up his sterling helmsmanship, but Ciela is quick to point out that Link did most of the work in getting them here. Unbowed, Linebeck tells the two to hurry up and find Astrid, then busies himself with the less-than-heroic task of looking after his ship.

The hut near the port is empty and there isn't much north of it other than a few trees and some tall grass. Hack up the grass for items if you like, but don't bother rolling into the trees; nothing comes of it! Follow the stone pathway that stretches east and read the stone tablet you encounter near some steps for directions to the fortune-teller's house. Climb the steps and then enter the building to the north.

> **NOTE**
>
> Did you spot a treasure chest on the tiny northern isle? You can't reach it yet, but you can mark its location on your map for future reference!

Looks like nobody's home! Smash the pots in the corners of Astrid's house for hearts, and know that hearts will always pop out of the two pots here. Whenever Link's heart meter is low, pay a visit here and fill it up! When you're ready, go downstairs to search the basement. You didn't come all this way for nothing!

A wall rises behind Link when he enters the basement, blocking off the stairs and trapping him inside. A number of monsters then burrow up from the floor and attack! These freaky beasties are called Octoroks, and they love spitting rocks at their enemies from afar. Use targeted and spin attacks to clear the room, doing your best to keep away from the Octoroks' dangerous projectiles.

Octorok

Threat Meter

Speed: Slow

Attack Power: 1/2 heart (contact); 1/2 heart (rock)

Defense Power: 2 hits to defeat

These hardworking hostiles have put in appearances in nearly every major Zelda title, and *Phantom Hourglass* is no exception! Octoroks are classic baddies that attack by firing rocks from their oversized snouts. They're also the most resilient foes Link has faced up to this point, requiring two targeted attacks to defeat (or one potent spin attack). Fortunately, Link can deflect an Octorok's painful projectiles and bounce these guys around by charging them with his shield. This makes Octoroks somewhat easy to handle, provided Link doesn't show them his back!

primagames.com

57

The wall slides away from the basement stairs, allowing you to return to the surface. Don't do so yet, though; approach the blue door in the north wall instead. Ciela senses a presence behind the door and advises Link to **call out** and see if anyone's hiding in the room beyond. Yell into the DS microphone to make Link give a holler!

TIP

If you're playing in a quiet environment, you can simply blow into the microphone to make Link call out.

Ciela's instincts were correct: someone is indeed hiding in the room beyond the blue door. It turns out to be the fortune-teller, Astrid! Apparently, Astrid sealed herself in the back room to hide from those pesky Octoroks but she forgot one important thing: the door to the room can only be opened from the outside. She's trapped herself!

*When Link agrees to help free the fortune-teller, he soon learns it won't be easy. Astrid tells him that the **map on the right** is the key to opening the door, but she doesn't know exactly how it works. Only her assistant, Kayo, knows the secret! Ciela assures Astrid that they'll find Kayo and learn how to free her.*

Task 2: Speak with Kayo; Find the Torches

A Ghost of a Chance

Kayo must be found! Head upstairs to return to the first floor. If you were wounded in the fight with the Octoroks, smash the pots in Astrid's house for hearts. Then exit the building and go south and enter the island's southern-most hut.

Astrid

A sage fortune-teller, Astrid has the unique ability to see far into the future. Link comes to her aid after she is assailed by monsters, and the wise woman repays his heroism with gifts of knowledge and precious artifacts. Astrid sees immense promise in Link and does her best to guide the boy along his just and noble path.

TIP

Tap the map in Astrid's basement for a clue about what must be done to open the door.

There's little to see inside the southern hut except a few clay pots, an open book sitting on a table, and a torch burning brightly in the corner. Smash the pots for hearts, then tap the book to read it. It's Kayo's journal! His most recent entry is somewhat grim, indicating that something may have happened to him on the eastern side of the island. Well, at least you know where to look!

Exit the hut and head east in search of Kayo, crossing a wooden bridge as you go. A few Red ChuChus pop up from the ground to ambush you on the other side. These little guys are no threat; unleash your sword on them and then continue eastward.

Link encounters a large stone gate a short distance ahead. The gate seems to be electrified, so it would be unwise to touch it! A nearby stone tablet indicates that beyond the gate lies a path to the top of the volcano, but the tablet warns that approval is needed for entry. Guess you'll have to come back here later!

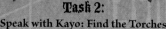

Task 2:
Speak with Kayo: Find the Torches

Press onward and cross another stubby wooden bridge. You're attacked by a new breed of enemy in the clearing beyond: spiderlike Tektites! Avoid their pounce attacks and dispatch each of these dangerous monsters with a few well-timed targeted attacks. They won't like it!

Tektite

Threat Meter

Speed: Fast

Attack Power: 1/2 heart (contact)

Defense Power: 2 hits to defeat

Resilient and tough to predict, Tektites can be a real handful for Link. Making fast, sudden leaps, these adversaries like to pounce on their quarry, then quickly hop away to safety. Don't play their game! Stay mobile to dodge their jump attacks and wait for the Tektite to land nearby. Then be quick to show it the sharp side of Link's sword! Targeted attacks work well enough, but powerful spin attacks are the fastest ways to put an end to these threats. Be especially careful around red Tektites; they're even tougher, requiring three hits to squash!

Those pesky Tektites are everywhere! Move with caution now as you continue moving eastward, slashing through each creature that lands in your path. Ciela soon notices the bones of a fallen adventurer on a tiny hill at the eastern edge of the island. Could these be the remains of Astrid's assistant?

As Link nears the pile of bones, a spirit suddenly materializes out of thin air. Creepy! Ciela screams at Link to attack the apparition, but the ghost quickly speaks up, insisting that it only looks scary. It assures the pair that it really is a good ghost—the ghost of Kayo, Astrid's assistant!

Realizing her mistake, Ciela apologizes to Kayo. The spirit dismisses the notion with a wave, saying it's not so bad being a ghost. He feels much lighter than before! Kayo is concerned for Astrid though, and when Ciela tells him that they've recently seen the fortune-teller, Kayo begs them to help his mistress. He then gives the duo a vital clue: The island's three torches are the key to freeing Astrid from captivity!

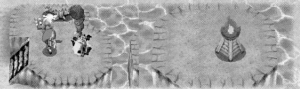

Kayo also shows Ciela and Link the location of one of the island's torches: it stands right behind his humble remains on a tiny isle to the east. He advises Link to mark the torch's location on his map. With a final whisper of concern for Astrid, Kayo vanishes, leaving the two to their task.

Freeing Astrid

You already know where two of the island's torches lie: one was inside Kayo's hut, and you've just learned that another one stands atop the tiny isle just east of Kayo's remains. Now you just need to find the last torch to save Astrid! Move north from your current position, slashing through the odd Tektite as you go. Watch out for a Crow in a tree not far ahead and make sure it doesn't steal your Rupees away!

TIP

Somersault into the tree the Crow was perched atop to knock three hearts from its branches. Lovely!

A new type of ChuChu emerges from the ground just beyond the Crow's tree. This is a Yellow ChuChu and it's a bit more dangerous than its red cousins. Yellow ChuChus like to surround themselves with pure electricity, and Link suffers damage if he tries to smack them when they're all lighted up. Wait for the Yellow ChuChu's current to die down, then tap it to unleash a fast targeted attack!

Yellow ChuChu

Threat Meter

Speed: Slow

Attack Power: 1/2 heart (contact)

Defense Power: 1 hit to defeat

Running into one of these ChuChus can be quite the shocking experience! Keep a distance from these electrified adversaries, who can leap toward Link from range to zap him with contact damage. Don't attack a Yellow ChuChu while it's lit up either, or its radiant current will flow through Link's blade for an unpleasant jolt. Wait for their charge to dissipate instead, then be quick about tapping them to retaliate with a targeted blow!

Keep heading north, following the island's edge as it curves westward. Watch out for Crows nesting in trees as you go! You eventually come to the third and final torch, which is guarded by another Yellow ChuChu. Lash out at the ChuChu when its energy

dwindles, then make a note of the torch's location on your map. Roll into the nearby tree afterward to knock a sparkly red Rupee from its boughs!

Red Rupee

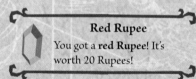

You got a **red Rupee!** It's worth 20 Rupees!

You've located all three torches and are now able to free Astrid from her panic room. Backtrack east and then south toward Kayo's remains. Take a slightly different route back to Astrid's house this time, climbing up some stone steps that lie just north of the

first wooden bridge you encounter. Smack the stone statue to the west atop the steps for a clue on how to open the summit gate: you need Astrid's help!

Continue north and then west, looping around the island once more on this taller tier. Shred through each Tektite and Yellow ChuChu that crosses your path, and roll into the two big trees you see to knock down a red Rupee from one and a trio of hearts from the other. Score!

Red Rupee

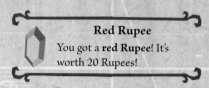

You got a **red Rupee!** It's worth 20 Rupees!

You eventually come full circle, arriving at Astrid's house from the north. Enter, smash the first-floor pots for hearts, then go downstairs. Approach the blue door and tap the map to the right of it to begin solving the puzzle that unlocks the door.

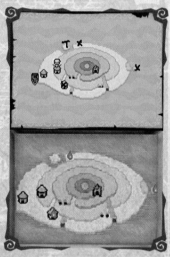

The puzzle asks you to mark the locations of the Island's three torches. No sweat! You've done the legwork and you know where they are. Tap the **southernmost hut**, the **easternmost isle**, and right near the end of the northernmost path. Voila! The map accepts your input and the door slides away.

A beautiful veiled woman with deep red hair steps out of the back room through the open door. This must be Astrid! Free from captivity at last, the fortune-teller gives Ciela and Link her heartfelt thanks.

Telling Astrid his name and purpose for visiting the island, Link is hopeful that the seer might have some insight as to where the Ghost Ship may have taken Tetra. Astrid imparts some shocking news: the haunted craft recently visited her island—just a few days ago, in fact! That was the primary reason she was hiding in her basement. That, and the recent influx of monsters!

Task 3:
Enter and Clear the Temple of Fire

It then occurs to Astrid that she hasn't seen Kayo since the Ghost Ship's arrival. Ciela is reluctant to tell the woman of her assistant's unfortunate fate. She doesn't need to say much, though; Astrid's uncanny insight has already told her of Kayo's untimely demise. She offers to direct her keen insight at Link and tell his fortune. When Link agrees, Astrid tells him to round up his companions and meet her upstairs.

Annoyed at being called away from his beloved ship, Linebeck demands that Astrid do the reading and be done with it. The seer soon arrives and, with everyone gathered, gazes deeply into her crystal ball. The visions she sees are bleak: darkness and evil shroud both land and sea. She issues Link a grave warning: to find the Ghost Ship, he must clash with the darkness itself!

Link assures Astrid that he's unafraid; she tells him to hasten to the Temple of Fire on top of the island. There, the young adventurer must defeat the power of darkness that haunts the palace. Only then will he find what he needs to open the path ahead.

Task 3: Enter and Clear the Temple of Fire

Reaching the Summit

Astrid's reading is both cryptic and clear. The very mention of dark forces and powers is enough to send Linebeck hurrying off to his ship again. What a shock! Speak with Astrid one final time to learn that she's released the seal on the summit gate. You're now free to scale the volcano and enter the Temple of Fire!

Exit Astrid's house and go south down the steps outside. Dash east toward the summit gate you noticed earlier. The electricity that previously surrounded the gate is now gone, so you can safely tap the door and open it. Do so and then head north, clobbering a Yellow ChuChu that pops up from the ground just beyond the gate to attack you. Remember to wait for its charge to dissipate before you strike!

Continue moving up the volcano, slashing away at any Tektites that bound into view. After you climb the next set of steps, the volcano suddenly begins to stir. Oh no, it's erupting! Huge, flaming boulders start flying out of the volcano's cone, shooting skyward and then tumbling back down with explosive results. From this point forward, watch for circular shadows that appear on the ground, and run away from them to avoid the forthcoming barrage!

CAUTION

Be careful not to fall off the edge of the volcano! If you do, you'll have to return to the summit gate and retry your ascent.

Keep circling around the volcano, winding your way ever upward. Be wary of red Tektites, which take three hits to defeat instead of the normal two, along with the occasional Crow perched in the surrounding trees. You soon come to a large doorway near the top of the volcano, but the passage has been walled up! This must be the temple's entrance, but how are you to open it?

Ignore the doorway for now and travel west to find more steps leading up. Looks like you haven't quite reached the top yet! Hack the patch of grass near the base of the steps for a heart, then climb up to reach the volcano's summit. Go northwest and tap the small chest lying on the ground to open it; claim a glimmering **red Rupee** from within.

Overworld Chest #3: Red Rupee

Red Rupee
You got a **red Rupee**! It's worth 20 Rupees!

Continue north and then east, looping around the summit. A stone tablet stands to the east; read it for an important message on how to proceed. The tablet hints that you must **blow out the flames** to illuminate the path ahead. Interesting....

There's nothing more to do up here, so run south and leap off this highest tier of the volcano, landing right near the walled-up passage you noticed just moments ago. Could the **"blow out the flames"** message be referring to the two candles that stand at either side of the passage? It's worth a shot! Move Link right in front of the doorway, then blow into your mic to make him blow out both candles at once.

It worked! The candles quickly go out, and the doorway opens. Now you can enter the Temple of Fire! There's no time to lose; hurry inside to face the darkness within.

Temple of Fire

Legend

-  **Dungeon Chest #1:** Small Key
- **Dungeon Chest #2:** Red Rupee
- **Dungeon Chest #3:** Boomerang
- **Dungeon Chest #4:** Boss Key
- **Dungeon Chest #5:** Heart Container #1
- Orb
- Floor Switch
- Lever
- Small Key

Temple of Fire: 1F

to 2nd Floor
x4
to 2nd Floor
to 2nd Floor
to Isle of Ember

Temple of Fire: 2F

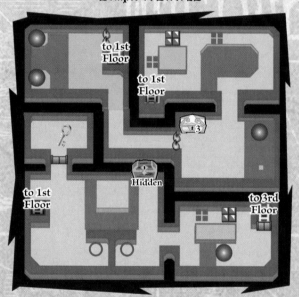

to 1st Floor
to 1st Floor
to 1st Floor
Hidden
to 3rd Floor

Items to Obtain

Boomerang — Boss Key — Heart Container #1 — Red Rupee — Small Key x3

1   2   3   4

Task 3:
Enter and Clear the Temple of Fire

Temple of Fire: 3F

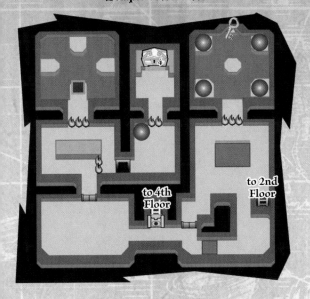

to 4th Floor

to 2nd Floor

Boss Chamber

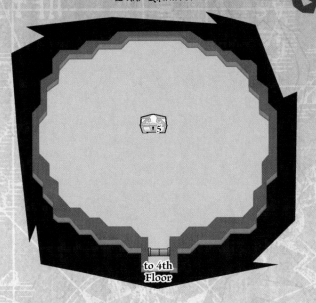

to 4th Floor

Temple of Fire: 4F

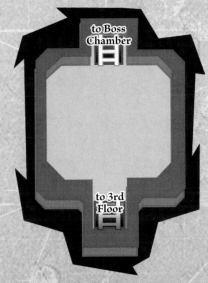

to Boss Chamber

to 3rd Floor

Temple of Fire: 1F

The searing heat of the temple is almost too much to bear. What a dreadful place! Noticing tall plumes of fire in the entry corridor, Ciela cautions Link to proceed slowly and try not to get burned. Smash the pot in the corner for a heart, then carefully proceed north, zigzagging to avoiding the flames in the hall.

CAUTION

Ciela isn't kidding! Keep away from open flames; Link loses 1/2 heart each time he get scorched.

The hall leads into a wide chamber. Be wary: a long column of fire slowly rotates about the center of the room. Wait for the fire column to move past, then follow close behind it. Smash the pots in the corners of the room for hearts as you work your way around the chamber, heading for the next room to the east.

TIP

After smashing a pot, you can hide in the corner of the room and avoid being scorched by the fiery column as it swings past.

Dungeon Denizens

Enemies

Fire Bubble	Fire Keese	Green Slime	Keese	Octorok

Boss

Rat	Red ChuChu	Yellow ChuChu	Blaaz, Master of Fire

Much of the floor is missing in this chamber. Make sure you don't fall into the abyss! Run to the north wall and then go east, leaping the gap and landing on a small chunk of floor in the middle of the room. There's a locked door to the north but you haven't a key to open it. Leap across the next gap ahead to reach the east side of the room.

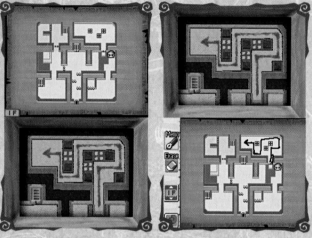

An old map hangs on the north wall. Tap the map to view it. The map shows you a path that leads you safely through the room to the north! The room lies beyond the locked door, so you can't reach it just yet. But take a moment to scribble the route on your map for future reference!

NOTE

The old map not only shows a safe path through the north chamber, it also shows where six trapdoors lie on the floor therein. Can you see them? They look like dark squares! You may find it easier to simply mark the locations of the trap doors rather than tracing the safe route through the room.

After jotting your notes, head south and whack the Red ChuChu that pops up from the floor to ambush you. Be ready when you enter the south chamber; a wall raises behind Link, trapping him inside the room! Four Keese then appear in puffs of smoke. Use targeted and spin attacks to beat back the Keese without delay.

Clearing the room causes the wall to retract, allowing you to escape. Don't leave just yet, though! To the west sits a chest containing a **small key**!

Dungeon Chest #1: Small Key

Small Key
You got a **small key**! Use it to open a door in this dungeon.

Alright! Now you can open that locked door you noticed just moments ago. Return to the door and tap it to access the chamber to the north. Remember the old map's warning: there's only one safe path through this room! Carefully follow the route you traced on your map to reach the west side of the chamber unharmed, and don't miss opening the treasure chest you pass when moving along the north wall!

TIP

The room's trapdoors trigger as you draw near. Slowly walk about to trigger each one, then simply avoid the pits!

Dungeon Chest #2: Red Rupee

Red Rupee
You got a **red Rupee**! It's worth 20 Rupees!

Task 3:
Enter and Clear the Temple of Fire

Four crystal orbs stand at the room's west end. Striking each one with the sword causes it to light up, but the orbs quickly darken once more. What a pain! To trigger them all at once, stand in the middle and trace a wide circle around Link to execute a spin attack. This is the only way to light them all!

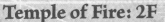

Activating all four orbs causes a door to open elsewhere in the dungeon, creating a new way forward. The newly opened doorway is temporarily shown on your map by a special icon, which fades after about 20 seconds. You can't go any farther in this direction, so backtrack through the chamber, being careful to avoid those sneaky trapdoors on your way. Jump across the pit and return to the central chamber, where the column of fire is still spinning away. Avoid the column and head north, taking the new route you've opened to reach the temple's second floor.

Temple of Fire: 2F

You enter the temple's second floor from the northeast stairs. So far, so good! A collection of large red blocks prevents you from moving north, so go east, quickly dispatching a Red ChuChu and a Yellow ChuChu when they pop up from the ground to attack. You

soon encounter more red blocks to the east; move west to locate a glowing red orb in the corner of the room. Whack the orb to turn it blue, causing the red blocks to lower and some blue blocks to rise just behind you. Wild!

Loop around to return to the east hallway. With the red blocks down, you're now free to explore the room's other side. Rip through another Red and Yellow ChuChu when they pop up from the floor, being careful not to fall into the room's central pit. Smash a pot near the south wall for a heart, then move south into the next chamber.

Look out: Link springs another trap when he enters the south chamber! A wall rises behind him, trapping him inside the room. Several green blobs then pop up from the ground and begin hopping about. These gelatinous foes are called Green Slimes, and

they can be a real pain in the rump! Keep near the doorway and let them come to you; use targeted attacks to slash them apart.

Green Slime

Threat Meter

Speed: Fast

Attack Power: 1/2 heart (contact)

Defense Power: 2-3 hits to defeat

Ew, gross! These revolting piles of goo leap about with surprising speed, relentlessly chasing Link. Maybe they're attracted to his stylish green outfit? In any case, be very wary of these foes; each time you strike one, it splits into two smaller, even more annoying blobs! Tiny Green Slimes don't damage Link when they leap onto him; instead, they slow him down and prevent him from drawing his sword. Naturally, this is a terrible burden when other monsters are about! Quickly rub the stylus left to right when hampered by bitsy slimes; this causes Link to shrug them off. Be quick to retaliate with spin attacks afterward!

Surviving this slimy ambush isn't easy, but the reward is great! A giant chest appears in one corner of the room, and it contains a fantastic prize: the **Boomerang**! This versatile item is the vital to progressing through this dungeon. You won't get any farther without it!

Dungeon Chest #3: Boomerang

Boomerang

You got a **Boomerang**! A great asset to any adventurer, this remarkable item has a wide variety of uses. Make Link ready the Boomerang by tapping the Item icon in the screen's upper-right corner, or by pressing and holding R or L. Then simply use the stylus to trace a path of flight! Link tosses the Boomerang when you lift the stylus off the Touch Screen, and the projectile flies outward, following the exact path you've traced. Amazing!

The Boomerang has a variety of uses, including:

- Stunning and defeating enemies.
- Activating distant orbs, switches, and the like.
- Smashing remote pots and retrieving out-of-reach items.
- Helping Link see what lies ahead. (You can pan your view of the environment a bit when tracing a flight path!)

Case in point: there's seemingly no way to lower the flames that block the hallway to the west. Not without the aid of the Boomerang, that is! Spy a darkened crystal orb sitting on a small platform across the pit to the east. You can't activate this orb without the Boomerang! Tap the Item icon in the upper-right corner of the screen, then trace a line toward the orb with your stylus. When you lift the stylus, Link hurls his newest item, which follows the route you've traced. Neat!

⟶ NOTE ⟵

You may also ready the Boomerang by pressing and holding L or R. Releasing either trigger causes Link to store the Boomerang once more.

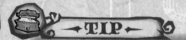
⟶ TIP ⟵

Toss the Boomerang at the pot just south of the orb to smash it open, revealing a heart. The Boomerang then retrieves this item for you on the rebound!

Striking the orb douses the flames to the west. You're now free to move on! Follow the corridor as it bends north, opening into a wide chamber. Two torches stand against the north and south walls and a wide pit lies to the west. Flames prevent you from hurrying down the nearby stairs; you'll have to find a way to get rid of them. Heads up, though: those two torches are mischievously enchanted, and they periodically shoot fireballs at you!

Keep near the south wall and dodge the south torch's fireballs. After dodging one of its flaming projectiles, hurry toward the pit and ready the Boomerang. Quickly trace a line due west; your view pans as you do so, and you can see a crystal orb beyond the pit! Target the orb and then release the stylus; the Boomerang flies out and smacks the crystal, dousing the south torch.

⟶ TIP ⟵

Be quick with your Boomerang and try to shut off the south torch before it launches another fireball.

One fireball-hurling torch is easier to handle than two, but don't get too hasty! Be patient and dodge one of the north torch's fireballs, then quickly ready the Boomerang. Trace a line toward the chamber's northwest corner, where another orb stands. Whack this northern orb with the Boomerang to put out the north torch!

With both orbs activated and both torches doused, the flames to the east die down, allowing you to proceed downstairs. Well, what are you waiting for? Get moving!

Temple of Fire: 1F Revisited

The steps lead down to the first floor's northwest chamber. Thrust your sword into the Yellow ChuChu that springs up from the floor, but only when it's safe to do so. Smash the pot in the corner for a heart, then whack the stone statue to the north. The statue says there are no treasure chests for you to find on this floor of the temple. Good to know!

⟶ TIP ⟵

Sick of waiting for Yellow ChuChus to lose their charge? Try smacking them with Link's Boomerang! This stuns the creatures, allowing you to follow up with quick targeted attacks.

The south passage is inaccessible because of a collection of raised blue blocks. A glowing blue orb is in the alcove to the west, but striking the orb with Link's sword causes the nearby red blocks to rise, trapping Link near the orb. Tricky! To proceed, stand near the raised blue blocks and then ready the Boomerang. Draw a line up and around so that the Boomerang flies past the lowered red blocks and strikes the orb. The blue blocks recede and the Boomerang returns to Link. Now you can travel south!

Task 3:
Enter and Clear the Temple of Fire

Yet another Yellow ChuChu pops up to attack just beyond the blue blocks. Dispatch it and then check out the pit to the west. There's another orb over there, seemingly out of reach. Not so! Use the Boomerang to whack the orb from range. This causes the flames to the east to die down, allowing you to return to the central chamber if you wish. There's no need to do so at the moment, so continue south instead.

Heads up! A wall rises behind Link when he enters the southwest chamber, trapping him inside with two all-new baddies. These scary-looking skulls are called Bubbles—Fire Bubbles, to be exact! Link's sword attacks don't seem to affect them, so try tossing the Boomerang at one instead. Presto! The Boomerang stuns the Fire Bubble, dousing its flames and sending it crashing to the floor. Hurry and finish it off with Link's sword before it recovers! Defeat both Bubbles to clear the way forward, then go upstairs to explore a new section of the temple's second floor.

TIP

You can often tell when Link will become trapped inside a room. Look at the floor before you enter and notice the wall that will rise behind him!

Fire Bubble

Threat Meter

Speed: Normal

Attack Power: 1/2 heart (contact)

Defense Power: 1 hit to defeat

Don't lose your head when faced with these frightening foes! These flaming skulls don't actually chase after Link; they simply hover about, blindly bouncing off walls and other objects. And although Fire Bubbles are immune to Link's sword while airborne, they are vulnerable to a quick toss of his Boomerang! It's best to trace a quick zigzag pattern between Link and the Fire Bubble to ensure the Boomerang strikes its target. Once it's grounded, quickly follow up with a targeted attack to burst that Bubble once and for all!

Temple of Fire: 2F Revisited

Link faces a new threat in the second floor's southeast chamber: Fire Keese! Like Fire Bubbles, these burning baddies can't be harmed by normal sword attacks. You must hurl Link's Boomerang to defeat them instead! Stick near the steps and thrash the nearest Keese with the Boomerang, then carefully move south, avoiding the two small, rotating columns of fire.

Fire Keese

Threat Meter

Speed: Fast

Attack Power: 1/2 heart (contact)

Defense Power: 1 hit to defeat (Boomerang)

Only Link's Boomerang is able to dispatch these dangerous dive bombers! Don't bother with cold hard steel; simply keep your distance, ready the Boomerang, and then trace a quick zigzag pattern between Link and the burning beastie. Fire Keese move in irregular patterns, so this is the best way to ensure that the Boomerang finds its mark! Like normal Keese, these little fry guys are too weak to withstand even one whack from the mighty Boomerang!

Another Fire Keese flutters about near the southern fire column. Run to the southeast corner and toss the Boomerang to eliminate this potential threat from a safe location. Smack the nearby statue afterward to learn that there's a treasure chest hidden on this floor of the temple! The statue even offers to show you the chest's location—for 20 Rupees, that is. No need to pay up; we'll show you where the chest lies very soon!

TIP

If you ever pay to have a stone statue show you the location of a treasure chest, make sure to mark it down on your map so you don't forget where it's hidden!

Wait for the southern fire column to spin past and then quickly dash east to reach a small alcove. There, a lever sticks out from the north wall! Tap the lever to make Link grab it, then tap the arrow that appears to pull the lever from the wall. Nice work! Another lever can be seen to the east on the other side of the wall. That's your next destination!

Head north, dodging the two spinning fire columns as you go. Carefully jump across a gap to the east and land on a wide platform where another long fire column is busy spinning away. Avoid the flames and continue eastward, leaping across another short gap. Quickly ready the Boomerang and hurl it at the Fire Keese that flutters about over here to extinguish it.

Eliminating the third and final Fire Keese in this area earns you a special treat: a treasure chest appears on the floor nearby! Open the chest to claim a **red Rupee** prize. Great! Now head south, smashing a nearby pot for a heart. Pull the lever you noticed a moment ago to open a door north of the stairs that brought you up to this area.

There's more to see to the east, but don't go there just yet. Instead, backtrack toward the door your lever-pulling has just opened, carefully avoiding those spinning fire columns along the way. Beyond that door lies a tiny chamber with two small holes in the north wall. A little Rat periodically darts out of one hole, quickly runs along, and then ducks into the other. You need to stop this Rat to claim the small key it carries, but the little guy won't emerge if you wait for him inside the room. He's a crafty one!

To outsmart the Rat, stand just south of the doorway and ready the Boomerang. Draw a line directly north and hold the stylus on the Touch Screen until the Rat pops out from one of the holes. The moment you see its beady little eyes, remove the stylus to make Link toss the Boomerang. Wham! The Boomerang dispatches the Rat, leaving you free to stroll in and collect its **small key**.

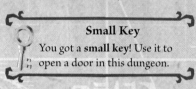

Small Key
You got a **small key**! Use it to open a door in this dungeon.

Onward and Upward

With the Rat's small key in hand, travel east once more to continue exploring where you left off. There's an odd scene going down at the southeast area: an Octorok stands its ground in the northern corridor, relentlessly firing rocks westward into a collection of red blocks. What a weirdo! Use the Boomerang to activate the glowing red orb across the pit to the south. This causes the red blocks to lower, granting you access to the angry Octorok.

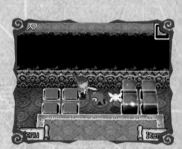

Approaching such an angry Octorok directly would be unwise, so let's calm it down a bit first. Keep out of sight and use the Boomerang to stun the Octorok from a safe vantage, blocking the Octorok's shots with your shield. While the Octorok is seeing stars, hurry toward it and finish it off with Link's steel.

Nice job! Now you just need to get rid of those pesky blue blocks that stand in your path. Position Link between the red and blue blocks, then trace a line with the Boomerang so that it loops around to strike the crystal orb. Bam! The orb changes color and the blue blocks retract into the floor. Smash the nearby pot for a heart, then use the small key you recently acquired to open the door that blocks the nearby stairs. You're doing great!

Task 3:
Enter and Clear the Temple of Fire

Temple of Fire: 3F

Things have been relatively easy so far, but they are about to heat up! Begin exploring the third floor by circling around the east chamber's central pit, dispatching the many Green Slimes that spring up from the ground. Remember that these slime balls separate when you slash into them, so be prepared!

Two candles stand against the north wall. You know you've got to blow these guys out, right? All in good time. For now, go south to explore the southeast area, carefully dashing past the fast-spinning column of fire. Dash into the southwest alcove to locate a wall map! This wall map contains a vital clue; tap it to check it out.

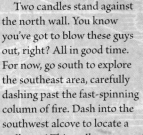

TIP

The corner pot near the fire column contains a heart, and after you smash it, you can stand in the corner and avoid the fire column!

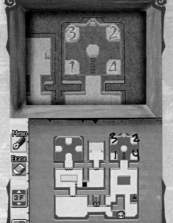

The wall map hints that you must activate four switches in the northeast chamber in a specific order. Study the map carefully to see that the numbers inscribed upon it show you the order in which the switches must be activated! Make a note of this clue on your own map, then return north to blow out those two candles.

As you did before when trying to enter the Temple of Fire, position Link near each candle and then blow into your mic to make him heave a mighty breath and extinguish each candle in turn. Way to blow! The flames on the ground between the candles go out and you're free to move on. Enter the northeast chamber to discover four crystal orbs sitting on four platforms, one in each corner of the room. These must be the switches the wall map was referring to!

Stand in the center of the room and then ready the Boomerang. Carefully trace a single line so that one toss of the Boomerang causes it to strike each of the four orbs, activating them in the following order:

1. Southwest orb first.
2. Northeast orb second.
3. Northwest orb third.
4. Southeast orb fourth.

Perfect! Activating all four orbs in one careful toss prompts a **small key** to fall from the ceiling, landing on the room's northernmost platform. Hurl the Boomerang to retrieve this vital item, then exit the room, heading south to open a nearby locked door with your newfound key.

Small Key
You got a **small key**! Use it to open a door in this dungeon.

Another stone statue stands just beyond the locked door, eager to tell you there's a treasure chest hidden somewhere on this floor. Save your hard-earned Rupees and read on; we'll make sure you get that chest! Continue west instead to encounter a creepy-looking block that's sealing up a passage to the north. Even Ciela is weirded out by this thing! Ignore the block for now and keep moving westward.

Once again, Link falls into a trap as he enters the southwest chamber. A wall rises behind him, trapping him in the room with two Yellow ChuChus and two Fire Keese. To make things worse, a fireball-spitting torch stands in the center of the room! Stay mobile and use Link's Boomerang to eliminate the Fire Keese. Stun the ChuChus with it as well, or simply hack them up when their electricity fades. Eliminate the room's four monsters to douse the central torch and unseal the north and east passages.

→ TIP ←

Smash the pots in the north corners of the room for hearts when necessary, but try not to waste them!

The passage to the north is dangerous, as two Fire Bubbles bounce aimlessly through its halls. Keep a distance and toss the Boomerang at these creatures to stun them, then hurry to finish them off with fast targeted attacks. Don't be afraid to retreat to the south chamber if one of the Bubbles draws too close for comfort! Wipe out both Fire Bubbles to lower the flames that block the north and east passages, then proceed north.

A stone tablet stands just inside the northwest chamber, providing you with a vital clue: three **torches** must be lit to open the way forward. Move to the room's central platform, where a pressure switch sticks up from the floor. Stand on the switch to cause one of the room's three torches to light up. That's one torch lit, but how are you to light the other two?

Use the Boomerang, of course! Trace a line so that the Boomerang strikes the burning torch first, then the north torch, and finally, the torch to the west. Because it's made of wood, the Boomerang catches fire when it hits the lighted torch, then shares this flame with the other two! When all three torches are burning, some flames that block a passage elsewhere in the temple are extinguished. (Their location is temporarily shown on your map.)

Task 3:
Enter and Clear the Temple of Fire

Obtaining the Boss Key

Backtrack south and then east, heading for the floor's central chamber. A wide pit prevents you from reaching it, and there seems to be no way of getting past. Time for a bit of recon! Ready the Boomerang and trace a line east to view the chamber ahead. There's a crystal orb in there! Activate the orb with the Boomerang to seal off the pit so you may proceed.

A three-pronged fire column spins about the central chamber, so proceed with caution! Avoid the flames and go north to reach another room. There you find a massive treasure chest! Open the chest to claim a very important item: the **Boss Key**!

> ### NOTE
>
> This massive chest is the one the stone statue was referring to.

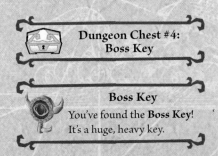

Dungeon Chest #4:
Boss Key

Boss Key
You've found the **Boss Key**! It's a huge, heavy key.

Unlike small keys, Link must carry the hefty Boss Key overhead, just like a barrel or rock. He can't run while carrying this item, so be careful when navigating the three-pronged fire column as you backtrack through the previous chamber. If need be, tap anywhere near Link to make him carefully set the Boss Key down. Tap farther away from Link to make him throw it!

Have you figured out what to do with the Boss Key? That's right! You must carry it back to that freaky-looking block you passed by a short time ago. You encounter no resistance on the way there, so simply tote the Boss Key over to the block and then tap the Block to make Link heave the key at it.

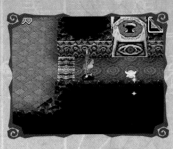

As if by magic, the Boss Key is sucked into the creepy-looking block. With a brilliant flash of light, the block slowly retracts into the floor, granting you passage up the staircase beyond. That's some trick! Now you can go upstairs and explore the rest of the temple.

Temple of Fire: 4F & 5F

There isn't much to see on the fourth floor of the temple; it's just a small chamber with a few pots and two stone tablets. Smash the pots for hearts and then read the nearby tablet. It informs you that this temple protects the **Spirit of Power**. Wonder what that could mean?

The other tablet tells you to step into the **blue light** to return to the temple's entrance. Right on cue, a small patch of blue light appears behind Link. No need to return to the temple's entrance just yet; there's one more floor to explore! Go upstairs for the final showdown.

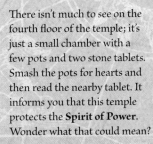

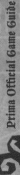

Blaaz, Master of Fire

Threat Meter

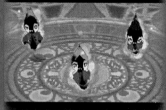

Speed: Normal

Attack Power: 1/2 heart (contact);
1/2 heart (fireball)

Defense Power: Multiple hits to defeat!

Ciela senses a powerful evil presence residing at the top of the temple, and as usual, she's not wrong! A wall rises behind Link the moment he enters the final chamber, trapping him within. A wicked sorcerer then appears in a giant puff of smoke! The sorcerer quickly divides himself into three smaller forms, and the battle begins.

Blaaz can be a real handful if you don't know how to handle him, but once you discover his secret, he's a pushover! For starters, he's completely invulnerable to all attacks while split into his triplet form. In this form, Blaaz chases Link about, periodically hurling fireballs at him from three separate angles. You've got to make him whole again, and fast!

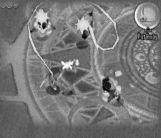

The Boomerang is the key to piecing Blaaz back together. Ready the Boomerang and then quickly trace a line to each micro-Blaaz so that all three are targeted. Try to do this before they toss their fireballs at you!

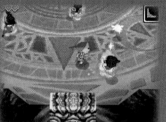

Quickly hurl the Boomerang as soon as all three mini-Blaazes are targeted. The Boomerang swoops them up, mashing them all together. Did it work? Sometimes it doesn't!

Blaaz has another secret, and this one's discovered by studying your map. Have you noticed how each mini-Blaaz's icon has a certain number of horns sticking out of its head? This is an important clue! To ensure Blaaz is made whole by a Boomerang toss, you must target the mini-Blaazes in the following order:

1. Target the one with only one horn first.

2. Target the one with two horns second.

3. Target the one with three horns third.

Fantastic! You've figured out how to merge Blaaz back together. Now show him the sharp side of Link's sword! Rip into Blaaz over and over by tapping him as fast as you can for huge targeted attack combos!

Keep the pressure on Blaaz and he soon falls to Link's unyielding heroism. If things ever become dicey, start smashing the many pots along the outside of the chamber for hearts. Defeat Blaaz to purify this sacred temple!

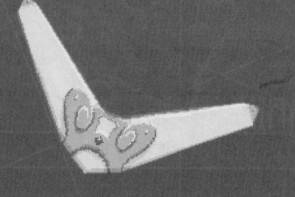

Task 4:
Return to Astrid: Sail to Mercay

Having suffered greatly, Blaaz has no choice but to succumb to Link's righteous blade. The evil wizard explodes in a blinding flash, becoming transformed into a column of sand! The sand flies skyward, whisked away from the temple to some unknown destination.

An odd insignia then illuminates on the floor. Out of it pops a small, red fairy. The fairy flutters toward Link and introduces itself as **Leaf, Spirit of Power**. Leaf thanks Link for saving him from the evil wizard. The fairy says he was locked away long ago, just like the Ocean King. How awful!

Leaf is concerned for the Ocean King and wishes to help in any way he can. He gladly joins up with Link, saying he will aid him as much as possible. How wonderful! Now it's time to hurry off and speak with Astrid. She'll want to hear all about your accomplishments!

Task 4: Return to Astrid; Sail to Mercay

Just Rewards

You've done it! The vile wizard Blaaz is no more, and Leaf, the Spirit of Power, has been saved. As a reward for your heroic efforts, a treasure chest suddenly appears in the chamber's center. Open it for a fantastic prize: a **Heart Container**!

Dungeon Chest #5: Heart Container #1

Heart Container #1

You got a **Heart Container**! Your heart meter has been increased by one heart!

It's time to leave this sweltering place. Step into the nearby patch of blue light to return to the temple's entrance, then head directly for Astrid's house. Don't dally!

Getting Some Guidance

Exiting the temple, Link and Ciela notice that the island's volcano has stopped growling. This must be because the temple has been cleansed of evil! Astrid confirms this, saying Link is to be commended for his courageous deeds. With Leaf, the Spirit of Power at his side, Link is now able to forge ahead in his quest!

The fortune-teller goes on to say that, ultimately, Link will need the help of three spirits: those of **Power**, **Wisdom**, and **Courage**. Once he has the aid of all three spirits, he'll be able to track down the Ghost Ship! Astrid believes the next clue awaits Link at the **Temple of the Ocean King** back at Mercay Island.

To aid him in his quest, Astrid bestows upon Link an item of great value: a **Power Gem**! She tells Link to find as many of these Spirit Gems as possible, and that when 10 such gems are collected, Link will be able to enhance the power of each spirit.

Sensing great fortune ahead, Linebeck is thrilled at the prospect of returning to Mercay. He hurries off to his ship, even as Ciela berates him for being so self-centered. Strangely, Astrid senses that Linebeck will be a great asset to their cause in the coming conflict. Now, **there's** a surprise!

There's no time to lose—the light that seeks Link's aid is growing fainter by the minute! Hurry to Linebeck's ship and cast off for Mercay Island. The Temple of the Ocean King awaits!

►NOTE◄

If you'd like to make a slight detour before visiting Mercay Island, board Beedle's Shop Ship and check to see if his supply of treasures and ship parts has been restocked!

Power Gem #2

You got a **Power Gem**! Collect these items and use them to power up the Power Spirit.

Tasks
Complete!

Chapter 3

Contents

Back Where We Started: Mercay Island & Temple of the Ocean King Revisited

Mercay Island

Temple of the Ocean King

Shop

Legend

Overworld Chest #4: Ship Part

Bomb Wall

Return to Mercay Island: Overview

Well, here we are again! Mercay Island hasn't changed all that much, though you'll be excited to learn that the Shipyard is now open for business. There, you can swap out bits and pieces of Linebeck's ship, customizing it just how you like. You'll need to find more ship parts, of course; you've only had a chance to obtain two so far. In any case, the real reason you're here isn't to tune up Linebeck's vessel; you're here to revisit that dreadful Temple of the Ocean King! Make haste to the temple; Tetra's fate hangs in the balance!

1 Obtain the Phantom Hourglass

2 Venture Deeper into the Temple

3 Buy a Cannon for Linebeck's Ship

4 Explore the Quadrant's West Half

A Link to the Present

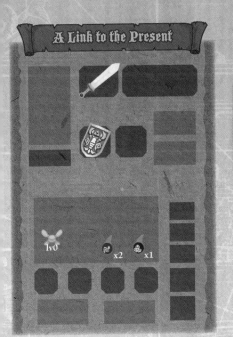

Items Already Acquired

Boomerang   Oshus's Sword   Wooden Shield   Power Gems x2   Wisdom Gems x1

Items to Obtain

Ship Part

Overworld Denizens

Characters   Enemies

Shipyard Worker   Red ChuChu   Crow

Task 1: Obtain the Phantom Hourglass

Open for Business

Disembark at Mercay Island and go across the pier. Hey, hey: Looks like the Shipyard is finally open! Speak with the man standing out front for confirmation, and to hear a hot tip that you already know: you can ready items like the Boomerang by holding Ⓛ or Ⓡ.

Stop into the Shipyard for a quick visit. Don't worry if you didn't buy that ship part Beedle was peddling from his Shop Ship; there's one to be found right here! Open the treasure chest in the corner to claim a **ship part**, which is completely random. That's right; you never know what you'll get!

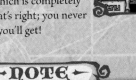
─NOTE─

View your ship parts by calling up the Collection menu and then tapping the arrow to the right to access the Ship Parts menu.

Overworld Chest #4: Ship Part

Ship Part

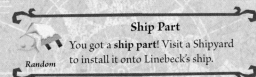

Random

You got a **ship part**! Visit a Shipyard to install it onto Linebeck's ship.

Next, speak with the nearby worker, who seems happy to have finished repairing the bridge and eager to start servicing vessels. The man offers you two choices: you may **Customize** Linebeck's ship, or simply **View** the ship to see how she looks.

Tap **Customize** to update Linebeck's vessel. Tap any class of ship part (prow, anchor, etc.) to view all the parts you've collected so far in that category. To install a ship part, tap its name, then tap the Attach button. It's just that easy!

─NOTE─

Tap the Explanation button for a brief description of the selected ship part.

Ready to admire your handiwork? When you've finished installing ship parts, tap **view ship** for a full 360-degree look at the newly customized craft. Tap and drag to rotate the view of the ship, and use the slider on the right to zoom in and out. Neat!

All ship parts belong to one of nine different sets. Sets are made up of eight parts of a kind. Outfitting Linebeck's craft with multiple parts from the same set makes it look sleek and stylish—and also makes it super strong! Combine parts from a set to enhance the craft's heart meter as follows:

Three of a Kind: One heart is added.

Six of a Kind: Two hearts are added.

Complete Set: Three hearts are added.

The rarest ship parts are the ones made of pure gold. This unique set of ship parts bestows exceptionally great benefits to Linebeck's craft:

Two of a Kind: One heart is added.

Four of a Kind: Two hearts are added.

Six of a Kind: Three hearts are added.

Complete Set: Four hearts are added.

Moving Right Along

When you've finished outfitting Linebeck's vessel, exit the Shipyard and then dash through town. Run north, traveling through the woods on your way to the Temple of the Ocean King. Be wary of those Red ChuChus and that sneaky Crow lurking in the forest! When you finally reach the temple, go directly inside.

Temple of the Ocean King, Revisited

Legend

Dungeon Chest #1: Force Gem

Dungeon Chest #2: Force Gem

Dungeon Chest #3: Force Gem

Dungeon Chest #4: Sea Chart #2

Orb

Floor Switch

Lever

Small Key

Red Jar

Yellow Jar

Items to Obtain

Phantom Hourglass   Force Gem   Sea Chart #2   Small Key

Dungeon Denizens

Characters   Enemies

Fallen Adventurer   Oshus   Phantom

Temple of the Ocean King: Entry Hall

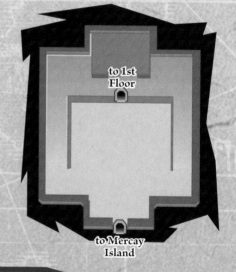

to 1st Floor

to Mercay Island

Task 1:
Obtain the Phantom Hourglass

Temple of the Ocean King: 1F

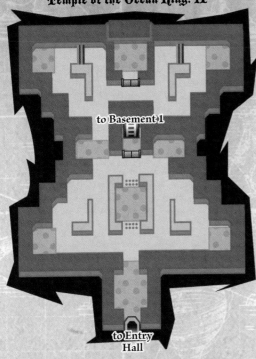

to Basement 1

to Entry Hall

Temple of the Ocean King: B2

to Basement 1

to Basement 3

Temple of the Ocean King: B1

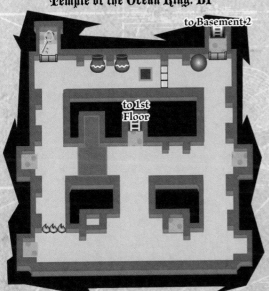

to Basement 2

to 1st Floor

Temple of the Ocean King: B3

to Checkpoint Chamber

to Checkpoint Chamber

to Basement 2

Temple of the Ocean King: Checkpoint Chamber

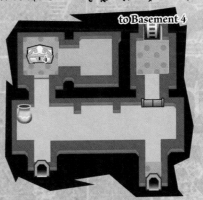

to Basement 4

No Time to Lose

His thoughts focused solely on finding a clue to tracking down the Ghost Ship, Link bolts recklessly through the temple's entry hall. In a rare act of selflessness, Linebeck suddenly calls out to his young companion, urging him to be careful not to end up like the fallen adventurers that line the hall. He reminds Link that the horrible curse still fills the temple, and it will slowly **drain** the life from Link if he isn't careful! Reluctantly, Linebeck admits that Link may not make it very far.

A familiar voice suddenly pipes up, saying Linebeck's fears may be unfounded. Spinning around at once, the group is surprised to see Oshus standing in the doorway! The old man has heard of Link's accomplishments at the Isle of Ember and is greatly impressed by the lad's valor. Growing excited, Oshus yells at Link, telling him to examine the altar atop the stairs!

Approaching the altar, Link is amazed to find an ornate hourglass sitting there. He hadn't taken much notice of it before! Suddenly, the hourglass begins to hover and spin, and a column of sand shoots up, surrounding the ancient timepiece. This must be the same mysterious sand Link noticed after rescuing Leaf at the Temple of Fire!

Yelling out from the hall below, Oshus tells Link to grab hold of the hourglass. When the boy does so, the surrounding sand suddenly flies into the hourglass as if drawn into it. The Phantom Hourglass is now in Link's possession!

Returning to Oshus, Link is told that he now owns the legendary Phantom Hourglass. As long as sand remains within the hourglass, Link is free to explore the temple without fear of its curse! However, when time has run out, Link must flee the temple and recharge the **Sand of Hours** inside the hourglass in the light of the sun. This is the only way to restore its mystical properties!

Oshus goes on to say that the Sand of Hours Link obtained by rescuing Leaf is only a fraction of the sand that fills the Phantom Hourglass. The young hero must rescue the other spirit fairies and find more sand for the ancient timepiece. Only then will he be able to fully explore the great depths of the Temple of the Ocean King.

Putting it all together, Linebeck recalls that the sea chart Link found during his first foray into the temple showed them the location of Leaf, the Spirit of Power. Perhaps there are other charts within the temple that might reveal the locations of the other two imprisoned spirits! Seeing fame and fortune on the horizon, the good captain urges Link onward.

Phantom Hourglass
You've found the **Phantom Hourglass**!
It's a mysterious hourglass filled with golden sand.

Task 2: Venture Deeper into the Temple

Temple of the Ocean King: 1F

Your course is clear! The spirits of **Wisdom** and **Courage** must be found if you're going to track down that evil Ghost Ship. The clues you need to find them are most likely hidden within this accursed temple. Go downstairs and proceed through the north doorway to reach the temple's first floor.

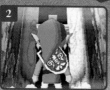

Task 2:
Venture Deeper into the Temple

The Phantom Hourglass flips over when you leave the entry hall, showing that you have just **10 minutes** to find the clue you seek. Don't worry though; time doesn't drain away while you stand in those purple-tiled **safe zones**. The hourglass only becomes active while you're traveling from one safe zone to the next. As long as sand remains in the timepiece, Link is completely safe from the effects of the temple's prevailing curse!

NOTE

Henceforth, the time remaining in the Phantom Hourglass is shown in the upper-left corner of your map screen. You have plenty of time to accomplish your goals here in the temple, but don't get sloppy! Keep to safe zones and make every second count.

The temple's first floor is exactly as your remember it from your first visit. This time, however, you aren't looking to explore the northern half of the floor; you simply need to open the central door with the odd marking to proceed. Run directly north from the entry safe zone to reach the door.

The symbol on the door is the same as the ones you've seen etched onto Power Gems. It's the **symbol of power**! Leaf appears and tells Link he's able to open the door for him. Tap the door to open it, then dash down the stairs beyond.

TIP

No need to linger in the cursed hallway; you can tap the door to open it from the safety of the central safe zone!

Temple of the Ocean King: B1

Unlike the Temple of Fire, the Temple of the Ocean King brings you ever downward, not up. The first floor's stairs bring Link down to the center of this first basement floor. It sure is creepy down here! Step off the central safe zone for an unwelcome surprise:

two brutish Phantoms appear in bursts of smoke, intent on keeping unwanted visitors out of their lair!

Phantom

Threat Meter

Speed: Slow (patrolling); Fast (alerted)
Attack Power: 1 heart (contact)
Defense Power: Seemingly invulnerable

Whoa, look at the size of these guys! Phantoms are the guardians of the Temple of the Ocean King, and they take their job *very* seriously. These brutes are so tough, Link has no hope of defeating them in combat! The young hero must instead outwit Phantoms, keeping out of sight and dashing to hide at safe zones whenever he's been spotted. Phantoms pack quite a wallop when they strike Link, reducing his health energy by one full heart. Worse, each Phantom's attack drains 30 precious seconds from the Phantom Hourglass and sends Link back to the entrance of the current floor. Yikes! Keep a distance from these dangerous watchmen, stick close to safe zones and monitor your map carefully.

Link has no ability to combat Phantoms, so you've got to keep out of sight. Study your map to learn that one Phantom patrols the far west hallway while the other circles the southeast corner of the floor. When it's safe to do so, dash east and then north, locating a locked door and a crystal orb. You've no key with which to open the door, so whack the crystal orb instead to activate it. This causes a torch to light at the south end of the floor.

TIP

Phantoms always move in certain patrol patterns. Watch their movements carefully on your map and bolt from safety when the moment is right.

NOTE

Phantoms can't see or reach Link when he stands in a safe zone. Retreat to one if you're spotted to give pursuing Phantoms the slip.

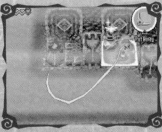

Turn around and run directly south toward the torch you've just lit. That ticking sound in the background means you're under a strict time limit to reach the torch, so don't dally! Run directly to the southeast safe zone and take cover there from the patrolling Phantom. Ready the Boomerang and trace a line west toward the lit torch, and then to the unlit torch you can barely see standing even farther to the west. The Boomerang catches fire when it strikes the first torch and carries the flame over to light the second one!

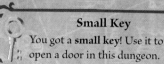

Small Key

You got a **small key**! Use it to open a door in this dungeon.

NOTE

You've got to move fast to light those torches! If the first one goes out, you'll have to reactivate the northeast orb and try again.

Lighting both torches causes flames in the southwest to die down, allowing you to explore the westernmost hall. A Phantom patrols that corridor, so be careful! Run west from the southeast safe zone and take cover in the one at the southwest alcove. When the nearby Phantom moves north, dash out and follow behind him, taking cover in the next safe zone ahead.

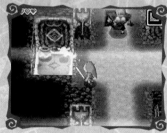

Wait for the Phantom to turn around and move past you before dashing north from the safe zone. You find the bones of a fallen adventurer and two red pots in the northernmost hall. The spirit of the fallen adventurer hints that breaking the pots will spill magical fluid onto the floor, which acts as a miniature safe zone! Quickly smash the nearest red pot with your sword and then step onto the resulting puddle. Sure enough, the Phantom Hourglass stops draining, and Link becomes invisible!

Smash the other nearby red pot if you wish, then move east and step onto a pressure switch that juts up from the floor. The switch lowers, causing a nearby door to open!

Return to one of the red pot puddles if you need to hide from the lurking Phantom. When all is clear, run west and then north, passing through the door you've just opened. Up the steps beyond the door lies a safe zone; in its center sits a **small key**!

Now you just need to travel to that locked door you noticed earlier in the northeast corner of the floor. Take your time, watch the Phantoms closely, and dash from one safe zone to the next when the guardians aren't looking. Head east along the southernmost corridor and then cut north to return to the central safe zone. Then simply run east, and then north, to reach the locked door. Tap the door to unlock it and then hurry down the steps beyond.

NOTE

You're doing great if you still have more than 8 minutes left in the Phantom Hourglass. Keep it up!

Temple of the Ocean King: B2

That wasn't so bad! This second floor of the temple's basement is a bit tougher, but nothing you can't handle. Watch out for the Phantom that stands just west of the entry safe zone; this guy's guarding a lever and he doesn't budge—that is, not unless he sees you! Wait for your map to show the Phantom is looking away from you, then dart south to locate a crystal orb. Smack the orb with Link's sword to activate it.

Striking the orb makes quite a racket. The noise draws the attention of the nearby Phantom, which quickly moves to investigate. Dash west and then north to locate another orb. Activate this one with a quick sword swipe as well. When both orbs are lit, a small key appears inside the floor's central chamber, as shown on your map. You'll get it soon enough!

TIP

Striking objects with the Boomerang makes less noise than hitting them with Link's sword. If you're having trouble with the Phantom here, keep out of view and use the Boomerang to activate the orbs instead.

Task 2:
Venture Deeper into the Temple

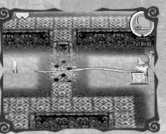

If the Phantom is hot on your trail, you may need to retreat to the entry safe zone to buy yourself some time. If the Phantom is still a ways off, hurry east and tap the lever it was guarding to make Link grab it. Quickly tap the arrow that appears below Link to yank the lever, which quells some flames to the south and allows you to proceed.

►NOTE◄

If you've retreated to the safe zone, you'll need to trick the Phantom into moving away from the lever. Step into view to attract its attention and then run about, looping around the corridors and pulling the lever when a chance permits.

Now that the flames are out of your way, run south and then west along the central corridor, speeding past a locked door. Hey, there's another one of those red pots in the far west alcove! Smash the pot to create a puddle of safe zone, then step onto the liquid to conceal yourself.

More flames block the passage to the south, and there seems to be no way to get rid of them. This calls for a little recon, Boomerang-style! Ready the Boomerang and trace a flight path south to see what lies ahead. Aha! A crystal orb stands just beyond the flames. Whack it with the Boomerang to douse the fire, then hurry to the southwest safe zone when no Phantoms are about.

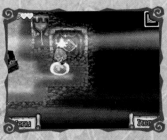

So far, so good! The floor's southeasternmost alcove is your next destination, but watch out: a fearsome Phantom patrols this southern corridor! Wait until the Phantom nears the southeast corner of the map, then start running east along the hallway. The Phantom moves north as you near the southeast alcove, and there you discover another red pot! Spill the pot's contents onto the floor and then quickly take cover; the sound of the pot breaking is enough to alert the nearby Phantom, which rushes over to investigate. Wait for the Phantom to leave westward and then go north.

Just a little ways north, a pressure switch sticks up from the floor. Step onto the switch to cause the spikes to the west to lower, granting you access to the **small key** in the room beyond. You've got to stand on the switch to keep the spikes down however, which presents a slight problem. Nothing the Boomerang can't fix! Toss the Boomerang to retrieve the small key, then duck into the nearby safe zone to hide from the patrolling Phantom.

►NOTE◄

Did you spy the cracked wall near the pressure switch? Better make a note of it on your map!

You're nearly finished! Return to the southernmost corridor when the resident Phantom is off to the west. This time, run north up the central hallway, crossing some lowered blue blocks. A fallen adventurer's remains lie just beyond the blue blocks. The spirit hints that you should watch the movements of Phantoms carefully. No kidding! Smack the nearby orb to lower the red blocks to the north and then hurry past them, returning to the central corridor.

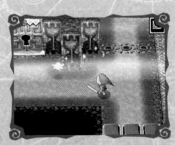

You're home free! Tap the nearby locked door to open it, then dash downstairs to reach the third basement floor.

►NOTE◄

How's your time? If you've got more than 5 minutes left, you're in great shape!

Temple of the Ocean King: B3

This is the final scary floor, we promise! Again, two Phantoms lurk down here and they're eager to chop down your time and send you packing back to the temple's entrance. The watchmen are a little ways off from your starting location, so dart east and then north, circling around the network of hallways until you encounter a fallen adventurer. This one's spirit lets slip that the contents of yellow pots restore sand to the hourglass. Handy!

As luck would have it, a yellow pot sits just to the west. That fallen adventurer almost made it! Too bad for him, but it's good news for you. Smash the yellow pot and collect the **time bonus** that pops out to add 30 seconds' worth of sand to the Phantom Hourglass. Every little grain helps!

Keep moving west to reach a safe zone where a small chest awaits discovery. Open the chest to claim an important item: a **Force Gem**! Link must carry this item overhead just like a Boss Key. It's pretty heavy and he can't run very fast with it, so don't be shy about tapping near Link to set it down when you need to run from a Phantom. Alternatively, have Link throw the Force Gem forward, then run up, grab it again, and repeat the strategy.

Dungeon Chest #1:
Force Gem

Force Gem
You got a **Force Gem**! Use this item to open a door within this temple.

Leaf appears to Link and explains how to use the Force Gem he's just found. The gem must be placed onto one of the three pedestals that stand at the large northeast safe zone. When all three Force Gems have been set on the pedestals, a new path will open. Guess that means there are two more gems to find!

Alright, bring this Force Gem over to those pedestals! Move south and then east, heading directly over to the large northeast safe zone where the pedestals stand. Time your movements carefully so that you aren't caught by the Phantom patrolling the floor's northwest section. When you reach the pedestals, tap any one of them to set the Force Gem onto it. The pedestal then retracts into the floor!

CAUTION

If a Phantom spots Link, flames rise to seal off the northeast safe zone where the pedestals lie. Hurry to a different safe zone and hide there until the Phantom leaves and the flames go down!

TIP

Stop and hide in the entry safe zone if the nearby Phantom gets too close for comfort.

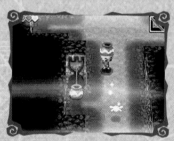

With the first Force Gem in place, return to the central corridor and dash west to discover a red pot at the far west end of the hall. Smash the pot and stand in the mystical fluid that pours out to hide from the patrolling Phantoms.

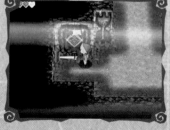

Head south when it's safe and locate a lever in the southwest alcove. Pull the lever to quell some flames to the east, which prevent you from climbing some steps. Those steps are your next destination, but a Phantom walks a tight patrol route all around them. Return to the puddle of safe zone you recently created and watch the Phantom's movements closely.

Prima Official Game Guide

Task 2:
Venture Deeper into the Temple

Did you notice that one of the Phantoms is carrying a key? You'll be retrieving it soon enough!

When the southern Phantom is moving east along the central hallway, dash south and then east, bolting across the southernmost corridor. Go directly to the southeast steps that the flames were previously blocking and run up them. Perfect; there's another red pot up here! Smash the pot and stand in the safe zone ooze that comes flooding out to give your hourglass a break.

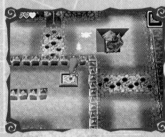

Time to get the key from that Phantom! There are two pressure switches up here, and they each control a trapdoor in the surrounding lower hallways. Wait for the Phantom to round the corner and start moving north up the nearby hall. Dash south to trigger the pressure switch on the floor. This causes a trapdoor to open in the hall to the west, plunging the Phantom into the abyss!

Flailing in his plight, the Phantom tosses the **small key** he was holding into the air just before he goes tumbling to his doom. Dash down the steps and retrieve the key. You'll soon need it! For now, run to the safe zone at the floor's southeast corner. Open the chest you find there to claim the second **Force Gem**!

Another strategy for obtaining the small key from the Phantom is to stand in a safe zone, then hit the Phantom with the boomerang. The Phantom drops the small key; run and pick it up!

Small Key
You got a **small key**! Use it to open a door in this dungeon.

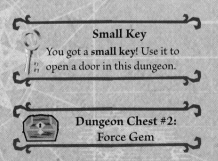

Dungeon Chest #2:
Force Gem

Force Gem
You got a **Force Gem**! Use this item to open a door within this temple.

With only one Phantom left to worry about, the rest of this area is a breeze! Simply carry the second Force Gem to the northeast safe zone and place it onto one of the remaining pedestals. Now there's just one more to find! Return to the southernmost corridor and tap the locked door to the west to open it using the key you lifted off the now-plummeting Phantom. The door leads to a safe zone and another chest. Wonder what could be inside this one? Why, the final **Force Gem**, of course!

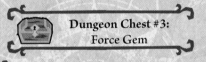

Dungeon Chest #3:
Force Gem

Force Gem
You got a **Force Gem**! Use this item to open a door within this temple.

Return to the pedestals and use the Force Gem to lower the final dais. The north wall then slides away, revealing a secret passage! Go through to reach the final portion of this floor.

Temple of the Ocean King: Checkpoint Chamber

Say, there's no inky purple fog down here. Looks like the temple's curse hasn't affected this area! A large stone door marked with an odd symbol stands just to the north, but you have no way to open it. You need to rescue another spirit fairy if you want to keep going!

Travel west and smash a yellow pot to add 30 seconds' worth of sand to your hourglass—but don't worry! You're right near the item you seek. Go north and open the giant chest that sits on the landing to claim another **sea chart**!

NOTE

No need to pass through the southern doorway; it just brings you to a tall ledge that overlooks the first part of this third floor.

Solve a Secret, Then Set Sail

There's little else to do on this island, so make tracks back to the harbor. A man stands at the pier and calls out to Link as he approaches. Speak with the man to learn that you can pick up a **cannon** for Linebeck's ship by visiting Eddo's Garage at Cannon Island. Makes sense!

Dungeon Chest #4:
Sea Chart #2

Sea Chart #2

You got another **sea chart**! This one reveals the northwest quadrant of the Great Sea.

The man says that, once outfitted with a cannon, a ship can defend itself from seafaring threats, smash apart boulders, and even dispel small cyclones. Wow!

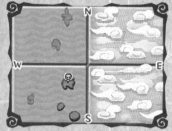

Awesome work! With this sea chart in hand, you're now able to explore the Great Sea's northwest quadrant! Linebeck should have a look at this chart. Hurry and show it to him!

As always, Linebeck is found standing next to his seaworthy vessel. Surprised that Link actually made it through the temple, he asks if his little friend found the sea chart they need to continue their exploration. Frustrated at the man's incredible arrogance, Ciela informs him that Link was indeed successful and retrieved a new sea chart.

You probably have loads of time left in the hourglass at this point, but there's no need to climb back up through the temple. A pool of blue light appears in the chamber to the east. It's ready to transport you back to the entry hall! Step into the blue light to be whisked away.

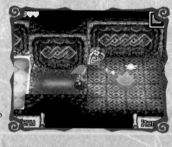

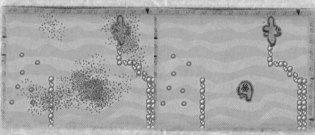

Looking at the chart, Linebeck determines that it's the chart they need to sail north. He can't tell much else, however: the chart is covered in heavy dust! Giving the map a few mighty blows, Link is able to brush off the dust and uncover a secret: one of the chart's islands is marked with a special symbol, just as the Isle of Ember was marked earlier! Another spirit fairy must be trapped there awaiting rescue. The group agrees to set sail and check it out.

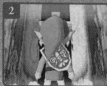

That giant cyclone still lurks about up north, and those pesky boulders still prevent you from exploring the west half of the quadrant. If only you had a **cannon**, you could probably find a way to venture onward. Hey, maybe Eddo has finally finished building the one he was working on! Plot a course to Cannon Island and pay Eddo a little visit.

Overworld Denizens

Characters — Enemies

Eddo | Fuzo | Bee | Rat | Red ChuChu

Taking the Scenic Route

If you previously dropped anchor at Cannon Island, you found that there wasn't much to see or do here. Well, that's all changed now! This time around, you're free to explore the entire isle. The gate leading toward the Bomb Garden is still shut tight, so go up the nearby steps and enter Eddo's Garage.

As before, Eddo isn't about, but his gargantuan assistant is. This time, he introduces himself as Fuzo, and he's a bit more chatty. Fuzo tells Link that his master is still locked away in his workroom, busy putting the finishing touches on his latest cannon. However, Fuzo also says that there's a back door to the workroom that's never locked, and he agrees to help Link get inside!

Cannon Island

Cannon Island

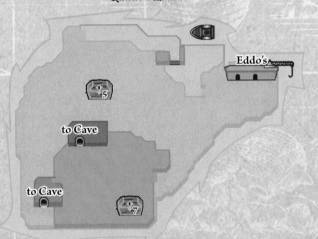

Eddo's

5

to Cave

to Cave

7

Legend

5 Overworld Chest #5: Treasure Map #1

7 Overworld Chest #7: Red Rupee

Fuzo

A friendly, bulging man, Fuzo lives a simple life on Cannon Island. He loves to do his master's bidding, but that isn't much of a job these days. Old Eddo has kept himself locked away inside his workroom for quite some time. Perhaps out of loneliness, Fuzo decides to help Link sneak into his master's workshop. Maybe once someone has purchased the cannon he's been working on, Eddo will finally choose to come out!

Items to Obtain

Big Red Rupee | Cannon | Power Gem #3 | Red Rupee | Treasure Map #1

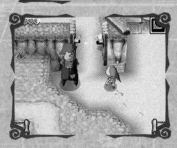

Follow Fuzo to the gate leading to the Bomb Garden. Fuzo opens the gate, then warns Link that monsters lurk in the grounds beyond. Be careful out there!

Fuzo wasn't lying; a pair of Red ChuChus pops up from the path just beyond the gate! These guys haven't gotten any tougher, so lay waste to them with Link's sword. Then continue up the steps ahead.

Bee-ware! Several beehives are stuck to the trees that stand beyond the steps, and their resident buzzers fly all about the nearby grounds. While Bees generally leave Link alone, they'll attack him if he messes with their hives. There's no real reason to harass these Bees, but if you feel like doing so, be prepared to face lots of them. If you're being swarmed, unleash spin attacks to make short work of the surrounding stingers.

→NOTE←

Somersaulting into the two western trees that feature beehives produces hearts, but this also angers the Bees in the hives!

Bee

Threat Meter

Speed: Fast

Attack Power: 1/2 heart (contact)

Defense Power: 1 hit to defeat

Be nice to Bees! These harmless buzzers don't aggressively pursue Link unless he angers them first, so why be mean to them? The only real way to tick off a Bee is to mess with its hive or walk near them; this prompts a large swarm to zip out and attack! Bees can hardly be considered enemies as they really just want to be left alone. Let them go about their bizzzness, will ya!

A small chest sits on the ground near one of the beehive trees. Don't miss opening this one; it contains a valuable **treasure map**! You'll find many more of these maps throughout the adventure, and each one points to lost riches that lie at the bottom of the sea!

Overworld Chest #5:
Treasure Map #1

Treasure Map #1

You got a **treasure map**! It reveals the location of a sunken treasure in the Great Sea.

Continue moving south to reach an entrance to a cavern in the side of the cliff. A nearby signpost informs you that the Bomb Garden lies ahead. Sounds like good times! Go into the cavern and get ready to blow some stuff up.

Bomb Garden Cavern

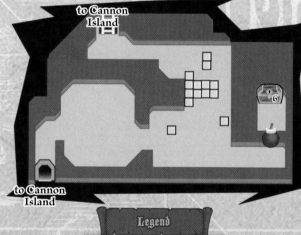

Bomb Garden Cavern

Bomb Garden Cavern

to Cannon Island

to Cannon Island

Legend

Overworld Chest #6:
Power Gem #3

Bomb Wall

This short cavern is the first place you get to make things go boom! Dispatch the two Rats running wild inside the entry chamber and then approach the blue and green plants growing nearby. These are called bomb flowers and they are, in fact, awesome. Tap one to make Link pluck up a Bomb from the plant, but watch out: the Bomb's fuse lights the moment you lift it!

Task 3:
Buy a Cannon for Linebeck's Ship

Notice the two strange blocks that plug the east passage. You've seen these blocks before; they were sitting in the woods at the northern tip of Mercay Island! These are called bomb blocks, and you've probably already guessed what to do with them. Tap the ground right near the blocks to toss your burning Bomb right next to them. The resulting explosion destroys the bomb blocks, clearing a way forward!

NOTE

Bomb flowers quickly sprout new explosives each time you take one, so don't worry if it takes a few tries to get the hang of tossing those Bombs.

Pluck another Bomb from one of the two bomb flowers and then dash into the east chamber. Another bomb block sits near a movable stone block, preventing you from shoving the stone block eastward. Again, quickly tap the ground near the bomb block to toss the Bomb right next to it, blasting the block to bits when the Bomb goes boom.

But wait, there's more! Before shoving the stone block about, spy a cracked wall at the end of the narrow east passage. Bet you know what to do with this! Snatch another Bomb and bolt toward the wall, tapping the ground in front of it to hurl the Bomb forward. The resulting blast blows a huge hole in the wall, allowing you to explore the chamber beyond! Therein lies a treasure chest; open it to claim another **Power Gem**!

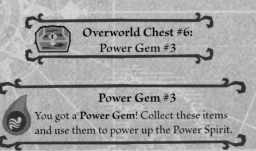

Overworld Chest #6:
Power Gem #3

Power Gem #3
You got a **Power Gem**! Collect these items and use them to power up the Power Spirit.

Now shove that stone block eastward to enter a small block maze. Ignore the nearby bomb flower for the moment and grab hold of the next stone block ahead. Pull this block south and then west. Move to the next stone block and pull this one east and then north. That's it!

Thrash the two Rats beyond the blocks and then return to the bomb flower you previously ignored. Pluck a Bomb and dash through the block maze, tossing the Bomb at the bomb block to blast it away. You're free! Exit the cavern to return to the outside world.

The Bomb Garden

At last! You've finally made it to Cannon Island's infamous Bomb Garden. It's easy to see where it gets its name; large patches of bomb flowers are growing all over the place! Be careful when slashing at the Rats running wild in the garden: striking a bomb flower instantly detonates its sprouting Bomb!

TIP

You may find the Boomerang to be a safer method of dispatching these pesky Rats, as you can throw it from a distance.

Use Bombs to destroy the surrounding bomb blocks, clearing pathways through the garden. Don't miss the chest near the rocks to the south; it contains a fabulous **red Rupee**! These extra funds will soon come in handy.

Overworld Chest #7:
Red Rupee

Red Rupee
You got a **red Rupee**! It's worth 20 Rupees!

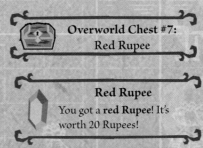

Toss more rocks to the east as you continue exploring the Bomb Garden's paths. Descend some steps to reach a lower clearing that is crawling with Red ChuChus. Lay into these monsters to secure the grounds. When you get a chance, carefully somersault into the lone tree just beyond the steps to knock a **big red Rupee** from its limbs!

—NOTE—

If you're feeling frisky, you can pluck Bombs from the bomb flowers that overlook the lower clearing and heave them at the Red ChuChus from up high!

Big Red Rupee

You got a **big red Rupee**! Just one of these is worth 200 Rupees!

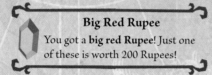

You eventually come to a path that's sealed off by three bomb rocks. Retrace your steps to the nearest bomb flower patch: the one that grows just atop the south steps. Grab a Bomb from a bomb flower and then leap off the ledge to reach the lower clearing. Dash to the east and hurl the Bomb at the bomb rocks across the fence to blast them out of your way. It may take a few Bombs to get the job done, so just keep trying!

With this final obstacle out of your way, you're free to enter Eddo's Garage from the rear. Eddo awaits inside. He is annoyed at the intrusion but impressed that Link chose to brave the isle's many dangers just to speak with him. After much ado, Eddo finally offers to sell Link a **cannon** for Linebeck's ship—for the colossal sum of 50 Rupees! You should have more than enough funds to cover the cost, so buy that cannon without delay.

Cannon

You got the **cannon**! This ship part from Eddo fits on the deck of Linebeck's ship.

Eddo

Small and squirrelly, Eddo is the genius inventor behind a variety of sea craft products and accessories. His latest and greatest achievement is a remarkable cannon that can be mounted on the deck of any good-sized vessel. A true workaholic, Eddo takes his calling very seriously, often locking himself away inside his workshop so he can achieve total concentration on the task at hand.

Way to go! You've finally cornered Eddo and purchased a cannon. Now you can blast those boulders away and continue exploring the Great Sea! Exit Eddo's Garage (through the front door this time) and speak with Fuzo one last time. The giant man warns Link that all sorts of monsters have been popping up from the sea lately, and to be extra careful on his journeys from this point forward.

—NOTE—

After selling Link the cannon, Eddo hints that he'll be devising a *salvage arm* next, which can be used to haul up sunken treasure from the depths of the Great Sea! Remember this for future reference.

Step outside Eddo's Garage for a special treat—or rather, a special delivery! The Postman swoops into view and lands on the nearby postbox. He's got an important message for Link that comes straight from the Postmaster himself: the Postman is a good guy, so please be nice to him! Of course, Link would never hurt such a friendly, hardworking fellow. After signing his receipt, Link watches the Postman fly off to continue his route.

Returning to the dock, Link shows Linebeck the cannon he purchased from Eddo. Impressed and eager to get on the move, Linebeck wastes no time installing the new hardware onto his ship. Heads up, sea monsters!

Task 4:
Explore the Quadrant's West Half

→NOTE←

Now that you've had your "official" introduction with the Postman, Link is able to receive letters at postboxes all across the sea! Big things come in small letters, so always keep your eyes peeled for a wiggling postbox.

Missing Links: Big Parts, Big Plays

By accomplishing the incredible in multiplayer Battle Mode, you're now able to unlock four of the most sought-after ship parts in the game. Acquiring and installing these four super-rare parts quickly adds up to two hearts to your vessel's heart meter!

Here's how it works: Battle Mode features 16 **Big Plays** that you can pull off during any match to earn Battle Mode score multipliers and, more importantly, **golden ship parts** for use in the main quest! Each time you manage to pull off four Big Plays that you've never completed before, Link gets a letter from Fuzo—Chairman of the Friends of Battle Mode—in the single-player adventure!

In his letter, Fuzo invites Link to visit him at Eddo's Garage. Sail to Cannon Island and speak with Fuzo, who rewards Link with a glorious golden ship part! Complete all 16 Big Plays to get four separate letters from Fuzo and gain half of the entire golden part set. Then visit the Shipyard at Mercay Island to customize your craft and enhance its defensive power!

Task 4:
Explore the Quadrant's West Half

Breaching the Reef

Now that you have a cannon, you can wage war at sea! Simply tap anywhere to start lobbing cannonballs toward that spot. The cannon has great accuracy, impressive range, and does a number on sea monsters, tiny cyclones, and certain types of boulders as

well! The giant whirlwind to the north is too much for your cannon to handle, so plot a course for the western reef instead.

→NOTE←

Although it's finally possible to blast those annoying Sea Traps out of the water, it's tricky. You must hit both urchins. Just keep leaping them instead!

→NOTE←

You can blast seagulls and that strange golden frog from the sky now, but nothing is gained from doing so at the moment. Spare these innocent creatures for the time being!

Be wary: as you near the reef, a new breed of aquatic enemy splashes up from sea! This little pest is called a Flying Fish and it's one of the weakest monsters in the ocean. Simply tap the baddie to lob a cannonball at it. One direct hit sends the fishy back to Davy Jones!

→NOTE←

Linebeck is exceptionally observant when sailing about, and he's quick to warn you when a new threat emerges. Pay attention to his warnings and be quick to react!

→NOTE←

Almost every sea creature you defeat gives up a reward. Typical prizes include hearts and Rupees. Some nautical hostiles even cough up valuable blue and red Rupees!

Flying Fish

Threat Meter

Speed: Normal

Attack Power: 1 heart (contact)

Defense Power: 1 hit to defeat

Finally, something to battle besides those practically harmless Sea Traps! Don't get too excited, though; Flying Fish aren't really much of a threat to your vessel. After emerging from the ocean, these little guys hover in midair for a moment before diving straight at you! Tap these fish out of water the second you spot them to blast them from the sky. Fish sticks, anyone?

Stop short of the giant brown boulders that plug the gap in the reef wall. Let's see what these stones are made of! Fire several cannonballs at the boulders until they're all destroyed. Now you can explore the western half of this sea quadrant! Set a course toward the southwest island. New adventures await!

CAUTION

You may be attacked by Flying Fish as you hammer away at the reef boulders. Stay alert!

A Ghostly Encounter

Link, Ciela, and Linebeck get more than they bargained for when they cross beyond the reef. Shortly after their ship passes through, dark clouds begin to gather and a dense fog rolls in. Suddenly, the Ghost Ship materializes out of thin air! Eager to catch the ship and claim its treasure, Linebeck yells at Link to plot an intercept course with the haunted vessel.

Holy smokes, it's the Ghost Ship! Now's your chance to catch it and save Tetra! Quickly tap the Route tab and then trace a course northward, directly toward the Ghost Ship. Fire on any enemies that pop from the ocean to attack you as you sail after the spectral craft. You may be attacked by Ocean Octoroks and Eye Plants as you give chase.

Ocean Octorok

Threat Meter

Speed: Normal

Attack Power: 1 heart (rock)

Defense Power: 1 hit to defeat

These aquatic Octoroks have adapted to life underwater. When an unsuspecting vessel happens their way, Ocean Octoroks surface and run into the vessel! It's tough targeting these nimble sea creatures, as they commonly circle around your ship. Sometimes they even dive underwater to give you the slip! Track an Ocean Octorok's movements carefully and aim just ahead of them. This gives your cannonballs time to travel through the air and strike the Ocean Octorok as it circles your craft. One hit is all it takes to sink these watery predators!

Eye Plant

Threat Meter

Speed: Immobile

Attack Power: 1 heart (contact); 1 heart (seed)

Defense Power: 2 hits to defeat

Some of the most dangerous creatures you'll encounter at sea are Eye Plants. These hideous villains resemble large eyeballs attached to tall stalks that poke up from the water when a tasty meal passes by. Eye Plants favor spitting large seeds at their prey to weaken them from afar, but they often surface directly in front of your ship, inflicting contact damage if you ram into them. It takes two direct cannon blasts to drop an Eye Plant, and their seeds can be shot down in midair as well. Blast these monsters the moment you spot them; they can inflict great damage in short order!

Mini Cyclone

Threat Meter

Speed: Slow

Attack Power: 1 heart (contact)

Defense Power: 2 hits to defeat

Mini Cyclones are tough to see, and this may be their most dangerous attribute! Keep a sharp eye out for these little devils, which can send your ship spinning if you sail into them. Being twirled by these whirlwinds drains one full heart from your ship's heart meter, so it's not a fun ride! Fortunately, dispelling Mini Cyclones is a breeze: just lob two cannonballs at one to make it quiet down.

Task 4:
Explore the Quadrant's West Half

The Ghost Ship doesn't wait up; it quickly sails off, heading north toward the sea's northwestern quadrant. The fog becomes much thicker as you follow the ship northward, so it's difficult to see very far ahead. Hey, no fair! Keep an eye on your sea chart and stay in close pursuit—you can't let that horrible Ghost Ship get away!

Not planning on being caught, the Ghost Ship flees all the way into the northwestern quadrant. Guess that island beyond the southwestern reef will have to wait! Keep chasing the Ghost Ship northward and make slight course corrections as it zigzags in an effort to lose you.

NOTE

To sail to the northwest quadrant, you must plot a course that takes you all the way up to the southwest quadrant's northern border. Once you reach the northwest quadrant, you must plot a new course northward to keep up with the Ghost Ship.

CAUTION

Watch out! Barrels filled with explosives float about in the sea, and they're tough to spot through the dense fog. Your ship suffers one heart's worth of damage if it rams into an explosive barrel, so be quick to blast these threats out of your path the moment you see them!

This long and arduous game of cat and mouse with the Ghost Ship ends abruptly. As your chase brings you near the Great Sea's northern end, the fog suddenly becomes so thick that Link and his companions can see nothing at all! When the fog lets up, Link and Linebeck are amazed to find themselves at the south end of the northwest quadrant. Hey, what gives?

Realizing what's happened, Linebeck suddenly recalls hearing rumors of the Ghost Ship leading vessels into such a fog. As the stories go, these unfortunate vessels are never seen or heard from again! It's best not to go any farther; the Ghost Ship is already gone.

Set a southward course and return to the southwest quadrant. Once there, plot a direct route to Molida Island to the south. Perhaps someone there knows how to navigate through this unholy mist!

CAUTION

Watch out for sea monsters and explosive barrels on your way to Molida Island! Waste no time blasting each one to bits as soon as you can.

Missing Links

Before you drop anchor at Molida Island, you have the option of exploring a few other places in the western half of the southwest quadrant. Sightseeing is purely optional at the moment, and you might want to dock at Molida first if your ship's nearly sunk. You can always check this stuff out later!

NOTE

Though the treasure map you found at Cannon Island shows a sunken treasure nearby, you can't drag it up without a salvage arm. Such an item is not currently available, so you'll have to come back another time!

Traveler's Ship

Set a course for the vessel, which is identified as a Traveler's Ship on your sea chart, floating to the south of Molida Island. Board the ship to see that its captain is in a terrible fix: a number of vicious Miniblins have taken over his craft!

Miniblin

Threat Meter

Speed: Fast

Attack Power: 1/2 heart (spear)

Defense Power: 2 hits to defeat

They travel in packs and attack from the back! Miniblins are easily bested in small numbers, but they can be quite a handful when they start to swarm. These little menaces love keeping *just* out of reach of Link's blade, quickly darting in to poke the young hero with their spears whenever chance permits. When faced with a group of Miniblins, it's usually best to pick one beastie and pursue it relentlessly with targeted attacks. Though Miniblins take two normal hits to defeat, their penchant for backpedaling often causes Link to lash out at them with double-damage jump attacks! Of course, your best option when you're being overwhelmed is the powerful spin attack. When properly timed, a spinning slash can wipe out multiple Miniblins at once!

Such scuttling cannot be tolerated! Teach these little devils a lesson by lashing out at the nearest one with Link's sword. Or stun a group of them from range with a quick toss of the Boomerang! However you choose to go about it, make mincemeat of the Miniblins and spare the ship's captain from their devious ways.

When the final Miniblin has fallen, tap the prone skipper to speak with him. The man doesn't seem responsive… you don't think he could be…? Tap the captain a few more times just to be sure. Whew! The man finally acknowledges your presence and stands up. What a relief! He was only *playing dead!*

The man stands up. Yikes! What an ugly mug! Seeing that the monsters have left, the captain thanks his lucky stars that he's so well-versed at playing dead. That's the only way to act when monsters are about! The man introduces himself as Nyave, member of the maritime defense force that patrols these waters. Hmm… not much of a defense force, now is it? Thanking Link for his help, Nyave hands him a treasure he managed to keep hidden from the Miniblins. Score!

Treasure

You got a **treasure**! Collect these items and sell them to the highest bidder!

Random

Speak to Nyave to learn that he isn't alone in this world. His older brother is also a member of the maritime defense force, and he patrols the waters in the **northwest quadrant**. Perhaps you'll meet him one day, if you can ever get past that gnarly fog! Nyave goes on to say he'd love to be a great hero like his bro, but he's lost his **guard notebook**! Poor guy…. He seems really nice! Why don't you keep your eyes peeled for his notebook and see if you can help out?

Task 4:
Explore the Quadrant's West Half

...continued

Nyave

Nyave is a loyal member of the maritime defense force. Sailing the southwest quadrant in his trusty vessel, this hard-featured soldier joined the force so he could learn to become a hero like his big bro. Unfortunately, Nyave's natural reaction when faced with danger is to play dead. This isn't exactly the type of posture that becomes a true hero!

Spirit Island

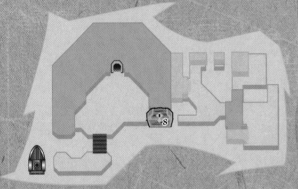

Legend

 Overworld Chest #8:
Courage Gem #1

Overworld Denizens

Enemies

Red
ChuChu

Items to Obtain

Courage
Gem #1

...continued

Notice that collection of small rocks jutting up to the south of Molida Island? They form the shape of a triangle. Something must lie between them! Plot a course and sail there to discover a tiny island that's not shown on your sea chart. How about that! Once you spot the isle, Ciela kindly marks it on your sea chart for future reference.

Dock at the island and start slashing the tall grass beyond the pier. Prepare to do battle: a number of Red ChuChus pop up and attack you here! Dispatch these minor threats as you clear away the surrounding greenery, and toss the nearby rocks as well to smash loose minor items.

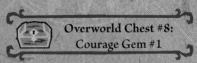

What's this? A small chest sits to the east! Open the chest to claim a fabulous prize: your very first Courage Gem! This is sure to come in handy down the road.

Overworld Chest #8:

Courage Gem #1

Courage Gem #1

You got a **Courage Gem**! Collect these items and use them to power up the Courage Spirit.

There's an entrance to a cavern in the north wall. Read the stone tablet near the cavern's entrance to learn that the servant spirits of **Power**, **Wisdom**, and **Courage** came to this little island long ago in search of the power to defeat an evil force threatening the land. Apparently, the spirits used **Spirit Gems** to gain the power they required. Interesting!

NOTE

There's a tiny portion of the island to the east of the chest, but you can't quite reach it with a jump. A short wooden peg sticks up from the area. You had better mark this on your map. You might find a way to get over there later.

Enter the cavern to pay a quick visit to the spirit shrine. Tap the door within the cavern to open it and gain access to the shrine ahead. Two tablets stand to the east and west beyond the door. One tablet informs you that 10 Spirit Gems will give great power to a spirit, while 20 Spirit Gems will fully realize its power. The other tablet tells you that Link may equip a powered-up spirit to increase his own abilities. Awesome!

A crystal-clear spring lies to the north. This must be the spirit shrine! As Link approaches, a voice suddenly calls out to him, telling Link to seek out **Spirit Gems** scattered about the world and bring them here to strengthen the spirits that travel along with him. The voice must be referring to spirits like Leaf, the Spirit of Power! Maybe all of those **Power Gems** you've been finding hold a secret to unlocking Leaf's true potential. Try coming back here when you find 10 gems or more!

Tasks:
Complete

Chapter 4

Contents

Great Explorations: Molida Island, Isle of Gust, & The Temple of Wind

Molida Island

Legend

 Overworld Chest #9: Treasure

 Overworld Chest #10: Shovel

 Overworld Chest #11: Treasure

 Overworld Chest #12: Treasure Map #2

Molida Island Overview

After narrowly surviving a hazardous game of cat and mouse with the nefarious Ghost Ship, Link, Ciela, and Linebeck find they are unable to venture onward. An incredibly dense fog clouds the only passage leading into the Great Sea's northwest quadrant—a mist so thick, it causes the trio to lose their way each time they try to pass through! With no place left to turn, the group decides to head south and eventually comes ashore at Molida Island. There's just got to be a way to get through that awful fog! Perhaps someone here will have a clue about how they can proceed.

1. Explore Molida Island

2. Navigate Through the Fog

3. Investigate the Isle of Gust

4. Enter & Clear the Temple of Wind

A Link to the Present

Max 10:00

x1
Lvl 0 x3 x1
x1

Items Already Acquired

Boomerang • Cannon • Oshus's Sword • Phantom Hourglass • Wooden Shield

Courage Gem x1 • Power Gems x3 • Wisdom Gem x1 • Treasure Map x1 • Sand of Hours: 10 Minutes

Items to Obtain

Big Green Rupees x3 • Shovel

Random Treasures x2 • Treasure Map #2

Overworld Denizens

Characters

Molida Shop Mistress • Romanos • Romanos's Mom

Enemies

Keese • Octorok • Red ChuChu • Yellow ChuChu • Zora Warrior

Task 1: Explore Molida Island

Words of the Wayfarer

There's got to be a clue around here somewhere! Speak with the friendly local near the dock, who welcomes you to the island and warns you about the fog to the north. Could have used that info a little earlier, thanks! Read the stone tablet to the south afterward, which is marked **Wayfarer's Words, No. 1**. It recounts the northern fog's ability to baffle and confuse seafarers, repeatedly sending them back to their starting locations. No kidding!

TIP

There's something special about that **stone tablet**! Mark its location on your map with the number 1 for future reference.

To the east stands a stone statue. Whack it for a hot tip: an unmarked island sits between the boulders to the south! The statue is referring to Spirit Island, and if you've been following this walkthrough carefully, you've already paid a visit to that tiny isle. If you haven't been there yet, mark your sea chart so you don't forget to check it out!

NOTE

Take the statue's tip to heart. Keep on the lookout for uncharted islands as you sail the Great Sea!

Speak with the tall, blue-haired woman north of the statue. She informs you that one of the island's inhabitants had a father who managed to get past the northern fog! The islander's name is **Romanos**, and he lives at the east edge of the village. Now we're getting somewhere!

While there's little to find in the village's westernmost hut except a few barrels and a pot, the next one over features a small chest! Pop open the lid to add a free random **treasure** to your collection. How nice!

Molida Island Shop			
Item	**Cost**	**Description**	**Notes**
Arrows (10)	50 Rupees	Arrows for the Bow	Require the Bow to carry.
Bombs (10)	50 Rupees	Volatile Explosives	Require a Bomb Bag to carry.
Purple Potion	150 Rupees	Recovery Item	Restores up to 8 hearts; used automatically if Link falls in battle.
Red Potion	50 Rupees	Recovery Item	Restores up to 6 hearts.

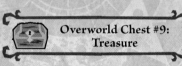

Overworld Chest #9: Treasure

Treasure

Random

You got a **treasure**! Collect these items and sell them to the highest bidder!

Another stone tablet stands just outside the chest hut. Tap it to read the **Wayfarer's Words, No. 2**. This tablet reveals that the mysterious Wayfarer somehow made his way through the northern fog and managed to reach the **Isle of Gust**, which he himself named upon landing there. Amazing! Now, speak with the large woman in yellow standing near the tablet. The woman says Romanos's father left these stone tables all over the island as testament to his journey through the all-but-impenetrable mist. So, *that's* who this Wayfarer character is!

Only one hut remains! Journey east to reach it and speak with the woman tending the garden out front. The woman is shocked to hear Link wants to visit the Isle of Gust. She says her husband left Molida to explore that place, spending many years discovering exactly how to pass through the northern fog and reach it. The woman hasn't seen her husband in over a year, but thinks her son, Romanos, might know more. She cautions Link that Romanos is angry at his father for leaving, however, and that her son may get upset if Link mentions the Isle of Gust.

Romanos's Mom

A hardworking woman with a big heart, Romanos's mom has done her best to raise her son alone. Her husband left long ago, selfishly pursing his dream of exploring the seas to the north. While she doesn't understand her husband's lust for adventure, she doesn't hold it against him like Romanos does. She simply yearns to be with her husband once more.

TIP

There's something very important about this second tablet left by the Wayfarer. Best mark its location!

Make a quick stop inside the tent to the east to visit Molida Island's local shop. You've seen all these wares before—all except one, that is! Bundles of **arrows** are sold here, but you can't carry them without a **bow**. That's a shame, but at least you know where to find arrows if you need them! You can also buy a Power Gem here if you didn't get one on Mercay Island.

Any attempt at entering the cavern to the north earns you a severe tongue-lashing from Romanos's mom. It's well known that monsters lurk within the cavern, and that's no place for a young man like Link! Head into the nearby hut instead to speak with Romanos himself.

 1
 2
 3
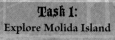 4

Task 1: Explore Molida Island

Hunched up against a table, Romanos seems pretty out of sorts. When Link mentions his desire to visit the **Isle of Gust**, years of pent-up aggression come pouring out of Romanos in the form of heated verbiage. After unloading on poor Link, Romanos tells him to leave his hut immediately. But as Link nears the door, the islander has a change of heart and calls him back.

Romanos apologizes for his outburst. He tells Link that his father did indeed find safe passage through the fog. There's a specific route one must take, but only his dad knew the way. Romanos guesses that clues to getting through the fog may be found within his father's secret **hideaway**, which lies somewhere in the cavern to the north. The trail's getting hotter!

Go outside and start toward the cavern. Romanos's mom is quick to holler at Link, but when she hears that Romanos told him to explore the cavern, she reluctantly allows Link to proceed. Hurry into the cavern; the clues you seek are just ahead!

Molida Island Cavern

Time for some action! This cavern is full of baddies, so be prepared to fight your way through. Your first targets are the Red ChuChus that bound up from the ground just inside. What's this? Some bomb blocks stand a short distance beyond the ChuChus and prevent you from exploring the north side of the cavern!

Not to worry! Backtrack a bit and climb some steps to reach a series of raised platforms. Be careful when jumping eastward from one platform to the next: Keese fluttering about up here, and they can easily knock you off! Make good use of the Boomerang and belt these pests from range before leaping too close.

←TIP←

A great way to use the Boomerang here is to hold L or R to ready it quickly and then simply tap the Keese. This is the fastest way to target them and take them out!

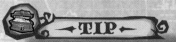
←TIP←

If the Keese drop any items, try to snag them with the Boomerang before they fall into the rushing waters below!

Notice a small chest sitting on a ledge beyond the raised platforms. Hmm… this chest seems unreachable! Mark its location on your map for future reference and then move north to initiate a fight against a powerful adversary!

Venturing deeper into the cavern, you suddenly hear a soft gurgling. What's this? A horrific sea monster leaps up from the murky waters ahead! Landing with a mighty roar, the creature moves forward to attack you!

Zora Warrior

Threat Meter

Speed: Normal

Attack Power: 1/2 heart (sword)

Defense Power: 5 hits to defeat

Lurking just beneath the water's surface, Zora Warriors suddenly pounce on unwary intruders! They also spit on their opponents to cause damage. These worthy combatants carry a large shield to defend themselves against all frontal attacks, and a huge sword to cleave apart their foes! Skilled in the art of combat, Zora Warriors are tough to handle head-on. Whack their backsides with a quick toss of the Boomerang to stun them, then follow up with a sword combo to their rear!

Head's up! This fearsome enemy is a Zora Warrior, and it's very accustomed to doing battle on land. It's nearly impossible to harm this creature with normal attacks, as the Zora Warrior is quick to block Link's blows with its heavy wooden shield. To best this mighty adversary, you'll need to stun it first with the Boomerang!

Keep a distance and dodge the Zora Warrior's attack by dashing to one side. Afterward, quickly ready the Boomerang and draw a fast line around and behind the creature. The idea is to make the Boomerang fly around it and strike it from the rear! A successful backside whack stuns the Zora Warrior, allowing you to circle around and assault it from behind with Link's sword.

⇥NOTE⇤

Don't attack the Zora Warrior from the front after stunning it! The creature simply blocks your blow and regains its composure.

Stun the Zora Warrior once with the Boomerang, circle around and unleash a furious barrage of sword strikes to quickly defeat it. Well done! A north wall slides away, revealing a hidden passage. What are you waiting for? Go on through!

⇥NOTE⇤

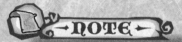

Did you notice that odd-looking patch of soil on the ground near the Zora Warrior battleground? You'll soon be able to dig up this soft patch of earth, so remember this location!

Be wary when exploring the hidden passage; many Octoroks lurk in this tunnel! Block their rocky projectiles with Link's shield and dispatch each one with fast targeted attacks. You can also use the Boomerang to stun them from afar! Smash the pots at the passage's northern tip for some hearts and then continue onward.

The passage leads back to the main chamber. You're now standing at its northern section, which you couldn't visit before! Whack the flapping Keese to secure your surroundings, then pluck a Bomb from the nearby bomb flower. Toss the explosive at those two bomb blocks to the south to clear the way so you can quickly return to the village. Don't head out there just yet, though!

Did you notice the large crack in the nearby wall? You know what that means! Snatch up another Bomb and heave it next to the bomb wall. Blammo! Go through the opening you've created to visit a supersecret chamber.

Hey, this looks like a little hideaway! Tap the open book on the table; it turns out to be a secret journal kept by Romanos's father. You've found the Wayfarer's hideaway! The journal informs you that Romanos's dad has yet another hideaway somewhere on the island. It goes on to say that the entrance to his second hideaway is at the spot where **the lines drawn between his stone tablets intersect**. Looks like you've got more exploring to do!

⇥NOTE⇤

See? We told you you'd want to mark down those stone tablets!

 1

2

3

4

Task 1:
Explore Molida Island

Before you leave, open the small chest sitting on the ground nearby to obtain a very useful item: the **Shovel**! With this vital item, you can now dig anywhere you like to uncover hidden goodies!

Overworld Chest #10:
Shovel

Shovel

You got a **Shovel**! Use it to dig in suspicious places and uncover fabulous prizes! You can even fill in holes you've dug, or ones you happen across. The Shovel may have other uses as well!

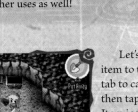

Let's put your newfound item to the test. Tap the Items tab to call up your list of items, then tap the Shovel icon. The Item icon in the Touch Screen's upper-right corner changes to show a picture of the Shovel instead of the Boomerang! Now you can tap the Item icon to equip the Shovel. Do so, then tap the suspicious-looking patch of soil right near the chest. Link digs a small hole in the ground, and out pops a **big green Rupee**!

Big Green Rupee
You got a **big green Rupee**! It's worth 100 Rupees!

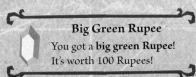

Leave the hideaway and run north, returning through the secret passage you took to reach this area. You haven't forgotten about that suspicious-looking patch of soil back where you fought the Zora Warrior, have you? Use the Shovel to dig there and uncover another **big green Rupee**. Talk about easy money!

Big Green Rupee
You got a **big green Rupee**! It's worth 100 Rupees!

Finding the Second Hideaway

Return through the passage once more, heading back toward the Wayfarer's hideaway. This time, go up the stairs just west of the hideaway entrance. This brings you outside to a small meadow where a stone tablet rests near a tree. Read the tablet, which is inscribed **Wayfarer's Words, No. 3**, to learn that the Isle of Gust is just one of many islands to be discovered beyond the northern fog. How exciting! Be sure to mark the tablet's location on your map!

A small chest sits just to the west of the tablet. Open it to claim a random **treasure**! Boy, your collection sure is growing fast! With the treasure in hand, turn around and run east through the woods.

Overworld Chest #11:
Treasure

Treasure
You got a **treasure**! Collect these items and sell them to the highest bidder!

Random

You eventually end up moving south toward the village. The fourth and final stone tablet stands on a ledge overlooking Romanos's hut. Read the tablet entitled **Wayfarer's Words, No. 4** for a hint that a massive, towering temple stands on the Isle of Gust. This temple must be the holding place of another entrapped spirit! Jot the location of this final stone tablet on your map, then leap off the south end of the ledge.

Alright! You've marked the locations of all four of the Wayfarer's stone tablets. Now you can find his second hideaway! Before you do so however, stop to dig at that suspicious-looking patch of grass just near the palm tree that stands just south of Romanos's hut. Out pops another **big green Rupee**! Cha-ching!

Big Green Rupee

You got a **big green Rupee!**
It's worth 100 Rupees!

Now it's time to find that second hideaway! Call up your map and draw two straight lines across it, connecting the west tablet with the east one, and the north tablet with the one to the south, making a cross. The lines intersect right at the heart of town!

Treasure Map #2

You got a **treasure map!** It reveals the location of a sunken treasure on the Great Sea.

Although there's no hallmark patch of loose soil to give its location away, the place to dig is right in front of the palm tree that stands just north of the village's central hut. (The *hut*, not the shop tent, mind you!) Dig there to uncover a hole that leads deep underground! You're right near the answers you seek. Drop into the hole without delay!

Hey, wait a second! Finding all this treasure has been lovely, but how do you get past that northern fog? Tap the map hanging on the wall near the chest to finally discover the clue you seek. It's a map showing you how to navigate through the mist! Tap the Sea Chart button in the screen's lower-right corner and trace this zany route down for future reference.

You've found it! The Wayfarer's second hideaway! Tap the book on the table to read a special message to Romanos from his wayfaring father. It expresses the Wayfarer's grief that he couldn't be a better father, along with a hope that his son has finally decided to forgive him and adopt the life of a true adventurer. How sad!

Now let's get out of here! Ascend the nearby steps and carefully hack through the Yellow ChuChus lurking in the passage beyond. Link notices a strange door in the north wall of the passage, but he can't seem to open it. The door has a unique marking.... Better make a note of it on your map!

But enough of this melancholy! Tap the chest near the table to flip its lid, claiming a **treasure map** from within. Nice! You've found two such maps so far, but you still need a **salvage arm** for Linebeck's ship to haul them up.

Although the map shows areas to the north beyond that strange mist, there's nothing else you can do here at present. Leap off the ledge to the east then go south to exit the cavern and return to the village. If you like, pay a quick visit to Romanos and his mom, and let them know what you've discovered! When you're ready to move on, speak with Linebeck at the pier and cast off. The treacherous fog awaits!

 1  2 3  4

Task 2:
Navigate Through the Fog

Missing Links

Fun with Squiddy

As you sail northward, keep an eye out for Squiddies that occasionally pop up from the sea. While these little purple dudes are harmless, blasting them with the cannon can be quite profitable! Each time you hit a Squiddy, you knock it higher into the air, and a **green Rupee** flies into your wallet! Keep hitting that Squiddy and it eventually splits into three; now you reap double the rewards! How long can you keep the combos going, swabbie?

Golden Frog #2

Another Golden Frog frolics just north of Molida Island. Have you seen this guy yet? You can blast him with your cannon if you like, but nothing much comes of it. There's definitely something peculiar about these frogs, though. Better mark this one down on your sea chart so you can find him later!

Treasures from Ember

Now that you have the Shovel, you're able to dig up a worthy prize from Astrid's basement at the Isle of Ember. Journey there, then dig at the suspicious patch of soil in the basement of Astrid's home to uncover a **treasure map**. Finders, keepers!

Treasure Map #3
You got a **treasure map**! It reveals the location of a sunken treasure on the Great Sea.

Ready for another treat? Visit Kayo's remains on the far east side of the island to find that they've been properly buried at last. Kayo's spirit is still hanging about, however, and it thanks Link for helping Astrid out of her plight. Kayo then points to the location of another buried **treasure map** on the island. Nice! Go there and dig up that map without delay.

Treasure Map #4
You got a **treasure map**! It reveals the location of a sunken treasure on the Great Sea.

Task 2: Navigate Through the Fog

A Crazy Voyage

As before, the fog becomes thick as you near the northwest quadrant of the sea. Not this time, fog! Plot a course to the northwest quadrant, and from there, plot the exact route you've traced on your sea chart. It's a curvy path to take, but it's the only way to get through this awful mist!

Expect to encounter the same enemies and hazards you faced while chasing the Ghost Ship before. Ocean Octoroks, Eye Plants, and explosive barrels are among the most common threats. Blast each one with the cannon as fast as you can, and remember to fire twice at those deadly Eye Plants to ensure you sink them.

> **NOTE**
> You may be tempted to try and outrun these sea villains, but that's unwise! Defeating them ensures you won't take much damage, if any. You also have a chance at acquiring healing hearts when you pummel these foes, which keep your ship in good repair.

The journey is long, but stay the course and you eventually reach daylight. Fantastic job! You've finally gotten past that dreary mist and are now free to explore the entire northwest quadrant of the sea! Be wary, though: two dangerous prowlers lie in the waters just east of the fog. These enemy vessels are called Cannon Boats, and they're the most dangerous nautical baddies you've faced to this point! Stay mobile, fire from range, and blast these boats from the water as fast as you can.

Cannon Boat

Threat Meter

Speed: Fast

Attack Power: 1 heart (cannon)

Defense Power: 5 hits to defeat

Sound the alarm! Cannon Boats are the terror of the high seas, firing on innocent vessels from afar the moment they spot them. Their cannons are just as powerful and accurate as Link's, and they unload their cannonballs at great speed! These mobile aggressors chase you all about, and never go down without a fight. Shoot the Cannon Boat cannonballs out of the air to protect yourself. Keep your ship sailing when facing with a Cannon Boat, and just keep firing away until you sink these dangerous craft!

Now that you've reached the Great Sea's northwest quadrant, you have the option to explore the waters, or simply set course for the Isle of Gust and get on with your quest. Check out the following Missing Links section if you'd like to scout the sea. If you'd rather just get a move on, flip ahead to the next task: investigating the Isle of Gust!

Missing Links

There sure is a lot to see and do on your first visit to the Great Sea's northwest quadrant! You can explore these waters later if you like, but now is your first chance to do so. Here we cover all of what you can do at present in this sizable sidebar!

Beedle's Shop Ship

Say, how did Beedle get up here? He must know how to get through that fog, too! Or perhaps he knows a different route. In any case, here he is, peddling his usual array of wares. Pick up that Wisdom Gem if you didn't before, and consider buying the random **ship part** and **treasure** he sells as well. Remember: all these purchases go toward membership points—and therefore, future savings!

...continued

NOTE

Beedle doesn't sell the Wisdom Gem here if you bought it from him down south before. He's only got the one!

Beedle's Shop Ship (NWQ)			
Item	**Cost**	**Description**	**Notes**
Red Potion	80 Rupees	Recovery Item	Restore up to 6 hearts.
Ship Part	Varies	Collectible Item (Ship Part)	A random upgrade for Linebeck's ship.
Treasure	Varies	Collectible Item (Treasure)	A random treasure. Collect and sell these for profit!
Wisdom Gem #1	500 Rupees	Collectible Item (Spirit Gem)	Used to power up the Wisdom Spirit.

 Ship Part

Random You got a **ship part**! Visit the Shipyard to install it onto Linebeck's ship.

Treasure

Random You got a **treasure**! Collect these items and sell them to the highest bidder!

Beedle's Assistant

If you're extremely fortunate, you may notice that Beedle's icon on the sea chart features a man wearing a **gold helmet**. Board Beedle's ship at these times to visit a rare version of his shop! When wearing his gold helmet, Beedle's Assistant offers precious valuables no other store ever sells. Take full advantage and buy everything you can afford!

NOTE

Beedle's Assistant warns that his special shop ship closes in just a matter of days, but this is merely hype. Though this shop ship appears very rarely, it never completely disappears!

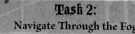

...continued

Beedle's Shop Ship (Gold Helmet)

Item	Cost	Description	Notes
Heart Container #2	1,500 Rupees	A rare and Precious Artifact	Permanently increases Link's heart meter by one heart.
Courage Gem #2	500 Rupees	Collectible Item (Spirit Gem)	Use to power up the Courage Spirit.
Red Potion	80 Rupees	Recovery Item	Restores up to six hearts.

Courage Gem #2

You got a **Courage Gem**! Collect these items and use them to power up the Courage Spirit.

Heart Container #2

You got a **Heart Container**! Your heart meter has been increased by one heart!

Bannan Island

That big island to the north sure seems enticing, doesn't it? Drop anchor there to pay a quick visit to Bannan Island—the Isle of Romance! You won't find much love from the local beasties, however, which include Red and Yellow ChuChus and those slithery Ropes! The Boomerang is a big help here; use it to stun ChuChus and defeat Ropes outright!

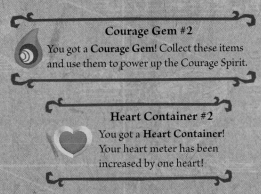

→NOTE←

Another one of those small wooden pegs is at the south end of the isle. Balance on it if you like, but make sure to mark it on your map!

Hack and slash your way to the tiny house to the north. The sign out front says this is the home of the infamous Wayfarer you've heard so much about! Let's go inside and see if he's about!

...continued

Sure enough, Link finds the old Wayfarer lounging about inside his home. The man is happy to see a fellow adventurer and welcomes the lad to Bannan Island. However, he mistakenly assumes Link has come here to track down the mythical **mermaid**, *who is said to reside somewhere nearby! He asks that Link tell him immediately if he should happen to encounter the wondrous creature. Right....*

Old Wayfarer

This guy lives for adventure! Having left his wife, son, and native island of Molida long ago, the man known only as the Old Wayfarer has sacrificed all in pursuit of his great dream: to venture forth into the thrilling unknown!

There's one last sight to see on this island: a cavern that lies to the south. Unfortunately, you can't venture very far into this place without the **power to shatter rock**, but a signpost hints that as soon as you're able to move forward, you'll gain access to some sort of exciting new game! A bit of investigation reveals a large crack running down the wall just beyond the signpost. No bomb flowers are about, though.... You'll have to come back here when you can carry Bombs with you!

→NOTE←

Now that you've had a chat with the Old Wayfarer, you'll soon be getting a letter from the man. In his message, the Wayfarer encourages Link to continue his wayfaring ways. He also includes a special gift: a **ship part**! What a nice gesture!

...continued

Fishing for the Mermaid

After your initial dialogue, speak to the Wayfarer a second time for a hot tip: apparently, the fabled mermaid he seeks won't show herself if monsters are nearby. How about that! Why not see if you can make her feel more welcome. Step outside and defeat all the various monsters near the pier and the Old Wayfarer's hut. Clear the area of villains and then begin your search for the mermaid!

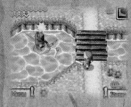

Although the monsters are gone, the mermaid is still rather elusive. She keeps away from dry land and quickly swims off if Link draws near. Run about the island's outskirts, hurling the Boomerang out to sea for a greater view of your surroundings. When you spy the mermaid floating out to sea, keep back and whack her with the Boomerang from range!

Stunned, the mermaid can't believe Link would strike her like that! She calls out for him to apologize, saying she's not really a mermaid: she's just a girl who loves to dress up as a mermaid!

Return to the Old Wayfarer's cabin and tell the man that you've found the mermaid. He thinks Link is pulling his leg about the mermaid paying him a visit, as he's yet to see any mermaid stop by. In fact, he fears that she may have already run into a different old man of the sea and completely forgotten about him! You don't think it could be….

Pay a visit to Linebeck to find that the Old Wayfarer's fears were well founded: the mermaid has indeed been speaking with the salty old captain! Linebeck says they didn't chat long; the girl quickly swam off. What a shame! Better check in on the Old Wayfarer and see how he's doing.

...continued

Return to the Old Wayfarer's hut. Link is shocked to see the mermaid lounging about in the pool inside! The Old Wayfarer couldn't be happier and gladly hands the boy a **Fishing Rod**. The mermaid says she's having a blast and decides not to tell the old man that she's really a girl in a mermaid suit.

Fishing Rod

You got a **Fishing Rod**! Now you can catch fish while sailing about the sea!

Fishing for Fun and Profit

Now that you've got a Fishing Rod, you can participate in a purely optional side quest that can earn you a fantastic prize: a new Heart Container! The road is long but the reward is great. Shove out to sea with your new Fishing Rod and get ready to reel!

Your sea chart should now show a large shadow of fish swimming about just beneath the water's surface. This icon represents a spot to which you can a sail, cast a line, and try to hook a fish! Plot an intercept course with the fish icon on your sea chart. Catch up to the shadow and then tap the Menu tab followed by the Fish button to commence fishing!

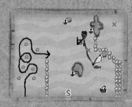

Tap the Menu tab and leave it open as you sail about chasing after the fish shadow. Then simply tap the Fish button when it lights up!

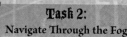

...continued

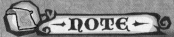

Link casts his line and the fish is quick to take the bait. Trace a fast line downward on the Touch Screen the moment the **Pull** message appears. This causes Link to pull up on the rod, setting the hook at just the right time. If you miss this initial hooking, the fish quickly escapes!

NOTE

Whether you land the fish or miss, the fish shadow disappears from the sea chart after you try to fish at that location. You have some options: you can wait for a new fish shadow, travel to a new quadrant of the sea to track a new fish shadow, or dock at the nearest island and then ship off again to reset the fish shadow in the area.

As soon as you've hooked a fish, the real excitement begins! Start reeling in the catch by tracing little circles with the stylus. Doing so quickly draws the fish toward you, but this also places great strain on the line! Ease the tension by tracing lines downward to make Link lift up on the rod.

The entire struggle boils down to a delicate balancing act between reeling in the fish and easing tension from the line. The meter along the left side of the top screen shows how close the line is to breaking. Reel in when the indicator is high but be quick to stop when it dips low. Trace lines downward to ease tension off the line until you can safely reel once more!

CAUTION

Fish sometimes jump out of the water and can throw the line. Don't let your catches escape so easily! Remove the stylus from the Touch Screen when the fish leaps up and the **Let Go** warning flashes to prevent the fish from fleeing the scene.

...continued

Landing the Big One

When it comes to fishing, you've got to start small. Begin by cruising the sea, searching to catch the three basic types of fish: a Skippyjack, a Toona, and finally, a Loovar. Catch one of each and show each one to the Old Wayfarer. The old timer can't believe Link's skill and hands the lad a Big Catch Lure, urging him to go out and catch an even bigger fish. No problem!

Big Catch Lure

You got a **Big Catch Lure**! You can catch huge fish with this quality lure!

Venture back out to sea and cast a line for a chance to land a big ol' **Rusty Swordfish** with your Big Catch Lure! These guys are huge, so expect a good fight. Take your time and work steadily to reel it in.

NOTE

Rusty Swordfish can also be caught in regular fish shadows, and Loovar can be occasionally caught in swordfish shadows.

Catch a Rusty Swordfish, then return to the Old Wayfarer and show off your accomplishment. The old man is ecstatic and begins to whisper to Link a whale of a tale about a legendary fish called Neptoona. Stories say that this fish was bigger than any other by far, and all but impossible to catch! The Old Wayfarer would obviously love a chance to admire one.

...continued

After the Old Wayfarer tells you the story of Neptoona, you'll have a small chance at landing the legendary fish each time you cast a line near a swordfish-shaped shadow. Neptoona is blazing fast and relentless in her determination to remain free, so prepare for an epic struggle between boy and fish! Pull out all the stops to help Link reel in this most wondrous of all catches, then hurry to show Neptoona to the Old Wayfarer. The old man is awestruck at Link's fishing prowess and hands him a worthy prize: a new Heart Container!

Heart Container #3

You got a **Heart Container!** Your heart meter has been increased by one heart!

Zauz's Island

Zauz's Hut

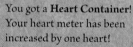

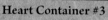

Legend

Overworld Chest #13: Wisdom Gem #2

...continued

Items to Obtain

Treasure Map #5   Wisdom Gem #2

Dungeon Denizens

Characters

Zauz, the Blacksmith

Did you happen to look north while sailing to Bannan Island? If so, then you surely spotted a secret island! Like Spirit Island, this tiny isle isn't shown on your sea chart. Sail west from Bannan Island to find it; Ciela kindly adds it to your sea chart as you draw near.

Linebeck feels there's something of value to find here, and when it comes to nabbing treasure, he's usually spot-on! The island isn't large, so have a look around. Cut down the grass for Rupees and travel north to a stone tablet standing at the edge of the isle. The tablet tells you to find the stone tiles that lie on the east and west ends of the island. It says to draw a line that connects the two east tiles, and then to do the same with the two west tiles. Finally, it hints that digging where the extensions of those two lines intersect will net you a prize. Well, that's clear enough!

The four stone tiles are easy enough to find; just search the east and west sides of the isle to locate the pairs. Mark their locations on your map, then draw a line to connect the two tiles on the east. Draw a second line connecting the two tiles on the west, then extend both lines southward until they cross each other. That's where you want to dig!

Whip out your trusty Shovel and start hauling up dirt! Dig around the south end of the island, just below the dusty pathway. Keep searching until you finally unearth a treasure map. Alright!

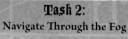

Task 2:
Navigate Through the Fog

...continued

Treasure Map #5

You got a **treasure map**! It reveals the location of a sunken treasure on the Great Sea.

 You probably spotted a small chest sitting atop the island's west hill. It seems out of reach, but you'll get there before you leave! For now, ascend the nearby steps to scale the central hill, then enter the hut you find there for a meeting with the island's one and only inhabitant: Zauz!

Hard at work pounding a piece of heated metal into shape, the man inside the hut doesn't seem to notice Link when he enters. After Ciela calls out to the man several times, he finally looks up from his labor and berates the little fairy for yelling at him. The man then addresses Link, saying he knows the boy is on a great quest to find the Ghost Ship. Whoa, he's intuitive!

*Shocked at his apparent psychic abilities, Ciela asks how the man can possibly know what they're searching for. The man simply states that people speak just as loudly with their hearts as they do with their mouths. Looking back to Link, he says Link is not yet ready to receive his aid. But, a time will come one day when Link will indeed require the help of **Zauz, the Blacksmith**! Link should pay him another visit then.*

Zauz

 A monster of a man, Zauz lives a life of solitude on his own, private island. Dedicated to his craft, he whiles away the days hammering out weaponry and tools of unrivaled quality. Intense and intimidating, yet kindhearted and wise, this burly blacksmith eventually plays an important role in helping Link unlock his true destiny.

...continued

Boy, is that guy intense! Good thing he's on your side, eh? Go outside after your chat with Zauz and corner one of the many Cuccos clucking about the grounds. Tap the Cucco to make Link lift it overhead. Time to fly!

Circle around Zauz's fence to reach the hilltop's east side. With Cucco in hand, make an eastward leap and glide over to the neighboring hill. Nice one! Now you can open that chest you noticed earlier. Do so to claim another Wisdom Gem!

Overworld Chest #13: Wisdom Gem #2

Wisdom Gem #2

You got a **Wisdom Gem**! Collect these items and use them to power up the Power Spirit.

Uncharted Island

Items to Obtain

Cyclone Slate   Treasure Map #6

Dungeon Denizens

Characters	Enemies		
Golden Chief Cylos	Miniblin	Crow	Yellow ChuChu

 Avast! Yet another unmarked isle lies due south of Bannan Island, nestled close to the eastern reef. Set a course there and Ciela adds this isle to your sea chart as you draw near!

...continued

Docking at the island presents a shocking discovery: No map appears on the upper screen! This island is completely uncharted! Linebeck assumes no one has ever set foot here before and concludes that big treasure must lie around somewhere. Seeing a flaw in the good captain's logic, Ciela points out that, if no one has ever been here, then how could there be any treasure to find? Well, who knows? There's only one way to find out!

Begin exploring the island, hacking up greenery and doling out punishment to the local hostiles, which include Miniblins, Crows, and Yellow ChuChus. Several stone statues stand at various spots on the isle, but none of them seems to have anything to say. How odd....

None of the statues says anything until you strike the central one, which stands near a small, U-shaped body of water. This statue pipes up, saying that a **Golden Chief** resides on this island. The chief won't speak

to just anyone, however; only those who solve the island's riddle are allowed to see him. The statue says Link must prove himself by striking four of its buddies in a specific order, and offers the following riddle as a clue: *It steers with a rudder, then makes a spray! And third, it paddles, then sees a way!* Unfortunately, that's all the statue has to say. Baffling!

Henceforth, Link may whack any of the other four statues on the island to hear information about the **golden frogs** you may have seen hopping about in various parts of the Great Sea. Apparently, there are six such frogs, and they each have the power to summon great cyclones! Very interesting, but this doesn't really get you anywhere. You still need to solve this island's riddle!

...continued

If you're completely lost, return to Linebeck for a hint on how to proceed. The savvy sailor advises you to sketch out the island so you can make sense of the layout. What a great idea! Start right where you are and slowly move Link along the very edge of the island, periodically calling up your map so you may trace its outline.

The island isn't shown on the upper screen, but Link's location is. Use this as a reference when charting the island.

You don't have to be a brilliant artist to sketch the outline of the island. Just take it nice and slow, and eventually, you'll come up with something resembling the above picture. Hey, don't laugh at our map! We aren't artists, either!

Gee, the shape of this island looks very familiar. Wait a minute, it looks just like a whale! *Now* the riddle makes sense. It's telling you the order in which you must whack the statues! Go ahead and smack them in the following order:

1. Hit the northeastern statue first (the one near the whale's **rudder**, or tail).

2. Hit the northwesternmost statue second (the one near the whale's **spray**).

3. Hit the southwesternmost statue third (the one near the whale's **fin**).

4. Hit the west statue fourth (the one near the whale's **eye**).

Presto! The riddle is solved, and a bridge extends near the central statue, granting you entrance to a cavern. Go inside and notice a small wooden peg near the entrance. These things are everywhere! Make a note on your makeshift map, then go down the steps to the west to a stone tablet. The tablet hints that something valuable is hidden beneath the statue near the whale's eye. You'll check that later; for now, run north and enter the passage ahead.

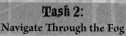

Task 2:
Navigate Through the Fog

...continued

Deep within the island's cavern, Link discovers a tranquil pond. Golden frogs swim about the waters, at peace with themselves and their surroundings. **Moving to the end of the walkway, Link is greeted by a giant golden creature. This must be the Golden Chief the statue was talking about!**

The creature introduces itself as Golden Chief Cylos, and says it's the only frog around that can travel about by **cyclone**. Sounds like fun! Noticing the **Phantom Hourglass** Link carries, Cylos realizes that the young lad must be a friend to Oshus. The Golden Chief tells Link that Oshus helped him find this very hideout, and agrees to aid Link in his quest to track down the Ghost Ship. He hands link a **Cyclone Slate**; a magical item that Link can use to warp about the Sea!

Cyclone Slate

You got the **Cyclone Slate**! Use it to travel about the sea by cyclone!

Golden Chief Cylos

Don't get the name wrong: this is Golden Chief Cylos, master of fast travel! A giant golden bullfrog living on an uncharted isle, noble Cylos grants Link the ability to warp about the sea with the aid of his "gilt minions"—those little golden frogs Link encounters while sailing the ocean blue! This method of travel is only possible through the use of his Cyclone Slate, which Cylos gives to Link when he recognizes the boy as a friend.

NOTE

Now that you've gotten your mitts on the Cyclone Slate, you can quickly traverse the Great Sea by way of golden frog. Henceforth, blast every golden froggy you see while sailing. Each one you hit will show you a special symbol that you may draw on the Cyclone Slate to warp about! Simply tap the Items tab, then tap the Cyclone Slate. Trace the symbol of the frog you wish to warp to and you'll soon be whisked away!

...continued

Way to go! Now you'll find traversing the Great Sea to be far less time-consuming. Exit the cavern and pay a short visit to the stone statue that sits near the eye of the whale. Pull out the Shovel and dig up the soil right in front of the statue to find a hidden **treasure map**! You've completely looted this island now. Time to set sail and pay a visit to those golden frogs.

Treasure Map #6

You got a **treasure map**! It reveals the location of a sunken treasure on the Great Sea.

The Great Golden Frog Hunt

Now that you have the Cyclone Slate, it's time to track down some froggies! Sail due west from the Uncharted Island and keep your eyes peeled for a golden frog hopping about. Blast this one with your cannon to make it stop and talk to you for a moment. The frog congratulates you on your marksmanship and shows you the symbol you must sketch on the Cyclone Slate to warp to this spot. Now you can return to the northwest quadrant of the sea at any time without having to sail through that awful fog!

TIP

Draw these warp symbols right on your sea chart for future reference.

Plot a course directly south to return to the southwest quadrant. You need not sail through the fog; just head south until you get down there. You're tossed even farther south by the giant cyclone, but that's a good thing; it brings you closer to the golden frog that hops about the small rocks north of the Isle of Ember! Track down this frog as well and blast it with the cannon to learn another warp symbol for your Cyclone Slate.

...continued

Now sail west, aiming to pass through the southwestern quadrant's rocky reef. Locate a third golden frog that swims north of Molida Island. You know what to do! Blast the frog from the sky to unlock another Cyclone Slate warp point.

Now that you've found three of the Great Sea's six golden frogs, let's give the Cyclone Slate a try. Tap the Menu tab and then tap the Slate icon to call up the Cyclone Slate. Trace the symbol of the golden frog you blasted near the Isle of Gust, which resembles a backward letter N. You must trace the symbol in one shot without lifting the stylus!

Whoa! As advertised, a giant cyclone materializes right above your ship and lifts it into the sky. Moments later, your ship is set down just north of the Isle of Gust. Incredible!

Traveler's Ship

Here's a stop you'll definitely want to make before venturing off to explore that dangerous Isle of Gust. After using the Cyclone Slate to return to the northwest quadrant, set an intercept course and board the Traveler's Ship that sails about to the south. Speak with the bearded fellow in the green garb who seems to be the ship's skipper.

Looking down at Link, the ship's captain can't help but notice a shocking similarity: The young lad is dressed just like him! Or is it the other way around? No matter! The man is pleased to meet such an obvious fan. He informs Link that he's a hero, traveling the world on his Red Lion ship to save all mankind from evil. Hmm… why does this sound so familiar?

...continued

After recounting his story, the self-proclaimed hero asks Link if he'd like an autograph. When Link says that yes, he would like one, the man suddenly realizes that he's run out of autograph paper. Such a shame! Knowing nothing can compare to getting a genuine autograph, the green-clad hero asks Link if he'd at least like to become his apprentice instead. What an honor! Everything is settled once Link tells the man that he couldn't hope for more—the young adventurer has found himself a mentor!

After the self-proclaimed hero agrees to take Link on as his apprentice, you can participate in a fun and profitable minigame. Speak with the man to receive a lesson in the fine art of swordsmanship! The man tells his young apprentice to come at him with everything he's got. Don't hold back! Tap the man repeatedly to assault him with targeted attacks!

After Link strikes the so-called hero, the man decides to take Link a bit more seriously. During the next round of battle, he holds up his spear to defend himself. Keep attacking the man with targeted strikes until he begs for mercy!

NOTE

The number of hits you've scored on the man is tallied in the screen's upper-right corner. Try to land lots of hits and improve on your high scores!

The man is impressed with Link's combat ability and designates him worthy of the title **Apprentice to the Hero**. How grand! As another reward for Link's efforts, the alleged hero gives his young trainee a valuable **treasure**. What a guy!

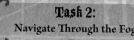

Task 2:
Navigate Through the Fog

...continued

Treasure

Random

You got a **treasure**! Collect these items and sell them to the highest bidder!

If you'd like another go, simply leave the ship and then quickly board it again. Speak with the self-proclaimed hero once more to initiate another battle. This fight isn't any more difficult than the last; just land a few blows to make the guy give up. He promotes Link to **Half a Hero** status and hands him another random treasure!

Treasure

Random

You got a **treasure**! Collect these items and sell them to the highest bidder!

Why not keep the gravy train rolling? Leave the ship and reboard for yet another fight against Link's "mentor." This fight is a bit more challenging, but not much. Just keep up the pressure until you land about 20 hits. The man then caves and admits that Link is at least **Two Thirds a Hero** now. He hands over yet another treasure as well. This is great!

Treasure

Random

You got a **treasure**! Collect these items and sell them to the highest bidder!

Things are a bit different the fourth time you face off against the green-clad hero. He now asks Link to strike him as many times as Link can before he lands **three hits** on Link. That's right! The so-called hero is going to start fighting back now!

Here are the two main tips to scoring high during swordplay practice:

Keep Up the Pressure: The so-called hero attacks faster and with greater ferocity if you don't give him something to worry about! Keep whacking him with targeted attacks and try to back him against a wall.

Be Ready to Dodge: The nameless hero often spins his spear just before stabbing it straight forward. When you see his spear start to spin, stop attacking and run to one side to avoid the coming blow!

...continued

Do your best to score **over 100 hits** against the alleged hero. Doing so nets you a fabulous reward: a Heart Container! This is by far the best prize you could have hoped for!

Heart Container #4

You got a **Heart Container**! You're heart meter has been increased by one heart!

→NOTE←

From this point forward, you may continue to combat the green-clad hero in an effort to better your high score. You don't even have to leave his ship to initiate a new round! Each time you show improvement, you're richly rewarded with a random **treasure**. Score really high and you may even start getting **ship parts**! Spend some time here and see how much loot you can rack up.

Task 3: Investigate the Isle of Gust

At last! You're finally able to explore the infamous Isle of Gust. According to that old **sea chart** you found inside the Temple of the Ocean King, you should find another entrapped spirit somewhere on this island! But boy, is that wind ever strong! You must watch out for those hurricane gales.

Isle of Gust

Windmill

Windmill   to Temple of Wind   Windmill

Legend

 Overworld Chest #14: Courage Gem #3

Overworld Chest #15: Treasure Map #7

Overworld Chest #16: Wisdom Gem #3

Overworld Chest #17: Power Gem #4

Overworld Chest #18: Treasure Map #8

Bomb Wall

Items to Obtain

Courage Gem #3 | Power Gem #4 | Red Rupees x3 | Treasure Map #7 | Treasure Map #8 | Wisdom Gem #3

Dungeon Denizens

Enemies

Miniblin | Red ChuChu | Sandworm

Blow Me Up, Blow Me Down

It's easy to see how this island got its name. Huge, powerful gusts of wind repeatedly batter Link from the east, shoving him westward like a green-clad tumbleweed. Head north from the pier and lay into the gang of Miniblins on patrol nearby. Be careful not to let the wind blow you off the edge of the island or you'll be dunked into the surrounding icy waters!

TIP

Run east toward the wind when it blows to keep from being shoved westward.

NOTE

The local monsters have spent their whole lives on this island and have grown accustomed to its powerful winds. They aren't affected by the mighty gales!

1

2

3

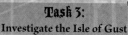
4

Go east and then south down some steps to come face-to-face with a Red ChuChu. Dispatch this minor threat and then climb the stairs to the east to reach a series of tall platforms separated by short gaps. Each platform has a group of monsters for you to tackle, and you must time your jumps between each one very carefully. Don't jump when the wind blows or you could take a nasty fall!

The wind picks up when you reach the island's southeast corner. Move down the steps to reach the lower grounds and take on the mob of Miniblins lurking down there. After securing the site, move to the pair of bomb flowers growing near a wall with a large crack running down it. You know what to do! Take hold of a Bomb and toss it right near the bomb wall to blast it wide open and reveal an entrance to a cavern.

Duck inside the cavern to momentarily escape the chaotic winds. Surprisingly, the small cavern is fully furnished, resembling a well-kept study! Smash the pots and barrels here for hearts, then tap the nearby chest to flip it open. Inside you find a **Courage Gem**!

Overworld Chest #14: Courage Gem #3

Courage Gem #3
You got a **Courage Gem**! Collect these items and use them to power up the Courage Spirit.

There's more to see in this small room! Tap the book on the desk to read it and learn that this is, in fact, another secret hiding place of the infamous Wayfarer! According to his journal, the Wayfarer traveled here during his adventures and also discovered smaller islands nearby. Tap the map on the wall to view it and learn the locations of two islands that aren't shown on your sea chart!

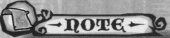

~NOTE~

If you've been following this walkthrough carefully, you've already been to the two islands shown on the wall map! They are Zauz's Island to the north and the Uncharted Island to the east. Check the previous Missing Links section to find out what you can do in those areas!

Exit the Wayfarer's hideout and then backtrack up the steps to the east. You must now leap across the tall ledges to the west, but these gaps are too wide to clear with normal jumps. Time to put all this wind to good use! Wait near the steps until a gust starts to blow, then run and jump westward, letting the wind carry you over to the next ledge ahead. Keep leaping westward until you reach a basin full of Miniblins.

There's no point in letting these monsters roam about! Show them the sharp side of Link's trusty blade and keep attacking until you've secured the grounds. Notice those three suspicious-looking patches of sand? Dig there to unearth three **red Rupees**!

CAUTION

Don't climb the tall steps to the west! They bring you to a ledge that overlooks the clearing near the pier and you'll have to come around again if you happen to fall off!

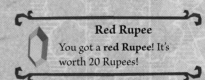

Red Rupee
You got a **red Rupee**! It's worth 20 Rupees!

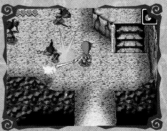

After digging up your Rupees, enter the cavern in the north wall to reach a wide chamber filled with a monstrous mob of Miniblins. Move around the ledge, being careful not to let the gust jars in the walls blow you into the Miniblin pit. Or just dive right in and make with the thrashing! There's good reason to dispatch the Miniblins here: wiping them all out causes a hidden chest to materialize in the pit! Open this chest to claim a **treasure map**, then open the chest that was already sitting in the center of the pit for a **Wisdom Gem**. Alright!

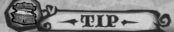

TIP

The spin attack makes mincemeat out of these Miniblins.

Overworld Chest #15: Treasure Map #7

Treasure Map #7

You got a **treasure map**! It reveals the location of a sunken treasure on the Great Sea.

Overworld Chest #16: Wisdom Gem #3

Wisdom Gem #3

You got a **Wisdom Gem**! Collect these items and use them to power up the Wisdom Spirit.

Gust Geyser Gorge

Exit the cavern with your loot and make short work of the two Red ChuChus you encounter just outside. Notice the powerful jet of wind blowing straight upward nearby. Such spouts are called gust geysers, and they're powerful enough to send Link soaring into the sky! Tap the gust geyser to move Link onto it, then watch as he's blown upward along the row of geysers beyond.

The gust geysers land Link on a high ledge. Go south and hack up the grass there for potential items. This is nice, but the real reason to trim the greenery here is to discover a hidden digging spot! Shovel up a **big green Rupee** to fatten your wallet, then travel north and leap across the gap to the west when the wind starts blowin'.

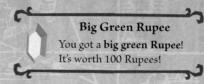

Big Green Rupee

You got a **big green Rupee**! It's worth 100 Rupees!

Have at the pair of Miniblins on the next ledge over, then scamper down the flights of steps that follow. Don't drop off the south ledge or you'll have to work your way around again! Descend to a lower area with a cobblestone floor, wipe out the Red ChuChus that attack you here, and then proceed north.

You're right near the entrance to some sort of temple, but a quartet of gust jars prevent you from moving any closer. Read the nearby stone tablet for a clue: the entrance stops gusting only when the **windmills have had their fill**. Strange.... You haven't seen any windmills around here! Tap the map on the wall nearby for another clue: it's a map of the Isle of Gust with an X marked on its northwest corner. Maybe that's where the windmills are!

Looks like your next stop is the island's northwest corner. Backtrack south and then use the nearby gust geyser to reach a higher ledge. Whee! Dash north and dice up two Red ChuChus that pop up to attack, then take note of a sealed door in the north wall. You can't open the door, so continue looping around and go south.

Drop down to a lower area where Ciela points out a few lumpy patches of dirt on the ground. You know what to do! Pull out your Shovel and dig up the loose, lumpy soil to uncover some gust geysers! You don't actually need to ride on these ones, however. Turn your attention—and Link's blade—on the nearby Miniblins instead!

Task 3:
Investigate the Isle of Gust

Two more lumpy patches of soil sit right near two northern ledges. Uncover the far west gust geyser first and sail up to reach a small ledge with a treasure chest! Claim another one of those **Power Gems** from the chest. Nice find! Now unearth the other geyser and sail northward to proceed.

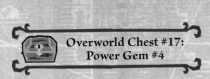

Overworld Chest #17: Power Gem #4

Power Gem #4

You got a **Power Gem**! Collect these items and use them to power up the Power Spirit.

Don't bother sailing up the next gust geyser ahead; it just leads you to a small fenced-in area with a Red ChuChu. Uncover the geyser to the west instead, then scurry down the steps that follow. An active gust geyser presents an obstacle ahead; it sends you up to another small fenced-in ledge you can't do anything with. How rude! Ready the Shovel and tap this pesky geyser to cover it up, then run west past it and sail up the next geyser ahead.

Are you getting dizzy yet? Don't worry; you're almost done! Descend the nearby steps and dig at that suspicious bit of sand to excavate a **big green Rupee**. Man, your wallet's gonna burst! Use the next gust geyser to reach the island's far northwest ledge, where a stone tablet and wall map await you. This is the spot the previous wall map told you to visit!

Big Green Rupee

You got a **big green Rupee**! It's worth 100 Rupees!

Read the tablet and the map to learn that you must activate **three sacred windmills** to open the path forward. As luck would have it, the map shows their exact locations! Mark them down on your own map, then drop down and bury with your Shovel the collection of gust geysers to the east so you may continue onward.

Sandworms & Sacred Windmills

Time to track down those windmills! Run up the north steps you find just beyond the final set of gust geysers, then smack the stone statue on the ledge for an eerie warning: horrible creatures dwell in the sandy desert ahead! The statue hints that the creatures sense by sound, and that Link should be able to fool them if he **slowly walks about**.

Heed the statue's warning and walk very slowly across the desert sand to the east. Running or walking at a brisk pace alerts the desert's guardians, who quickly burrow toward you at frightening speed! If you draw the attention of one of these scary Sandworms, start running for higher ground! And if you happen to get gobbled up, quickly rub the stylus left to right to wiggle Link free!

Sandworm

Threat Meter

Speed: Very Fast

Attack Power: 1 heart (devour)

Defense Power: 1 Bomb to defeat

Guardians of the sacred windmills on the Isle of Gust, Sandworms are completely docile until an unwelcome visitor happens across their peaceful habitat. Owning a keen sense of hearing, even the slightest noise alerts these fearsome beasts, who burrow to the site of the disturbance with alarming speed! When they've caught up to their quarry, Sandworms burst up from the desert sands, swallowing the intruder whole! Wise travelers keep very silent when crossing into Sandworm country, walking slowly to create as little noise as possible. The craftiest wayfarers have learned to throw Bombs to distract Sandworms, potentially tricking the beasts into swallowing the explosive by mistake!

Creep directly east across the desert to reach a northern platform where another stone statue is located. This one hints that Sandworms can be tricked into devouring Bombs! Pluck one up from a nearby bomb flower and then hurl the explosive at the desert floor. Sure enough, a Sandworm quickly burrows toward the disturbance and devours the Bomb, giving itself a nasty case of indigestion!

More bomb flowers grow on the northeasternmost platform, but you don't really need to use them. Simply walk Link very, very slowly about the desert, moving to each of the three windmills you must activate. When you reach a windmill platform, position

Link right near the device and then **blow into your mic** to start it spinning. Make sure to give a good gust so the windmill starts whirling at a good clip!

→ TIP ←

Smash the pots on the windmill platforms for hearts if Link's getting chewed up by the Sandworms.

Activate the two western and southeasternmost windmills to shut off the gust jars near the temple entrance you noticed earlier. The sealed door you spotted a moment ago also slides away, along with another one you couldn't see. Traveling through either passage lets you quickly reach the temple. How convenient! But before you leave, make sure to open the chest at the desert's southeast corner to claim a **treasure chart**. You wouldn't want to miss out on that!

Overworld Chest #18: Treasure Map #8

Treasure Map #8

You got a **treasure map**! It reveals the location of a sunken treasure on the Great Sea.

Task 4: Enter & Clear the Temple of Wind

Great explorations! You've been over every square inch of the Isle of Gust and can now enter the temple in the center of the island. The Wayfarer would be so proud! Stride to the desert's southwest corner and go through one of the two passages you've just opened to quickly return to the temple entrance. Pass directly inside; a spirit fairy in there needs your help!

Temple of Wind

Legend

Dungeon Chest #1: Courage Gem #4	Dungeon Chest #6: Heart Container #5
Dungeon Chest #2: Treasure	Bomb Wall
Dungeon Chest #3: Power Gem #5	Orb
Dungeon Chest #4: Bombs	Floor Switch
Dungeon Chest #5: Boss Key	

Temple of Wind: 1F

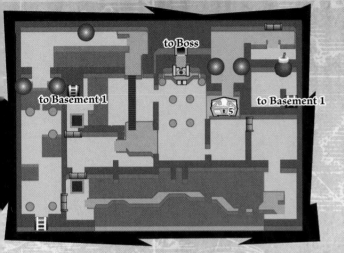

Temple of Wind: Mid-Level Passage

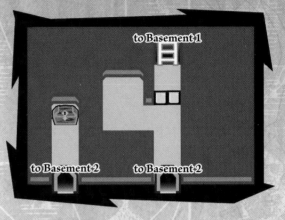

Temple of Wind: B1

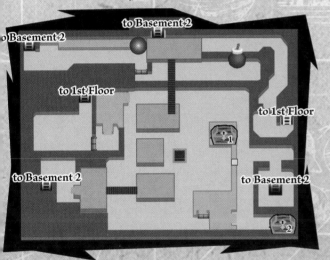

Temple of Wind: Boss Chamber Outer Hall

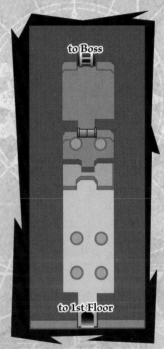

Temple of Wind: B2

Temple of Wind: Boss Chamber

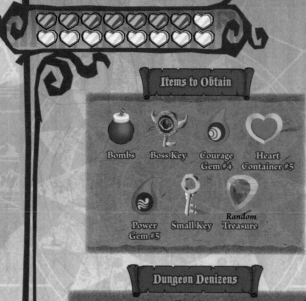

Items to Obtain

Bombs | Boss Key | Courage Gem #4 | Heart Container #5

Power Gem #5 | Small Key | Random Treasure

Dungeon Denizens

Enemies

Keese | Miniblin | Red ChuChu | Rock ChuChu

Rope | Sandworm | **Boss** Cyclok, Stirrer of Winds

Temple of Wind: 1F

Upon your entering the temple, Ciela warns Link that they haven't escaped the island's sudden gusts of wind quite yet. Numerous gust jars line the hall ahead; they are fully capable of sending Link tumbling into the surrounding pits. Stand near the gust jars and wait for them to stop blowing, then quickly dash past them.

TIP

At the second set of gust jars, wait for the middle one to stop blowing and then dash across.

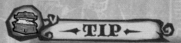

TIP

The strong gales produced by gust jars are shown on your map as little puffs of wind. Take advantage of this and check your map before venturing into the unknown!

Beyond the initial set of gust jars, Link finds a bomb flower growing near a large pit. Across the pit lies a row of bomb flowers that stretches between two crystal orbs. Wait a minute, there's a space between that row of bombs! Let's fill up that space, shall we? Snatch up a Bomb, then quickly tap the space between the Bombs ahead to make Link toss the explosive across the pit. When the Bomb goes off, it detonates the others in a rapid chain reaction, lighting both crystal orbs and extending a bridge across the chasm. Neat!

Dispatch the pair of Red ChuChus that springs up from the ground to attack just beyond the bomb flowers, then notice the pair of gust jars in the north wall to the east. These ones don't stop blowing! Fortunately, a stone block rests just in front of the first gust jar. Grab the block and shove it eastward, stopping when the block is in front of the first gust jar. That did the trick! Now simply run around the block and whack the crystal orb standing between the two gust jars. Presto! The gust jars stop blowing. You can now proceed.

Head south across the narrow, raised footbridge and then scamper down the stairs beyond. Wipe out the Red ChuChus at the foot of the steps. A northern door is sealed up tight, but the gate to the south opens with a tap of the stylus. Get through and cut down the fluttering Keese, then step on the nearby floor switch. A door in the west wall slides away. Return to the temple's entrance without having to loop around. You're far from finished here, though, so ascend the tall flight of stairs nearby.

TIP

Smash the pots nestled in the alcove near the northern stairs for hearts if Link's wounded.

Task 4:
Enter and Clear the Temple of Wind

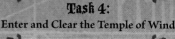

Next, carefully traverse a narrow walkway. Dangers include several Keese and a few gust jars that try to blow you into the southern pit. Take it slow and time your dashes past the gust jars carefully. Nail the Keese with Link's sword or Boomerang, but don't worry about them too much; you can bump them away with Link's shield!

Smash the pots on the other side of the walkway for hearts, then go into the northern chamber. Look out! A wall rises behind Link, trapping him in the room with four Ropes! These slithery villains can be dangerous, so waste no time unleashing a few spin attacks to wipe them out. Clear the room to lower the southern and western doors, then move west into the next room, which is filled with pots and Rupees!

After looting the chamber, shove the nearby stone block west to reach the floor's central hall. Be quick to eliminate the many Ropes in the area, then examine the north portion of the room. Two gust geysers try to catapult you northward here, but a pair of bomb blocks makes it impossible to move any farther. Go west instead.

You've come to the bottom floor of the chamber you crossed earlier via the elevated footbridge. Whack the statue in the corner to learn that there's only one chest to find on this floor. Save your 20 Rupees, though; we'll make sure you get that chest! Instead, tap the gust jar sitting on the floor for a surprise: Link can shove this gust jar around just like a stone block!

Have you guessed what you need to do with the gust jar? Just push it along the tile path on the floor until you reach the symbol on the ground to the west. Now you can use the gust jar to reach the western ledge! Run into the path of the gale to soar over the chasm and land safely on the other side. Before you go downstairs, stomp on the pressure switch to lower the nearby wall. Now you can easily return to the temple's entrance! There's no need to do so yet, of course; head downstairs to reach the first floor of the temple's basement.

Temple of Wind: B1

This temple isn't so bad, now is it? Don't speak too soon! Entering the first chamber of the basement lands Link in trouble: a wall rises behind him, trapping him inside the chamber with…a bunch of bomb flowers and rocks. What gives?

Your map shows enemies in the room where the rocks are sitting, but don't try to lift those rocks! Instead, hurl Bombs at them from afar to expose a new type of monster hiding beneath: Rock ChuChus! These guys lumber about wearing stone body armor to protect them from normal attacks. Use Bombs to blow off their shells, then finish them off with cold steel!

⚠ CAUTION

Rock ChuChus deal Link a quarter heart's worth of damage if he's stands too close when they burst from their hiding spots. Henceforth, if you approach a normal looking rock and see it start to quiver, run away fast!

Rock ChuChu

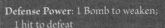

Threat Meter

Speed: Slow

Attack Power: 1/4 heart (burst from rock); 1/2 heart (contact)

Defense Power: 1 Bomb to weaken; 1 hit to defeat

Be careful when lifting up rocks: you never know what you might find! Rock ChuChus are tough nuts to crack. They hate being hit so much that they often hide under large boulders and wait for trouble to come find them! Once exposed, a Rock ChuChu relies on its strong stone shell to protect it from Link's sword. While sword attacks can keep a Rock ChuChu at bay, the only way to remove their rocky armor is to blast it off with a Bomb! After they've been stripped of their stone coatings, Rock ChuChus are nothing more than run-of-the-mill Red ChuChus. Finish them off in the usual fashion!

Crushing all three Rock ChuChus lowers the eastern wall. Continue your exploration of the temple. Smash the pots in the room beyond for hearts, then ascend the nearby steps. Use one fast spin attack to instantly defeat the three Red ChuChus that spring up

from the floor. Nice! Now descend the east steps and begin exploring the basement's large central chamber.

Be wary! This huge room is packed full of Miniblins, and they love sneaking up on you! Your first order of business is to secure the room so you don't have to worry about surprise attacks. Afterward, examine the stone tablet near the center of the room for an odd message: "When **two wings flutter**, the door will swing wide." How strange! Could it be referring to the two windmills standing atop the nearby platform? Perhaps, but for now, step on the nearby pressure switch to lower a wall to the southeast.

Climb the southeast steps and notice a movable stone block. Leave it for the moment and ride up the row of gust geysers instead to reach a northern ledge. There's a treasure chest over here! Open the chest to claim a valuable prize: another **Courage Gem**!

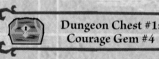

Dungeon Chest #1:
Courage Gem #4

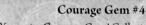

Courage Gem #4
You got a **Courage Gem**! Collect these items and use them to power up the Courage Spirit.

Drop down off the ledge and circle around to climb the southeast steps once more. Ignore the stone block yet again; this time descend the steps to the east. Smash two pots in a narrow passage ahead to locate another chest in the southeast corner of the floor. Pop the lid on this little guy for a random **treasure**!

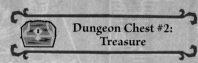

Dungeon Chest #2:
Treasure

Treasure
You got a **treasure**! Collect these items and sell them to the highest bidder!

Random

Now let's see what this stone block is all about! Grab the block and shove it north twice, then push it east twice to block off the second gust geyser from the top of the row. You can't bury these using your Shovel, as the floor is solid tile! Move to the far south geyser and ride across until you're dropped on top of the stone block. Now you can drop off to the east and reach a set of stairs leading even lower into the basement!

Temple of Wind: B2

You're doing well! This second basement floor is even more dicey, though, as the huge central chamber is guarded by those dreadful Sandworms. Smash the pots in the southeast chamber from which you enter, then use a Bomb from one of the nearby bomb flowers to blow a hole through the cracked north wall. Slowly walk to the main chamber's central platform; you don't want to rouse the ire of the slumbering Sandworms!

→NOTE←
You can toss bomb flower Bombs into the central chamber to dispatch the Sandworms, but know that you'll never be able to defeat them all.

→TIP←
If you don't feel like sneaking about, you can run in short dashes, then stop when the Sandworms start to draw near to give them the slip. This is somewhat risky, however!

 1  2  3  4

Task 4:
Enter and Clear the Temple of Wind

Check out the central platform's wall map for a clue on what you must do here: find and uncover four **pillars of wind** to open the way forward. The location of these important objects is shown on the map by four red Xs placed about the central chamber. Looks like you've got some exploring to do! Jot down these locations on your map, then start off toward one.

A bit of investigation reveals that the wall map's Xs point to various loose piles of sand on the ground. Whip out your Shovel and dig at these spots to uncover four gust geysers! **Pillars of wind**…how clever! Each time you uncover a gust geyser, a torch lights in one of the floor's four corners. Light all four torches to open the main chamber's north door, along with another door in the southeast corner chamber.

Don't leave this area just yet! Take a moment to investigate the west side of the main chamber, where a small chest awaits discovery. Open the chest to add another **Power Gem** to your collection. That's your fifth one! There's nothing else to do around here for now; return to the first basement floor.

NOTE

Did you notice the cracked wall in the northwest corner? Mark its location for future reference!

Dungeon Chest #3: Power Gem #5

Power Gem #5
You got a **Power Gem**! Collect these items and use them to power up the Power Spirit.

When Two Wings Flutter…

You have the choice of returning to the first basement floor via the northern or south-western staircase. Go with the southwestern stairs, then cross the walkway to the east to locate a gust jar. Link can grab this one and shove it around! Tap the gust jar to grab it, then drag it west, stopping on the special tile on the ground. This lines up the gust jar with the windmill ahead, causing the windmill to start spinning like crazy!

Backtrack to the second basement floor and cross the main chamber as carefully as you can. You don't want to become Sandworm food! Go through the north passage and then use a nearby bomb flower to remove those pesky bomb blocks from your path. Climb the stairs beyond to return to the first basement floor.

You know what to do here! Go south to reach another movable gust jar and slide it west, lining it up with the crest on the floor. The gust jar starts twirling the second windmill, causing a **small key** to fall onto the ground in the chamber below. Super! Simply drop from the ledge, run over, and collect the key. That's progress!

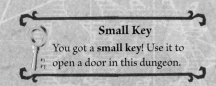

Small Key
You got a **small key**! Use it to open a door in this dungeon.

You must now return to the basement's second floor. Cross the row of gust geysers to the east just as you did before to get down there. Sneak through the Sandworms' lair and head directly for the northeast corner where a locked door prevents you from accessing the floor's northeast chamber. You're now the proud owner of a small key, so tap the door to open it.

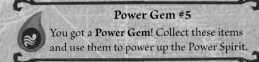

A great treasure awaits you in this small chamber. Climb the steps and kick open that big chest to finally obtain some **Bombs**! You now have a **Bomb Bag** and can carry up to 10 lovely little explosives around with you. Joy!

Dungeon Chest #4:
Bombs

Bombs

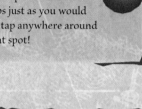

You got **Bombs**! Now you can blow up all kinds of stuff! Tap the Item tab and then tap the Bomb icon to equip them. Ready the Bombs just as you would the Boomerang or Shovel, then tap anywhere around Link to toss a Bomb right to that spot!

Having a Blast

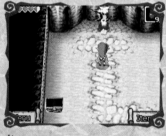

Yes! Now you've got a bundle of Bombs and a burning desire to use them. You don't have to wait very long! Exit the room, cross the central chamber, and approach the cracked wall in the northwest corner. Ready a Bomb and then toss it right in front of the wall to blow a hole right through it! Ah, that felt good!

— NOTE —

You can now feed Bombs to Sandworms whenever you like! Don't use them all up, though. Remember: you can carry a maximum of only **10 Bombs** at a time! Your current number of Bombs is shown in the Item icon while your Bombs are equipped.

Enter the hole you've created to reach a small chamber. A gust geyser blows steadily upward, but you can't reach the ledge above due to an unsightly bomb block. Blast the block from your path by tossing a Bomb directly at the gust geyser. The Bomb is lifted into the air and explodes, destroying the block! Smash the pots in the corner to replenish your supply of Bombs, then ride up the geyser and go upstairs.

— NOTE —

Now that you've got a **Bomb Bag**, you'll regularly find Bombs inside pots and the like. All the more reason to smash everything you see!

The stairs take you to the northwest corner of the first basement floor. First, let's secure the area. Run west down the hall, tearing through the few Red ChuChus that emerge to give you grief. Now, return to the gust geyser near the stairs and chuck a Bomb at it. As before, the Bomb flies up and explodes in midair, setting off the row of bomb flowers that stretches eastward! The final bomb flower's detonation lights an otherwise unreachable crystal orb, causing a southern wall to slide away. Brilliant!

Pass through the newly opened passage. Before reading the stone tablet, toss a Bomb at the rock sitting next to it. Out pops a Rock ChuChu! Quickly hurl another Bomb to blast off its protective shell, then follow up with a fast sword attack. In the same fashion, dispatch another Rock ChuChu hiding in the rock on the other side of the tablet, and a third hiding in one of the boulders at the passage's far end. With the area secure, tap to read the tablet for an important clue: not all bomb walls are marked with cracks!

Task 4:
Enter and Clear the Temple of Wind

Case in point: notice the small bit of tile on the floor near the north wall. This is a clue that the wall isn't quite as sturdy as it appears! Toss a Bomb onto the tile patch and watch as a large hole is blown open. Sneaky! Dash through the opening and clear the pathway beyond of Red ChuChus as you head for the far stairwell.

Back on Top

Finally! You're out of that musty basement and back on the temple's main floor. Use caution when exploring this northwestern chamber: two of those innocent-looking rocks to the west are actually Rock ChuChus in disguise! Heave Bombs at them to reveal and weaken them both, then move in with Link's blade to administer the final blows.

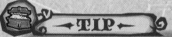

TIP

If you need more Bombs, backtrack and start smashing pots to find some.

Wait a minute; there's no way out of this room! Or is there? Stand near the north wall. You can just make out a small patch of tile in the neighboring room. Could this be a clue that the wall is susceptible to bombing? It's worth a shot! Plant a Bomb right in front of the north wall, directly opposite the tile. Blammo! A huge hole opens up, so move on.

Climb the steps ahead and smash the surrounding pots to refill your Bomb Bag. Notice two strings of bomb flowers nearby, each one leading to a crystal orb. You must light both orbs simultaneously to open the way forward, but one Bomb won't do the trick. Instead, quickly toss two Bombs at the pair of crests on the floor between the bomb flowers to solve this puzzle. When both orbs are glowing, the south door retracts into the ground.

A huge chest awaits you just beyond the door. Open it up to find a vital item: the dungeon's **Boss Key**! You know this means you're nearly finished with this place. Grab the Boss Key overhead and drop off the west edge of the platform to return to the floor's central hall.

Dungeon Chest #5: Boss Key

Boss Key
You've found the **Boss Key**! It's a huge, heavy key.

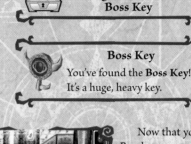

Now that you've got Bombs, you can finally get rid of those pesky bomb blocks sitting on the north ledge. Set down the Boss Key and then toss a Bomb at one of the gust geysers to send it upward to blow away both blocks in short order. Pick up the Boss Key once more and then sail up the gust geysers to reach the ledge. With Boss Key in hand, tap the Boss Key block to remove the massive obstacle. Now is a good time to save your game!

Travel steadily north through the long, elegant chamber, smashing the pots at the far end for hearts and Bombs. Tap the statue to summon a patch of blue light that can whisk you away to the temple's entrance if you so desire. Don't back out now! The Temple of Wind's boss lies just ahead!

Cyclok, Stirrer of Winds

Threat Meter

Speed: Normal

Attack Power: 1/2 heart (contact); 1/2 heart (cyclone)

Defense Power: 1 Bomb to weaken; multiple hits to defeat!

Catching Cyclok with a midair Bomb sends him crashing to the ground. He's down, but not out! Rush toward Cyclok and tap the monster as fast as you can to administer a righteous beating!

Just as when Link reached the top of the Temple of Fire, a wall rises behind the young adventurer when he enters this final chamber, trapping him inside the boss's lair. A massive Octorok awaits Link here. It quickly envelopes itself in a whirlwind and takes to the sky. The battle begins!

You must drop Cyclok several times, following up each time with loads of sword strikes until you finally best the beast. A quick scan of the arena shows pots containing recovery hearts and Bombs, and even a few bomb flowers you may use to conserve your own stockpile of explosives. Just make sure you don't hold onto a bomb flower's Bomb for too long; the worst damage you can take in this battle is a close-range Bomb blast!

Cyclok is a massive Octorok with the power to summon cyclones! The beast hovers high in the air, keeping well out of reach of Link's sword. How will you ever manage to bring such a huge monster down? Cyclok only lowers himself to make swooping attack runs at our young hero! Run to one side the moment you see Cyclok dive or you'll be struck hard!

To keep Link on his toes, Cyclok also periodically summons tiny cyclones that twirl about on the ground. You don't want to get caught up in one of these little twisters! Instead, use them to your advantage: toss a Bomb into a mini cyclone to send it spiraling skyward to erupt in a violent blast!

Task 4:
Enter and Clear the Temple of Wind

Beaten to a pulp by Link's trusty blade, Cyclok finally succumbs to his wounds. Exploding in a brilliant flash, the beast is suddenly transformed into a collection of sand! The Phantom Hourglass then flies out of Link's pack, and the **Sand of Hours** is drawn into it, adding a full **two minutes'** worth of time!

Suddenly, a giant crest on the floor begins to glow. Out flies a blue fairy! The tiny being introduces herself as **Neri**, the **Spirit of Wisdom**. She thanks Link for releasing her from captivity. Seeing Leaf fluttering about nearby, Neri is quick to join Link in his quest. Only one more fairy remains to be found!

A Hearty Reward

Fantastic job! The Spirit of Wisdom has been rescued, and you're now one step closer to tracking down that slippery Ghost Ship. That's not all: a large chest suddenly materializes nearby! Open the chest to claim a wondrous prize: a new **Heart Container**! Collect this precious gift, then step into the shimmering pool of blue light to return to the temple's entrance. Well done!

Dungeon Chest #6:
Heart Container #5

Heart Container #5
You got a **Heart Container**! Your heart meter has been increased by one heart!

Let's return to Linebeck and see what he thinks of your accomplishment. The fastest way back to the pier is to travel south from the temple entrance, scale the steps to the east, and then drop off the south ledge that follows to reach a lower clearing. From there, go west and then climb a tall staircase, leaping off the west side of the high ledge. Bingo! You're back at the dock. Speak with Linebeck, who's eager to return to Mercay Island and continue scouring the **Temple of the Ocean King** for treasure. Yeah, right; like that old barnacle will be doing any scouring inside there!

You *could* go sailing off to Mercay Island without delay, but what's the rush? Let's spend a little time seeing the sights first. Now that you've gotten your hands on some Bombs, you're able to explore a new area on Bannan Island, where you may partake in a fun and profitable minigame!

Bannan Island: Cannon Game

Remember that cracked wall you couldn't Bomb back inside the cavern at Bannan Island? Well, it's still there, and this time it's going down! Set sail for Bannan Island, then go east to enter the cavern. Toss a Bomb at that bomb wall and blast it apart!

Slash through a few Keese in the tunnel beyond the bomb wall as you head for the far opening. Exit the cavern to reach the island's east side, where a dreadfully bored man has set up some sort of stand. The sign indicates that this is some sort of Cannon Game...pay the man 20 Rupees to learn how to play!

→ NOTE →
Did you notice the short wooden peg near the shore? Boy, these things are everywhere! Better make a note of it in case you find a way to use it later.

Salvatore

Though he runs an exciting Cannon Game challenge from his little stand at Bannan Island, Salvatore is an extremely bored, downtrodden individual. This is most likely because his stand sees very few customers, but what can he expect? He couldn't have chosen a more remote spot to run his attraction! Link is able to cheer the man up considerably by playing—and winning—Salvatore's Cannon Game.

When you slide some Rupees his way, the man suddenly perks up, explaining the rules of the game with a fun puppet show! Apparently, the game takes place on the open sea. You'll be sailing along a short course lined with red and blue **targets**. Blue targets blow up when you shoot them, adding 100 points to your score. Red targets are indestructible, and every hit you land on them nets you 20 points. That's all there is to know!

...continued

The game's record high score is 2,500 points. Beat that and you're sure to win something special! You don't have to beat this score to win prizes, though. There are fabulous concession gifts just for giving it a shot! Pick one of the three chests the man presents to you and see what you get.

Based on your score, here's what you might find within the concession prize chests:

Less than 1,500 Points: green or blue Rupee.

1,500–1,999 Points: green, blue, or red Rupee, or a random treasure.

2,000–2,499 Points: red or big green Rupee, or a random ship part.

2,500 Points and Higher: Bomb Bag #1. Afterward, big green Rupee or a random ship part.

Of course, there's an even greater prize to win if you manage to score over 2,500 points. Doing so is no easy feat, however. You've got to pull out all the stops! Tap those targets as fast as you can to keep your cannon blazing away. Blast every blue marker for 100 points apiece and hammer each red one as many times as you can to bolster your score. Pan your view around your ship to blast targets from port to starboard!

Beat that high score to land yourself a fabulous prize: a bigger **Bomb Bag**! Now you can carry twice as many Bombs! Your new maximum is 20. You also get an extra prize: a red Rupee to cover the cost of your game. Bonus!

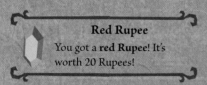

Red Rupee
You got a **red Rupee**! It's worth 20 Rupees!

...continued

Bomb Bag #1

You got another **Bomb Bag**! Now you can store up to 20 Bombs!

NOTE

After winning the Bomb Bag, you can continue to play the Cannon Game to score even more concession prizes.

NOTE

Now that you've spent some time making friends with Salvatore, he'll soon be sending you a letter in the mail. In it you'll find **Wisdom Gem #4**!

Astrid's Gift of Wisdom

Ready for a real treat? Use the Cyclone Slate to warp southward, then sail to the Isle of Ember. Go directly to Astrid's house and speak with the fortune-teller. She's pleased to hear of Link's accomplishments at the Isle of Gust and bestows a **Wisdom Gem** upon him in praise of his heroic efforts. Very cool!

Wisdom Gem #5

You got a **Wisdom Gem**! Collect these items and use them to power up the Wisdom Spirit.

1

2

3

4

Tasks:
Complete!

Chapter 5

Contents

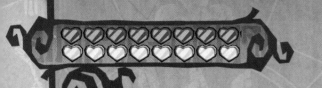

Digging Deeper: Temple of the Ocean King 3 & Temple of Courage

Mercay Island

to Temple of the Ocean King

Treasure Teller

Shop

Legend

19	Overworld Chest #19: Power Gem #7
💣	Bomb Wall

Digging Deeper: Overview

Things are starting to look up for Link! Our hero has now rescued two of the three spirit fairies needed to track down the Ghost Ship. Only one more spirit fairy remains! With Neri, the Spirit of Wisdom at his side, Link can finally return to the Temple of the Ocean King on Mercay Island and delve deeper into its labyrinthine basement. Another vital clue that will lead him to the final fairy must be hiding in that temple!

1. Return to Mercay & the Temple

2. Find a Clue About What to Do

3. Obtain the Salvage Arm & Sun Key

4. Enter & Clear the Temple of Courage

A Link to the Present

Max 12:00

Max 20

x4

Lvl 0   Lvl 0   x5   x5

x8

Items Already Acquired

Big Catch Lure   Bomb Bag #1   Bombs   Boomerang   Cannon   Fishing Rod   Oshus's Sword   Phantom Hourglass

Shovel   Wooden Shield   Courage Gems x4   Power Gems x5   Wisdom Gems x5   Treasure Maps x8   Sand of Hours: 12 Minutes

Items to Obtain

Power Gem #6   Power Gem #7

Overworld Denizens

Enemies

Rat   Crow   Red ChuChu

Task 1: Return to Mercay & the Temple

Be It Ever So Humble

Ah, there's no place like home! Now that you're back at Mercay Island and most likely are toting a swollen wallet, why not pay a visit to the local shop? Or spend some time customizing your vessel at the Shipyard? With all those parts you've just won at the Cannon Game, you might be able to attach several parts of the same category and enhance your ship's defensive capabilities!

TIP

You can now buy Bombs at Mercay Island's shop. Do so if you're low; you'll need some very soon!

Since you're back at Mercay, why not check in on old man Oshus and see how he's doing? Cross the bridge to reach the island's west side and enter Oshus's house. The old man congratulates Link for rescuing Neri from the Temple of Wind and hands over a valuable prize: another **Power Gem**!

Power Gem #6

You got a **Power Gem**! Collect these items and use them to power up the Power Spirit.

NOTE

If you don't stop by and see Oshus, he eventually tires of waiting and simply mails the Power Gem directly to Link.

When you've finished reacquainting yourself with the good people of Mercay, travel north from the village, starting off toward the Temple of the Ocean King. Now that you've got Bombs, you can finally blast those two pesky bomb blocks near the stairs in the forest out of your way. This creates a small shortcut, saving you a few steps through the woods.

You also can finally deal with that cracked bomb wall in the northern cliff just beyond the stairs. Plant a Bomb there and blast the wall wide open to reveal an entrance to a small cavern. Go right inside!

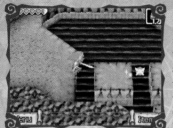

This cavern's crawling with Rats! Best the pests on the small entry ledge, then whack the nearby statue for a tip you already know: you can speak with the spirits of fallen adventurers within the Temple of the Ocean King. Understood! Now leap across the small platforms to the east, using your Boomerang to wipe out the Rat on the far ledge before hopping onto it.

Jump to the chest on the north ledge and kick it open for a great prize: a sparkly **Power Gem**! Good find, but did you notice that odd eye crest on the north wall? Creepy; but there must be something special about it! Better make a note so you'll remember its location for future reference.

 Overworld Chest #19: **Power Gem #7**

Power Gem #7

You got a **Power Gem**! Collect these items and use them to power up the Power Spirit.

Temple of the Ocean King, Third Visit

Temple of the Ocean King: B1

to Basement 2

to Mercay Island

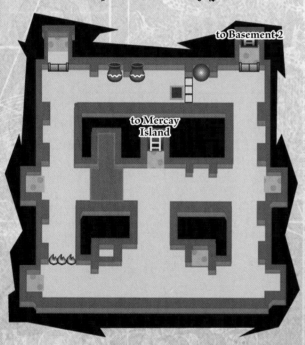

Temple of the Ocean King: B2

to Basement 1

to Basement 3

Legend

Dungeon Chest #1: Force Gem	**Dungeon Chest #2:** Force Gem	**Dungeon Chest #3:** Force Gem
Dungeon Chest #4: Power Gem #8	**Dungeon Chest #5:** Red Potion	

Bomb Wall	Orb	Floor Switch	Lever
Red Jar		Yellow Jar	

Task 1:
Return to Mercay & the Temple

Temple of the Ocean King: B3

Temple of the Ocean King: Checkpoint Chamber

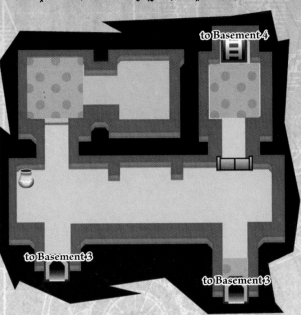

Temple of the Ocean King: B4

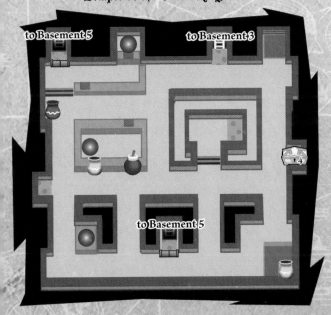

Temple of the Ocean King: B5

Temple of the Ocean King: B6

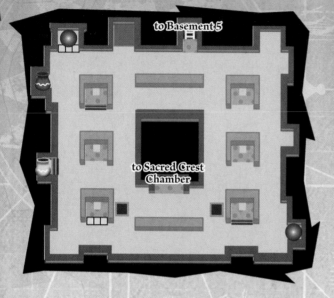

to Basement 5

to Sacred Crest
Chamber

Temple of the Ocean King: Sacred Crest Chamber

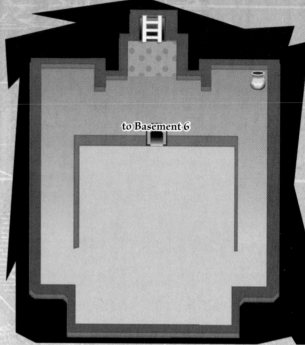

to Basement 6

Items to Obtain

Force
Gem x3

Power
Gem #8

Red Potion

Small
Key x4

Dungeon Denizens

Enemies

Phantom
Eyes

Miniblin

Phantom

Yellow
ChuChu

You've done all there is to do
around these woods. Now it's
time to revisit that temple!
Waste no time getting there
and going inside. Smash the
pots in the entry hall for items
if need be, then go directly
downstairs. Cross the first floor
as you did before and dash

straight down the central staircase to reach the first basement floor.

→ NOTE ←

The Phantom Hourglass now features 12 minutes'
worth of sand. The extra two minutes comes from the
Sand of Hours you claimed by defeating that horrible
beast Cyclok at the Temple of Wind.

Temple of the Ocean King: B1

Alright, it's time to outwit those lumbering Phantoms! Remember
how to get through this floor? You had better because all the traps
and locked doors have been reset! Don't worry, though: Your new
Bombs make a great shortcut.

When it's safe to do so, dash
east and then north, heading
for the locked door and crystal
orb at the northeast corner
of the floor. You don't need
to mess with that little orb
anymore: just toss a Bomb at
the nearby bomb blocks to
clear the way westward! Move

west and step on the floor switch in the hallway. As before, this
opens the door at the hall's far end and grants you access to a safe
zone and a **small key**. Nab the key and then open that northwest
door to head downstairs.

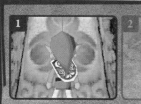

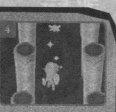

Task 1:
Return to Mercay & the Temple

Small Key
You got a **small key**! Use it to open a door in this dungeon.

Missing Links
Diggin' for Bombs

Low on Bombs? Never fear! Just run to the southeast corner of the floor and spy a small pile of dirt on the ground near a wall. When no Phantoms are about, whip out the Shovel and dig there to unearth a gust geyser! Ride it up to reach a tiny ledge where a little pot sits all by itself. Smash the pot to add a few Bombs to your Bomb Bag!

Temple of the Ocean King: B2

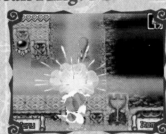

Your Bombs helped you make short work of that first basement floor, and they're just as handy here on floor B2! As before, wait for the nearby Phantom to look westward, then dash south toward a crystal orb. Simply heave a Bomb at the south bomb wall to blow a hole right through it to the southern chamber!

TIP

The bomb wall is easily identified by the large crack running down in its south side.

Be wary: the sound of the explosion will draw the ire of the Phantoms! Dash through the bomb wall and hole up in the safe zone to the east, waiting for the Phantoms to disperse. Afterward, position Link on the pressure switch to lower the west spikes, then toss the Boomerang westward to nab the **small key** in the chamber beyond as you did before.

Small Key
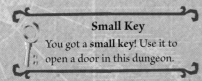
You got a **small key**! Use it to open a door in this dungeon.

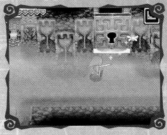

Super! Now you just have to get to that central locked door. Go south for the easiest route, looping around to the west and then heading northward again past a row of lowered blue blocks. Whack the crystal orb that stands in the east alcove to raise the blue blocks and lower the red blocks to the north, then simply go north to open the locked door.

Missing Links
Every Second Counts

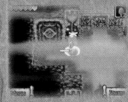

If you're looking to add some sand to your Phantom Hourglass, smash the red pot in the alcove west of the central locked door and wait on the safe zone puddle until no Phantoms are about. When it's clear, pull out a Bomb and toss it at the wall to the north, blasting a hole right through to a safe zone! Here you may smash a yellow pot to add 30 seconds to your timer, but that's all for the moment. A tiny hole in the north wall seems very peculiar though, doesn't it? It sure does, and you'll find out what it's used for on a future visit!

Temple of the Ocean King: B3

Unfortunately, this floor doesn't feature big-time shortcuts like the previous two. Instead, you must work your way around to those three **Force Gem** chests, avoiding the Phantoms as you did before. Since little has changed here, we'll just cover the new stuff you can do.

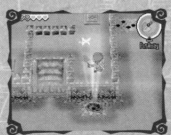

There's only one shortcut here at present, and it's not a huge one. Now that you've got the Shovel, you don't need to pull the floor's southwest lever to lower the flames to the southeast. Instead, simply dig up the soft patch of soil near the flames to uncover a gust geyser that lifts you up and onto the platform above! Then use the pressure switches as you did before to dunk that patrolling Phantom and claim his **small key**. Use this key to get at the Force Gem that's locked away behind the southern door.

Small Key
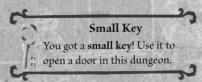
You got a **small key**! Use it to open a door in this dungeon.

Missing Links

More Sand, Less Spikes

A full minute can be added to the Phantom Hourglass via two yellow pots found on this floor. The first is directly north of the entry stairs; just loop around to find it sitting against the northern wall, then smash it apart to add 30 seconds' worth of sand to your timer.

The other yellow pot couldn't be reached before. To get at it, you need Bombs! Blast away the northeast bomb blocks to reach the yellow pot, then smash it to extend your timer by another 30 seconds. Nice!

Finally, you can disable the spike traps that surround the southeast platform as long as you have the boomerang. Move south from the bomb blocks and stand at the edge of the tall ledge. Ready the Boomerang and trace a line south and then east to strike the nearby crystal orb. Whacking the orb deactivates the spike traps, making the area a little bit safer for young adventurers.

Temple of the Ocean King: Checkpoint Chamber

Use the three Force Gems to open the sealed north doorway and proceed to the second half of the floor. (Check our map to locate the Force Gems if you've forgotten where they are.) This is where you found the second sea chart during your last trip through the temple! You're far from finished with this awful place, however. Now that Neri is with you, you can open the sealed east door marked by a strange symbol—the **Crest of Wisdom**! Tap the door to open it, then proceed downstairs.

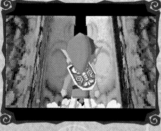

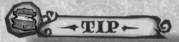

Before you leave, go west down the hall and smash a yellow pot for another 30 seconds' worth of sand!

At this point, you're doing just fine if you've got more than eight minutes' worth of sand in your hourglass. If you have significantly less than that, consider using the blue light in the northern chamber to warp to the temple's entrance, then do your best to hurry through these first few floors.

Temple of the Ocean King: B4

You're now venturing into unexplored temple depths! Things become a bit more difficult from this point forward. Keep your wits about you, think carefully before you act, and stick close to those safe zones!

Neri warns you of a new threat when you reach this fourth basement floor of the temple: Phantom Eyes! These ugly creatures serve as surveillance cameras for Phantoms, alerting the temple's guardians whenever they spot Link slinking about. Fortunately, Link can dispatch Phantom Eyes to continue his infiltration. It's usually best to keep out of sight and stun these creatures with the Boomerang from range, then hurry in to finish them off with Link's sword before they recover.

Phantom Eyes are shown on the map just like Phantoms. Keep track of them and plot routes that allow you to sneak up on them!

Phantom Eyes

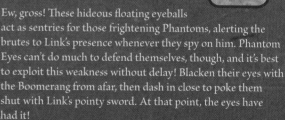

Threat Meter

Speed: Normal

Attack Power: None

Defense Power: 1 hit to defeat

Ew, gross! These hideous floating eyeballs act as sentries for those frightening Phantoms, alerting the brutes to Link's presence whenever they spy on him. Phantom Eyes can't do much to defend themselves, though, and it's best to exploit this weakness without delay! Blacken their eyes with the Boomerang from afar, then dash in close to poke them shut with Link's pointy sword. At that point, the eyes have had it!

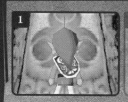

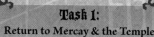

Task 1:
Return to Mercay & the Temple

A gust jar blows steadily to the west, forcing you to go east from the entry point. Make your way southeast until you encounter another pair of gust jars that block your path. This just won't do! Ready the Boomerang and hurl it southward, striking a crystal orb beyond the southern gust jar. This deactivates the southern gust jar and you can then continue southward. Watch out, though: one of those disgusting Phantom Eyes lurks just around the corner!

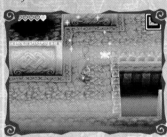

Before proceeding southward, ready the Boomerang for a second time and toss it at the nearby Phantom Eye. The Boomerang makes contact, momentarily stunning the creature. Now's your chance! Bolt right up to the Phantom Eye and tap it to unleash a fast targeted attack. Poof! The creature is defeated in a puff of smoke.

TIP

To add 30 seconds' worth of sand to your hourglass, use the Boomerang to smash a yellow pot that sits on the tiny southeast ledge. If necessary, toss the Boomerang a second time to retrieve the bonus time that pops out!

Carefully proceed south and then west. A Phantom patrols the nearby corridors, so look out! Watch his movements carefully and then sneak along behind him as he moves northward up the nearby hall. A row of spikes blocks access to the floor's central chamber, so continue following the Phantom as he turns and lumbers westward.

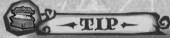
TIP

If the Phantom happens to notice you, make tracks toward the eastern safe zone!

When you reach a gust jar, stop following the Phantom and turn north. Check your map to see that a Phantom Eye patrols the hall to the west. Ready the Boomerang and wait for the creature to draw near, then quickly trace a line around the corner to whack it without being seen. Race forward and quickly dispatch the stunned peeper with a swipe of Link's sword.

CAUTION

If a Phantom Eye notices you, it not only alerts the roaming Phantom, but also calls up reinforcements: another Phantom materializes near the northeast entry stairs!

You're safe from detection for the moment, but your hourglass has been draining away all this time! Catch a break by breaking the red pot at the hall's far west end. Stand on the safe zone puddle that emerges and watch the patrol path of the Phantom Eye to the south. When the moment is right, dash to the southwest safe zone and eliminate this third and final Phantom Eye just as you did the first two.

Wiping out all three Phantom Eyes not only makes life easier, it also reveals a hidden prize: a giant treasure chest materializes at the floor's far east safe zone! Let's make a few important stops on the way over there. First, shut off those annoying gust jars. Locate a soft patch of earth near a ledge at the floor's southwest corner. Shovel there to reveal a gust geyser, then use it to reach the ledge above. Smack the crystal orb on the ledge to deactivate all the gust jars on this floor. Nice!

Backtrack to the west safe zone and from there, go east along the nearby corridor. As you move along, notice a large crack running down one of the north walls. You know what that means! Bomb open the wall to gain entry to a small chamber with yet another crystal orb. Whack this orb to deactivate the spike strip to the east that you passed a short time ago.

CAUTION

Blasting open the wall may alert the nearby Phantom. If this occurs, dart to the west safe zone before entering the chamber. You don't want to get cornered inside there!

Now that the spikes are down and the gust jars are no longer blowing, you have a clear shot to the floor's central chamber where a **small key** awaits. Dash into that chamber when no Phantoms are looking and claim the key from within, then continue moving eastward to reach the big treasure chest you revealed just moments ago. Open the chest to add yet another **Power Gem** to your collection!

Small Key
You got a **small key**! Use it to open a door in this dungeon.

Dungeon Chest #4: Power Gem #8

Power Gem #8
You got a **Power Gem**! Collect these items and use them to power up the Power Spirit.

Now bail out of here! Go south to locate a locked door and tap the door to open it using the small key you've just found. Great work! Descend the stairs beyond the door to reach the basement's next floor.

NOTE
How's your time? Do you have more than five minutes left in the hourglass? If so, you're doing great!

Temple of the Ocean King: B5

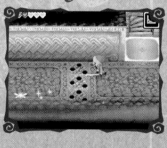

Now we're getting somewhere! This floor is far more straightforward compared to the last few, but it's scarce on safe zones. You can't enter the far southeast chamber yet—it's blocked by spikes that you can't lower—so wait for the spikes to the west to retract and then dash north into a large chamber.

Alternatively, the orb in the southwest shuts off those spikes and can be hit with the boomerang.

Yikes! A wall that rises behind Link when he enters this chamber traps him inside with four crackling Yellow ChuChus! Resist the urge to attack them until their electrical charges fade, then wipe out a few to create some breathing room. Use the Boomerang to stun the other two and finish them off with Link's steel. Defeat all four Yellow ChuChus to lower the south and east doors, along with a row of spikes to the west. Smash the yellow pot in the west alcove for an extra 15 seconds' worth of sand before speeding eastward into the next chamber ahead.

CAUTION
Don't linger about in these chambers; sand is steadily draining from your hourglass!

Oh no. Not again! The moment he enters, Link becomes trapped in the east chamber, and four Miniblins pop in to attack. No point in waiting for these guys to make the first move! Charge into the fray, utilizing targeted attacks and spins to wipe out the monsters fast. Clearing the room causes the east and north doors to open, and another row of spikes to retract to the east. Smash another yellow pot to gain 15 more seconds of time, then hurry through the north doorway.

You can't get very far: a gust jar blocks access to the west hallway, preventing you from reaching the safe zone that lies just beyond. There's got to be a way to shut that thing off! It's recon time: ready the Boomerang and draw a line over the pit to the east to discover a hidden crystal orb. Smack the orb with the Boomerang to shut off the gust jar, and also reveal a small chest in the north alcove. Quickly open the chest to claim a valuable **Red Potion**, then bolt to the nearby safe zone. Whew!

Dungeon Chest #5: Red Potion

Red Potion
You got a **Red Potion**! Gulp it down to replenish up to six hearts whenever Link's health energy is low.

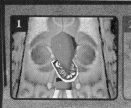

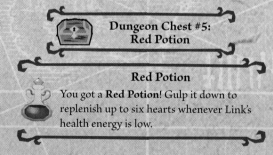

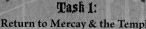

NOTE

Sometimes Link is already carrying two potions and has no room for more. In these cases, he often finds a Rupee prize inside chests that would normally contain a potion. He never comes up empty-handed!

A big treasure chest sits on a ledge just across a gap to the west. A gust jar blows constantly in your face, so there's no way to cross. You know something good's in there! Perhaps you'll be able to open it later. For now, simply head down the north stairs to reach the next floor of the temple.

NOTE

This floor shouldn't have taken you too long to clear. Feel proud if you've got at least three minutes left to work with: there'll be no stopping you!

Temple of the Ocean King: B6

Alright, last floor! Neri encourages you onward, but a quick look at your map shows that this floor is a doozy, featuring two brutish Phantoms and two Phantom Eyes. Fortunately, there are loads of safe zones for you to hide in as well! Begin by waiting for the nearby Phantom Eye to move close, then hurl the Boomerang at it from the comfort of the entry safe zone. Whack!

Hurry to finish off the Phantom Eye with Link's sword, then dash to the northeast safe zone. A massive stone tablet stands here; tap the tablet to read it and learn that it's the **second tablet governing the crest**. What a strange message… wonder what that's about? Whatever it is, it must be important. Let's make a note on the map! Call up your map and **draw the number 2** on this safe zone.

Now move to the next safe zone to the south. Be careful that the patrolling Phantom doesn't see you! Another large tablet standing at this safe zone simply says that **four stone tablets govern the crest**. Good to know! No need to make a note of this one, though.

From the central east safe zone, rush to the southeast corner of the floor, where a crystal orb stands in the alcove. Whack the orb to lower the spikes that block the nearby safe zone, then dash over there to find yet another stone tablet. This is the **fourth tablet governing the crest**. Make a note on your map by **writing the number 4** at this location!

A pressure switch sits just to the west of this southeast safe zone. When no Phantoms are about, move onto the switch to disable the gust jar ahead. This grants you access to the central safe zone. Dash there and tap the bright red door to learn that you must **reveal the sacred crest** to open the way forward. Unfortunately, you don't have enough information to draw the crest just yet. More exploration is in order!

A gust jar blocks your progress to the west, so loop around when it's safe to do so, taking the southernmost hallway toward the southwest safe zone. Be wary, though: this corner safe zone is walled off by bomb blocks and patrolled by a Phantom Eye! Avoid detection

and move to step on the pressure switch in the corridor between the central and southwest safe zones. This disables the other gust jar. Hurry back to the central safe zone before you're spotted!

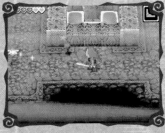

From the central safe zone, ready the Boomerang and trace a line westward to strike the nearby Phantom Eye. Once it's stunned, quickly finish off the creature and then plant a Bomb near the southwest safe zone's bomb blocks. Blammo! Step onto the safe zone and tap the tablet to learn that this is the **third tablet governing the crest**. Great! **Draw the number 3** at this spot on your map. Only one more tablet to mark down!

TIP

Dispatching both Phantom Eyes lowers a row of spikes to the west. Now you can reach a yellow pot in the western alcove! Smash the pot to add 30 seconds to your time.

If you're running low on Bombs, smash the pot in the floor's southwest corner to find more.

The northwest safe zone's tablet holds the key to solving this floor's puzzle. Read it to learn that the sacred crest both begins and ends here. That's it! Now you know how to draw the crest! Call up your map and label this spot **1**, then trace a single line that connects each

of the tablets you've numbered, in their proper order. Draw the line to the tablets you've numbered as 1, 2, 3, and 4. It looks like you've drawn a big Z! The crest both **begins and ends here** though, so finish it off by returning the line to this spot. Look at that! The crest looks just like the **Phantom Hourglass**!

Go northward next, toward the northwest corner. The northwest safe zone is guarded by spikes, but a red pot sits in the floor's northwest alcove. Smash the pot to create a puddle of safe zone to stand in while you decide what to do next.

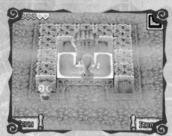

Now you can open the floor's central door and finally claim what you've been searching for. Hurry to the central safe zone and tap the red door. When prompted, draw the design of the sacred crest upon the door by tracing a big Z and then connecting the final line. Presto! The door opens to the central chamber.

CAUTION

Ignore the central west safe zone entirely. Reading its cursed tablet causes two more Phantom Eyes to appear on the floor!

Did you notice the soft patch of dirt on the ground nearby? You know what to do! Dig there with the Shovel to uncover a gust geyser that blows at regular intervals. Good find! Unfortunately, a collection of bomb blocks prevents you from using the gust geyser to reach the ledge above. How rude!

Task 2: Find a Clue About What to Do

Temple of the Ocean King: Sacred Crest Chamber

Hey, sand is no longer draining from the Phantom Hourglass. The temple's curse doesn't seem to work here! Smash the yellow pot in the northeast corner for 30 extra seconds of sand if you like, then approach the large portrait on the north wall. Tap the portrait for an odd instruction: you must **press the sacred crest against the sea chart** to transfer it. Wild!

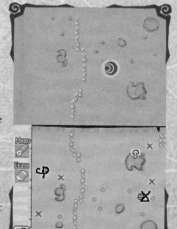

To solve this puzzle, begin by readying your Bombs. Wait for the gust geyser to stop blowing, then toss a Bomb onto it. When the geyser starts spewing once more, the Bomb is lifted upward and explodes in midair, blasting away the bomb blocks! Good work; now use the gust geyser to reach the ledge above, where you find a crystal orb. Light the orb to lower the spikes that block the northwest safe zone. Talk about a procedure!

Have you figured out what you need to do? Here's a hint: the portrait on the wall looks a lot like one quadrant of the Great Sea! While looking at the portrait, tap the Sea Chart button in the Touch Screen's lower-right corner. Then tap the chart's **southwest quadrant** for a closer view of that portion of the sea. Hey, look. The portrait matches this quadrant, but it's all upside down! That's a big clue: to transfer the **sacred crest** onto your sea chart, you must **close your DS**. No joke!

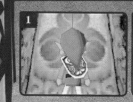   

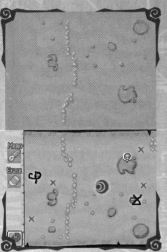

Open your DS again for a delightful surprise: the sacred crest has been pressed onto your sea chart! Amazing! The crest seems to be right in the middle of the sea, but there's just got to be something there for you to find. Let's return to Linebeck and see what he thinks! Step onto the shimmering blue light that appears in the room to quickly return to the temple's entrance. Now rush to speak with Linebeck at the harbor. Great work!

Lots to Do at Mercay Village

Whoa, Mercay Village is jumping! For starters, that peculiar Treasure Teller shop at the north end of town is finally open for business. Go inside to speak with the Treasure Teller himself, who gladly appraises all the **treasures** and **ship parts** you've accumulated thus far. If you're in need of cash, feel free to sell your excess goods for huge profits!

Each ship part and piece of treasure has its own value. Some of these collectibles are hard to find, and are therefore more valuable to the Treasure Teller than others. Simply tap any one to have the man appraise it for you, then decide if you wish to sell or not.

All treasures and ship parts fit into one of four different categories of rarity:

Rarity Values	
Rarity	**Value**
Common	50 Rupees
Uncommon	150 Rupees
Rare	800 Rupees
Super-Rare	1,500 Rupees

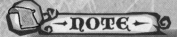
NOTE

Some ship parts, such as the ones that came stock with Linebeck's ship, are of no value to the Treasure Teller.

NOTE

To review the value of any ship part or treasure at any time, refer to the treasure and ship part checklists that appear near the end of this guide.

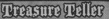
Treasure Teller

Hold fast your valuables! The Treasure Teller makes his living buying and trading collectible commodities, including all the various treasures and ship parts Link acquires during his travels. This makes the Treasure Teller a great guy to know when you need some fast cash. If you find you're carrying around multiple identical ship parts and treasures, feel free to pawn some to the Treasure Teller and fatten your wallet for future buys.

After visiting the Treasure Teller, travel south to see the town's postbox bouncin'. You've got mail! Approach the box to prompt a visit from your friendly neighborhood Postman, who's pleased to make another special delivery.

Landing with a huff, the Postman informs Link that this latest letter comes straight from Eddo at Cannon Island. Eddo writes to tell Link he's got big news—big, big news! It appears that the old inventor has finally finished his work on the salvage arm he'd started building right after Link purchased his well-crafted cannon. This is another crazy gadget for Linebeck's ship—one that enables the craft to haul up sunken treasure from the seafloor! Eddo says he'll sell his salvage arm to the first person to pay him a visit. Ready, set, sail!

There's no time to waste! You've already found a number of treasure maps leading to sunken goodies—now's the time to buy a **salvage arm** and start hauling up that loot! Dash for the dock and speak with the man in the green tunic for a tip on the use of the salvage arm. As if you needed any more prodding! That beauty is gonna be *yours*! You can also buy a treasure map from this man if you answer "yes" when he asks if you have the salvage arm.

As usual, Linebeck isn't far from his trusty ship. Hearing that Link and Ciela have discovered where to go next, the good captain is keen to go. Climb aboard Linebeck's ship and hurry to Cannon Island!

Task 3: Obtain the Salvage Arm & Sun Key

A Visit with the Master

Your course is clear: go directly to Cannon Island without delay! There's little to worry about on the short trip there, but be ready to blast anything that might poke up from the water. After you drop anchor, dash up those steps and barge right into Eddo's Garage!

Standing near the counter, Fuzo reaffirms that his master has indeed finished his work on his latest invention, the **salvage arm**. The door to Eddo's lab is wide open, so enter. Sure enough, Eddo is eagerly awaiting his first customer: you!

Shocked at seeing Link again, Eddo can't believe how such a young man could have the need (and the Rupees) for his expensive, top-of-the-line equipment. Even after Link **agrees that he's a real fan of Eddo's work**, Eddo still demands that he prove it by **shouting out** his desire for the salvage arm. Sheesh, what a character! Better do what he asks, though. **Shout as loud as you can** into the DS microphone!

→NOTE←

Remember: if you're in a quiet place, you can blow into the DS microphone and achieve a similar result.

Thrilled at hearing Link scream out his passion for ingenious gadgetry, Eddo decides to sell the boy his **salvage arm**. The price depends on how loud you've shouted! The louder you shout, the more excited Eddo gets, and the lower the cost. Feel free to back out of the deal if you think you can really impress old Eddo with a deafening roar!

→NOTE←

We were happy to shell out 200 Rupees for our salvage arm. How much did you spend? Don't worry if it was more; the vast amount of treasure you'll find with this device is worth any price!

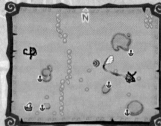

Salvage Arm

You got the **salvage arm**! Now you can pull up sunken treasure from the bottom of the sea! Tap the Menu tab while sailing on Linebeck's ship, then tap the Salvage icon to ready this awesome gadget. Let the hunt begin!

Obtaining the Sun Key

The salvage arm is yours! Now let's put this baby to work and start hauling up some *treasure*. First on your list of places to search is that strange crest you pressed onto your sea chart at the Temple of the Ocean King. Something must be hiding in the waters there! Set a course for the crest and be ready to defend your ship as you sail there.

When you arrive at your destination, tap the Menu tab at the screen's lower-left corner and then tap the Salvage icon to ready the salvage arm. Bingo! The salvage arm pops into place on the deck of your ship, and the hunt for treasure begins!

Using the Salvage Arm

Equipping the salvage arm draws you into a short and challenging minigame. You didn't think finding sunken treasure was going to be easy, did you? The goal here is to lower the arm toward the treasure chest on the seafloor while avoiding rocks and dangerous underwater creatures called Octomines. To dodge such threats, steer the arm using the **control bar** at the bottom of the screen. Tap the central **control box** with the stylus and then drag the box left or right to make the arm do the same. Drag the stylus up or down to increase or decrease the speed of the arm's descent. Though these controls seem simple, it takes a steady hand and sharp reflexes to master the fine art of underwater salvaging!

Task 3:
Obtain the Salvage Arm & Sun Key

TIP

Try to burst Rupee bubbles with the tip of the arm for a bit of extra cash, but don't put your arm at risk!

CAUTION

Make sure to tap and drag the **control box**! If you don't, you'll find steering the arm far more challenging.

The salvage arm's state of health is shown by a row of diamonds in the screen's upper-left corner. You start with five diamonds and must make each one count! Any sort of underwater collision removes one diamond from the arm's health meter. If all five diamonds are lost, the salvage arm becomes too damaged to be useful. You'll have to visit the Shipyard at Mercay Island and cough up some serious Rupees to get it fixed!

TIP

Don't focus on the salvage arm's chain. You only need to worry about keeping the red tip of the arm safe from underwater threats.

TIP

If you miss a valuable Rupee or see an unavoidable collision on the horizon, tap the Escape Arrow button at the screen's lower-left corner to quit the salvage op and try again.

The game's not over once you land the chest. You've still got to haul your prize back up to the surface! Fortunately, the arm faces the same hindrances on the way up as it did during the plunge down, so you know what to look out for.

CAUTION

Make sure to grab the chest with the salvage arm! If you miss and hit the ocean floor, you'll have to try again!

TIP

If your salvage arm takes damage but isn't completely broken, you can still repair it at Mercay Island's Shipyard. It's far more expensive to fix a broken salvage arm, so repair minor damage regularly to keep costs down!

Here are some important tips for successful salvaging:

- Take it slow! Moving too fast is the most common mistake made by rookie salvagers. Remember: this is a salvage operation, not a race!

- Look for openings! You may be faced with a tough group of obstacles that forces you to bob and weave the arm about. Always search for the safest route through.

- Keep away from the edges! Octomines commonly swim across the screen and some move quite fast. It's nearly impossible to avoid these volatile creatures if you don't give yourself time to react.

- Look closely at what's coming! Some obstacles blend in with the background, particularly Octomines you encounter at the ocean's darker depths. Be ready for anything down there.

- Watch those Octomines! Some of them are faster than others. Pay attention to how they move and learn to avoid them.

Catch! You've pulled your first treasure chest up from the seafloor! Inside rests the **Sun Key**, a vital item you need to open the door with the strange crest at Molida Island. If you're in a rush to get going, use the Cyclone Slate to warp over to Molida Island without delay.

Sun Key

You got the **Sun Key**! Now you can explore the north half of Molida Island!

Missing Links

High adventure awaits you at Molida Island, but that big hunk of rock isn't going anywhere. Why not take a short detour and put your new salvage arm to use? If you've been following our walkthrough carefully, you've already found eight treasure maps that point to six pieces of sunken treasure scattered about the Great Sea. And now that you've found the Sun Key, you can find a whole new map! Let's go hunting and track down that loot!

...continued

Treasure Map #9

First thing's first: there's another treasure map for you to claim back at Mercay Island! Drop anchor there and speak with the man in the green tunic at the pier, who hollers out to Link from afar. Now that you've gotten your  hands on a salvage arm, the man offers to sell you a **treasure map** for just 50 Rupees! Snap up that map to learn the location of another valuable sunken treasure chest.

Treasure Map #9
You got a **treasure map**! It reveals the location of a sunken treasure on the Great Sea.

Sunken Treasures 1-9

Now set sail for each of the sunken chests listed in the following table, which are marked on your sea chart by bold red Xs. For your convenience, the table also lists all the bonus Rupees you can try to obtain during these salvage efforts. You might not be able to claim them all, but try landing the big ones!

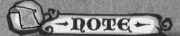

NOTE

Sunken Treasure #4 is currently unreachable. It lies in the as-yet unsailable waters to the east of Bannan Island! You won't be able to claim this sunken goodie for quite some time, but don't worry: we'll remind you about it when the time comes!

...continued

Sunken Treasure Chests

Number	Contents	Bonus Rupees	Location
1	Ship Part	Green (9)	SWQ; SW of Molida Island
2	Sand of Hours (1 minute)	Green (12); Red (1); Big Green (1)	SWQ; NE of Mercay Island
3	Ship Part	Green (12); Big Green (1)	NWQ; SW of Isle of Gust
4	Ship Part	Green (5); Red (1); Big Green (1)	SWQ; North of Molida Island
5	Treasure	Green (12); Big Green (1)	NWQ; West of Bannan Island
6	Ship Part	Green (5); Red (1)	NWQ; East of Isle of Gust
7	Ship Part	Green (21)	SWQ; SE of Mercay Island
8	Sand of Hours (1 minute)	Green (5); Red (1)	SWQ; West of Cannon Island

NOTE

Treasures and ship parts obtained through salvage operations have a higher chance of being rare compared to ones you find at stores or inside Overworld chests.

Molida Island Revisited

Items to Obtain

Wisdom Gem #6

Legend
 Overworld Chest #20: Wisdom Gem #6

Dungeon Denizens
Enemies

Giant Eye Plant | Miniblin | Crow

Red ChuChu | Yellow ChuChu | Zora Warrior

Task 3:
Obtain the Salvage Arm & Sun Key

Molida Island

to Temple of Courage

20

Romanos

Shop

Fortunately, the monster doesn't have many tricks up its sleeve. It simply spits out green, spiked projectiles from afar, usually in volleys of three. These projectiles are similar to cannonballs, and race through the air at high speed. Each spiked ball that strikes your vessel inflicts one heart's worth of damage, so be quick to blast these threats from the sky with your cannon. Stay defensive out there!

To damage this cretin, you must batter the large eye that sits atop its head with cannonballs. The monster's eye closes while it attacks however, so always be ready to blast its volleys from the sky. After avoiding a projectile barrage, be quick to return fire and smash its eye with a blast from your cannon. Strike the creature's eye five times to send it flailing into oblivion!

Linebeck congratulates you on a job well done, then pulls up to dock at Molida Island. Nice job!

Ambushed at Sea

Reaching Molida Island isn't as easy as you'd think. Dark clouds gather as the party nears the harbor, and a massive monster surfaces from the depths of the sea! This horrific creature must be defeated at all costs—there's no way to sneak past it. The fight won't be easy though, so get ready for a brawl!

Exploring Up North

Armed with the **Sun Key** you dredged up from the depths of the Great Sea, you're now able to open the sealed door within Molida Island's central cavern and explore the northern half of the isle. Remember how to get to that strange door? Take the secret passage through the Old Wayfarer's second hideaway! Dig **in front of the palm tree that's just north of the village's second hut** to access the Wayfarer's supersecret underground hideout, then drop inside.

Giant Eye Plant

Threat Meter

Speed: Immobile

Attack Power: 1 heart (spike ball)

Defense Power: Multiple hits to defeat!

Storm clouds gather and a massive monster erupts from the oceanic depths! This gigantic eyesore wants nothing more than to ruin your chances of reaching land. It must be battled via cannon at sea, and it's going not going down without a fight! The fiend's fast spiky projectile attacks can easily tear through a ship's hull and must be thwarted at all costs. Keep afloat by keeping in motion. Blast spiky balls from the sky as you look to put out the monster's eye!

NOTE

Pay a call on Romanos and his mom to hear some shocking news: Romanos has found his father's hideaways and now yearns to become a great explorer just like his old man!

Once inside the Wayfarer's underground hideout, go west and climb the nearby steps. This brings you back into the island's central cavern—watch out for Yellow ChuChus in the passage ahead! Make your way north toward the sealed door, which you may now open with a tap of the stylus. Bingo! The Sun Key works like a charm and the door opens. Bolt up the stairs beyond to head outside.

Take Linebeck's advice to heart: keep your ship sailin' throughout this battle. Otherwise, you're a sitting duck! The easiest way to keep your vessel mobile is by plotting out a semicirclular route back and forth around the monster. Overlap the route several times so that your ship stays in motion throughout the fight. This allows you to concentrate solely on combat!

You're now in the northern half of the island. Few have set foot here before! Resist the urge to rush off or you'll miss a digging spot in the grass nearby. You can just barely see it if you look carefully! Whip out the Shovel and dig there to uncover a hole leading back into the cavern. How strange!

Drop into the hole to land on a ledge you couldn't reach before. Hey, there's a treasure chest up here! Pop the lid on the chest for a great find: another **Wisdom Gem** for your collection! After pocketing the gem, drop off the ledge and dash up the north stairs to return outside.

Overworld Chest #20: Wisdom Gem #6

Wisdom Gem #6
You got a **Wisdom Gem**! Collect these items and use them to power up the Wisdom Spirit.

Be careful as you explore the north woods: a mean-spirited tribe of Miniblins makes its home here! Show the fiends no mercy as you fight your way northward. You eventually find a stone statue near the island's edge; whack it to learn that something valuable is buried under the tree near Oshus's storehouse back at Mercay Island!

NOTE

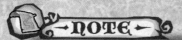
You can rush back to Mercay right now and retrieve the buried treasure, but there's no need to do so right now. We'll take you there in the next Missing Links section!

The path only becomes more dangerous beyond the stone statue. Yellow ChuChus pop up from the ground here and there, and nesting Crows dive bomb you from their treetop perches. Don't rush forward; take your time and deal with each threat in turn. The Crows are particularly nasty. Run away from them until they drop low enough for you to clobber with a well-timed spin attack!

Press on until you reach the northernmost tip of the island. There stands a massive temple! Unfortunately, the entry door is sealed off by a giant stone wall. There's got to be a way to get inside! Tap the nearby stone tablet to learn that **only statues can urge the temple door open**, and that you must **focus their light gaze upon it**.

Lighting the Way Forward

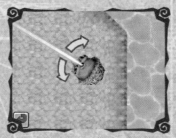

Continue past the temple, being wary of Crows nested in the surrounding trees. You soon come to a large tribal statue in the shape of a person's head. How strange! Whack the statue with Link's sword to cause a ray of blue light to shine out from the jewel in its forehead. Now *there's* something you don't see everyday!

Have you figured out what you need to do? Tap the tribal head statue a second time to make Link grab hold of it. Now you can turn the statue about! Drag the stylus to spin the statue, rotating it so its beam of light shines directly at the temple's sealed door. Good work!

TIP

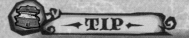
Use your map as a reference when lining up the statue's light beam.

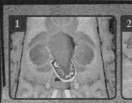

Task 4:
Enter and Clear the Temple of Courage

After rotating the statue, continue your exploration of the woods ahead. Upon reaching a wide clearing, Link is assaulted by *two* fearsome Zora Warriors! Yikes! As before, you must use the Boomerang to whack these monstrous enemies from behind, then quickly attack their backsides with fast sword combos while they're stunned. This is a difficult fight against two worthy foes, so try to single out one by luring it away from the other. Keep out of range until you manage to stun one of the monsters, then dash around behind it and unleash a furious barrage of sword strikes!

TIP

Try holding L or R to quickly ready the Boomerang during this frantic fight.

CAUTION

Be careful not to fall off the island's edge during this struggle!

The battle becomes much easier after you defeat one of the brutes. Continue to keep your distance from the remaining foe and toss the Boomerang from range. Dispatch both Zora Warriors to cause another tribal head statue to rise from the ground in the middle of the clearing. Wild!

TIP

The Zora Warriors won't chase you very far. If you're having trouble with this fight, backtrack into the woods and hurl the Boomerang from a safer vantage!

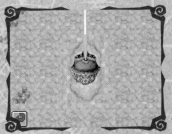

As before, whack the tribal head statue to activate its laser, then rotate the head so its light beam shines on the temple door to the north. Use your map as a reference while spinning the statue. Well done! Just one more statue to find!

The third statue is actually back near the temple itself. Return to the temple and cross the southern footbridge, then move west to the edge of the ledge. The final statue stands on the neighboring ledge to the south! You can't reach the statue with Link's sword, so hurl

the Boomerang at it to activate it instead. Whack! Luckily, the statue is already pointing right at the temple's door; no need to shift it!

Task 4: Enter & Clear the Temple of Courage

With all three tribal head statues shining their beams of light toward the temple, the sealed door slowly opens, granting Link access to the temple's mysterious halls. No point in hanging about! Hurry inside and begin the search for the third spirit fairy!

Temple of Courage

Temple of Courage: 1F

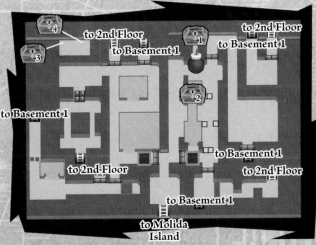

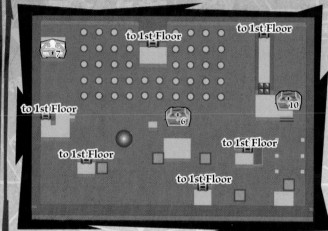

Temple of Courage: B1

to 1st Floor

to 1st Floor

7

to 1st Floor

to 1st Floor

6

to 1st Floor

10

to 1st Floor

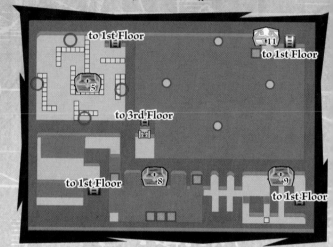

Temple of Courage: 2F

to 1st Floor

11

to 1st Floor

5

to 3rd Floor

to 1st Floor

8

9

to 1st Floor

Temple of Courage: 3F

12

to Boss Chamber

to 2nd Floor

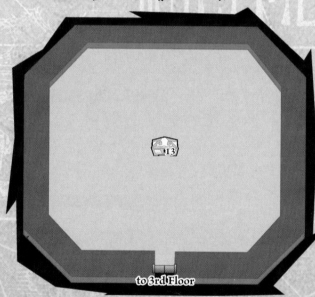

Temple of Courage: Boss Chamber

13

to 3rd Floor

Legend

Dungeon Chest #1: Treasure	Dungeon Chest #2: Small Key	Dungeon Chest #3: Power Gem #9
Dungeon Chest #4: Ship Part	Dungeon Chest #5: Square Crystal	
Dungeon Chest #6: Big Green Rupee	Dungeon Chest #7: Bow	Dungeon Chest #8: Power Gem #10
Dungeon Chest #9: Treasure	Dungeon Chest #10: Wisdom Gem #7	
Dungeon Chest #11: Boss Key	Dungeon Chest #12: Courage Gem #5	Dungeon Chest #13: Heart Container #6
Orb	Lever	

Task 4:
Enter and Clear the Temple of Courage

Items to Obtain

Boss Key | Courage Gem #5 | Heart Container #6 | Power Gem #9 | Power Gem #10

Random Ship Part | Small Key x3 | Square Crystal | Random Treasures x2 | Wisdom Gem #7

Dungeon Denizens

Enemies

Beamos | Green ChuChu | Green Slime | Moldorm | Pols Voice

Shell Beast | Winder | **Boss** Crayk, Bane of Courage

Temple of Courage: 1F

You've done well to make it this far, but have you the courage to conquer the challenges that lie in wait for you here? We're certain you do! If Link could use a bit of healing, smash the four pots in the temple's small entry chamber for up to four hearts before proceeding north and passing a pair of tall sealed doors.

Be careful when exploring the north hall: huge, spike-covered pins roll back and forth, ready to crush you like a grape! When the first pin rolls north, dash forward and take cover in the tiny alcove to the east. Wait for the pin to roll south again and then bolt past it, stopping short when you reach a patch of floor tiles. You're safe while standing on the tiles, so wait here until the next pin rolls away northward. Run right behind the second pin, ducking into the east side hall.

Again, pause on the floor tiles and wait for a third pin to roll eastward. Before chasing behind it, quickly toss a Bomb next to the north wall. The Bomb blasts open a secret passage, granting you access to a hidden chest! Run to open the chest and claim a random **treasure** from within.

CAUTION

Don't toss the Bomb while the spike pin is rolling toward you or it might shove the explosive right into your lap!

Dungeon Chest #1: Treasure

Treasure

You got a **treasure**! Collect these items *Random* and sell them to the highest bidder!

After claiming your treasure, carefully return to the floor tiles in the outside hall while the spike pin is in the east. Wait for the spike pin to return and then roll eastward away from you, then quickly chase after it, ducking into the south passage to finally escape this dangerous area. Temple of courage, indeed!

Be wary when traveling south: a new brand of trap awaits! Stepping in front of this bladed device causes it to fly toward you at high speed, inflicting half a heart's worth of damage if you're struck. The blade trap then retracts to its original position—and it's right in your way! To get past this sentry, you must dash in front of it, tricking the blade trap to fly northward. While it's out of position, quickly circle around behind it and run south before the trap resets itself.

CAUTION

Once reset, the blade trap is also capable of flying southward at you if you draw near. Hurry onward before that nasty trap comes sailing your way!

Whew! Fortunately, you won't have to go that route again. Proceed to the stairs beyond the blade trap and step on a nearby pressure switch to lower the sealed door to the west. Now you can quickly return to the temple's entrance! If you left any pots at the entry chamber and need to heal, head over there and smash the pots for hearts. Afterward, climb the nearby stairs to discover a treasure chest that holds a **small key**!

**Dungeon Chest #2:
Small Key**

Small Key
You got a **small key**! Use it to open a door in this dungeon.

Now you can open a locked door to the north. Leap off the east edge of this upper walkway and then dash to the east wall to quickly escape the blade trap. When it's safe to do so, bolt north and then open the locked door beyond the rolling spike pin. Smack the stone statue in the hallway beyond if you'd like to pay Rupees to learn how to find the two remaining chests on this floor. This isn't required, of course; we'll guide you to every chest in this dungeon!

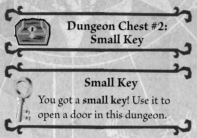

Look out! Link becomes trapped in the large chamber south of the statue and must face off against two of the most dangerous enemies he's yet encountered. These centipede-like beasts are called Moldorms, and they deserve your utmost respect. Their armored heads and hides provide great protection against Link's blade, so target their pink tails instead! Lure one Moldorm away from the other, then run circles around it, keeping well clear of its pincers. Whack each beast's tail three times to defeat it and pass this test of courage!

TIP

As always, when faced with two or more tough enemies, it's best to single one of them out. This fight becomes much easier as soon as you defeat one of the Moldorms!

Moldorm

Threat Meter

Speed: Normal
Attack Power: 1/2 heart (contact)
Defense Power: 3 hits to defeat

Watch out when combating these creepy crawlers! Although slow, Moldorms are relentless and tough to handle in groups. Link's greatest advantage against them is his superior speed and mobility. The young hero must outmaneuver Moldorms so he can stick them where it hurts: their soft, pink tails! It takes three regular sword strikes to a Moldorm's tail to dispatch the monsters, so be prepared for a tactical battle. Keep away from their pincers and run circles around these dangerous foes, and hack at their vulnerable tails at every chance!

Temple of Courage: B1

After you eliminate the Moldorm threat, descend the south stairs to reach the temple's basement. Looks like this place is undergoing repairs! A look at the map shows that most of the floor is missing, leaving just tiny fragments of footing for you to navigate. Fortunately, a network of moving platforms allows you to traverse this otherwise impassible floor. Smash the nearby pots, then step onto the moving platform when it approaches from the west.

TIP

The moving platforms are shown on your map as well. Watch them to learn how to move about this basement.

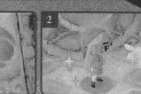

Task 4:
Enter and Clear the Temple of Courage

Heads up! A new breed of monster awaits you on the next bit of floor. Fortunately, this little guy isn't nearly as challenging as those creepy Moldorms. This is a Shell Beast and it's a tough nut to crack! In fact, Link's sword has almost no effect on this monster—except to bump it backward. Say, that'll do just fine! Whack the creature a few times until you knock it into the surrounding abyss. Bye-bye, little guy!

Shell Beast

Threat Meter

Speed: Slow

Attack Power: 1/2 heart (contact)

Defense Power: Invincible

For these guys, slow and steady wins the fight! Though incapable of moving very quickly, Shell Beasts pursue their prey with steady determination. They damage Link if they manage to touch him, so keep these creatures at bay! Although well shielded by their thick, natural armor, Shell Beasts can be knocked about by Link's stiff sword attacks. Beat these beasts backward and try to knock them off ledges and the like—they weren't built to take a fall!

Step onto the next moving platform to continue traveling westward. You soon pass near a platform to the north, which features a glowing red crystal orb. Whack the orb with the Boomerang to change its color to blue. This lowers some red blocks you'll soon encounter. Step onto the next moving platform when its path crosses yours and ride along to a set of stairs to the west. Climb up to return to the temple's first floor.

Temple of Courage: 1F Revisited

Beware! The square-shaped network of hallways that lies beyond the stairs is filled with Green Slimes of all sizes, along with a dangerous new adversary: a Winder! You've faced Green Slimes before and know how treacherous they can be. Expect them to split when hit, spawning smaller slimes that try and latch onto Link, holding him in place so the Winder can snake by and shock him for heavy damage. It's best to remain near the stairs and let the surrounding Green Slimes come to you, splattering each one with fast spin attacks. The Winder should simply bounce along the corridors, oblivious to your presence. Let it pass, then follow along behind it, dispatching Green Slimes as you go.

CAUTION

Don't strike the Winder! Their electrical current races up Link's blade and zaps Link for damage, just like Yellow ChuChus.

Winder

Threat Meter

Speed: Slow

Attack Power: 1/2 heart (contact)

Defense Power: Invincible

Always steer clear of Winders! These electrically charged baddies snake through halls and corridors, bouncing ever onward to zap anything in their path. A Winder's current is always active, and it races up Link's sword if he tries to attack them. It's best simply to avoid these shockingly dangerous foes!

The red blocks to the north should be lowered to the ground so you can escape the Winder. Aren't you glad you activated that crystal orb in the basement? Smash the pots in the room beyond for Bombs and a heart, then read the two stone tablets against the north wall. One tablet hints at how to weaken an enemy you've yet to encounter. The other gives you a vital clue about how to solve this temple's puzzles: remember the order of **up, down, right, then left**. You'll soon discover why these clues are so important! For now, plant a Bomb right between the tablets. This blasts a hole in the north wall; then enter a very special chamber.

This room's loaded with goodies! Smash both pots for more Bombs, then open the two chests near the north wall for a random **ship part** and a **Power Gem**. What a haul!

Dungeon Chest #3:
Power Gem #9

Power Gem #9

You got a **Power Gem**! Collect these items and use them to power up the Power Spirit.

Dungeon Chest #4: Ship Part

Ship Part

You got a **ship part**! Visit the Shipyard to install it onto Linebeck's ship.

Random

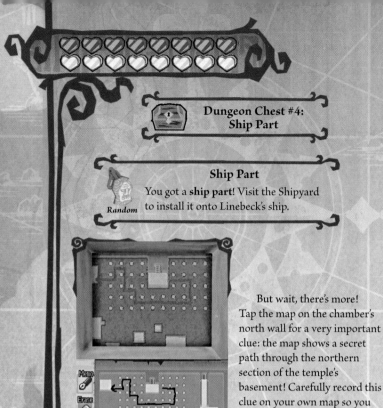

But wait, there's more! Tap the map on the chamber's north wall for a very important clue: the map shows a secret path through the northern section of the temple's basement! Carefully record this clue on your own map so you can reference it later.

Time to move on! Heave a Bomb at the bomb blocks to the west to blast them out of your way, then prepare to battle a new type of ChuChu. This Green ChuChu likes to shrink into a small puddle and then creep along the floor, inching toward its quarry. You can't harm it while it's in its puddle form, so keep a distance and wait for it to pop back up. Then be quick to tap it for a fast targeted attack!

Green ChuChu

Threat Meter

Speed: Slow

Attack Power: 1/2 heart (contact)

Defense Power: 1 hit to defeat

These guys come in green, too? Wild! Whatever you do, don't take Green ChuChus lightly: they can make themselves invincible by shrinking into tiny puddles! None of Link's attacks affect a puddled Green ChuChu, so it's best to keep away and wait for it to reform once more. The moment you see the ChuChu return to its normal shape, tap it to unleash a fast targeted attack. Splat!

The next wide chamber beyond features two raised platforms. Several Green ChuChus guard the lower area; make mincemeat out of each one as you move to climb up the northernmost platform's steps. There you find an odd, square-shaped floor switch and a stone tablet. The tablet says that crystals can only fit onto **same-shaped pedestals**. Surely this will make sense soon!

Go to the southern platform, dispatching Green ChuChus that spring up to attack you on the way. Look out: this platform is home to a new, giant enemy, a Pols Voice! This massive, bloblike head seems quite formidable, but there's a sneaky way to weaken it. Notice its gigantic ears? While these help the Pols Voice hunt down its prey, they're also its greatest weakness: **shout into the DS microphone** to bombard this bouncy beast with a sonic blast!

TIP

If you're in a quiet place, remember that you can simply **blow** into the DS microphone to defeat the Pols Voice without having to raise your own.

Pols Voice

Threat Meter

Speed: Normal

Attack Power: 1 (contact)

Defense Power: 1 good scream to weaken; 1 hit to defeat

These big-eared baddies appeared in the very first *Legend of Zelda* game way on the original NES. Arrows were the key to dispatching Pols Voices in those days, but Link finds loud noises work even better against them here in *Phantom Hourglass*! When faced with one of these long-eared foes, simply holler into your DS microphone. This sonic assault forces the Pols Voice to shrink into a tiny ball! Follow up with a fast sword attack to finish the creature off in style. Make sure to deal with Pols Voices quickly; they hop about with surprising speed, yearning to crush Link under their incredible bulk!

After weakening the Pols Voice with a shout, quickly administer a sword attack to deal the final blow. Wiping out the monster earns you a vital prize: a **small key**! Collect the key, then step onto a nearby pressure plate to open another sealed door leading back to the temple's entrance. How convenient! Again, feel free to return to the entry chamber and smash those pots for hearts. When you're ready to move on, backtrack north and open a locked door in the north wall to access some stairs leading upward.

Temple of Courage: 2F

The stairs lead up to the northwest corner of the temple's second floor. Watch your step up here: you face a dangerous maze patrolled by a pair of zap-happy Winders! A number of laser-emitting Beamos statues also present significant threats to Link's health: if their rotating eyes catch a glimpse of him, they're quick to start firing away. It's tough getting through here without losing health, but you must navigate the maze: four separate levers need pulling here!

TIP

If Link suffers grave injury, simply retreat to the first floor and then quickly return upstairs to reenter the maze. This causes the pots near the stairs to reappear, both of which contain hearts! Repeat this until you've filled up Link's heart meter, then take another crack at solving the lever maze.

Beamos

Threat Meter

Speed: Immobile

Attack Power: 1/2 heart (laser)

Defense Power: Invincible

These immobile stone sentries are something to be feared! A Beamos's only moving part is its laser eye, which rotates 360 degrees around the top of the statue, scanning the vicinity for intruders. When a threat is identified, a Beamos quickly fires a powerful laser from its eye, carving a line into the floor—and into anything caught standing in its path! Steer clear of Beamoses you see, moving past them when their scary eyeballs aren't watching. Don't linger if you're about to be spotted: quickly run away to safety!

Remember what that stone tablet told you back on the first floor? **Up, down, right, and left.** This is the secret to solving this deadly maze! Four levers must be pulled in that exact order. Do your best to keep away from the Winders, and keep out of the Beamoses' sight as you move to pull the north, south, east, and west levers in turn.

TIP

The Winders keep near the walls, so move to open ground to avoid them. Watch the Beamoses' eyes carefully and keep out of sight. Dash past the sentries when their eyes aren't watching.

Yank all four levers in the proper order to reveal a hidden chest in the center of the maze. Go to it and flip the chest's lid to claim an important item: a **square crystal**! This must be the item you need to place in the pedestal you noticed just moments ago!

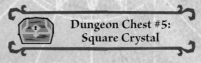
Dungeon Chest #5: Square Crystal

Square Crystal
You've found the **square crystal**! Take it to the same-shaped pedestal.

The square crystal must be carried overhead just like a Boss Key. Carefully transport the crystal downstairs and place it onto the pedestal that stands atop the nearby raised platform. Bingo! The crystal slides perfectly into place, and a sealed door slides away to the north. This grants you access to another set of stairs leading down into the temple's basement. Nice work!

TIP

If danger rears its ugly head, you can set the square crystal down or toss it away just like a Boss Key.

Temple of Courage: B1 Revisited

Downstairs, you arrive at the basement's northern platform. Smash the surrounding parts for hearts and other goodies, but be wary: another Shell Beast is lumbering your way from the east! Hey, how's it walking across the abyss like that? No matter! Move to the north wall and attack the monster until you knock it off the south or west sides of the platform. See ya!

Whack the nearby stone statue for a clue about how to proceed: an **invisible path** winds through the surrounding chasm! So *that's* how the Shell Beast was able to cross over here! Check your map to see the route you traced before when you discovered that wall map on the first floor. This is the path you must follow!

If you didn't copy down the wall map clue before, return upstairs and visit the first floor's far northwest chamber by Bombing it open.

Take a deep breath, count to three, then step off the east side of the platform. Holy smoke! You're walking on thin air! At least that's how it looks; you're really moving across an invisible pathway. Carefully follow the route you traced on you map, using the surrounding pillars as landmarks to guide you. The path is narrow, so stay right between the pillars as you go. You may take a few falls, but you'll get to the northwest platform eventually!

You encounter another Shell Beast along the invisible path. Stand your ground and smack it when it draws near to send it tumbling off the trail!

The pots on the northern platform often produce hearts when smashed. If the going has been rough, keep moving upstairs and then back down to respawn the pots, smashing them each time to refill Link's heart meter.

About halfway through the trek across the invisible pathway, you can take a secret detour to reach one of this basement's treasure chests! After you loop around from the starting ledge and begin heading westward, move south toward a tiny ledge that's directly south of the ledge you started from. Open the chest here to claim a **big green Rupee**!

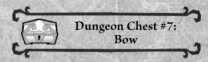

**Dungeon Chest #6:
Big Green Rupee**

Big Green Rupee

You got a **big green Rupee**! It's worth 100 Rupees!

Made it! Reaching the northwest platform, you see that your efforts have not been in vain: a huge treasure chest is over here! Open this chest to claim a new and extremely cool item: the **Bow**, which comes stocked with 20 arrows. Fantastic!

**Dungeon Chest #7:
Bow**

Bow

You got the **Bow**! Now you can fire arrows at distant enemies and objects. Ready the Bow as you would Bombs or the Boomerang, then tap anywhere on the Touch Screen to fire an arrow in that direction. Tap and drag to aim your shot! Use your arrows wisely; you can only hold 20 at a time.

Prima Official Game Guide

156

Task 4:
Enter and Clear the Temple of Courage

Ignore the stone statue near the chest; it just wants you to cough up Rupees to learn the locations of the floor's two remaining treasure chests. We'll show you where those lie, so save your cash for later. Instead, equip the Bow and take aim at the creepy eye crest that sticks out from the north wall. Strike the eyeball with an arrow to change its color from blue to red. This causes a footbridge to extend southward, bridging the gap to a nearby platform!

Cross the footbridge carefully and stop short as you near the end. Another one of those dangerous Moldorms crawls about on the tiny platform ahead! Battling the Moldorm in such a small space is risky, so why not put your new Bow to good use? Fire at the Moldorm's pink tail from range, striking it twice to defeat the beast with ease.

> **→ TIP ←**
>
> The Bow inflicts significant damage from range. When you've got a good supply of arrows, use the Bow to keep away from enemies as you pierce them from afar.

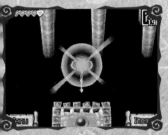

Smash some nearby pots for arrows. Before you ascend the nearby stairs, examine the strange object at the platform's west edge. This device is called an arrow orb, and it'll send your Bow's projectiles flying much farther than normal! Whack the orb three times to spin it so that its head is facing west, then ready your Bow and fire an arrow into its tail. Voilà! The arrow flies westward, strikes another arrow orb, then zips south to strike the floor's central crystal orb, changing it from blue back to red. Now go upstairs to continue your exploration of this bizarre temple.

Temple of Courage: 1F Third Visit

You arrive at the first floor's southwest corner. Be wary: two more Moldorms crawl about up here! Dash past them and up some nearby steps to reach a raised platform, where the Moldorm's can't reach you. Then simply pick them off with your Bow from here! After dispatching the Moldorms, read the platform's stone tablet to learn that you must retrieve the square crystal you found earlier and bring it to this spot, where another square pedestal sits. Oh, bother!

Fortunately, you don't have to return to the basement and take the long way around to get that crystal. Instead, go east down the hall, slashing apart an attacking Green ChuChu. Two sealed doors stand at the hall's far end, and there's a pit to the east. Across the pit lies another eye crest! Fire an arrow into the eye to lower one of the two nearby doors. Proceed north to the chamber where the square crystal lies. Watch out for Green ChuChus up there!

Move to the northern raised platform and tap the square crystal to remove it from the pedestal. This causes the north door to rise once more, but that's OK: you're all done exploring that portion of the basement anyway! Carry the crystal to the floor's southwest corner and place it onto the square pedestal you found just moments ago. Voilà! The other sealed door at the hall's east end slides away to reveal some stairs leading upward.

Temple of Courage: 2F Revisited

Now, you're back on the second floor. The chamber to the west is filled with danger, so look out! A hoard of Octoroks have made their den here and they're milling about and firing high-speed rocks from their snouts. This wouldn't be so bad if there weren't three others across the south gap, who regularly fire rocks northward! It's easy to become caught by the south Octoroks' crossfire, so don't go dashing into the fray. Keep a distance and pick off as many Octoroks as you can with your Bow. Just one arrow bests each beast!

> **→ TIP ←**
>
> This is a frantic battle, so it's best to use L or R to quickly ready the Bow. Then simply tap each Octorok to pelt it from afar!

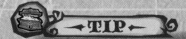

> **→ TIP ←**
>
> Remember that Link automatically blocks these beasts' rocks with his shield! He won't block if his Bow is drawn however, so release the trigger buttons to lower it whenever you need to defend.

Eradicate all Octoroks—including the three across the south pit—to cause a bridge to extend eastward across the north gap. Cross over to find a chest-revealing stone statue and a few pots. Smash those pots to restock your supply of arrows and then wait near the gap at the far end of the hall for a moving platform to drift your way.

Step onto the moving platform and ride it southward to a tiny ledge. Watch out: a pesky Keese flutters about over here! Pick it off with an arrow or the Boomerang before moving onto the ledge, then ride eastward on a second moving platform. Pause on this platform and aim at the north wall, firing on a distant eye crest to change it from blue to red.

TIP

Remember, when combating foes with the Boomerang or Bow, it's easiest to hold L or R, then simply tap the enemy for a fast ranged attack! Simply release the trigger to quickly return to a defensive state.

Ready the Boomerang and then cross over to the next moving platform when it drifts near. This platform moves north and south. Hurl the Boomerang to dispatch another Keese that flaps about the tiny north ledge. Don't disembark onto the ledge; instead, step onto yet another moving platform to the east, again using the Boomerang to eliminate another nearby Keese. Beating these Keese is important—they can easily drive you batty!

Spy another eye crest on this section of the north wall. Launch an arrow at this second eyeball to redden it as you did the one before. When both eye crests are activated, a small chest pops into existence on the north ledge you passed by a moment ago. Return to the ledge and claim your tenth **Power Gem** from the chest!

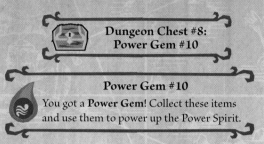

Dungeon Chest #8:
Power Gem #10

Power Gem #10

You got a **Power Gem**! Collect these items and use them to power up the Power Spirit.

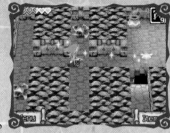

Excellent work! Now carefully navigate the floating platforms, making your way to the east corridors. Be very careful when passing through here: two active blade traps cruise by at high speed, ready to slice you into tiny portions of hero. Don't let those traps do their work! Wait for the first one to speed past and then bolt across, stopping right in front of the next trap ahead. Again, wait for the second blade trap to zip by before dashing past.

Watch out: a Beamos stands guard in the tiny chamber just beyond the blade traps! It's tough finding a safe place to stand in the Beamos's chamber, so your best bet is simply to run circles around the sentry statue, keeping away from its scary laser eye. If you're low on Bombs, smash the two pots against the north wall to claim some, then leap across the small southwest pit to reach the south hall.

A bomb block plugs up the south hall and prevents you from moving onward. However, it's also preventing an active blade trap from zipping down the hall and making mincemeat out of you! To survive this scenario without taking a scratch, plant a Bomb near the bomb block, then retreat into the side hall near the gap you've just leaped across. The bomb block is destroyed and the blade trap beings zipping along the full length of the hall.

Now return to the Beamos's chamber. Wait near the gap until the statue's eye passes you by, then leap over to revisit the room. Quickly dash eastward and then leap across another gap, landing right in front of a movable stone block. Tap the bock to grab it and then shove it southward when the blade trap is in the east. The stone block plugs up the south corridor, again preventing the blade trap from reaching the west side!

Task 4:
Enter and Clear the Temple of Courage

TIP

Remember: you can use items such as the Bow and Boomerang to pan your view of the environment and see farther in all directions. Do this if you're having trouble spying on the Beamos statue.

When it's safe to do so, leap back into the Beamos chamber and dash westward, then leap across the other gap to return to the west end of the south hall. Talk about getting the runaround! Fortunately, the rest of this scenario is simple: just shove that stone block eastward, slowly cornering the blade trap into the east alcove. Take that, you dirty trap! Dash up the hall that stretches north to locate three pots and a small chest. Raid everything for hearts, arrows, and another random **treasure** for your collection! Proceed down the nearby stairs afterward to return to the temple's first floor.

Dungeon Chest #9:
Treasure

Treasure

Random — You got a **treasure**! Collect these items and sell them to the highest bidder!

Temple of Courage: 1F, Fourth Visit

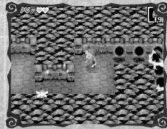

Although this is a short trip through the first floor's southeast corner, it still features its share of dangers! Two frightening Winders creep along the narrow corridors here. They're capable of draining away some of Link's health. Avoid them as best you can while making your way westward. Leap across a narrow gap to finally escape the Winders.

Stairs leading downward sit just across the gap. Before you bolt downstairs, step on a nearby pressure switch to lower the north sealed door. This creates yet another fast path to the temple's entrance! If the Winders taxed Link's health, streak to the entry chamber and break the pots there for hearts. Now, return to the stairs and descend to the basement one last time.

Temple of Courage: B1 Third Visit

Are you getting dizzy yet? All these stairs are enough to confuse anyone! You're nearly finished with this dreadful place though, so don't lose heart! Step onto a moving platform when it slides nearby and ride it eastward toward the basement's southeast corner ledge.

Another moving platform carries you north from the corner ledge, but a collection of raised spikes prevents you from setting foot on the next ledge ahead. Well, that's not very nice! The secret to lowering these spikes lies all around you: the cold torches! Only one of the six torches is burning, and you must spread its flame to the other five. While riding along the moving platform, use the Boomerang to target each torch in turn, starting with the burning one to the south. Light all six torches with the Boomerang to lower the spikes and reach the north ledge!

A lumbering Shell Beast awaits you on this final ledge, so be quick to knock it out of your hair! Well done, but now you've got to get rid of those tall red blocks to the north. Equip the Boomerang and hurl it at the arrow orb to the west. Whack the orb twice with the Boomerang to spin it westward, then fire an arrow into its tail. The arrow zips along, eventually striking the crystal orb in the center of the floor! This changes the orb's color from red to blue and lowers the red blocks to the north so you can proceed up the stairs beyond.

Don't dash up those stairs just yet; you're right near a hidden treasure chest that you don't want to miss! After lowering the red blocks, smack that arrow orb once more with the Boomerang so that it faces north. Then hit it with an arrow to activate a hidden eye crest up north! This makes a chest appear on your ledge; open it up to claim another glowing **Wisdom Gem**!

Dungeon Chest #10:
Wisdom Gem #7

Wisdom Gem #7

You got a **Wisdom Gem**! Collect these items and use them to power up the Wisdom Spirit.

Temple of Courage: 1F, Fifth Visit

Are you ready to rumble? Another evil Pols Voice awaits you in the small chamber upstairs! Waste no time: yell (or blow) into your DS microphone to assault the creature with a sonic blast. After the Pols Voice has curled up, quickly unleash a fast sword attack to finish it off. Great job! Grab the **small key** the monster was guarding and use it to open the nearby door so you may continue upward to the temple's second floor.

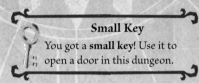

Small Key
You got a **small key**! Use it to open a door in this dungeon.

Temple of Courage: 2F Third Visit

Only one final chamber needs solving, but boy, it's a big one! Break the pots at the foot of the stairs for hearts and arrows, then smack the nearby stone statue for a hot tip: you must control the moving platform in this chamber by drawing its flight path on your map! Step onto the platform, then call up your map. Draw a curvy line so you may explore the vast chamber to see what's about.

→ NOTE ←

You may need to step off the moving block and then step back on again to get it started. Sometimes the thing's got a mind of its own!

A bit of exploration reveals four tall pillars that stretch up from the surrounding chasm: one in each direction. Each of these four pillars features an eye crest that must be shot with the Bow. However, there's a specific order in which the eye crests must be activated. Do you recall the clue? **Up, down, right, and left** is what a stone tablet once told you. Draw a line on your map so that you visit the pillars in that order (north, south, east, then west), activating each one in turn with a shot from Link's Bow.

Great work! Solving this chamber's riddle reveals a giant treasure chest back at the northeast ledge. Return to that ledge and open the chest to claim this dungeon's **Boss Key**! Now you're home free!

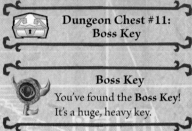

Dungeon Chest #11: Boss Key

Boss Key
You've found the **Boss Key**! It's a huge, heavy key.

Carry the Boss Key onto the moving platform and then trace a line on your map that runs directly over to the chamber's southwest ledge. Ride over to that ledge, where the Boss Key block awaits. The stone tablet near the block hints at how to solve the chamber's puzzle and obtain the Boss Key, but you've already figured it out! Hurl the Boss Key into the block to remove the obstacle, then go up the staircase beyond.

Temple of Courage: 3F

You've finally solved this puzzling temple and are on the cusp of facing off against its ruling boss! Tap the nearby stone tablet to trigger the appearance of a pool of blue light that can warp you back to the temple's entrance. No need to leave just yet, of course: you have unfinished business here! Smash the surrounding pots for a variety of useful items.

Don't rush up those stairs just yet! Instead, circle around behind them and plant a Bomb against the north wall. Kaboom! The blast blows a hole through the wall to a hidden treasure chest! Open the chest to add a shiny new **Courage Gem** to your collection. Very nice! Now move up those steps and get on with your boss fightin'!

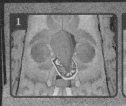   

Task 4:
Enter and Clear the Temple of Courage

Dungeon Chest #12:
Courage Gem #5

Courage Gem #5

You got a **Courage Gem**! Collect these items and use them to power up the Courage Spirit.

Crayk, Bane of Courage

Threat Meter

Speed: Normal

Attack Power: 1/4 heart per second (grab and shake); 1/2 heart (contact); 1/2 heart (Craykling)

Defense Power: Multiple hits to defeat!

Upon reaching the temple's apex, Link becomes trapped in a wide, circular chamber. Inside awaits a hideous, crablike monstrosity! This vile creature puts Link's courage and resolve to the ultimate test, so prepare for the worst!

Seeing the young intruder enter its lair, Crayk suddenly vanishes in a puff of smoke. Hey, what gives? Look at the top DS screen to see the monster closing in on Link. You're witnessing the fight through Crayk's beady eyes!

Crayk's main method of attack involves snatching Link up in its powerful claws and then shaking the daylights out of him. Link loses a quarter heart for every one or two seconds he's shaken, so you must free him fast! Whenever Crayk grabs hold of Link, quickly rub the stylus back and forth across the screen. The faster you rub, the faster Link manages to wiggle free!

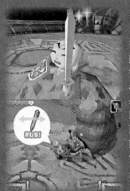

CAUTION

Crayk can also toss Link backward for half a heart's damage, and Link suffers this same amount of damage if he accidentally runs into the monster. Keep away from this fearsome beast!

During this first phase of the battle, your goal is simply to strike Crayk with an arrow from Link's Bow. A successful hit forces the monster to reveal itself once more! Begin by circling around the arena, running far away from the creature. Glance at the upper screen to gauge Crayk's relative position. When the monster seems distant, turn around and then fire arrows at it as it closes in. This is somewhat awkward at first, but you'll get the hang of it!

Just keep launching arrows, glancing at the top screen as you aim arrows straight into the fiend's eyes.

TIP

Break the pots scattered about the walls for hearts and arrows, but don't waste them!

Striking Crayk in the face with an arrow forces it to reappear. The monster then tucks into its shell and begins turning in place. Rush forward and unleash a barrage of sword strikes on the creature, inflicting steady damage to its outer shell. Keep punishing Crayk's shell with Link's sword until it finally shatters apart!

CAUTION

Watch out for little Crayklings that skitter about the arena. These little baddies pursue Link on sight and can inflict up to half a heart of contact damage if they manage to strike him! Dispatch each one you see with a few sword strikes. They occasionally drop hearts and arrows for you to use!

Continued on next page!

Crayk, Bane of Courage (Cont.)

After you've managed to remove Crayk's outer shell, the fight becomes far more straightforward. The beast is no longer able to turn itself invisible and must stalk after Link in its birthday suit. How revolting! Attack the monster's face with a barrage of sword attacks, then quickly circle around behind while it covers up. Batter its bright blue tail with more sword attacks to inflict serious damage!

TIP

If you're having trouble getting Crayk to cover up, try shooting it with an arrow. This usually stuns the creature for several seconds, allowing you to land several blows on its vulnerable tail.

Keep up the pressure on Crayk, punishing its tail at every opportunity. Just keep slashing away until the beast finally collapses. If your situation becomes grim, use Link's superior speed to run away from Crayk and seek out pots and Crayklings to batter for needed hearts and arrows. Defeat this terrible monster to pass Link's final test of courage!

Delivering a powerful blow to Crayk's wounded hide, Link is finally victorious over the dreadful fiend. The test of courage has been passed! Crayk explodes into a cloud of sand, which quickly streaks into the Phantom Hourglass. Two more minutes' worth of sand have been added to the ancient timepiece!

*The seal on the chamber floor soon begins to glow a soft green, and out flies a fairy! Spreading its wings, Link and Ciela are surprised to find the fairy bears a striking resemblance to Ciela herself! How peculiar. The fairy says nothing and simply flutters into Link's hands. The **Spirit of Courage** has been rescued at last!*

Hearts for the Brave

Outstanding performance! You've bested a very challenging adversary and have earned the right to call yourself a true hero. Open the large chest that shimmers into existence in the center of the room for another precious **Heart Container**! Excellent! Now hurry back to Linebeck's ship and let's hunt down that Ghost Ship!

Dungeon Chest #13: Heart Container #6

Heart Container #6

You got a **Heart Container**! Your heart meter has been increased by one heart!

A Reunion with Friends

*Returning to the dock, Link and Ciela are met with a pleasant surprise: Oshus has paid them a visit! The old man must have something very important to tell them to come all this way—it's a dangerous voyage here from Mercay Island! Indeed he does: Oshus tells Ciela that she's no ordinary fairy. In fact, she's really a **spirit**!*

Stunned, Ciela finds this news hard to believe. She doesn't even have any powers! Oshus consoles her, saying he knows it's hard to accept such news without being able to recall her past. However, the old man tells Ciela that the time has come for her to return to her true form. Turning to Link, he asks the boy to release the fairy he found within the Temple of Courage.

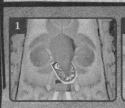 1
 2
 3
 4

Task 4: Enter and Clear the Temple of Courage

The fairy flutters toward Ciela, and the two begin an intoxicating dance, spiraling higher and higher into the sky. Powerful magic begins crackling all about, and with a blinding flash, the two fairies merge into one! Ciela's true form has finally been revealed: she's the **Spirit of Courage!**

Laughing with delight, Ciela is thrilled to at last be her old self again. She feels alive! Leaf and Neri float to Ciela; they're overjoyed at being reunited once more. After their brief reunion, the spirit fairies get right down to business: focusing their energy together, they catch a brief message from Tetra!

"Link… help me!"

Oshus informs Ciela that one of her gifts is the ability to sense evil. And there's great evil coming from that awful Ghost Ship! Ciela rushes over to Link, urging him to hurry and rescue his friend. There isn't a moment to lose! The three spirit fairies flutter about Link, assuring him that they'll help him track down the Ghost Ship. It's now clear that Tetra's fate hangs in the balance!

Eager to get moving, Link and the fairies dash aboard Linebeck's ship. Before joining his crew, the salty old captain turns toward Oshus, amazed at the secrets the old man has kept all this time. Asking Oshus who he is and how he knows so much, Linebeck's question is met with more mystery: the old man isn't quite ready to reveal such personal secrets just yet!

A Slightly Less Pleasant Reunion

The time has finally come to set after that accursed Ghost Ship! But where could it be? In a rare stroke of genius, Linebeck comes up with a bright idea: why not head into the fog up north, where the Ghost Ship escaped to before? Sounds like a plan! Set course for the northern fog!

Unfortunately, the party doesn't get very far. Linebeck suddenly gets an awful chill down his spine, then spots a vessel on the horizon. Is it… the Ghost Ship? No! It's a battleship belonging to someone Linebeck calls **Jolene**!

Shouting at Linebeck from her vessel, Jolene seems thrilled that she's found the old captain at last. Say, what's going on here? Before anyone can react, the Jolene fires a torpedo toward Linebeck's ship, which narrowly misses its mark. Yikes!

Totally freaking out, Linebeck tells Link that this woman is crazy. Crazier than a rabid squid! He hints that the two knew each other when they were kids, but says no more on the matter. There are more pressing priorities at hand—like getting out of here! Linebeck tells Link to **always run from Jolene**, saying she'll attack their ship with torpedoes that must be dodged by jumping. Sounds like you've got a new threat to worry about at sea!

Prepare to Be Boarded!

Jolene's right on top of your ship, and there's little hope for escape! The irate woman steams forward at a full clip, launching torpedoes in an effort to slow you down. Jolene's got the drop on you here, so you're better off just letting her sail up and board your ship. Just make sure you're prepared for a brawl!

NOTE

If you're quick on the draw, you might be able to whip out the Cyclone Slate and use it to escape Jolene's wrath. You don't have to flee the scene, though, and you'll miss out on some interesting bits of story if you do!

Now that she has caught up with her quarry at last, Jolene wastes no time in storming Linebeck's vessel. Although her quarrel is with the old barnacle himself, she doesn't hesitate to bring the fight to Link when the young lad refuses to give Linebeck away. Wow, she must really be upset!

Jolene

Threat Meter

Speed: Fast

Attack Power: 1/2 heart (sword swipe); 1 heart (dash attack)

Defense Power: Multiple hits to defeat!

This is one woman whose fury truly has no equal! Fast and accurate with her curved blade, Jolene is a very dangerous adversary. While her normal attacks are potent, she enjoys dashing forward at lightning speed to deliver an extremely punishing blow. Link must keep away from this woman's curved blade at all times and try to circle around behind her when she prepares to unleash a powerful dash! This helps Link avoid the coming blow, and also positions him to retaliate with some fancy swordplay of his own!

Jolene's attacks are swift and powerful, so don't be a stationary target. Keep a distance and keep moving around her, waiting until she prepares to unleash one of her fast dash attacks. Circle around Jolene to avoid these assaults, then quickly strike her backside with a powerful spin attack!

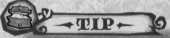

TIP

Jolene shouts and twirls her sword just before executing a dash strike. Learn to anticipate and be quick to counter!

You can only hit Jolene once each time she misses with a dash, so make the effort count! Don't try to be greedy after scoring a hit, either: retreat after the blow lands so you aren't caught by the woman's fast counters. Keep up this strategy until you finally manage to wear Jolene down. A final test of skill determines the outcome of the fight: when called upon, **rub the stylus left to right** as fast as you can to disarm Jolene and send her packing back to her ship.

TIP

Lift and toss the surrounding barrels at Jolene to keep her at bay and create more room to move.

Voicing her severe displeasure before storming off, Jolene assures Linebeck that their business is far from over. Approach the large wooden box nearby to prompt Linebeck to pop out. What a coward! The good captain assures Link that crouching in boxes is great for the back, but it's hard to believe such an exercise could ever cure a back so spineless. Linebeck isn't without gratitude, though: he hands his young savior a sparkly **blue Rupee** as a reward!

Blue Rupee

You got a **blue Rupee**! Well, it's better than nothing.... What a cheapskate!

Returning to the bridge, the group sees that Jolene has sailed off. It's high time you did the same! The Ghost Ship awaits you somewhere in the northern fog, but there's lots of optional stuff to do at this point as well. Check the Missing Links section if you're interested in obtaining some precious treasures. If you're eager to chase after the Ghost Ship, feel free to skip past the Missing Links and continue on with the story. You're the skipper!

   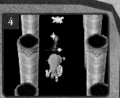

Tasks:
Complete!

CAUTION

Henceforth, Jolene's ship will patrol the Great Sea in search of Linebeck's vessel. If she spots you sailing about, she'll immediately open fire with her torpedoes and attempt to board your ship all over again! Fortunately, Jolene's location is always shown on your sea chart. Keep well away from this feisty pirate until you find some way to calm her down!

Missing Links

Glad you could make it! We've got a fantastic assortment of goodies for you to nab in this Missing Links section, and you'll find each one of them well worth the time. Let that Ghost Ship sit and hide; it's not going anywhere!

Romanos's New Venture

The first place to check for new and exciting adventure is closer that you might expect! Turn around and drop anchor at Molida Island once more to find the village's postbox wobbling away. Time for some fun with the Postman!

*Special delivery for Mr. Link! This letter is from Romanos, who is happy to say that he's finally found his true calling in life! Though Romanos can't find the words to describe his newest venture, he urges Link to stop by and pay him a visit sometime. He even includes a fabulous **ship part** as a present to his young friend. Boy, it's a good thing the Postman didn't have to carry this message very far!*

Ship Part

Random — You got a **ship part**! Visit the Shipyard to install it onto Linebeck's ship.

NOTE

This letter may be delivered to you elsewhere. Like most letters, you can receive it at the first island a postbox that you dock at.

...continued

Well since you're here, why not pay good old Romanos a visit? Go to the east side of the village and enter his hut for a shocking surprise: Romanos has transformed his humble abode into some sort of exciting attraction! Speak with Romanos to learn that he's decided to go the way of his father and become an explorer. Doing so takes capital however, so Romanos has decided to start up a Shooting Range game to earn a few bucks. What a novel idea! Why not pay the man 20 Rupees and give his game a try?

The rules for the Shooting Range are simple. Twenty Rupees buys you 70 seconds to shoot as many targets as you can with unlimited arrows. **Ghost targets are worth 10 points** each time you hit one, up to a maximum of 50 points apiece (if you were to shoot five in a row without missing). However, shooting a girl target will break your combo multiplier and also subtract 50 points from your score. Beat the game's high score of **1,700 points** to win an amazing prize!

TIP

Only one girl target crosses the range at a time. So, if you can see a girl target moving past, you know all the rest are going to be ghosts until the girl target reaches the other side! Use this to your advantage. When a girl target's in play, feel confident about shooting the other targets the moment they flip over.

Take your mark and get read to test your skill and accuracy! The targets move by slowly at first, puttering along until they spin to show their picture. If you see a white ghost, quickly tap it to fire away! If the target shows a girl in a red dress, don't shoot! Break all the ghost targets and avoid missing when you shoot to keep your point multiplier going!

NOTE

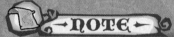

You cannot shoot a target before it flips around to show its picture. Don't even try! Doing so counts as a missed shot and resets your multiplier.

TIP

You can hold the stylus on the Touch Screen and simply release it to fire. Some find this faster than tapping!

Here's how the point multiplier system works:

One-Ghost Combo: 10 points are added to your score.

Two-Ghost Combo: 30 points are added to your score (10 + 20).

Three-Ghost Combo: 60 points are added to your score (10 + 20 + 30)

Four-Ghost Combo: 100 points are added to your score (10 + 20 + 30 + 40).

Five-Ghost Combo: 150 points are added to your score (10 + 20 + 30 + 40 + 50).

Six-Ghost Combo: 200 points are added to your score (10 + 20 + 30 + 40 + 50 + 50, and so on).

Naturally, the game speeds up and becomes increasingly difficult as the seconds tick away. Remember: shoot only the ghost targets without firing a wayward shot to build up your point multiplier and keep it at 50 points per ghost! This is the best way to earn the highest scores. Set a record high score of more than 1,700 points to win Romanos's first grand prize: a backup **Quiver** for your Bow!

TIP

Because accuracy is critical, it helps to ensure you're looking straight at your DS's Touch Screen while playing this game. Angled views may cause you to miss your mark!

Quiver #1

You got a **Quiver!** Now you can carry 10 more arrows for your Bow, for a new maximum of 30!

Romanos is a good sport, of course, and he offers a wide selection of concession prizes. Even if you don't set the high score, you have a chance to win **treasures**, **ship parts**, and **Rupees** just for playing! The better your performance, the more valuable the prize. Keep trying until you manage to accumulate more than 2,000 points and snag Romanos's ultimate prize: a brand new **Heart Container!**

Heart Container #7

You got a **Heart Container!** Your heart meter has been increased by one heart!

You can keep playing Romanos's Shooting Range challenge even after you claim the Heart Container prize. Here are some of the goodies you can expect to win from this game based on your score:

0–1299 Points: Keep trying!

1,300–1,699 Points: Random treasure.

1,700–1,999 Points: Quiver #1, then random ship parts.

2,000 Points and More: Heart Container #7, then random ship parts.

Quiver for Sale

Pay a stop to Molida's local shop to find a very special item for sale: another **Quiver** for your Bow! The price is steep at 1,000 Rupees, so you may need to visit Treasure Teller at Mercay Island and sell off some of those ship parts you recently won from Romanos. You'll find Mercay's shop carries this Quiver as well! The Quiver is no longer sold at either shop once you buy it, however.

Quiver #2

You got another **Quiver!** Now you can carry 20 more arrows for your Bow, for a new maximum of 50. You're now at maximum arrow capacity!

1

2

3

4

Tasks: Complete!

...continued

Power Spirit Upgrade

You're in the neighborhood, so why not swing by Spirit Island to the south and put those hard-found Power Gems to good use? You've already collected 10 Power Gems if you've been following this walkthrough carefully, and that's enough to power up Leaf, the **Spirit of Power**! Dock at Spirit Island and go north into the cavern to revisit the spirit shrine you stumbled upon a while ago.

Returning to the shrine, Link proudly shows his collection of Power Gems to the mysterious forces that be. Leaf, the Spirit of Power, slowly flutters out above the spring and begins drawing strength from the sacred gems. The fairy soon unleashes a brilliant flash of light: the Spirit of Power has been powered up!

You've powered up Leaf, the **Spirit of Power**! Now Link's sword burns with searing flames, looking much cooler and inflicting a bit more damage to his enemies. Smokin'!

More to Do at Mercay

Mercay Island

...continued

Items to Obtain

| Big Green Rupee | Courage Gem #6 | Ship Part | Treasure Map #10 | Wisdom Gem #8 |

Dungeon Denizens

Characters

| Rat | Crow | Red ChuChu | Zora Warrior |

Oshus's Lost Map

Now that you've explored this section of the quadrant, let's set sail for Mercay Island and see what's shakin' over there. Remember that stone statue you saw just before you entered the Temple of Courage? It hinted that something valuable might be hiding under the tree in front of Oshus's storehouse! Return to Mercay Island and travel to the cavern just east of Oshus's house. Whip out your Shovel and dig in front of the tree outside to unearth a long-forgotten **treasure map**!

Treasure Map #10

You got a **treasure map**! It reveals the location of a sunken treasure on the Great Sea.

Mercay Bomb Caverns

You're far from finished with this place! Now that you have the Bow, you can finally activate that eye crest you noticed inside the island's north cavern. Dash through the woods north of town and reenter the cavern you Bombed open awhile ago. Dispatch the Rats inside as you hop east toward the far ledge. Arm the Bow and shoot out the eye crest on the north wall. This causes a footbridge to extend southward!

...continued

TIP

If you're short on arrows, pay a visit to Mercay Island's local shop to pick some up.

Steel yourself before crossing the bridge: a formidable Zora Warrior awaits you on the other side! Combat this cretin as you have others past, stunning the monster by whacking its back with the Boomerang. Defeat the Zora Warrior and then continue south to exit the cavern.

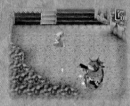

TIP

If you don't want to fight, simply dash past the Zora Warrior and flee the cavern at once.

You find a stone tablet and another eye crest just outside the cavern. The tablet hints that a nearby cliffside has a hidden weak spot. To find it, the tablet hints that you must **shine a beam** parallel with a line drawn between the **temple** and **Mercay Tavern**. This will all make sense in a moment! For now, simply run up the steps to the east, then turn around and fire an arrow at the eye crest on the west cliff.

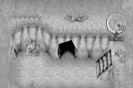

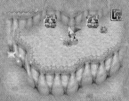

Thwack! The arrow strikes the eye crest, causing a tribal head statue to rise from the grass nearby. Neat! Ignore the tribal head statue for the moment, however, and run past it, turning south to locate two treasure chests on a small ledge that overlooks the village. Open both chests to claim a **big green Rupee** and a random **ship part** to add to your collection.

Overworld Chest #21: Big Green Rupee

Big Green Rupee

You got a **big green Rupee**! It's worth 100 Rupees!

...continued

Overworld Chest #22: Ship Part

Ship Part

Random

You got a **ship part**! Visit the Shipyard to install it onto Linebeck's ship.

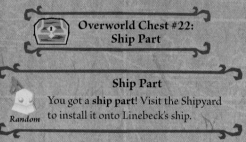

Return to the tribal head statue and smack it with Link's sword. A ray of light shines out from the statue's forehead! Before rotating the statue, call up your map and draw a straight line that connects the **Temple of the Ocean King** with the **Milk Bar** in Mercay village. (The Milk Bar is the largest building in town.) Now spin the tribal head statue so that its ray of light shines northwest, running parallel to the line you've just drawn. The light shines at a northwest cliff!

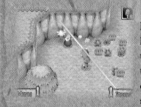

Move north past the tribal head statue and drop to the lower clearing. Blaze through the Red ChuChus and Crow in the surrounding woods as you continue heading northwest up some steps. Toss a Bomb at the cliff where the statue's light beam is shining. Boom! The Bomb blows a huge hole in the cliffside, revealing a hidden cavern!

No scary monsters lurk inside this second bomb cavern. Move to the long wooden footbridge and hurl Link's Boomerang southward when you're halfway across. Smack a hidden crystal orb with the Boomerang to cause a secret treasure chest to appear at the far end of the bridge. Sneaky! Open the chest to claim another Courage Gem.

Overworld Chest #23: Courage Gem #6

Courage Gem #6

You got a **Courage Gem**! Collect these items and use them to power up the Courage Spirit.

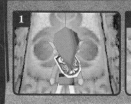

Tasks:
Complete!

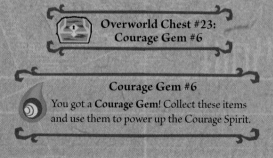

...continued

Freedle and Tag Mode

Proceed through the cavern's far exit to return outside. Hey, you've finally reached Mercay's small northeast isle! Climb up the north stairs to meet up with a friendly character named Freedle, who sings Link a happy song about **Magic Boxes**. Afterward, Freedle shows Link a group of three boxes behind her. Freedle says Link can place ship parts and treasures he no longer wants into the boxes and exchange them with others. Interesting!

⟶NOTE⟵

Visiting Freedle unlocks a special new mode in *Phantom Hourglass* known as **Tag Mode**. Now you can share your treasures and ship parts with other players who connect to your DS! Any items you place into Freedle's Magic Boxes are free for the taking, and you can browse other players' Magic Boxes as well. For details, please see the Tag Mode section in the Training portion of this guide.

Freedle

This free spirit has a fondness for fun! Freedle whiles away the days at Mercay Island's northeast islet, strumming a guitar and singing praises about Magic Boxes to all who'll listen. Freedle just wants folks to share the love—of treasures and ship parts, that is! Meeting Freedle for the first time unlocks Tag Mode, a special mode that allows players to share their excess collectibles with folks who connect to their DS. When everybody pitches in, no one's left out!

You can place items in Freedle's boxes if you wish, but you might want to hang onto your goods for now. Treasures and ship parts can be sold for Rupees, after all, and you can always return to Freedle later if you'd like to share with others! Before moving on, make sure to open the treasure chest that sits just east of Freedle. Inside you find a shiny **Wisdom Gem**!

⟶TIP⟵

Step on the pressure switch at the base of the isle to extend a bridge leading back toward the village. No need to take the long way around anymore!

...continued

⟶ Overworld Chest #24: Wisdom Gem #8 ⟵

Wisdom Gem #8

You got a **Wisdom Gem**! Collect these items and use them to power up the Wisdom Spirit.

Rupees from Linebeck

Now that you're able to combat Linebeck's greatest nemesis, Jolene, you can actually win free Rupees from the old tightwad! The good captain rewards you each time you cross swords with Jolene and save his hide: save him once to gain a blue Rupee, twice for a red one, and a third time to make Linebeck cough up a big green Rupee as thanks to his young bodyguard.

⟶ Big Green Rupee ⟵

You got a **big green Rupee**! It's worth 100 Rupees!

A Letter for Joanne

Crossing swords with Jolene is not only profitable, but also a great way to increase your Spirit Gem collection! After your first fight with Jolene at sea, the Postman soon delivers Link a letter from the girl. Unfortunately, the letter is actually addressed to Jolene's sister, Joanne! The Postman could obviously use some help, so why not deliver the letter to Joanne for him? You've already met Joanne: she's the girl dressed up as a **mermaid** back at Bannan Island!

⟶NOTE⟵

If you don't have Jolene's Letter, you can get it by letting her board Linebeck's ship and then defeating her in combat. The next time you dock at an island with a postbox, the Postman delivers the letter to Joanne to Link by mistake!

→NOTE←

Haven't seen the mermaid? Don't know what we're talking about here? You must not be following our walkthrough very carefully! Never fear. Simply flip back to the previous Missing Links section that appears before the Temple of Wind walkthrough. That's the first time you're able to meet the mysterious mermaid!

Jolene's Letter

You got Jolene's Letter! It's addressed to her younger sister, Joanne.

Warp to the sea's northwest quadrant and set sail for Bannan Island. Enter the Old Wayfarer's hut when you arrive and speak with the mermaid to hand her Jolene's Letter. Joanne couldn't be happier and gives Link a glimmering Wisdom Gem as thanks for being so thoughtful. How sweet!

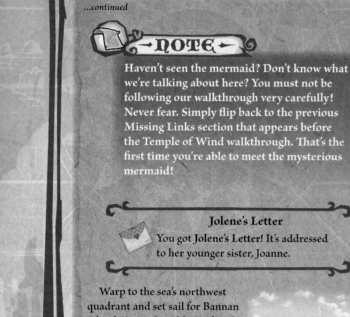

Wisdom Gem #9

 You got a **Wisdom Gem**! Collect these items and use them to power up the Wisdom Spirit.

→NOTE←

That's not all you get from Joanne! She soon mails Link a thank you letter that includes a random ship part. Who knew mermaids were so nice?

Sunken Treasure #10

Since you're already sailing about the sea's northwest quadrant, why not take a moment to dredge up another sunken treasure chest from the depths? The treasure map you found buried beneath the tree near Oshus's storehouse indicates that something precious lies in the waters just southeast of the Isle of Gust. Cruise to that bright red *X* and put your salvage arm to work hauling up another prized **ship part**. Just be sure to watch out for those pesky Octomines!

Ship Part

Random You got a **ship part**! Visit the Shipyard to install it onto Linebeck's ship.

Tasks: Complete!

Chapter 6

Contents

Fog and Fear: Ghost Ship & Temple of the Ocean King 4

Fog and Fear: Overview

Link's deeds of courage and valor have brought him far. At long last, the young hero has finally managed to rescue all three spirit fairies from imprisonment. And as it turns out, Ciela was one of them all along!

Link's heroic efforts have gained him the spirits' friendship, trust, and support. United at last, these spirits of **power**, **wisdom**, and **courage** are now able to combine their abilities and help Link track down the slippery Ghost Ship. With any luck, Tetra will soon be safe among friends once more!

A Link to the Present

Max 16:00

Max 20

Max 50

Lvl 1   Lvl 0   x10   x9   x6   x10

Items Already Acquired

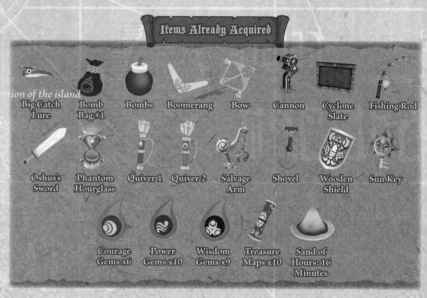

portion of the island

Big Catch Lure	Bomb Bag #1	Bombs	Boomerang	Bow	Cannon	Cyclone Slate	Fishing Rod
Oshus's Sword	Phantom Hourglass	Quiver 1	Quiver 2	Salvage Arm	Shovel	Wooden Shield	Sun Key
Courage Gems x6	Power Gems x10	Wisdom Gems x9	Treasure Maps x10	Sand of Hours: 16 Minutes			

Task 1: Board & Search the Ghost Ship

Into the Fog

That sneaky Ghost Ship can't hide from you anymore: you've rescued all three spirit fairies and are finally able to track it down! The Ghost Ship seems to enjoy hiding out in the sea's thick northwest fog, so that's the best place to start your search. Use the Cyclone Slate to warp to the northwest quadrant, then plot a westward course into the soupy mist.

1 Board & Search the Ghost Ship

2 Speak with Zauz the Blacksmith

3 Return to Temple of the Ocean King

4 Sail to the Southeast Quadrant

The sailing is smooth through the fog until Linebeck's ship suddenly comes to a jarring halt. What's going on? Heading into the engine room, Link finds Linebeck unable to get the ship moving. It must be the influence of that awful Ghost Ship! Linebeck assures Link that he can get the ship moving again, and asks the lad to take the helm.

At first, Link wonders how he'll be able to find the Ghost Ship. The fog is too thick to see through! Ciela quickly flutters close and tells Link not to worry: she and the other spirit fairies will help guide the ship along! Everything's been decided. Link will steer the ship, and with the spirits' help, that Ghost Ship will soon be found!

Alright, time for some precise helmsmanship! Ciela gives you some basic pointers: tap the engine controls on the right to start the ship moving, then drag the stylus right or left to steer the vessel accordingly. No sweat! Set the engine controls to **Go** and start off!

The fairies are here to help, so pay close attention to their reactions as you sail through the fog! They can sense the presence of the Ghost Ship through the fog, and they'll start jingling louder and louder when you're sailing toward the haunted craft. They even sparkle when you're right on course! Let the spirit fairies guide you along and simply steer Linebeck's ship in the proper direction.

CAUTION

Watch out for explosive barrels! It's tough to avoid them, but do your best if you see one coming. Each collision with a barrel inflicts one heart's worth of damage to Linebeck's ship!

If you've warped to the northwest quadrant and entered the fog from the east, you don't have very far to go: the Ghost Ship floats just north of the tiny boulders shown on the sea chart. Sail directly toward the Ghost Ship the moment you see it and board it without pause. Hang on, Tetra; help is on the way!

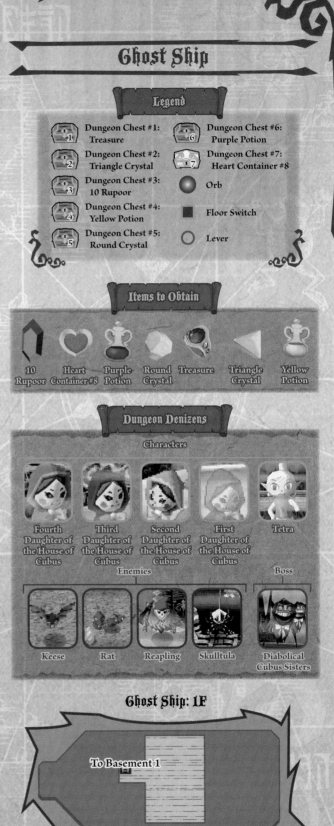

Ghost Ship

Legend

Dungeon Chest #1: Treasure	Dungeon Chest #6: Purple Potion
Dungeon Chest #2: Triangle Crystal	Dungeon Chest #7: Heart Container #8
Dungeon Chest #3: 10 Rupoor	Orb
Dungeon Chest #4: Yellow Potion	Floor Switch
Dungeon Chest #5: Round Crystal	Lever

Items to Obtain

10 Rupoor — Heart Container #8 — Purple Potion — Round Crystal — Treasure — Triangle Crystal — Yellow Potion

Dungeon Denizens

Characters

Fourth Daughter of the House of Cubus — Third Daughter of the House of Cubus — Second Daughter of the House of Cubus — First Daughter of the House of Cubus — Tetra

Enemies

Keese — Rat — Reapling — Skulltula

Boss

Diabolical Cubus Sisters

Ghost Ship: 1F

To Basement 1

Ghost Ship: B1

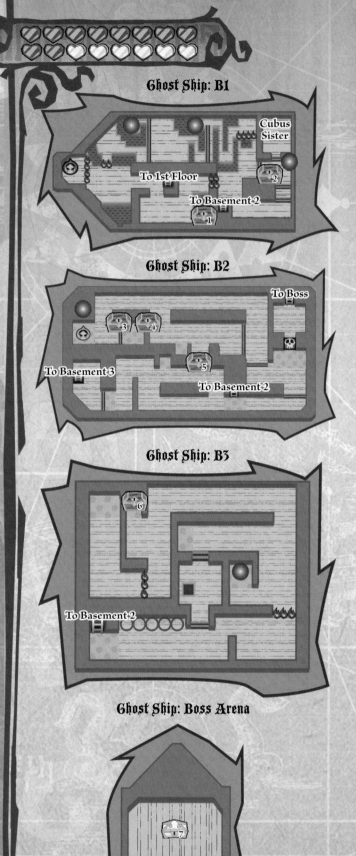

Cubus Sister

To 1st Floor

To Basement 2

Ghost Ship: B2

To Boss

To Basement 3

To Basement 2

Ghost Ship: B3

To Basement 2

Ghost Ship: Boss Arena

Ghost Ship: 1F

With the invaluable aid of the spirit fairies, Link and Linebeck finally manage to track down and board the nefarious Ghost Ship. The place is dreadfully cold and gloomy, and Linebeck quickly comes down with a case of the shivers. Ciela berates him for being such a coward, but his fear is quite understandable aboard this awful vessel! Hissing at Ciela to clam up, Linebeck urges Link to hurry and find his friend.

There isn't much to do on the Ghost Ship's main deck. Feel free to have a quick look around after chatting with Linebeck. You encounter some Keese here, but that's all. When you're ready to move on, go down the stairs in the west to reach the lower decks.

Ghost Ship: B1

The first basement floor has a lot more going on than the top deck. Go south from the stairs and wipe out the Rats that scurry past. Some blue flames block your progress to the east, but you can leap across a short gap to reach a narrow ledge with a treasure chest! Open the chest to claim a random **treasure**. Linebeck will be thrilled!

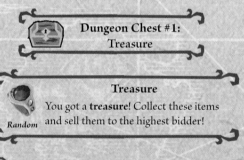

Dungeon Chest #1:
Treasure

Treasure

Random You got a **treasure**! Collect these items and sell them to the highest bidder!

→NOTE←

Link can lift and toss the surrounding steel drums just like wooden barrels. Tap one and see!

Task 1:
Board & Search the Ghost Ship

You can go no farther in this direction. Return to the stairs and then head west, but look out: Link becomes trapped in the west chamber, and three scary ghosts suddenly materialize from thin air! These vile spirits are called Poes, and they're tricky to deal with. Poes commonly vanish just before Link can strike them with his sword, so take them out with ranged attacks instead. Use the Boomerang or Bow, or simply lift and toss the surrounding pots at the Poes from afar.

TIP

Poes are tough to hit if you're not quick! The moment you see one appear, quickly press and hold L or R to ready the Bow or Boomerang, then tap the Poe to attack it from range.

Poe

Threat Meter

Speed: Slow

Attack Power: 1/2 heart (fireball)

Defense Power: 1 hit to defeat

You can never be sure if a room is empty anymore! Poes are evil spirits with the frightening ability to disappear and reappear right under Link's nose. These wicked ghosts float just out of reach, often vanishing before the young hero can strike them with his blade. If a Poe gets a chance, it quickly spits out a blue fireball that cannot be blocked. Dodge these dangerous projectiles and look to retaliate with a fast attack from Link's Boomerang or Bow.

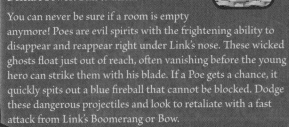

Defeat the three Poes to lower the sealed door behind you, along with flames to the north and west. Enter the west holding cell to find a young girl in a red cloak. Could this be Tetra?

The sobbing girl looks up at Link's approach. It's not Tetra! Perking up, the girl recognizes Link as a legendary hero, and seems to have been expecting him. She introduces herself as the youngest daughter of the House of Cubus, and says that she and her three sisters have all recently been abducted by the Ghost Ship. They've been locked away on this haunted vessel, waiting for someone to save them! The girl becomes overjoyed when Link agrees to rescue the Cubus sisters. Now's his chance to prove his heroism!

NOTE

From this point on, the locations of the daughters of the House of Cubus are shown on your map.

Ciela suspects that Tetra must be in one of the Ghost Ship's cells on a lower deck. Go north from the holding cell and smash some pots for items. Be careful when moving eastward: a giant spiderlike creature periodically drops from the ceiling! These critters are called Skulltulas, and they love making snacks out of unsuspecting heroes. Wait for the Skulltula to drop in, then whack it with Link's sword to dispatch it.

CAUTION

Skulltulas don't stay defeated for long: new ones soon drop in to take the place of fallen brethren! Loads of these crawlies lurk on the Ghost Ship, and many other traps besides, so it's best to walk about slowly instead of running. This ensures you won't be caught off guard!

Skulltula

Threat Meter

Speed: Immobile (drop and hang)

Attack Power: 1/2 heart (contact)

Defense Power: 1 hit to defeat

These freaky creepers are nothing to fear, as long as they don't get the drop on you! Skulltulas periodically plunge down from the rafters, attempting to snare Link by surprise. However, their positions are given away by their shadows, and by the rattling sound they make just before they fall! Link does well to walk slowly when Skulltulas are about, dispatching each one after they drop in to say hello.

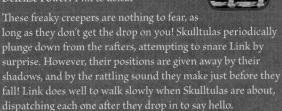

A row of spikes sticks up from the floor just beyond the Skulltula. Don't touch these pointy obstacles or Link suffers a full heart's worth of damage! Instead, ready the Boomerang and trace a line north, curving around some steel drums to whack a nearby crystal orb. This lowers the spikes so you may proceed. Carefully navigate past the blue twirling fire column beyond, and use the Boomerang once more to eliminate a Poe that harasses you after you cross.

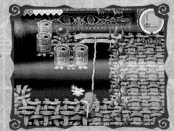

Your map shows a prisoner in the north holding cell, but ignore her for the moment. Instead, open the nearby treasure chest to claim a **triangle crystal**. You know where this goes! Carry the crystal westward and jump across the west gap. Leap across and lift the crystal once more, then carry it north toward the triangle-shaped pedestal beyond the blue flames. Place the crystal onto the pedestal to lower the flames at last, along with the spikes that block the south stairs.

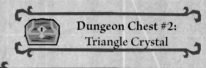

Dungeon Chest #2: Triangle Crystal

Triangle Crystal

You've found the **triangle crystal**! Take it to the same-shaped pedestal.

Rescuing the Third Daughter

Return to the holding cell you passed by earlier and speak with the girl in the blue cloak standing inside. She's another lost sister! The girl introduces herself as the third daughter of the House of Cubus, and asks Link to escort her to her younger sister. No sweat!

Carefully lead the girl back to the floor's west holding cell, where her younger sister awaits. You've removed the blue flames to the north, so traverse the northern walkways so that the girl follows close behind. Take it slow, being wary of Skulltulas and lingering Poes as you guide the girl to her sister.

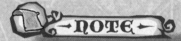

The Cubus sisters can't leap across gaps, so you must use the triangle crystal to lower the north flames and guide her to the west holding cell.

Although they can't actually be harmed, the Cubus sisters still become frightened whenever monsters are about, and quickly duck for cover. Eliminate any nearby enemies and then speak with the shaken girl to ease her fears and coax her into following Link once more.

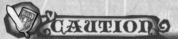

TIP

Take the time to defeat the Poe or it continues to spit fireballs at you from range.

The narrow walkways that follow are packed with dangers, so tread lightly! Another Skulltula drops from the ceiling, right in front of a second row of spikes ahead. Dispatch the Skulltula after it falls, then quickly ready the Boomerang. Trace a line north along the spikes, targeting another crystal orb behind some steel drums. After tracing the flight path, hold your stylus on the orb until the spikes lower, then quickly release to hurl the Boomerang. Time this right and you activate the orb and permanently lower the spikes.

CAUTION

Remember that the Skulltula will come back after a short time. Don't linger about where it drops!

Navigate the next few walkways, moving slowly to avoid being surprised by Skulltula ambushers from above. Smash some pots near a triangle-shaped pedestal for hearts and items, being careful not to touch the blue flames to the south. To get past the flames, simply leap across the short gap between the two narrow walkways.

More spikes block your progress to the east, so walk south and loop around. Eliminate more Rats and another Skulltula in the southern passage. This place is just full of pests! Carefully cross the two spike traps that follow, dashing past each one when they retract into the floor. Whack the crystal orb beyond to lower some spikes to the north and west. Now you can enter the north holding cell!

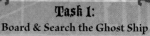

Reunited at last, the two youngest Cubus sisters share a squeal of glee. They ask Link to continue to search for their two older sisters and bring them back up here as well. No problem, ladies! Retrace your steps to the east end of the ship, then descend the south stairs to reach the next floor below.

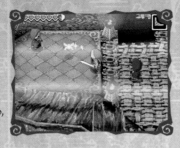

►NOTE◄

Did you notice the circle-shaped pedestal near the stairs? Remember it for future reference!

Ghost Ship: B2

Notice anything strange about the Ghost Ship's second basement floor? There are safe zones down here, just like in the Temple of the Ocean King! Wonder why? Just step off the entry safe zone to find out! When you do, a terrifying Reapling suddenly appears to the north and it's eager to seek out and punish any intruders. Needless to say, you don't want to get caught by that thing!

Reapling

Threat Meter

Speed: Normal

Attack Power: 2 hearts (scythe)

Defense Power: Invincible

The terror of the Ghost Ship and bane of all would-be heroes, Reaplings scour the lower decks of their haunted craft in search of trespassers. Similar in many ways to Phantoms, these massive wraiths are faster and more menacing by far. A Reapling's ethereal form allows it to see and travel right through solid walls; it can spy intruders from afar and quickly cross great distances. Fortunately, Reaplings still can't see or pass through safe zones! Link must keep well out of sight and stick close to safe zones so he can quickly reach cover whenever he is spotted. Risk takers don't last long when Reaplings are about!

A look at your map shows that the Reapling merely prowls this basement's northern section, so you don't need to fear it at first. Walk east from the entry safe zone, being watchful for telltale Skulltula shadows that appear on the floor. Dodge or slice through each spidery menace that plummets into your path, and carefully dash past the floor spikes you encounter as you begin moving northward.

►NOTE◄

Ignore the large stone block marked with a skull pattern near the far eastern safe zone. You'll find a way to get past this obstacle later!

Plenty of safe zones are about, so you should have little trouble outmaneuvering the lone Reapling. Keep out of sight as you navigate the north halls, moving eastward toward the far safe zone. There you find another Cubus sister! The yellow-cloaked girl introduces

herself as the second daughter of the House of Cubus, and although she hasn't heard of Tetra, she does ask Link to escort her upstairs. Can do!

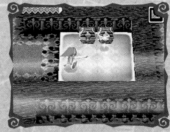

Before heading out, whack the crystal orb standing behind the Cubus sister to lower all the spike traps across the entire floor. This grants you access to a nearby safe zone, where two treasure chests await your discovery! Start moving toward them. The girl suddenly advises you to open the **chest on the left**. Don't take her advice, though: the left chest contains a **10 Rupoor**, which drains 10 Rupees from your wallet! Worse, opening that cursed box causes a second Reapling to appear at the south end of the basement floor! Leave the left chest alone and only open the one on the right, which contains a valuable **Yellow Potion**.

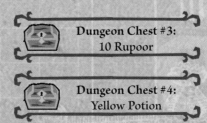

Dungeon Chest #3:
10 Rupoor

Dungeon Chest #4:
Yellow Potion

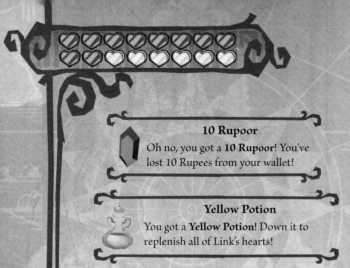

---

10 Rupoor
Oh no, you got a **10 Rupoor**! You've lost 10 Rupees from your wallet!

Yellow Potion
You got a **Yellow Potion**! Down it to replenish all of Link's hearts!

Rescuing the Second Daughter

Now escort the second daughter back to her sisters! With the girl in tow, begin making your way westward. All the floor's spike traps are now disabled, so you can easily reach the south stairs without being detected. On your way, stop to open a treasure chest near the middle of the floor, one that you couldn't have reached before. Inside you find a glimmering **round crystal**!

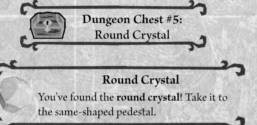
Dungeon Chest #5:
Round Crystal

Round Crystal
You've found the **round crystal**! Take it to the same-shaped pedestal.

Carefully carry the round crystal overhead as you lead the girl toward the south steps. Climb the stairs to return to the first basement floor. Now that you've found the round crystal, you can take a huge shortcut through here! Place the crystal onto the round-shaped pedestal just north of the stairs to douse the nearby blue flames. Now, simply lead the girl westward to reunite her with her sisters!

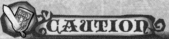
CAUTION

There are Rats and Skulltulas beyond the blue flames. Eradicate these threats to keep your ward going.

Thrilled at seeing their older sister safe and sound, the Cubus daughters praise Link for his heroic efforts. There's still one more girl to find, though! Backtrack eastward and go downstairs to continue searching the Ghost Ship. When you're back on the second basement floor, simply walk west and proceed down the southwest stairs.

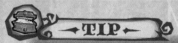
TIP

The three pots near the southwest stairs all contain hearts. Remember their location and take full advantage of them!

Ghost Ship: B3

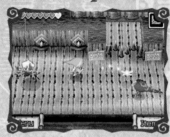

Oh no, even more safe zones are down here! That means there must be more Reaplings! Go east from the entry safe zone, battling a Skulltula and a Poe. Whoa, look at all those levers on the north wall! Two nearby signs indicate that there's some sort of **steel drum storage** nearby, but a row of spikes blocks the pathway to the north. Ignore the spikes and levers for now, and continue moving eastward.

Look out: Link becomes trapped in the southeast corner of the basement floor and five Skulltulas plunge down from the ceiling! Dash through the room and hide in a corner, waiting for the spidery villains to fall. When all five have dropped, quickly  set about defeating each one with Link's blade. The spin attack works wonders! Clear out the Skulltula infestation to douse the blue flames to the north.

TIP

As always, the Skulltulas' shadows and rattling sounds give them away. You can also see them on your map!

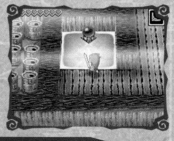

Move north and then duck into a side passage with a safe zone on your left. Hey, there's a crystal orb over here! Ignore it to avoid releasing a Reapling.

Task 1:
Board & Search the Ghost Ship

Dash north and head for the floor's far northern hallway. Move to a tiny northwest safe zone, where a treasure chest lies. Pop open the chest for a handy **Purple Potion**!

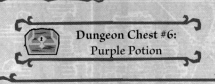

Dungeon Chest #6:
Purple Potion

Purple Potion

You got a **Purple Potion**! Drink it to replenish up to eight hearts whenever Link's health energy is low. If Link falls in battle, this item is used automatically to bring him back!

Carefully return to the safe zone with the crystal orb you activated just moments ago. Don't let that awful Reapling see you! When it's safe to do so, dash to the floor's central safe zone, where a stone tablet stands. This tablet gives a clue as to how you must pull the levers in the southern passage: **2, 4, 5, 1, 3**. Write this sequence down on your map so you don't forget it!

Dart out from the safe zone when the Reapling isn't about and return to the levers. Pull all five in the exact order indicated by the tablet, working left to right. Here's exactly what you must do:

1. Pull the fourth lever first.
2. Pull the first (farthest west) lever second.
3. Pull the fifth (farthest east) lever third.
4. Pull the second lever fourth.
5. Pull the third (middle) lever fifth.

Pulling the levers drops the spikes to the north and grants you access to the steel drum storage chamber. Don't rush up there, though: there's a trapdoor in the room's southern entrance! Instead, go to the floor's east side again, looping around to enter the steel drum storage room from the north. Be careful not to let that scary Reapling see you on the way!

When the Reapling is nowhere nearby, start lifting and tossing the steel drums in the storage chamber. Hey, there's a pressure switch near the storage room's west wall! Step on the switch to lower some blue flames in a passage to the west. Now you can access the floor's farthest northwest safe zone.

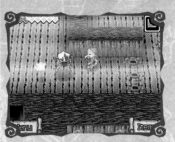

When it's safe to do so, dash east and then south, looping around to the safe zone that's just east of the steel drum storage room. Wait for the Reapling to move close to the storage chamber, then dash north and west, directly toward the northwest corner of the floor. Watch out for Skulltulas that drop down along the way!

The farthest northwest safe zone features nothing more than a collection of steel drums. Hey, wait a minute: one of those drums is jiggling! Lift it up and toss it aside to find a girl in a green cloak hiding underneath. It's the first daughter of the House of Cubus! The girl is happy to see a friendly face and asks Link to lead her back to her younger sisters. Here we go again!

Rescuing the First Daughter

Like the other Cubus girls, the first daughter becomes frightened by Skulltulas and the like, so you must make a slow, methodical journey across the floor. Soon into the trip, the girl gives Link an important tip: **Reaplings' backs are sensitive to arrows!** Equip the Bow and try shooting the wandering Reapling in its back with an arrow. This stuns the fiend for quite some time, helping you slip past!

TIP

Keep the Reapling stunned as long as is needed by firing more arrows into its back!

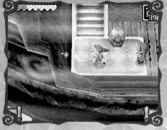

Take it slow and you should have little trouble guiding the girl to the floor's southwest stairs. If the Reapling notices you, rush to a safe zone as always—Reaplings have no interest in the Cubus daughter, so don't worry about her! Simply avoid or stun Reaplings you see, and dispatch all Skulltulas as you backtrack through the lower decks. Escort the girl all the way up to her sisters on the first basement floor.

 **CAUTION**

Remember: there's a trapdoor just south of the steel drum storage room! Don't lead the girl that way.

At last, Link manages to fight his way upstairs and reunite the final Cubus daughter with her sisters. The girls are delighted to be together once more, but surprisingly, the reunion isn't as cheery as Link had anticipated! One of the girls suddenly hisses at Link, muttering that the Reaplings should have scared the wits out of him by now. Another says that Link must play along with their little game, just as they made Tetra play with them before. Squealing with glee, the Cubus sisters suddenly transport their young plaything topside for a high-stakes game of dead man's volley!

Diabolical Cubus Sisters

Threat Meter

Speed: Normal

Attack Power: 1/2 heart (laser); 1/2 heart (energy balls)

Defense Power: 2 hits to defeat each sister

It seems that no good deed goes unpunished! Revealing their true forms, the evil Cubus sisters suddenly take flight and hover high above the deck of the Ghost Ship. Without warning, three of them begin firing lasers down at Link!

 **TIP**

The four pots at the edges of the ship contain hearts. Try to save them until you really need them.

...continued

Naturally, you don't want to touch those powerful lasers. Keep well away from their points of contact with the ship deck, and notice that one of the Cubus sisters doesn't fire a steady laser beam. Instead, she periodically lobs large balls of crackling energy toward Link! These energy balls are the key to besting the Cubus sisters: You've got to play their deadly game to beat them!

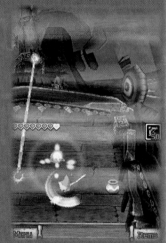

Dodge the three laser beams and keep below the lone sister who isn't firing one. When she unleashes an energy ball, stand your ground and execute a fast side slash or spin attack just as the ball draws near. If you time this just right, Link's blade acts as a bat and knocks the dangerous projectile back at the Cubus sisters!

CAUTION

If you miss the energy ball, it explodes against the back wall of the ship, sending out one or more smaller balls that cannot be deflected. Make sure to dodge these little orbs!

Whack! The energy ball smacks into one of the four Cubus girls, striking her for damage. Bat another energy ball back at the same girl to defeat her. One fiendish sister down, three to go!

Task 1:
Board & Search the Ghost Ship

...continued

...continued

TIP

The evil sisters occasionally swap positions with one another. Keep track of the ones you've hit by the color of their cloaks!

The game becomes a bit more intense after you defeat the first Cubus sister. Two of the girls continue firing steady lasers while the third launches more energy balls. This time, when you knock the ball back at the Cubus sisters, they'll pass it to each other before volleying it back at you! Whack the energy ball a second time to send it back at the devilish sisters, this time scoring a hit on one of them.

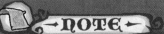

NOTE

Any of the sisters can return the second volley at you. Stay on your toes: you never know which one will return the ball!

CAUTION

After you defeat one of the four sisters, the other three may launch a new type of energy ball that resembles a collection of smaller orbs. These ones explode if you strike them with Link's sword, so don't try returning them! Dodge them instead.

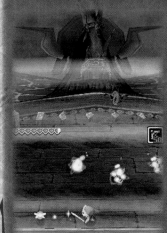

Expect the volleys to become more and more intense as the game nears its climax. Keep moving and keep returning those energy balls at the evil sisters. Eventually, you're left with just one Cubus sister, and the fight becomes far more challenging: the remaining girl floats closer to Link and begins firing three energy balls in a single shot.

Two of the energy balls are made up of smaller orbs and will explode on contact with Link's sword. The other is a whole ball that must be volleyed back at the final Cubus sister! The spin attack is the best way of ensuring you don't miss batting the proper ball—return it and keep the volley going until you finally manage to score a hit. Strike the final Cubus sister with three energy balls to win this terrible contest!

Game, Set, and Match

Beaten at her own game, the last of the Cubus sisters spirals downward and collapses to the ground. She gives Link his due respect and then vanishes with a laugh, leaving behind a creepy-looking **Ghost Key**. Now you can probe the ship's lowest decks and finally rescue Tetra! A giant treasure chest soon appears, along with a pool of blue light. Open the chest for another prized **Heart Container**, then step into the blue light when you're ready to go belowdecks once more.

Dungeon Chest #7: Heart Container #8

Heart Container #8

You got a **Heart Container**! You're heart meter has been increased by one heart!

Ghost Key

You got the **Ghost Key**! Now you can fully explore the Ghost Ship!

Questing for Tetra

The blue light brings you back to the main holding cell, where the Cubus sisters first jumped you. Head east and go downstairs to reach the second basement floor. Hey, the Reaplings are gone! Proceed to the farthest east safe zone and tap the giant stone block engraved with a skull design. Now that you've got the Ghost Key, you can remove this obstacle and proceed to the northeast stairs!

Storming into the Ghost Ship's cargo hold, Link and Ciela are met with a shocking sight: Tetra stands at the far end of the room, stone stiff! She's been turned to stone!

Oshus goes on to explain that Bellum used the life force he stole from the Ocean King to spread his evil across the sea, creating all manner of wicked minions to carry out his bidding. His fiends soon managed to imprison the noble spirits of Power and Wisdom, but Ciela was able to split her soul, allowing a small portion of her identity to escape. This is why Ciela's memory had been lost for so long!

As Link stares wide-eyed at his friend, Linebeck scurries into the cargo hold, saying that the surrounding fog has disappeared. Completely oblivious to Tetra's plight, the old sea dog asks if Link has managed to find the Ghost Ship's treasure yet. Talk about self-centered! As Ciela yells at Linebeck, a voice suddenly calls out from behind them. It's Oshus!

With his strength nearly gone, the Ocean King had but one option: he used his last ounce of power to create a clone of himself, just as Ciela had done! Naturally, this clone is Oshus. As Oshus, the Ocean King made a humble home for himself on Mercay Island. He wanted to keep an eye on Bellum, who still resides deep within the accursed temple. Oshus used the Sand of Hours to create the Phantom Hourglass so he could enter the temple and keep watch over Bellum, waiting for a chance for vengeance.

Oshus explains that the Ghost Ship has used its vile influence to ensnare Tetra and drain her life force away. He begins to tell Link all that he knows, revealing one shocking secret after another. The first is that he isn't an old man at all: Oshus is actually the great and powerful Ocean King!

Oshus finishes his tale by explaining that the evil Bellum has wrought will stop at nothing to devour every ounce of life force in the world. That's why the Ghost Ship was created: to seek out living beings and steal their life force away! Tetra's soul was so bright and pure, the Ghost Ship was inevitably drawn to her. It was no accident that she stumbled across this haunted craft—the Ghost Ship came to her! Still, Oshus can sense that some of Tetra's life force yet remains. If Link can defeat Bellum in time, the girl may yet be saved!

Using story cards, Oshus explains that, as the Ocean King, he was attacked by an unfathomable evil long ago: a wretched being known as Bellum. This vile monstrosity was drawn to the Ocean King's incredibly strong life force, and to the life force of the many noble beings inhabiting the surrounding islands. Although the Ocean King struggled valiantly against Bellum in a mighty battle, the great beast's evil was so pervasive that it drained the Ocean King's life force away even as they fought. Bellum won the clash, and Oshus's true identity has been sealed away ever since in the sunless depths of the cursed temple on Mercay Island, where his life force continues to dwindle.

Oshus advises Link to visit a man named Zauz, who lives nearby on a small island north of the Isle of Gust. Zauz is an infamous blacksmith with the knowledge and ability to help Link defeat Bellum and purify the world of his wickedness. Only then will Tetra and the Ocean King be spared their dreadful fate.

Task 2:
Speak with Zauz the Blacksmith

Learning that the promise of treasure aboard the Ghost Ship was nothing more than fiction, Linebeck yells, screams, and storms off in a childish rage. The treasure was the only reason he put his life on the line to begin with! Now that there's none to be had, Linebeck sees no point in continuing to let Link use his ship. The deal's off!

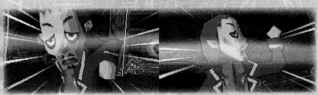

Astonished, Ciela can't believe that a "real man of the sea" would turn his back on the Ocean King himself. Oshus chuckles, knowing that Linebeck won't help without suitable compensation. The old man tells Linebeck that if he continues to help them, he'll grant the good captain one wish—anything his heart desires. Experiencing a remarkably fast change of heart, Linebeck suddenly begins shouting orders at his crew, urging them to hurry and set sail for Zauz's Island. Time's a-wasting after all, and that awful Bellum must pay for his crimes!

Task 2: Speak with Zauz the Blacksmith

All Aboard!

Seeing no reason to linger aboard the creepy Ghost Ship, Link and company depart, returning to Linebeck's vessel. They carry Tetra's stony form along with them and store her belowdecks. Linebeck encourages Link to hurry to **Zauz's Island**. You've been there before if you've been following this walkthrough carefully: set a course for the waters north of the Isle of Gust and aim for Zauz's Island!

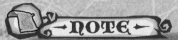

Zauz's Island doesn't appear on the sea chart until you draw near. It's pretty small, but you shouldn't have much trouble finding it!

A Meeting with Zauz

Entering the small hut at the island's center, Link and Ciela see big, burly Zauz hard at work, hammering away at a hunk of steel. The blacksmith has been expecting them, and tells Link that, for generations, his ancestors have devoted their lives to serving the just and noble Ocean King. They forged weapons and fought in epic battles to protect both land and sea. To save the Ocean King and banish evil, he will need a precious artifact called the Phantom Sword!

Unfortunately, Zauz no longer has the legendary weapon. Ciela becomes alarmed, but Zauz quickly calms her. He's a blacksmith, after all—he can make a new one! However, no ordinary metals can be used to make a sword with such incredible power. Zauz requires three special types of metal: Aquanine, Azurine, and Crimsonine. He recalls that the Ocean King gave these precious metals to three tribes long ago.

Thinking it over, Ciela admits that no tribe they've encountered thus far is likely to have any of these metals. Zauz advises that they return to the Temple of the Ocean King once more and search for another sea chart so they can explore more of the world. The blacksmith goes on to say that a special symbol can be drawn on a door within the temple, a door that will open a pathway to a new portion of the palace. He points to a pattern hanging on the wall of his hut, advising Link to try drawing the same symbol on the temple's door.

What a guy! Zauz has shared his vast knowledge of the Phantom Sword with you, and has pointed you in the proper direction: you must now return to the Temple of the Ocean King! Tap the wall map in Zauz's hut for a closer view of the symbol etched upon it, then copy that same symbol onto your map for future reference. When you're ready to go, return to Linebeck and sail to Mercay Island!

Legend

Dungeon Chest #1: Force Gem		Dungeon Chest #10: Wisdom Gem #10	
Dungeon Chest #2: Force Gem		Dungeon Chest #11: Ship Part	
Dungeon Chest #3: Force Gem		Dungeon Chest #12: Sea Chart #3	
Dungeon Chest #4: Power Gem #11		Bomb Wall	
Dungeon Chest #5: Red Potion		Orb	
Dungeon Chest #6: Treasure Map #11		Floor Switch	
Dungeon Chest #7: Round Crystal		Lever	
Dungeon Chest #8: Triangle Crystal		Red Jar	
Dungeon Chest #9: Courage Gem #7		Yellow Jar	

Task 3: Return to the Temple of the Ocean King

Back at Mercay

Ready for another visit to the cursed temple? Sure you are! But first, take a moment to check the postbox when you arrive at Mercay Island. What's this? You've got another piece of mail!

The Postman has an extra-special delivery for Link this time: a letter from Linebeck! The captain stumbles over his words at first, but eventually manages to shake out a surprisingly thoughtful "thank you" to Link for all his help. Guess he's really starting to take a liking to his young swabbie! The good captain even includes a shiny new ship part in his letter. Wait a second…who are you, and what have you done with Linebeck?

Ship Part

You got a **ship part**! Visit the Shipyard to install it onto Linebeck's ship.

Random

Spend a moment visiting the local shop to stock up on items and the Shipyard as well, if you like. When you're ready to move on, go north toward the temple.

Temple of the Ocean King: Fourth Visit

Items to Obtain

Courage Gem #7 · Force Gems x3 · Power Gem #11 · Red Potion · Round Crystal · Sea Chart #3 · Ship Part · Small Keys x4 · Square Crystal · Treasure Map #11 · Triangle Crystal · Wisdom Gem #10

Temple of the Ocean King: B1

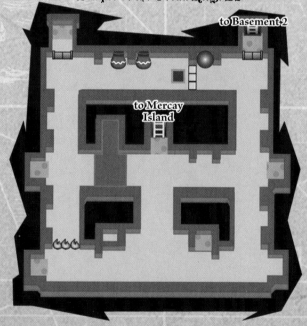

to Basement 2

to Mercay Island

Dungeon Denizens

Enemies

Phantom Eye · Fire Bubble · Moldorm · Phantom · Wizzrobe

Temple of the Ocean King: B2

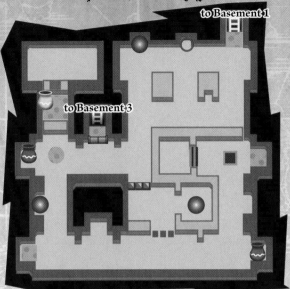

Temple of the Ocean King: B4

Temple of the Ocean King: B3

Temple of the Ocean King: B5

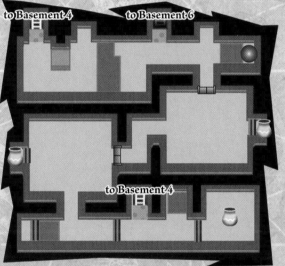

Temple of the Ocean King: Checkpoint Chamber

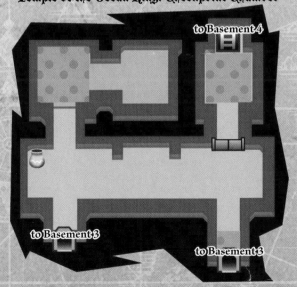

Temple of the Ocean King: B6

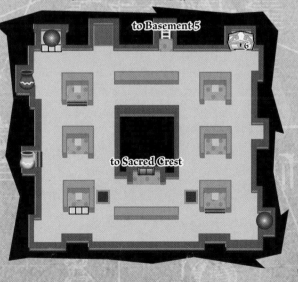

Temple of the Ocean King: Sacred Crest Chamber

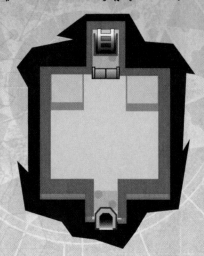

Temple of the Ocean King: B9

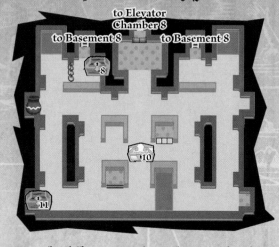

to Elevator
Chamber 8

to Basement 8   to Basement 8

Temple of the Ocean King: Elevator Chamber

to Basement 9

Temple of the Ocean King: B7

to Basement 8

to Basement 6

to Basement 8   to Basement 8

Wisdom of the Fallen

Here we are, back in this awful temple! Nothing much seems to have changed in the entry hall, but that's not exactly true! Speak with the spirits of the three fallen adventurers to learn that each one now offers to sell you information; they know a variety of tricks that can help you get through the temple with less hassle! Save your Rupees for later, though. We'll make sure you're well informed as you explore the temple's depths!

→ NOTE ←

If you've been following this walkthrough carefully, then you've got 16 minutes' worth of sand in the hourglass at this point. Some of this time comes from the Sand of Hours that can be hauled up from sunken chests at the bottom of the sea. Sixteen minutes is more than enough time to get the job done here!

Temple of the Ocean King: B8

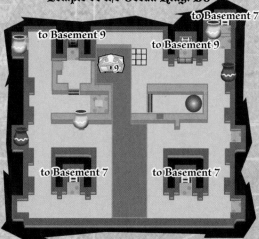

to Basement 7

to Basement 9   to Basement 9

to Basement 7   to Basement 7

Task 3:
Return to the Temple of the Ocean King

As you revisit the temple's first few basement floors, you find that everything's pretty much the same as it was before. There is one important difference, however: those scary Phantoms are now wearing bright red suits of armor! These red Phantoms are faster than the blue ones, able to pursue Link almost as quickly as he can sprint. All the more reason to keep well out of sight!

Temple of the Ocean King: B1 & B2

The first two basement floors offer nothing new, so focus on blazing through as fast as you can. To save time, remember to use Bombs and take the following key shortcuts in B1 and B2:

B1 Shortcut: Destroy the north bomb blocks to access the northwest small key.

B2 Shortcut: Blast open the south cracked wall to quickly reach the central small key.

Temple of the Ocean King: B3

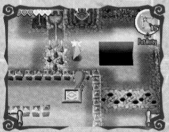

Now that you have the Bow, you can see and do a few things within the temple that you couldn't before. The first of these occurs at the third basement floor: there's an eye crest on the wall just south of the large northeast safe zone! Use the Shovel to unearth a gust geyser near the south platform and bypass the flames on the stairs, then fire an arrow northward into the eye crest. Bull's eye! The eye turns red and a big old treasure chest appears near the giant safe zone.

Hurry up: there isn't much time to reach that chest! If you don't open it quickly enough, it disappears. Run south and drop off the platform, then dash north, darting past the spike traps when they retract. Bolt to the safe zone and open that chest to claim another **Power Gem!**

TIP

If you're having trouble reaching the chest in time, try shutting off the spike traps by tossing the Boomerang at the crystal orb that stands atop the high eastern ledge. Also, dunk the patrolling Phantom into one of the trapdoors to remove him as an obstacle.

Dungeon Chest #4:
Power Gem #11

Power Gem #11
You got a **Power Gem!** Collect these items and use them to power up the Power Spirit.

Temple of the Ocean King: B4

While there's no new treasure for you to find on the fourth basement floor, you're now able to take a pretty huge shortcut. Go east from the entry safe zone and locate an eye crest on a wall beyond a pit in the floor's northeast corner. Shoot this eye crest to instantly shut off all the gust jars in the area! Now you can quickly make your way to the west bomb wall, blast it open, and strike the crystal orb inside the chamber beyond to lower the spikes blocking access to the floor's small key.

CAUTION

Remember not to let any of those Phantom Eyes see you! If one does, it calls in for a backup Phantom.

NOTE

You still can't get at that yellow pot atop the wall near the west crystal orb. Don't let it bother you; you'll snag it later!

Temple of the Ocean King: B5

Armed with the Bow, you can now access a special storage room on this floor that you couldn't reach on your first run-through. (You may have obtained this earlier in the room through the use of your boomerang plus good timing.) Take aim at the eye crest on the wall just east of the entry safe zone and nail it with an arrow to lower the surrounding spikes. Thwack!

Now check out the room to the east! Inside you find a large number of blue pots filled with an assortment of hearts and items. There's also one yellow pot containing a time bonus good for 30 seconds' worth of extra hourglass sand. Not a bad haul!

Heads up: instead of Yellow ChuChus and Miniblins, you face Fire Bubbles and Moldorms in the next two chambers! Remember to use the Boomerang to knock those Fire Bubbles to the ground and then quickly smash their skulls apart with Link's blade. The Moldorms can be tricky and you can't afford to waste time on them. Don't worry too much about Link's safety; just run about and unleash spin attacks as fast as you can, ripping into their pink tails for maximum damage!

After clearing these rooms, don't forget to claim the time bonuses from the yellow pots in the east and west alcoves!

Even if you found it last time, that hidden chest containing a Red Potion is still up for grabs! Use the Boomerang to strike the crystal orb in the floor's northeast corner to make the chest appear.

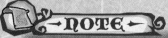

You still can't get at that large treasure chest across the west pit. Not to worry: it will be yours one day!

Temple of the Ocean King: B6

Hope you're ready to find some more treasure! When no Phantoms are about, shoot the eye crest on the floor's northwest wall to cause a huge treasure chest to appear in the northeast alcove. Nice! Now rush over to the chest before it vanishes and open it to claim another valuable **treasure map**!

Dungeon Chest #6:
Treasure Map #11

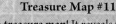

Treasure Map #11
You got a **treasure map**! It reveals the location of a sunken treasure on the Great Sea.

Finally, this is the floor with the sacred door Zauz mentioned! Move toward the central safe zone, stepping onto one of the two nearby pressure switches to shut off the blowing gust jars at either side. Tap the door for a closer view, then trace the symbol you saw on Zauz's wall, which resembles a large triangle with an upside-down triangle in its center.

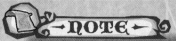

As before, the symbol must be drawn in one motion without letting the stylus up from the screen. It's easiest to start at the top and then draw a diagonal line downward, filling in the middle of the triangle when you reach the bottom. After tracing the upside-down triangle in the middle, continue the line upward to the top, completing the outer triangle.

Can't remember what the symbol looks like? If you traced it on your sea chart before, simply tap the Menu tab, then tap the Sea Chart button. Tap the northwest quadrant of the sea, then tap on Zauz's Island. This calls up the island's map and the note you made should still be there!

Temple of the Ocean King: Sacred Crest Chamber

Hey, this room looks different than before. Tracing the symbol Zauz showed you must have brought you to a different section of the temple! Speak with the nearby fallen adventurer to learn that dark terrors lurk in the floors ahead. The spirit decides to help you by summoning a magical pool of yellow light nearby! This yellow light acts as a **midway checkpoint**: you can step into it right now to return to the surface, and your current hourglass time will be saved. Afterward, you may step onto the yellow light that henceforth appears within the temple's entry hall to return to this chamber. In short, you never have to visit those first six floors again!

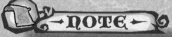

Even if you aren't planning on leaving, definitely use the yellow light to return to the entry hall. Doing so records your current time and allows you to instantly return to this spot at any point in the future. If you're determined to explore further, simply step into the yellow light in the entry hall to warp back here with the exact same time.

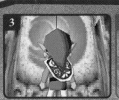

TIP

Consider buying potions at Mercay's shop if you don't have any: the next few floors are going to be rough!

Before moving onward, take a moment to dig at the soft patch of soil near the fallen adventurer to uncover a gust geyser. Ride up to the ledge above and smash the pots there for hearts. If you need Bombs or arrows, hurl the Boomerang at the pots on the adjacent ledge to smash them open, tossing it a second time to nab the goods that pop out, if necessary.

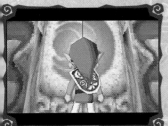

Ready to move on, hero? Just tap the large door to the north. Ciela uses her power as the **Spirit of Courage** to open the massive gateway so you may explore deeper into the temple. Get in there and find that sea chart!

NOTE

You've got three more floors to go through, so here's hoping you've got a good eight minutes left on the clock. If not, consider using the yellow light to return to the entry hall, then try blazing through those first six floors again to record a better time. If you've been finding treasure maps and hauling up Sand of Hours from the seafloor, you can easily set a midway point with more than 10 minutes to work with!

Temple of the Ocean King: B7

One look at the seventh basement floor's map shows it to be a crazy place! You're in no immediate danger from the start, as the Phantoms are quite far away. Step onto the moving platform and ride across the surrounding abyss, moving from one platform to the next as you head to the small patch of safe zone to the northwest.

Stop on the tiny safe zone ledge and use the Boomerang to smash two pots to the west. One of the pots is a yellow one that provides 30 seconds' worth of bonus time! Though you can't quite reach it, make a note of the chest near the pots, then cross over to the floor's west side.

The west floor is covered in a thin layer of water, and Ciela is quick to notice that the sound of Link's footfalls will most likely alert any nearby Phantoms! She thinks he'll be OK if he **slowly walks** when Phantoms are nearby, though.

No Phantoms are about, so dash for the southwest stairs, keeping well clear of the Phantom that patrols near them.

Temple of the Ocean King: B8

Well, that was fast! You've already reached the eighth basement floor. Wait on the entry safe zone and pay close attention to the movements of the nearby Phantom. Watch him move along your map until you see him float across the central chasm. There must be an invisible footbridge! Make a note on your map by tracing a line where the Phantom crossed.

Cross the central chasm, when it's safe to do so, using the invisible pathway that the Phantom has so kindly revealed. You can explore this half of the floor if you like, but there isn't much you can do here at present. Have a look around if you wish, then bound up the southeast stairs to return to the seventh basement floor.

CAUTION

Remember that Link's footfalls make noise when he's running across water. Walk silently when Phantoms are nearby!

CAUTION

Keep off the eastern "safe zone" near the bones of a fallen adventurer: it's actually a trapdoor in disguise!

Temple of the Ocean King: B7 Revisited

You're not going in circles. Really! Sure, you're back on the seventh floor, but now you've reached its eastern side. This portion of the floor is heavily guarded, so you've got to make each movement count. Wait on the entry safe zone and watch your map closely, monitoring

the nearby blue and red Phantoms. Wait until the stationary blue Phantom turns to face north and the red Phantom is heading eastward along the central hall, then dash westward, circling around to follow after the red Phantom.

CAUTION

Keep a distance from the red Phantom and start walking if you catch up to him. The ground's covered in water here and Link's footsteps make too much noise if he runs!

TIP

If you're having difficulty outmaneuvering the Phantoms, fire arrows at their backs to stun them for a time.

Move to the central hallway as quickly as possible and lift the red pot in the east alcove. Carry the pot a few paces south and then toss it in front of the stationary blue Phantom. The noise draws the Phantom's ire, so quickly move onto the puddle of safe zone and wait for the guards to resume their posts. Afterward, ready the Boomerang and trace a line southward to strike the crystal orb in the alcove near the blue Phantom.

TIP

If you're quick with the Bow, you may find it easier to shoot the blue Phantom in the back when he turns to face eastward, then dash forward to activate the orb before he recovers.

Smack! The orb lights up and some flames to the north die down. Now you can travel across some more moving platforms! Make your way over to the moving platforms when it's safe to do so, then step on the nearest one to start riding north across the chasm. Face eastward as you travel along: two traps fire arrows at you from the east wall, but Link can deflect the projectiles with his trusty shield!

CAUTION

The north flames light up if the Phantoms spot you. Make sure to stay out of sight!

Step west off the final platform to reach the farthest north ledge. You've finally reached the chest you noticed before! Flip its lid open to claim a **round crystal** from within. This'll come in handy.

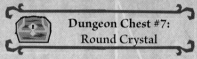

Dungeon Chest #7:
Round Crystal

Round Crystal

You've found the **round crystal**! Take it to the same-shaped pedestal.

You can't return south on the moving platforms: those searing flames have flared up again! Fortunately, snagging the round crystal has doused another set of flames to the east. Use the northernmost moving platform as a stepping stone to reach the floor's northeast corner, then carefully move southward, carrying the round crystal overhead as you make for the southeast stairs.

NOTE

Did you take note of the small wooden peg in the northeast corner? Make sure to mark it on your map for future reference!

Temple of the Ocean King: B8 Revisited

Now we're getting somewhere! Again, wait for the nearby red Phantom to cross the invisible walkway before dashing northward with your round crystal in hand. Walk to the central safe zone and drop the crystal into the circle-shaped pedestal you find there. Presto! The nearby spikes retract into the floor; you now have access to the northwest stairs.

Task 3:
Return to the Temple of the Ocean King

Two yellow pots are now within your grasp, if you want them. Head north and climb a short flight of steps to the west, then ready the Boomerang when you reach the top. Hurl the Boomerang westward to smash a yellow pot on a tall ledge. Nice one!

Next, step on the nearby pressure switch to activate a gust geyser just south of the circle-shaped pedestal. Move to the gust geyser when the patrolling blue Phantom isn't about and sail upward, landing on top of the nearby wall. Hey, here's a yellow pot up here!

Smash the pot for another 30 seconds' worth of sand, then quickly drop to the ground and dash down the northwest staircase.

Temple of the Ocean King: B9

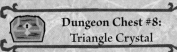

Your first visit to the ninth basement floor is a short one. A wide spread of flames to the west corners you near the stairs. The trip isn't a total loss, however: open a small chest down here. Inside you find another crystal—a **triangle crystal**, to be exact!

Dungeon Chest #8:
Triangle Crystal

Triangle Crystal
You've found the **triangle crystal**! Take it to the same-shaped pedestal.

Smash the nearby pots for items if you like, then carry the triangle crystal back upstairs. Just before you go up, Ciela flutters past the flames to the west, pointing out a square-shaped pedestal on the other side. Too bad you can't cross those flames so easily! Make a note of the pedestal's location, then return to the floor above.

Temple of the Ocean King: B8 Third Visit

This next bit's a breeze! Simply avoid the Phantoms as you carry the triangle crystal south, using the invisible pathway to move eastward across the central chasm once more. This time, go north toward the door's farthest northeast safe zone. Remember to avoid the safe zone along the east wall: It's really just a trapdoor!

Upon reaching the farthest northeast safe zone, drop the triangle crystal and move to pick up the nearby red pot against the east wall. Carry the pot a few paces westward and toss it in front of the sealed north door. Use the safe zone puddle as a midway point between the northeast safe zone and the bomb block to the west. Pull out a Bomb and plant it near the bomb block when the patrolling Phantom isn't about, then quickly move to collect the triangle crystal.

Well, what do you know? That bomb block was covering up a triangle-shaped pedestal! Carry the triangle crystal there and place it onto the pedestal to lower some spikes to the south and cause a giant treasure chest to appear to the north. The chest seems to be floating in midair over the central chasm!

→ NOTE ←

There's one little square of safe zone in front of the triangle pedestal. You're safe from the wandering Phantom as long as you stand there.

Allow the Phantom to move away eastward, then dash north, crossing the floor's farthest north hallway as you make for the treasure chest. Though you can't see it, there's a short invisible pathway leading south toward the chest! The darkest portion of the floor shows where the path lies. Open the chest for a special reward: another glowing **Courage Gem**!

→ NOTE ←

There's no rush to reach this chest. It won't disappear on you!

Dungeon Chest #9:
Courage Gem #7

Courage Gem #7
You got a **Courage Gem**! Collect these items and use them to power up the Courage Spirit.

Very nice! Now it's time to move along. Return to the nearest safe zone and then dash past the spikes you've just lowered. A crystal orb stands just beyond the spikes! Whack it to lower the sealed north door, granting you access to another set of stairs. Take the triangle crystal from its pedestal before heading downstairs: you'll soon need it again!

How's your time, hero? You shouldn't have any trouble reaching your goal if you've got more than five minutes left to work with.

Temple of the Ocean King: B9 Revisited

Great work! You've made it to the ninth basement floor's east side. Now you can fully explore this area! Leave the triangle crystal at the entry safe zone and speak with the spirit of a fallen adventurer who lies right nearby. The fallen adventurer gives you an eerie warning: there are things other than Phantoms to fear down here! Creepy.

Take a look at your map and notice that it now features four skull icons, one at each corner of the floor. These icons represent a new breed of baddie that the fallen adventurer warned you about: Wizzrobes! These fiendish ghouls are completely invisible until just before they strike. As soon as they slip into range, a Wizzrobe unleashes a fast attack that chops 15 seconds of time off your clock! Keep an eye on your map screen as you explore this floor, and be wary when Wizzrobes draw near!

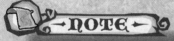

After striking Link, a Wizzrobe disappears for a short time, eventually reappearing at its starting corner of the floor.

Wizzrobes are cowardly villains and they disappear if you turn to face them. When one prepares to attack you from behind, quickly unleash a spin attack to defeat it, then collect the time bonus it drops. Defeat all the Wizzrobes on the floor to gain a full two minutes' worth of extra time!

Wizzrobe

Threat Meter

Speed: Normal

Attack Power: 15 seconds drained (scythe)

Defense Power: 1 hit to defeat

Feel a chill in the air? Better take a look behind you: a Wizzrobe may be close on your heels! These ghouls remain invisible until they slip behind Link, then they swing at him with their scythes. Each hit they score instantly drains 15 seconds from the Phantom Hourglass! Wizzrobes can pass through walls and the like to get close to Link with frightening speed. The young hero must keep tabs on them by glancing at his map, and make good use of safe zones to escape the Wizzrobes' wrath. Fortunately, each time a Wizzrobe draws near, Link has a chance to retaliate by unleashing a quick spin attack! One spinning blow from Link's sword is all it takes to wipe a Wizzrobe from existence.

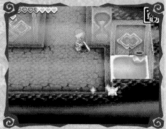

From the entry safe zone, dash south, heading for the distant safe zone at the floor's southeast corner. Dodge any Wizzrobes that materialize nearby, or better yet, execute spin attacks to defeat them and claim the time bonuses they drop!

Catch your breath at the southeast safe zone before readying your Boomerang. Dash westward when no enemies are about, then whack the arrow orb that hovers over the nearby pit. Strike it just once to point it northward and then quickly ready your Bow.

Fire an arrow into the orb to send it flying northward to strike the eye crest on the nearby wall.

This eye crest closes when Link looks toward it! To open it up, stand north of the arrow orb so that Link is facing south when firing at the orb.

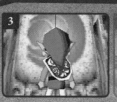

Task 3:
Return to the Temple of the Ocean King

Activating the eye crest lowers some spikes that block another safe zone to the west. Go over there, destroying the bomb blocks in front of a nearby safe zone to give yourself some refuge from the patrolling Phantom. Dash to the western safe zone when you're ready, checking your map for Wizzrobes as you go.

This safe zone features a pressures switch that controls a nearby trapdoor. Did you notice how the map shows that the Phantom is carrying a square crystal? Sure you did! Use the trapdoor to dunk the Phantom and so you may retrieve the crystal he guards.

Square Crystal

You've found the **square crystal**! Take it to the same-shaped pedestal.

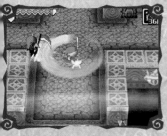

Well done! That Phantom didn't know what hit him. Before grabbing that square crystal, let's first secure the rest of the floor. Move about and get those Wizzrobes to chase you, then use fast spin attacks to defeat each one as it approaches from behind. Wipe out all four Wizzrobes to reveal a large treasure chest near the floor's center of! Pop that sucker open to add another glimmering **Wisdom Gem** to your collection.

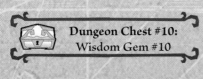
Dungeon Chest #10:
Wisdom Gem #10

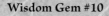
Wisdom Gem #10
You've found your tenth **Wisdom Gem**! Now you can visit Spirit Island and power up the Spirit of Wisdom!

You may have noticed another little chest in the floor's southwest corner. Move to that safe zone and open the chest for a random **ship part**. Don't you just love surprises?

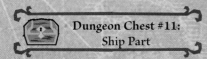
Dungeon Chest #11:
Ship Part

Ship Part
Random You got a **ship part**! Visit a Shipyard to install it onto Linebeck's ship.

Obtaining the Sea Chart

Alright, time to wrap things up! Retrieve the triangle crystal you left near the northeast stairs and bring it to the large northern safe zone. Three pedestals stand there, one in the shape of a triangle, one in the shape of a square, and one in the shape of a circle. Set the triangle crystal onto its pedestal and then move to collect the square crystal that the Phantom left behind after you dropped him through the trapdoor.

Don't bring the square crystal to the northern safe zone. Instead, carry it to the northwest corner of the floor, where the square-shaped pedestal that Ciela noticed awhile ago still stands. You know what to do! Drop the square crystal onto the pedestal to lower the nearby flames and get fast access to the floor above. Race upstairs without delay.

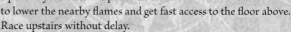

You're back at the eighth basement floor and very near the round crystal. Dash to collect the crystal when the Phantom isn't about. Naturally, this causes the nearby spikes to rise, preventing you from reaching the stairs. Nothing is ever easy!

The south gust geyser is your ticket to reaching the stairs. Dash to the gust geyser when it's safe to do so and ride up to reach the top of the surrounding walls. Nice! Now simply cross the walls and drop off near the stairs to return to the ninth floor with the round crystal in hand.

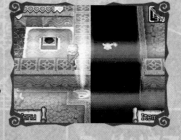

You're home free! Drop each crystal onto its proper pedestal at the northern safe zone. When all three crystals have been inserted, the north door slides away.

Temple of the Ocean King: Elevator Chamber

Well done! You've solved the puzzles and have seen much of this dreary temple. Now a great prize is within your grasp! The giant chest on the north platform contains the item you seek: another **sea chart**. Now you can explore the Great Sea's southeast quadrant!

Dungeon Chest #12:
Sea Chart #3

Sea Chart #3
You got another **sea chart**! This one reveals the southwest quadrant of the Great Sea.

After collecting the sea chart, Ciela hints that you should be able to explore deeper into the temple if you so desire. The nearby fallen adventurer gives you a clue on how to do just that: exit this chamber and then reinsert the crystals in the following order: **square**, **circle**, and then **triangle**. Doing so opens the sealed door as before, but this time, reentering the sea chart chamber causes the whole room to lower just like an elevator! When you exit the chamber once more, you find you're on the temple's tenth basement floor. Wild!

➤NOTE➤

Though you don't need to go any farther, you're now free to explore the rest of the temple. In fact, if you're really good, you can keep going and obtain the fourth sea chart right here and now! Only the most skillful will be able to obtain the fourth sea chart at present, however. We strongly recommend that you stop for the moment: you'll soon return here armed with new talents and abilities—and several additional minutes' worth of sand for your hourglass! However, if you're determined to take the hard road and continue on, skip ahead in the walkthrough to the next visit to the Temple of the Ocean King. Otherwise, just keep on reading!

Task 4:
Sail to the Southeast Quadrant

Shovin' Off

Unlike the first two sea charts, this one doesn't hold any secret crests or markings for Link and Linebeck to decipher. It merely reveals the southeastern portion of the sea, allowing you to explore the region as you see fit. Of course, there are a number of beneficial side tasks for you to undertake at the moment! Check the following Missing Links sections for complete details, or simply skip past it to continue on with the main adventure.

Missing Links

Hope you're up for a bit of optional adventuring, because the payoffs are huge this time around! Completing the Missing Links that are currently available lets you enter the next dungeon with more Bombs and two more powered-up spirit fairies. Talk about gaining an edge!

Treasure Huntin'

Your first optional find lies right at Mercay Island and can be nabbed before you set sail for the southeast quadrant of the sea. Before shoving off, pay a short visit to the northeast isle and speak with Freedle, who stands near her magic boxes. She has heard of Link's brave deeds and hands the boy a **treasure map** she'd been holding onto. What a nice gesture!

Treasure Map #11
You got a **treasure map**! It reveals the location of a sunken treasure on the Great Sea.

If you feel like paying a quick stop to Molida Island, a treasure map is available to you there as well. No need to venture far to get it: simply speak with the young girl running about near the pier. Sure enough, she hands over a **treasure map** to aid Link in his quest. Pay dirt!

Treasure Map #12
You got a **treasure map**! It reveals the location of a sunken treasure on the Great Sea.

...continued

Now that you've found a few maps, why not head out to sea and haul up some loot? You have three new maps since your last salvage expedition and can now haul up sunken treasures 11 through 13. Here's what you'll get:

Sunken Treasure Chests 11-13

#	Contents	Bonus Rupees	Location
11	Sand of Hours (1 minute)	Green (21)	NWQ; North of Isle of Gust
12	Ship Part	Green (5); Blue (1); Red 1)	SEQ; North of Dee Ess Island
13	Ship Part	Green (9)	SEQ; East of Harrow Island

Spirit of Wisdom Upgrade

If you've been following this walkthrough carefully, you found your tenth Wisdom Gem on your last dive into the Temple of the Ocean King. You know what that means! Plot a course for Spirit Island and visit the spring there to power up Neri, the Spirit of Wisdom. Now you can equip Neri at the Collection menu to increase the defensive ability of Link's shield! When powered up by Neri, Link can block stronger attacks than he could before.

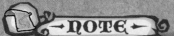

> **NOTE**
>
> Link can only equip one spirit fairy at a time. Call up the Collection menu and tap the spirit you wish to use.

Pirating Some Courage

The first time you sail out to explore the southeast quadrant of the sea, you're likely to encounter a ship full of dangerous pirates! This pirate ship is easy to identify from regular Cannon Boats: it's a bit bigger and features a large sail. The pirate ship tries to slow you down with long-range fire and attempts to board Linebeck's vessel just like that crazy pirate girl, Jolene!

There's treasure to be had from the hands of these pirates, so let them close in. When they board Linebeck's ship, a host of Miniblins floods into the cabin. Wipe them all out and then speak with Linebeck, who hides inside a nearby crate as usual. He's glad to have Link on his side and hands over a glimmering **Courage Gem**!

...continued

Courage Gem #8

You got a **Courage Gem**! Collect these items and use them to power up the Courage Spirit.

Bombs from Beedle

After you've dealt with the southeast quadrant's few initial nautical threats, you're able to explore the waters and discover a number of valuable goodies. Set your first course for Beedle's Shop Ship to find the man sells, among other things, a precious **Bomb Bag** for the high price of 1,000 Rupees. Get some funds together and buy that Bomb Bag without delay!

Bomb Bag #2

You got another **Bomb Bag**! Now you can carry 10 more Bombs, for a new maximum of 30. You couldn't possibly carry more!

More Golden Froggies

While exploring the southeast quadrant, keep your eyes peeled for two little golden frogs that hop about the waters. The first is near the middle of the sea, a little way east of Goron Island. Blast this playful fellow from midair with the cannon to learn a new warp symbol for your Cyclone Slate!

Another golden frog hangs out to the northeast, right near the ice-covered Isle of Frost. Sail about and pop him with a cannonball to learn yet another Cyclone Slate warp symbol. Travel will be a breeze from this point forward!

Traveler's Ship

Hey, another Traveler's Ship sails around these south-eastern waters! Pay a visit to the southeast quadrant's Traveler's Ship to meet up with a group of unique treasure-seeking explorers called Ho Hos. These intrepid travelers have a keen eye for valuables: speak to the Ho Ho who stands at the north end of the cabin to learn that he seeks rare and precious items. He'll pay top dollar if you manage to bring him a prized treasure!

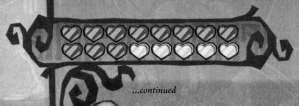

...continued

NOTE

Regal Rings are the rarest of all treasures. If you're lucky enough to have found one by this point in the adventure, feel free to sell it to the Ho Hos. They pay out far more for these special treasures than the Treasure Teller at Mercay Island!

Speak to the rest of the Ho Hos to learn bits and pieces about their mysterious culture. One of the men mentions that he seems to have misplaced something, but he doesn't get into specifics. Curious...perhaps you'll be able to help find what he seeks in the future!

Digging for Riches: Harrow Island

A small island to the north is uncharted. Sail northward until you spy the isle, which Ciela quickly jots down on your sea chart. Let's see what this place has to offer!

There isn't much to see or do at the island until you whack a stone statue that stands near the pier. The statue welcomes you to the island and offers you a chance to dig for fortune and glory, all for the small price of 50 Rupees. Pay the statue and then step onto the gust geyser that starts blowing nearby to be blown northward and reach a huge sand pit that dominates most of the island!

This desert is actually a huge sandbox filled with wondrous prizes. What a find! Dig about to unearth up to 10 random treats, including the following:

| Blue Rupees | Red Rupees | Big green Rupees | 10 and 50 Rupoor |

NOTE

You can also dig up four separate treasure maps in the sandbox, but we've got more important things to worry about; namely the pure metals! Check back here after finishing the Temple of Ice to get two treasure maps, and again after obtaining the fourth and final sea chart to get the other two.

While digging for loot, you'll periodically uncover an invisible spirit named Lucky Lee who resides here at Harrow Island. Lucky Lee always offers to let you play a special game of chance: for just 50 more Rupees, you can open one of two chests and win even greater prizes! Here's what you can win:

I'm Lucky Lee, the lucky spirit that dwells on this island!

Tiny winner: 40 Rupees. Uh-oh!

So-so winner: 150 Rupees. Nice!

Big winner: 300 Rupees. Whoa!

CAUTION

Whatever you do, make sure you stop digging after uncovering your tenth prize at Harrow Island. If you keep digging for more loot after being told to stop, you suffer a harsh 100-Rupee penalty! If you continue to dig, you lose all your Rupees. If you keep digging, you're banned from playing here. You'll then need to pay 300 Rupees to get out of the ban and play again.

Dee Ess Island

Legend

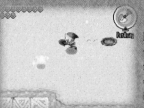 Overworld Chest #25: Courage Gem #10

  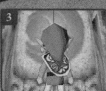 

Task 4:
Sail the Southeast Quadrant

Prima Official Game Guide

196

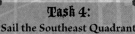

...continued

Items to Obtain

| Big Green Rupee x2 | Big Red Rupee | Courage Gem #9 | Courage Gem #10 |

Overworld Denizens

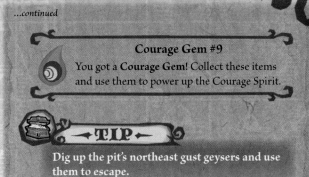

| Characters | | Enemies | | |
| Gorons | Bee | Eye Brute | Rock ChuChu | Rope |

There's another small, uncharted island to the south. Scour the seas east of Goron Island to find a bit of land with a familiar shape called Dee Ess Island. The name is certainly fitting: the whole island is shaped like a DS!

Ciela marks the island's location on your sea chart for future reference. Drop anchor there and have a quick look around. Some Gorons are preparing to set up a business in the wide southern pit, but they aren't quite ready to accept customers yet. Say hello and remember this spot for future reference!

Whack the stone statue to the north for an unusual tip: something good is buried beneath the lower screen's Menu tab. How strange! Could this tip have something to do with the island's shape?

It does! Drop into the southern pit, which resembles the Touch Screen of the DS on the map. Move to the pit's southwest corner, where the Menu tab would normally appear. Dig right in the corner to unearth a long-forgotten Courage Gem!

...continued

Courage Gem #9

You got a **Courage Gem**! Collect these items and use them to power up the Courage Spirit.

←TIP←

Dig up the pit's northeast gust geysers and use them to escape.

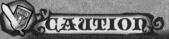

Next, wander about and spend some time digging things up with the Shovel. There are a number of suspicious-looking patches of soil lie about the island, but be careful: you may uncover nests of Bees and Ropes in addition to Rupees! Mostly you uncover minor items here, but there are a few worthy finds. Move to the northern "top screen" part of the island and dig beneath the rocks amidst the bomb flowers to the east and west to uncover two **big green Rupees** and one sparkly **big red Rupee**. Cha-ching!

CAUTION

Watch out for Rock ChuChus hiding among the bomb flowers!

Big Green Rupees

You got two **big green Rupees**! They're worth 100 Rupees apiece!

Red Rupee

You got a **big red Rupee**! Just one of these is worth 200 Rupees!

...continued

There's one last thing to do before you leave. Drop into the "top screen" pit and prepare to battle two fearsome monsters known as Eye Brutes! These fiends put up a tough fight if you try to fight on their terms. Tip the odds in your favor by firing arrows into their huge eyeballs to stun the creatures before ripping through them with fast sword attacks!

Eye Brute

Threat Meter

Speed: Slow

Attack Power: 1/2 heart (contact); 1 heart (Bomb)

Defense Power: Multiple hits to defeat

What an eyesore! These big, blue, one-eyed brutes may not have much in the way of looks, but they make up for that in sheer strength. Eye Brutes like to batter Link up close and hurl Bombs at him from afar. It's tempting to try to run from such frightening creatures, but Link's best option is to simply stare these foes right in the eye. Or better yet, let lose a few arrows! Poking out an Eye Brute's one and only eye is a surefire way to calm them down. Then Link can rush forward to inflict serious damage with his trusty blade.

...continued

Dispatch both Eye Brutes to prove your valor and cleanse Dee Ess Island of their wickedness. Of course, there's another good reason to beat them: Doing so causes a treasure chest to appear in the middle of their pit! Open the chest to claim a very precious reward: your tenth **Courage Gem!**

Overworld Chest #25:
Courage Gem #10

Courage Gem #10

You've found your tenth **Courage Gem!** Now you can visit Spirit Island and power up the Spirit of Courage!

Spirit of Courage Upgrade

This one's a no-brainer! You've found ten Courage Gems and now have the ability to power up **Ciela**, the **Spirit of Courage**. Drop anchor at Spirit Island and visit the spring to show off your gems and imbue Ciela with their sacred might. Now you can equip the Spirit of Courage from within the Collection menu! Henceforth, while Ciela is selected, a small shockwave flies outward from Link's sword, significantly increasing its attack range. Awesome!

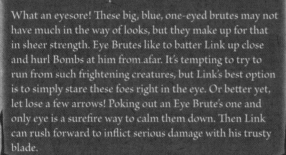

1 2 3 4

Tasks:
Complete

Contents

Goron
Temple

Shop

Rockin' and Rollin': Overview

The path has not been easy, but Link's fate has finally been made clear: Bellum must be destroyed so that Tetra and the Ocean King can be freed from his terrible curse. Three pure metals must be found so that the Phantom Sword may be reforged—for only with that sacred blade will evil finally come undone!

Fortunately, new paths offering high adventure amidst new waters have opened up to Link. An entirely new section of the sea awaits discovery, and what better place to start than that massive body of land to the south: Goron Island? The Gorons are said to be a most proud and ancient tribe.... They just might know where one of those pure metals can be found!

1. Explore Goron Island

2. Gain Access to the Temple

3. Enter & Clear Goron Temple

4. Return & Speak with Biggoron

A Link to the Present

Max 17:00

Max 50

Max 30

Lvl 1

x10

Lvl 1   Lvl 1   x11   x10

x13

Items Already Acquired

| Big Catch Lure | Bomb Bag #1 | Bomb Bag #2 | Bombs | Boomerang | Bow | Cannon | Cyclone Slate |

| Fishing Rod | Oshus's Sword | Phantom Hourglass | Quiver #1 | Quiver #2 | Salvage Arm | Shovel | Wooden Shield |

| Sun Key | Ghost Key | Courage Gems x10 | Power Gems x11 | Wisdom Gems x10 | Treasure Maps x13 | Sand of Hours: 17 Minutes |

Items to Obtain

| Big Red Rupee | Power Gem #12 | Treasure Map #14 | Treasure Map #16 | Wisdom Gem #11 |

Overworld Denizens

Characters

Biggoron   Gongoron   Gorons   Goron Shop Mistress

Enemies

Blue ChuChu   Like Like   Rock ChuChu

Task 1: Explore Goron Island

Waylaid at Sea

The crew comes under sudden attack just as they begin to near the quadrant's massive southwestern island. What's this? A giant cyclone sweeps up Linebeck's ship, and a massive creature surfaces from the water to attack! The brief yet wild cyclone ride is enough to soak the ship's engines, preventing Linebeck from propelling the craft. What a nightmare!

There's no escape! The huge sea monster begins flying about, spitting large yellow fireballs from up high. You can't hope to dodge, so stay put and simply let loose with your ship's cannon. The monster is covered with six large eyeballs: three on each side. Aim to blast out each eye, striking each one with cannonballs to redden them. Hit all six eyeballs to defeat the monster and calm the sea once more. The ship's engines become useable after the fight, and Linebeck finally manages to find harbor at the island.

TIP

Shoot down the sea monster's fireballs at every chance or you'll soon be sunk! Each one you destroy occasionally restores one heart to your ship's health.

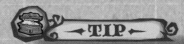

Goron Island

Meet and Greet

Arriving at the island at last, Ciela flutters about excitedly. There's just got to be some **pure metal** around here! Linebeck's instincts tell him that such a large island must be hiding vast amounts of treasure. While he can't be certain they'll find any pure metals, he's eager for Link to begin poking around. The good captain remains near his ship as always. He already has enough on his plate: He's got to think about what to wish for from old man Oshus when all this is over!

Not every inhabitant of the island is a Goron: a friendly woman has set up a small shop tent at the tiny southwest isle! Stop by and browse her wares to find a unique selection of goods, including some interesting-looking **Bombchus** that you can't purchase just yet. Stock up on goods before continuing your exploration of the island.

Speak with the funny-looking islander near the pier to learn that you've landed at Goron Island, home of the Goron tribe. The young Goron advises Link to make himself known to everyone on the island, saying that Gorons don't play with outsiders. What a great idea! Let's take a quick tour and say hello to the Gorons.

Goron Island Shop			
Item	**Cost**	**Description**	**Notes**
Arrows (10)	50 Rupees	Arrows for the Bow	Require the Bow to carry.
Bombchus (10)	50 Rupees	Mobile Explosives	Require a Bombchu Bag to carry.
Purple Potion	150 Rupees	Recovery Item	Restores up to 8 hearts; used automatically if Link falls in battle.
Yellow Potion	150 Rupees	Recovery Item	Drink to restore all hearts.

Gorons

A proud and ancient race of noble beings, the Gorons make their home on a giant island at the south end of the Great Sea. These large, rotund creatures are exceptionally strong and naturally resistant to harsh climates. They're so tough that they're perfectly comfortable living amongst the cliffs of their rocky island home! Link must prove himself to this quiet tribe in order to gain their trust, for only with their aid can he banish evil from the land.

Make your way westward, stopping to chat with Gorons you see. Some of them live within their cliffside homes; others simply stroll about in the sun. Speak to each Goron you see to learn more and more about their unique culture!

NOTE

The store also carries Wooden Shields if Link happens to lose his to a shield-devouring monster.

North of the harbor, Link finds a young Goron standing in fear of some nearby monsters on a high cliff. A gang of crackling Yellow ChuChus is giving the guy a hard time! Let's see if we can help him out. Whip out the Shovel and dig at the loose patch of soil on the ground to uncover a gust geyser, then ride it up to the north ledge.

Attack the nearby acorn for arrows, then move to the edge of the ledge. Switch to the Bow and aim at the Yellow ChuChus to the south, picking off all three from range. Take that! The Goron becomes thrilled by your marksmanship and happily hands you a **treasure map** as thanks. Well done!

 1
 2
 3
 4

Task 2:
Gain Access to the Temple

Treasure Map #14

You got a **treasure map**! It reveals the location of a sunken treasure on the Great Sea.

—NOTE—

Like bomb flowers, acorns grow back after a short time. Just one acorn can be a never-ending supply of goods!

Exploring Eastward

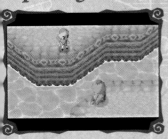

One little Goron sits on a remote ledge east of the harbor. Hey, how'd he get over there? There seems to be no way across! A nearby sign hints that you should **give a shout** if you need anything. Go on: **Shout into the DS microphone** to get the Goron's attention! The creature snaps to and kindly extends a bridge so you may cross over and explore the east half of the isle. No toll, of course!

—TIP—

As always, you can simply blow into the DS microphone to make less noise if you're in a quiet place.

More Gorons are milling about to the east. One of them helpfully points out the location of the Goron elder's home. Great! Now you can speak with the man in charge. Visit with the other Goron in his nearby home before heading northward.

Taking the easternmost trail toward the northern end of the island results in your meeting stiff resistance: A large Goron guard won't allow an outsider to explore any more of the island up north. Guess you'll just have to pay a visit to his chief and see he'll make an exception to the rule!

—TIP—

Shovel into the small digging spot near the elder's house to unearth a sparkly **red Rupee**!

Task 2: Gain Access to the Temple

The Goron Elder

Stepping into the elder's house, Link finds two Gorons standing before him: one small and one massive. The larger creature welcomes Link and introduces himself as Biggoron, leader of the Goron tribe. The smaller Goron is Gongoron, the elder's son. Neither creature has much to say to Link until they hear that he's spoken with **each and every Goron on the island**.

—NOTE—

If you're having trouble getting the elder to open up to you, leave and make sure you've talked with every Goron on the island. Barge right into their homes and speak with every creature you see! There are 14 Gorons for you to speak with in all. Chat with each one until Ciela hints that you've probably spoken with all the Gorons on the island.

Biggoron

Noble leader of the proud Goron tribe, Biggoron has seen much in his long tenure as elder. His great size and strength are matched only by his great heart—and his vast love of Goron culture! To gain acceptance among his tribe, Link must prove that his affinity for all things Goron runs just as deeply as the gentle elder's. Only then will the lad gain the help he needs to carry out his great quest!

Gongoron

Gongoron is Biggoron's one and only heir. Brash and immature, he doesn't warm up to Link at first. Instead, Gongoron resents the young outsider for trying to become a brother to the Goron tribe for selfish reasons. Gongoron soon learns that Link's heart is in the right place however, and the two end up relying on each other to get through a variety of harrowing trials.

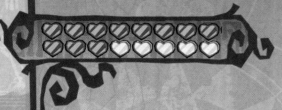

After you've spoken with all Gorons on the island, Biggoron warms up a bit. He says he'd be happy to help Link get hold of the **pure metal** he seeks, if only Link were a part of the Goron tribe. Fortunately, for just 20 Rupees, Biggoron invites Link to participate in a brief initiation quiz. If Link can pass the test, Biggoron will recognize the boy's commitment and look upon him as a true brother to the mighty Goron tribe!

Pay the 20 Rupees to begin Biggoron's quiz. The elder asks you six questions, handing out a prize each time you get one right. Answer all six questions correctly to pass the test and impress Biggoron! However, if you miss just one question, the game ends and the elder takes back all the prize money you've won. Talk about high stakes!

Here's what you win for getting each question right:

> First Question: Green Rupee
>
> Second Question: Blue Rupee
>
> Third Question: Red Rupee
>
> Fourth Question: Red Rupee
>
> Fifth Question: Big green Rupee
>
> Sixth Question: Wisdom Gem #11

All of Biggoron's questions revolve around the Gorons and their island home. He picks his questions at random, so you never know which ones he'll ask. A bit of legwork and careful note taking is all that's required to answer his questions correctly, but we'll save you some time. Here's what the elder might ask, along with the proper answers:

> Q: How many Gorons live on this island?
> **A: 14.**
>
> Q: How many homes are on this island?
> **A: 6.**
>
> Q: How many Gorons are in their homes right now?
> **A: 7.**
>
> Q: How many Gorons are outside?
> **A: 7.**
>
> Q: Of those Gorons outside, how many are adults?
> **A: 4.**
>
> Q: How many Goron children are on the island?
> **A: 6.**

> Q: How many rocks are in this home?
> **A: 3.**
>
> Q: The Goron at this spot! What is he staring at?
> **A: Ship.**
>
> Q: What color were the odd creatures on the cliff?
> **A: Yellow.**
>
> Q: Easy one, stranger! What number question is this?!
> **A: Hope you've been paying attention!**
>
> Q: How many Rupees have you won so far? Easy!
> **A: Hope you've been paying attention!**

Success! You are now an official brother of the proud Goron tribe. However, Biggoron isn't quite finished yet: he asks for a one-time payment of membership dues equaling 146 Rupees. Hey, that's the exact number of Rupees you've just won! Oh well. Pay up to make everything nice and legally binding.

The elder then tells you that the **pure metal** you seek is being kept safe in the **temple** at the north end of the island. Now that you're a full-fledged member of the Gorons, you're free to visit the temple and claim the pure metal! Speak with the elder's son, Gongoron, who has been told to guide you to the temple. The young Goron scoffs at Link and then bolts outside, taunting his charge to try to keep up. Better hurry after him!

Chasing Gongoron

Where did that little runt get to? Gongoron is nowhere about, so you'll have to track him down. You can't journey northward without your guide! Start wandering about and speaking to each Goron you see. Someone must have seen where the elder's son went!

Follow the clues that lead you westward to a tall cliff. Sure enough, Gongoron is hiding out atop the high ledge! He laughs at Link for being such a slowpoke and then quickly runs off once more. What's this guy's problem?

 1  2  3  4

Task 2:
Gain Access to the Temple

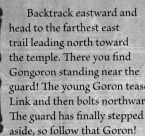

Backtrack eastward and head to the farthest east trail leading north toward the temple. There you find Gongoron standing near the guard! The young Goron teases Link and then bolts northward. The guard has finally stepped aside, so follow that Goron!

North Maze

What's this? The trail beyond the guard leads to a dead end! Surely Gongoron must have come this way. Examine the stone wall to the north to find it badly cracked in two places. These spots are weak enough to destroy with Bombs! Pluck some from the nearby bomb flower or use your own explosives to blast open the way forward, starting with the cracked wall on the left.

A new breed of ChuChu attacks you in the passage you enter. These blue ones are the most dangerous forms! They chase after Link more aggressively than others and are electrified just like Yellow ChuChus. A Blue ChuChu's electricity never fades however, so stun these villains with a quick toss of the Boomerang before moving in to swing Link's sword.

Blue ChuChu

Threat Meter

Speed: Normal

Attack Power: 1/2 heart (contact)

Defense Power: Stun with Boomerang; 2 hits to defeat

This most dangerous form of ChuChu is nothing to toy with! Blue ChuChus stalk Link with surprising ferocity, leaping and bounding forward to zap the young hero with their electrified frames. As with Yellow ChuChus, Link suffers harm if he tries attacking these guys while they're powered up. Stun them with a Boomerang toss to make them safe to strike, or simply dispatch Blue ChuChus with Bombs or arrows from a distance.

Be careful when removing rocks from your path around here: most are actually Rock ChuChus in disguise! Hurl Bombs to weaken these sneaky adversaries from afar, then finish them off with Link's sword after removing their rocky armor. Make your way

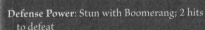

to a pressure switch to the west and step on it to lower some spikes near a nearby chest. You can't reach the chest just yet but you'll get to it soon enough!

~NOTE~

Did you notice that crystal orb all tucked away to the south? You can't reach it at present, but you'll soon discover a way!

Backtrack eastward and blast through the other bomb wall to explore more of the maze. Continue bombing through cracked walls you see, and blasting apart ChuChus you encounter. The path winds westward, eventually leading to a treasure chest! Open the chest to claim a **big green Rupee**. Score!

Overworld Chest #26: Big Green Rupee

Big Green Rupee
You got a **big green Rupee**! It's worth 100 Rupees!

It's always nice to pocket some cash, but you now seem to be stuck: the trail has ended at the treasure chest! Backtrack eastward a short distance until you notice a large ornate symbol on the ground of the neighboring passage to the north. This symbol must mean something! Maybe there used to be a passage here? Place a Bomb near the wall right below the symbol to blast a hole clean through.

Now you can run westward and escape the maze. That wasn't so bad! Don't forget about that chest you noticed earlier, though: re-enter the maze through the nearby southern passage to finally reach the chest, which contains a gleaming **Power Gem**. Nice!

Overworld Chest #27: Power Gem #12

Power Gem #12
You got a **Power Gem**! Collect these items and use them to power up the Power Spirit.

Breaching the Temple

Link comes face-to-face with a terrible new foe just beyond the maze: a Like Like! Don't go anywhere near this funny-looking monster: it can quickly suck Link up and eat his Wooden Shield! Keep a distance and ready the Bombs, then toss one at the Like Like when it starts sucking in air. The creature sucks up the Bomb and suffers great harm; hurry to finish it off with Link's blade while it's stunned!

CAUTION

Like Likes eat shields! If one sucks Link up, hurry to defeat it and then quickly grab the Wooden Shield it drops before it vanishes. If you aren't able to recover the shield, you can always buy another one at the Goron shop.

Like Like

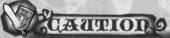

Threat Meter

Speed: Slow

Attack Power: 1/2 heart (devour)

Defense Power: 1 Bomb to weaken; 1 hit to defeat

Keep well away from Like Likes: they quickly suck Link up and start digesting him. Getting sucked up by a creepy Like Like is bad news because these cylindrical villains love snacking on shields! They don't do so well after munching down Bombs though, and Link can trick these hungry uglies into doing just that!

Wipe out the Like Like to prove your worth and open the way forward. The long row of spikes to the west soon retracts, granting you entry to the Goron Temple! Approach the temple's entrance and step on the nearby pressure switch to span a footbridge that leads back toward the harbor. Feel free to hit the local shop one last time to gear up: the Temple is a very dangerous place!

Task 3: Enter & Clear the Goron Temple

You've done it! The Gorons have accepted you as one of their own and you've gained access to their sacred temple. Hopefully that pure metal is somewhere safe inside!

Goron Temple

Goron Temple: 1F

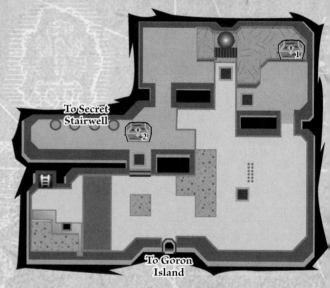

To Secret Stairwell

To Goron Island

Legend

Dungeon Chest #1: Treasure Map #15	Dungeon Chest #6: Treasure
Dungeon Chest #2: Red Rupee	Dungeon Chest #7: Boss Key
Dungeon Chest #3: Bombchus	Dungeon Chest #8: Heart Container #9
Dungeon Chest #4: Treasure	Orb
Dungeon Chest #5: Red Rupee	Floor Switch

Goron Temple: Secret Stairwell

to Basement 1

to 1st Floor   to 1st Floor

Goron Temple: B1

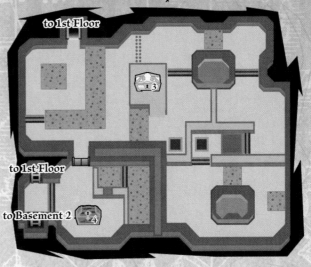

to 1st Floor

to 1st Floor

to Basement 2

Goron Temple: B2

to Basement 3

to Basement 3

to Basement 1

Goron Temple: B3

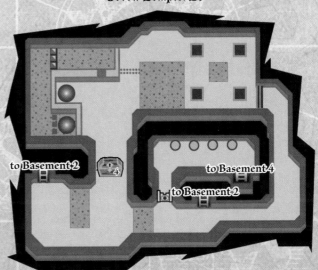

to Basement 2

to Basement 4

to Basement 2

Goron Temple: B4

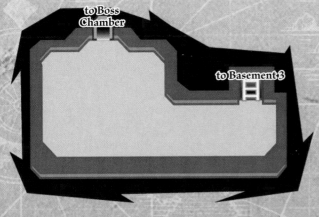

to Boss Chamber

to Basement 3

Goron Temple: Boss Chamber

to Crimsonine Chamber

to Basement 4

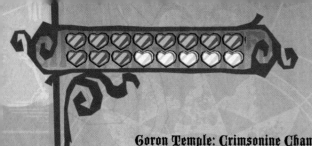

Goron Temple: Crimsonine Chamber

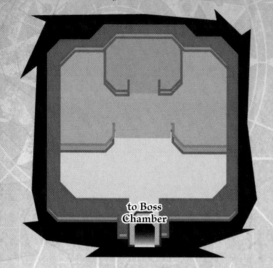

to Boss Chamber

Items to Obtain

Bombchus · Boss Key · Crimsonine · Heart Container #9

Red Rupees x2 · Treasure Map #15 · Random Treasures x2

Dungeon Denizens

Characters — Enemies

Gongoron · Armos · Beamos · Blue ChuChu · Eye Slug

Boss

Fire Bubble · Green Slime · Miniblin · Rock ChuChu · Dongorongo, Armored Lizard

Goron Temple: 1F

Gongoron is nowhere in sight, but he must be hiding in the temple somewhere! A nearby stone tablet offers you an important initial warning: **keep away from quicksand.** Keep this in mind and steer clear of deep-looking sand, as falling in inflicts half a heart's worth of damage! Move eastward past the sign, defeating Blue ChuChus while you carefully avoid being tagged by the nearby Beamoses.

A row of spikes blocks your progress through the Beamos maze. This is a dangerous place to hang out, so let's hurry up and get rid of those spikes! Tap the large statue near the maze's center to make Link grab it, just like a stone block. Shove the statue eastward and then south, following the line of dark floor tiles. Carefully avoid the Beamoses' laser eyes as you maneuver the giant statue onto the pressure switch, lowering the spikes so you can escape.

Be careful when venturing northward: a new enemy lies in wait! The next large dark statue you encounter springs to life as you draw near, producing spikes from its base and hopping after you wherever you go. Run away from this threat and ready a Bomb, then quickly toss the explosive at the statue to permanently disable it from range.

Armos

Threat Meter

Speed: Normal

Attack Power: 1/2 heart (contact)

Defense Power: 1 Bomb to disable

Huge and intimidating, these statue-like sentries remain completely docile until an intruder draws near. As soon as it detects a trespasser, an Armos suddenly comes to life, stomping about in pursuit to eliminate the threat! While these massive beings are too sturdy to take damage from Link's sword, they're highly vulnerable to explosives. Just one blast from a Bomb shuts down an Armos for good!

Task 3:
Enter and Clear the Goron Temple

Whew, that was close! After you disable the Armos, you can grab it just like the giant statue you previously saw. Grab this one and shove it onto the pressure switch to the north. A steel door then rises to the east, granting you access to a nearby chamber.

NOTE

Never mind the crystal orb across the north quicksand or the eye crest hanging up on a nearby wall. You'll deal with these objects soon enough!

Ready your Bombs before proceeding into the next chamber: another Armos statue quickly comes charging your way! Heave a Bomb at the statue to shut it down with a bang, then shove its hulking remains westward along the floor tiles. Position the statue on a nearby pressure switch to extend a bridge across the chasm to the west.

Backtrack a bit and dig at the soft patch of soil nearby to uncover a gust geyser. Ride upward to the ledge above so you may cross the bridge you've just extended. Pluck up a Bomb from a nearby bomb flower, step onto the bridge, and then toss the Bomb at the crystal orb in the quicksand below.

Boom! The Bomb activates the orb and causes a hidden treasure chest to appear to the east. Dash over to the chest and open it before it disappears once more. The prize you find is worthwhile: a **treasure map** is inside!

Dungeon Chest #1: Treasure Map #15

Treasure Map #15

You got a **treasure map**! It reveals the location of a sunken treasure on the Great Sea.

Keep your Bombs at the ready: more Armoses are ahead! Cross the bridge and drop into the west chamber beyond, which is guarded by two active Armoses. Blast each one with a Bomb to secure the chamber and open the sealed south door. There's no need to shove these statues around after the fight; just leave them and continue going southward.

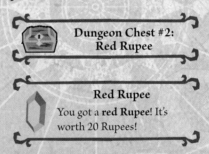

Step on the pressure switch ahead to lower some spikes at the foot of the nearby stairs. Now you can quickly return to the entrance! But you don't need to do so at present. Instead, move to the east balcony and fire an arrow at the eye crest on the east wall.

Thwack! The crest activates, revealing a nearby chest that contains a shiny **red Rupee**!

Dungeon Chest #2: Red Rupee

Red Rupee

You got a **red Rupee**! It's worth 20 Rupees!

Goron Temple: Secret Stairwell

Now, run west down a nearby passage and use a Bomb to blast a hole through a cracked portion of the north wall. Blammo! You've gained access to a secret chamber, but you can't do much from your current vantage: a pit of quicksand blocks the east half of the room! Smash the nearby acorn for items and then step back through the wall.

There's got to be another way into that area! Move east a few paces and then place another Bomb between the two far right pillars along the north wall. Sure enough, you're able to blast right through to the east half of the secret chamber. Sneaky! Smash the pots and acorn as you make for the north stairs.

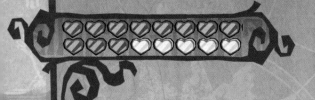

Goron Temple: B1

Watch out: Link is ambushed just seconds after he reaches the basement! The door seals shut behind him and two Fire Bubbles begin bouncing in his direction. Stay near the entry door to avoid becoming a target for the two nearby Beamoses and unleash the Boomerang on the Bubbles as they draw near to knock them both to the ground. Quickly lash out with Link's sword to finish the Bubbles off when no Beamos is watching.

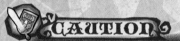

CAUTION

Be careful not to fall into the surrounding quicksand during the fight!

Defeating the Bubbles lowers the door near the stairs, along with a row of spikes to the south. Equip the Bow, then dash south past the spikes, carefully avoiding the Beamoses as you go. Follow the path eastward until you finally catch up to a familiar character.

Trapped!

*Gongoron calls out to Link from beyond a pit of quicksand. It seems that the young Goron hasn't been hiding at all: he's been captured by the monsters in the temple! Despite how mean Gongoron has been to Link, the young hero still **agrees to help him out** of his predicament. Overwhelmed with joy, Gongoron thanks Link and apologizes profusely for his recent behavior.*

You don't have much time to chat with Gongoron: a vicious Eye Brute suddenly appears behind you and attacks! You've seen these guys before on Dee Ess Island and know what to do: get some distance and then fire an arrow into its eye! As the creature staggers in pain, rush forward and finish it off with a blazing barrage of cold steel.

TIP

The nearby acorn yields arrows if you're low.

Amazed at his friend's display of heroism, Gongoron happily agrees to work with Link so they can both escape this awful place together. His help is certainly needed: a row of spikes to the south prevents Link from exploring any farther! Tap the icon that appears at the top of the Touch Screen to switch control between Link and Gongoron.

NOTE

Link and Gongoron's fates are now joined! Henceforth, the two share the same heart meter. If one of them falls in battle, so will the other!

Take a moment to get used to steering Gongoron before moving much farther. Notice that he tucks and rolls as you move him faster: Gongoron smashes right through objects like pots and rocks while rolling along at a good clip! Send him crashing through the collection of rocks to the south to uncover three hidden Rock ChuChus. Each time one pops out, stop rolling and tap the creature to make Gongoron smash it with a fast jump attack! Smash all three Rock ChuChus to pieces to lower the spikes near Link.

Switch control over to the boy in green and move south beyond the spikes that Gongoron has so kindly lowered. Be careful, though: two Like Likes lurk just ahead! Feed them a Bomb from range and then bring the full weight of Link's sword to bear. Be quick to reclaim your Wooden Shield from the Like Likes if they happen to gobble it up!

Teamwork Time

A bit of exploration shows that Link has come to another dead end. This time he must help clear the way for his partner! Move Link onto the nearby pressure switch to lower some spikes on Gongoron's side of the floor, then switch control back to the elder's son.

1

2

3

4

Task 3:
Enter and Clear the Goron Temple

As Gongoron, roll down to the spikes Link has lowered. There's a pit beyond them, but it's not too wide for a fast-moving Goron to clear! Run up and send Gongoron rolling right over the pit and onto the ledge beyond. Once there, position Gongoron onto the nearby pressure switch.

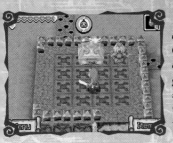

Poof! A giant treasure chest appears near Link. Leave Gongoron at the switch and change control back to our green-clad hero. As Link, approach the chest and open it to claim an awesome new tool: the **Bombchus**!

Now that Gongoron's surroundings are secure, switch back over to Link and then make a dash for the door that has just opened. Oh, no. More Eye Slugs! These creepy crawlers pose little threat to Link, so wipe them all out with some fancy swordplay to cause a hidden chest to appear nearby. Pop the chest open to claim a lovely **treasure**—a Goron Amber!

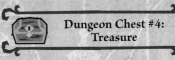
Dungeon Chest #4: Treasure

Treasure
Random
You got a **treasure**! Collect these items and sell them to the highest bidder!

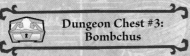
Dungeon Chest #3: Bombchus

Bombchus

You got the **Bombchus**! Now you can blow stuff up from long range! Ready the Bombchus as you would any other tool, then trace out a route for the Bombchu to follow. The Bombchu then rolls along the exact path you've drawn and explodes on contact with whatever it strikes!

Acquiring the Bombchus causes a row of spikes to lower near Gongoron. Swap control over to Gongoron for the moment and roll southward. Whoa! A number of Eye Slugs slither about down here, searching for their next meal. Don't become it! Tap each Eye Slug or simply roll Gongoron into these minor threats to clear the area. Defeat all the nearby Eye Slugs to lend a hand and open a sealed door for Link!

You've done all you can around here, but how are you to proceed? With the help of a Bombchu, that's how! Notice a small hole in the nearby wall. Move Link close to the hole and then ready a Bombchu. Tap the Item icon to pause the in-game action and call the map down to the lower screen. Now you can plot out your Bombchu's path with your stylus! Carefully trace a line north through the tiny hole, east across the quicksand beyond, and then south toward the nearby crystal orb. Accept your decision to send the Bombchu rolling!

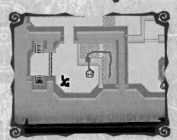

→NOTE←

If you make an error, simply cancel the current path to start a new one.

Eye Slug

Threat Meter

Speed: Normal

Attack Power: 1/2 heart (contact)

Defense Power: 1 hit to defeat

These slithering fiends sure look mean, but they barely register on the threat meter. Link has faced far more dangerous creatures already in his adventures and can easily wipe out these small-time pests however he chooses. The spin attack usually works quite well, as Eye Slugs tend to attack in groups and can quickly swarm Link.

Excellent work! The Bombchu rolls through the tiny hole, crosses the quicksand, and then detonates on impact with the crystal orb. This lights the orb, which lowers the final set of spikes to the west. You've done it! Now you can continue onward.

Gongoron sees Link is doing well and decides to venture on without him. Finding a small hole he can just barely squeeze through, Gongoron thanks Link for his help and then departs. Proceed down the southwest stairs to reach the next basement floor below.

You may also return to the first floor using the stairs to the north. The only reason to do so is to extend a footbridge leading back to the temple entrance, and this is a purely optional venture.

Goron Temple: B2

Blast and carve your way through the Like Like and two Rock ChuChus in the second basement floor's first few halls. Lift and toss the southeast rock to reveal a small hole in the nearby wall. Remember the hole's location: you'll soon be using it!

Go north and whack the nearby stone statue for a hot tip: you must **light two crystal orbs** at the same time if you want to progress any farther. One of the orbs stands in the alcove to the east. The other orb stands just east of that one, but beyond a wall. How will you ever manage to strike both at once?

With Bombchus, of course! Stand near the orb and whip out a Bombchu, then start tracing a line on your Touch Screen map. Send the Bombchu south and into the tiny hole you uncovered just moments ago. Guide the Bombchu from there into another small hole that leads into a tiny alcove, where the second orb stands. Accept your path to send the Bombchu puttering off toward the orb.

Although your viewpoint usually follows the Bombchu to its destination, you can change all of that with a touch of the stylus. Tap anywhere on the Touch Screen to center the action back on Link. Watch your map closely as the Bombchu moves along its path, and tap the crystal orb near Link to make him whack it just as the Bombchu blasts the other one nearby.

Smooth! Both orbs light simultaneously and the spikes to the west quickly retract into the floor. Your path to the next basement floor is clear! Go downstairs to continue your search for the pure metals.

Goron Temple: B3

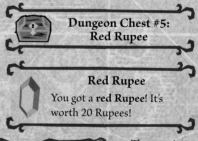

Wow, this is one deep temple! The third basement floor is as large as the first two and equally dangerous. Carefully move about the large western chamber, bringing Link's blade to bear against the hoard of Miniblins hopping about down here. Eliminate all the Miniblins to cause a hidden chest to appear in the room's center. How nice! Open the chest to claim a lovely **red Rupee**.

CAUTION

Watch the pots near the Miniblins: they'll come flying right at you! Smash them with the Boomerang from a safe distance.

Dungeon Chest #5:
Red Rupee

Red Rupee
You got a **red Rupee**! It's worth 20 Rupees!

The area is now secure, but there seems to be no way of getting past a strip of spikes to the north. Not so! Approach the nearby crystal orb, which glows a bright red. Smack the orb with Link's sword to change its hue to blue. This lowers some red blocks in the sand-filled chamber to the west while raising some blue ones there as well. Interesting!

Task 3:
Enter and Clear the Goron Temple

Now that the orb is glowing blue, ready a Bombchu and then trace its path through the small hole in the north wall. Send the Bombchu west into the sand-filled chamber and then south, crossing the blue blocks and ending at the darkened crystal orb beyond them. Accept the course to release your volatile assistant.

The Bombchu skitters along as predicted. Tap the touch screen to switch the view back to Link. Remain near the glowing blue orb and smack it after the Bombchu moves past the red blocks to lower the blue ones ahead. This clears the way for the Bombchu to strike the orb in the sand-filled chamber, lighting it and lowering the north spikes.

Well played! Now equip Link's Bombs and hurry past the spikes. Four wary Armoses guard the next wide chamber and you've got to disable each one to proceed. Try to alert them one at a time so as not to become overwhelmed; heave Bombs at each one until all four have been shut down.

Now you can drag each smoldering Armos onto one of the four pressure switches on the floor! When all four switches are depressed, the spikes that block the east passage withdraw into the ground, allowing you to proceed.

CAUTION

Be careful when venturing down the east passage: the pots along the hall begin to float, then suddenly fly at Link, attempting to smash into him for damage! Smash the pots before they come forward or simply run away.

You've finally located the Boss Key block, but you've yet to find the Boss Key! Remember the block's location for future reference and then charge up the nearby stairs to return to the basement floor above.

Goron Temple: B2 Revisited

You're doing great! Now you're free to explore the east half of the second basement floor. Begin by stepping on the pressure switch to the west. This extends a footbridge across the west pit, which grants you a fast route back to the rest of the floor. No need to go backward, though! Ignore the bridge, equip the Bow, and run eastward instead.

A wall rises behind Link, trapping him in the floor's southeast chamber. Two burly Eye Brutes then shuffle forward with cruel intentions. Release an arrow into each one's eye as fast as you can, then dash into close quarters to slice them up with Link's faithful blade.

→ TIP ←

The acorn in the room's northeast corner always produces arrows when smashed. Stick around for a while and top off Link's Quiver!

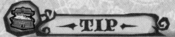

The passage north of the Eye Brute chamber is chock-full of Blue ChuChus and Green Slimes. Take it slow as you methodically eliminate each gooey adversary that bounds into range. Ignore, for the time being, the crystal orb you encounter midway down the passage and simply work at securing your surroundings.

Your progress is eventually blocked by a northern spike strip. Assuming the area is free of baddies, stand near the spikes, then ready a Bombchu and trace its path south toward the crystal orb you recently passed. When the Bombchu blasts into the orb, the spikes near Link momentarily drop! Skip past them without delay.

Shred the few Eye Slugs that slither your way as you move westward toward a large sandpit. Many other Eye Slugs creep about the quicksand, presenting obstacles for the Bombchus you must send out to strike two crystal orbs against the far west wall. Start sending Bombchus westward in an effort to light both orbs.

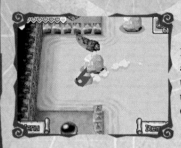

As a bonus, destroy all the Eye Slugs in the area to reveal a hidden chest nearby. Open the chest to claim a fabulous **treasure**: another precious Goron Amber!

Dungeon Chest #6: Treasure

Treasure

Random

You got a **treasure**! Collect these items and sell them to the highest bidder!

Lighting both orbs by Bombchu reveals an ornate chest on a raised platform back east. You'll have to send another Bombchu to activate the south orb and lower the spikes as before, but this time you can simply send the Bombchu south across the

quicksand. Dash past the spikes and open up that treasure chest to get your mitts on this dungeon's **Boss Key**. Standing near the quicksand, you can also activate the switch using the Boomerang or Bow and Arrow.

Dungeon Chest #7: Boss Key

Boss Key

You've found the **Boss Key**! It's a huge, heavy key.

Goron Temple: B4

The rest of the trek is fairly straightforward. Carry the Boss Key back downstairs and use it to remove the giant Boss Key block you noticed earlier. Proceed down the staircase beyond the Boss Key block to reach the fourth basement floor. Load up on Bombchus at the pair of acorns down here and then tap the stone tablet to summon a pool of blue light. You aren't finished with this place yet, so ignore the blue light and go through the large doorway to face off against a big, bad boss.

Dongorongo, Armored Lizard

Threat Meter

Speed: Slow

Attack Power: 1/2 heart (contact); 1/2 heart (fireball); 1 heart (charge); 1/2 heart (Eye Slugs)

Defense Power: Weaken with Bombchus; multiple hits to defeat!

As Link and Ciela enter the final chamber, they notice a massive armored lizard roaring at them from across a wide sandpit. Whoa, that thing's huge! As Link ponders how he'll cross the quicksand to reach the monster, a friendly voice suddenly calls out from ahead: it's Gongoron! The young Goron has arrived just in time! He yells to Link, saying that he'll try to trip up the beast while Link attacks from his location. The battle begins!

As before, you must use the button that appears at the top of the Touch Screen to switch control between Link and Gongoron throughout this battle. Begin as Gongoron and roll around the huge monster, looking to strike it from the side with Gongoron's jump attack. Make sure you aren't struck by the spread of fireballs Dongorongo periodically spits out!

CAUTION

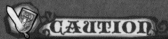

Don't move Link or Gongoron into the southern quicksand or they'll sink and suffer damage!

While attempting to circle around Dongorongo as Gongoron, be wary of Eye Slugs that periodically creep out to attack Link. Whenever one draws near, Gongoron and Ciela are quick to issue warnings.

Task 3: Enter and Clear the Goron Temple

...continued

Pay attention and quickly switch control back to the green-clad hero so you may deal with the Eye Slugs before they inflict much damage.

Eye Slugs are shown by skull icons on your map.

Your best opportunity to circle around Dongorongo comes when the beast stops spitting fireballs and tries to ram Gongoron. Dongorongo always opens his mouth wide for a moment before rushing forward. Learn to anticipate this attack and quickly roll Gongoron to one side to avoid the forthcoming charge. After dodging the assault, quickly **tap Dongorongo's midsection** to make Gongoron jump attack repeatedly.

If Link and Gongoron's heart meter runs low, quickly switch control back to Link so you can drink a potion and recover. Several nearby pots contain hearts as well.

Keep hammering away at one side of Dongorongo's belly until the whole monster is finally knocked over on its side. Now's your chance! Gongoron yells to Link to make his move. Switch control to Link, ready a Bombchu, and then **trace a line across the sandpit and into the recumbent Dongorongo's mouth**. Release the Bombchu to force-feed the giant lizard an unpleasant snack!

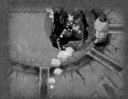

Burp! The Bombchu erupts inside Dongorongo's belly, giving the monster a nasty case of indigestion. Nice work, but it'll take more than that to beat this massive lizard. Continue to avoid Dongorongo's fireballs and charging attacks as Gongoron, and look for a chance to knock the boss onto its side. As Link, keep those Eye Slugs at bay and be ready to send out a Bombchu whenever Dongorongo takes a tumble!

When you've run out of pots to smash, defeating Eye Slugs becomes a great way to obtain hearts and Bombchus.

CAUTION

Eye Slugs begin assaulting Link with more regularity as the fight wears on. Pay close attention to your map and Ciela's warnings!

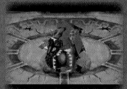

Coordinate Link and Gongoron's efforts until you manage to feed Dongorongo three Bombchus. The monster finally collapses and a bridge extends across the quicksand. Great work! Gongoron speeds off to scout for the pure metal. Cross the bridge and make for the north door.

Hold everything: that giant lizard isn't finished quite yet! As you cross the chamber, the bridge suddenly vanishes from behind you and the north door slams shut, trapping you in the room once more. Dongorongo's eyes open, and the monster returns to his feet. The fight's second half begins!

You don't have Gongoron to rely on for this last bit, so it's all up to Link! Dongorongo is a bit more aggressive now and his Eye Slug minions just keep coming, so it's important to stay on the move. Ready your Bombs and run circles around Dongorongo, avoiding his fireballs and waiting for the creature to stand upright on two hind legs. When it does so, Dongorongo soon begins to inhale deeply to unleash a wide stream of flame. Quickly toss a Bomb into the monster's mouth while it's breathing in!

Blammo! The Bomb badly upsets Dongorongo's stomach and the monster topples over onto one side. Now's the time to strike! Circle around behind the creature and unleash a vicious barrage of sword strikes onto the large blue crystal on its back. Inflict as much punishment as you can before Dongorongo returns to its feet once more.

It takes a great number of sword attacks to finally best the beast, so repeat this procedure as necessary. If Link's heart meter ever becomes dangerously low, stop fighting Dongorongo and start hunting Eye Slugs for hearts. Otherwise, keep looking for chances to feed the monster a Bomb and bury Link's blade into its back.

Victory!

Having felt enough of Link's righteous wrath, Dongorongo at last succumbs to his wounds. The monster collapses in a heap, then slowly transforms into a collection of sand. The granules fly around Link and quickly become sucked into the Phantom Hourglass. Evil has been vanquished and two more minutes' worth of time have been added to the sacred timepiece!

Fantastic job! You've defeated a dangerous monster and restored peace to the Goron Temple. A giant treasure chest appears in the chamber's center and the north door slides open. Crack the lid on that chest for a wonderful new **Heart Container** and then hurry through that door!

Dungeon Chest #8:
Heart Container #9

Heart Container #9
You got a **Heart Container**! Your heart meter has been increased by one heart!

The First Pure Metal

*Gongoron awaits Link and Ciela just beyond Dongorongo's chamber. The young Goron apologizes for hurrying off so fast, but Link and Ciela simply thank him for all his help. After working together through so many troubles, the group of friends have gained each other's trust and respect. Gongoron is happy to call Link a true brother and proudly offers him the **pure metal** he seeks.*

After speaking with Gongoron, dash up the nearby steps and collect the sparkly red crystal on the top pedestal. You've found the **Crimsonine**! Just two more pure metals left to find!

Crimsonine

You got the **Crimsonine**! It's one of the pure metals you need to make the Phantom Sword.

Thanking Link once again, Gongoron gets ready to leave. Before he departs, Gongoron asks Link to stop by his father's house and tell the elder all about what has happened. Link agrees and the two go their separate ways once more. Step into the blue light to return to the temple's entrance. Well done!

Task 4: Return & Speak with Biggoron

Making It Official

Before you do anything else, take Gongoron's advice and return to Biggoron's chamber. You can't leave with the Crimsonine without permission from the Goron's elder! After hearing of Link and Gongoron's heroic deeds at the temple, Biggoron is happy to let Link sail off with the tribe's pure metal. It has become clear to the elder that the lad stands tall and proud among the Gorons! As a parting gift, Biggoron refunds all the tribe initiation fees back to Link, plus interest: he hands Link a **big red Rupee**!

Big Red Rupee
You got a **big red Rupee**! It's worth 200 Rupees!

You've had a very successful stay here at Goron Island. You've made some good friends and the first pure metal now rests in your hands. Although you're free to go after the next pure metal now, why not take a moment to complete a few optional tasks? Check the Missing Links section for details on all the new activities that have become available to you, and when you're ready to move on, set a course for the Isle of Frost to the northeast. The second pure metal awaits you there!

Missing Links

There isn't a whole lot to do after clearing the Goron Temple, but your newfound Bombchus open up a few very important optional adventures. Before rushing off to that chilling Isle of Frost, why not undertake a few optional tasks and give yourself an advantage?

Fan Mail from Gongoron

Now that you've made nice with the Goron elder's son, you soon get a friendly letter from Gongoron thanking you for helping him battle the monsters inside Goron Temple. The letter sure is nice, but the real treat is what's inside: a sparkly new **Courage Gem**! It may take some time for the letter to reach you, but rest assured that it's in the mail.

Courage Gem #11

You got a **Courage Gem**! Collect these items and use them to power up the Courage Spirit.

Bigger Bag, More Bombchus

Before leaving Goron Island, stop by the local shop to find that it's now selling a lovely **Bombchu Bag** for just 1,000 Rupees. What a steal! Buy that Bombchu Bag, if you can, to increase your mobile explosive storage capacity.

TIP

Light on cash? Pay a visit to the Treasure Teller at Mercay Island, then sell some treasures and ship parts to pad your wallet. You may find the Bombchu Bag on sale at Mercay's local shop as well.

...continued

Bombchu Bag #1

You got a **Bombchu Bag**! Now you can carry more Bombchus, for a new maximum of 20!

Heart for Sale

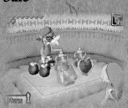

Clearing the Goron Temple and purchasing the quiver and Bombchu Bag from the store gives you the opportunity to purchase a valuable item from any island's local shop. Swing by the store at Goron Island, Mercay Island, or Molida Island to find that each one now sells a **Heart Container**! The price is high at 2,000 Rupees, so you may need to sell some treasures and ship parts to the Treasure Teller to amass enough cash. Make sure to purchase this precious item to gain an advantage in the coming dungeon!

NOTE

There's only one Heart Container for you to buy at this time. After you purchase this Heart Container from any shop, the rest of the shops stop selling it.

Heart Container #10

You got a **Heart Container**! Your heart meter has been increased by one heart!

Treasure Map #16

Now that you've got some Bombchus, you can finally activate that dark crystal orb you noticed within Goron Island's north maze. Head toward the maze and bomb the cracked wall on the left to get inside it once again. Loop around to find the crystal orb sitting in a small area to the south you couldn't get to before. Well, you still can't, but your Bombchus can! Set one rolling southward, through the small hole in the cliff and directly into the crystal orb.

...continued

 Boom! The orb lights up when the Bombchu collides with it, and a hidden treasure chest appears up north! Bomb your way toward the chest and kick it open to claim a brand new treasure map. Nice!

Overworld Chest #28: Treasure Map #16

Treasure Map #16

You got a **treasure map**! It reveals the location of a sunken treasure on the Great Sea.

...continued

Sunken Treasures 14–16

Ready to haul up some loot? You've found three more treasure maps since your last salvage expedition, so get out there and find some sunken goodies. Happy hunting!

Sunken Treasure Chests

#	Contents	Bonus Rupees	Location
14	Ship Part	Green (8); Big Green (1)	SEQ; NE of Goron Island
15	Ship Part	Green (5); Red (1)	SEQ; South of Isle of Frost
16	Ship Part	Green (9)	SWQ; South of Cannon Island

Tasks
Complete!

Contents

Chill Wind a-Blowin': Isle of Frost & Temple of Ice

Isle of Frost

Anouki Estates

Chiefs Home

Temple of Ice

33

32

30 31

29

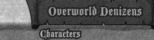

Legend

29	Overworld Chest #29: Big Green Rupee
30	Overworld Chest #30: Red Rupee
31	Overworld Chest #31: Red Rupee
32	Overworld Chest #32: Power Gem #13
33	Overworld Chest #33: Wisdom Gem #14

Items to Obtain

Big Red Rupee	Power Gem #13	Red Rupees x2	Treasure Map #17	Wisdom Gem #14

Overworld Denizens

Characters

Anoukis	Aroo	Island Chief	Yook Imposter

Enemies

Yook

There's a Chill Wind Blowin': Overview

Things are looking up for our young hero! After proving his courage and valor to the Gorons, Link has become fast friends with the whole tribe. The Gorons have given Link their precious pure metal and only two more pure metals await discovery! Link's next stop is a small frozen isle to the northeast. It's hard to imagine that anyone could possibly live at such a freezing place, but it's certainly worth a look!

1

Explore the Isle of Frost

2

Discover the Imposter

3

Enter and Clear the Temple of Ice

4

Return and Speak with the Chief

A Link to the Present

Max 19:00

Max 30

Max 50

Max 20

Lvl 1

x11

Lvl 1 Lvl 1

x12 x11

x22

Items Already Acquired

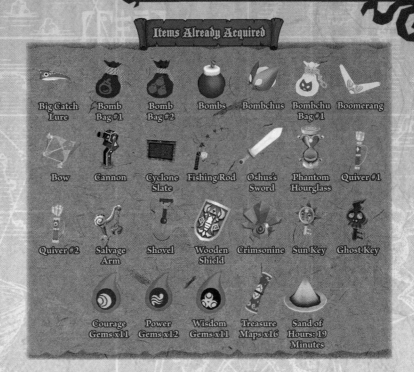

Big Catch Lure	Bomb Bag #1	Bomb Bag #2	Bombs	Bombchus	Bombchu Bag #1	Boomerang
Bow	Cannon	Cyclone Slate	Fishing Rod	Oshus's Sword	Phantom Hourglass	Quiver #1
Quiver #2	Salvage Arm	Shovel	Wooden Shield	Crimsonine	Sun Key	Ghost Key
Courage Gems x11	Power Gems x12	Wisdom Gems x11	Treasure Maps x16	Sand of Hours: 19 Minutes		

Task 1: Explore the Isle of Frost

Breaking the Ice

Docking at the southeast quadrant's Isle of Frost isn't as easy as one might think! As you approach the island, you can easily see that the entire land mass is encased in a thick sheet of solid ice. There's no way of reaching its port!

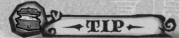

Linebeck suddenly comes up with a brilliant idea: Why not put the ship's cannon to use and blast those ice chunks to bits? Sounds like a plan! Plot a circular course around the isle so that your ship sails all the way around it, then simply open fire on the ice as you putter along. You must blast each ice chunk multiple times to finally sink it.

Beware: you'll need to use the cannon against the gang of Eyeball Monsters that attacks your ship while breaking the ice as well!

Eyeball Monster

Threat Meter

Speed: Normal

Attack Power: 1 heart (contact)

Defense Power: 1 hit to defeat

Some airborne entities you encounter in eastern waters of the sea are actually Eyeball Monsters that flutter high above the surface of the ocean. These fiends travel in tight packs, eager to swoop down and assault unwary wayfarers by slamming into their vessels. Fortunately, these minor threats are somewhat slow and easy to blast from the sky. Just unleash a barrage of cannonballs until you've obliterated the whole pack!

TIP

Each individual ice chunk is shown on your map. Make a second trip around the island if you missed a few and need to finish them off.

Well done! The island has been fully uncovered and you're finally able to explore it. There must be some pretty cool stuff around there! Hurry and dock without delay.

Isle of Frost

The Anouki Tribe

The moment he sets foot on the Isle of Frost, Linebeck feels the presence of great treasure. He feels the terrible cold even more however, and asks Link to venture on without him. Dash north from the dock and speak with the odd-looking creature in the thick fur coat nearby.

The creature is amazed to see an outsider. He tells Link that he's a member of the **Anouki**, a tribe that lives here on the island. This Anouki doesn't know much about pure metals though, and he advises Link to speak with the **Island Chief** for more information. Can do!

The Island Chief's house stands on a hilltop to the northeast. Climb the nearby steps and enter the house to visit with the chief. You can tell he's important by the length of his beard!

The Island Chief welcomes Link to his home. He already seems to know that the boy seeks the Anouki tribe's pure metal. The chief hints that he'd be willing to part with the pure metal, provided Link can help him out of a tricky situation. Oh boy, here we go again!

It seems that the Anouki have been living under a shaky peace treaty with a neighboring tribe called the Yook. The Yook live in the Great Ice Field to the east, and they've always been jealous of the Anouki's half of the land. In fact, one Yook has recently managed to sneak into Anouki territory and is currently disguised as one of the locals! The Island Chief asks Link to sniff out the Yook intruder and kick him out of Anouki territory.

Island Chief

The long-bearded leader of the Anouki tribe is known only as the Island Chief. This thick-skinned chieftain has seen much hardship in his time, and many of his recent burdens stem from the Yook: a nasty tribe of wicked creatures that reside in the Great Ice Field to the east. The Island Chief hopes that Link can help him settle things between the Yook and Anouki once and for all in an "I scratch your back, you scratch mine" bargain. If peace can be achieved, perhaps he'd be willing to part with his tribe's pure metal!

Task 2: Discover the Imposter

To Catch a Yook...

Looks like you've got your work cut out for you! One of the Anouki living on the island is actually a Yook intruder, but which one could it be? Begin questioning the locals near the chief's house to gain some insight into the whole messy situation between the Anouki and the Yook.

→NOTE→

You'll notice a number of wooden pegs and out-of-reach treasure chests as you explore the island. Make notes of each one so you don't forget about them!

Talk to just a few Anouki and you soon get the picture: The Yook are evil, ferocious creatures, and they've been at odds with the harmless Anouki for centuries. They lie, cheat, and steal. They're just bad news! And now that one of them has snuck into Anouki land, no one can trust anyone. What a disaster!

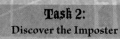

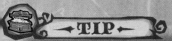

TIP

Hop onto the wooden peg just east of the chief's house and then speak with the nearby Anouki. The creature is impressed with Link's agility and hands over a **red Rupee**!

TIP

While questioning the locals, dig around with the Shovel to unearth a variety of valuable Rupees. Try digging in front of signs, houses, and the signs of the Anouki estates!

After exploring around town, go north to visit the Anouki Estates. There are six homes up here, each with a sign out front that tells you whose house it is. Enter each estate and speak with the resident Anouki to get to the bottom of this quandary. One of these Anouki is no Anouki at all!

Speaking with each Anouki at the estates elicits the following statements:

Dobo: The Yook are liars! And Mazo's honest. The guy never lies!

Kumu: The Yook you're looking for is a liar. Either Mazo or Aroo is lying to you.

Fofo: The Yook do nothing but lie. Gumo never lies.

Mazo: I don't care if you believe me, but me and Dobo only tell the truth.

Aroo: Between you and me, Kumu is lying.

Gumo: Either Fofo or Aroo has been lying to you.

Have you determined who the imposter is? Here's a hint: As many Anouki have told you, **the Yook always lie**. Therefore, the imposter has to be **someone who accuses someone else**! From their statements, you can tell that this rules out Dobo, Fofo, and

Mazo. Knowing that, and looking at Gumo's statement, it becomes clear that the imposter must be **Aroo**! Visit Aroo's house and speak with him a second time to accuse him.

Aroo puts up a smooth act at first, but he eventually folds in the face of **intense questioning**. He's the Yook! The creature thought its ingenious disguise would fool anyone, but its act wasn't good enough to fool Link! Shedding its fur coat and mask, the Yook roars out with tremendous force, blowing Link clear out of the house. Loudmouth!

Missing Links

Words of Wisdom

During your investigation, you may have noticed a stone statue standing on a tiny isle northeast of the estates. Whack the statue for an odd message: If you draw a line between here and the Island Chief's house, you'll find something buried near the middle. How about that!

Call up your map and trace the line to the village chief's house, then dash south and start digging. Sink your Shovel right in front of the east stone tablet that reads "Anouki Estates" to claim your prize: a big red Rupee!

Big Red Rupee

You got a **big red Rupee**! It's worth 200 Rupees!

Into the Ice Field

The Yook imposter managed to escape, but a deal's still a deal! Link returns to the Island Chief's house and informs the head Anouki of his success in sniffing out the intruder. The chief is thrilled at the news and finally offers Link a chance to go after the pure metal he seeks. He grants Link passage into the Great Ice Field, which leads east toward the Temple of Ice. That's where the pure metal lies, but retrieving it won't be easy: The temple is smack in the middle of Yook territory!

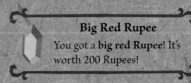

The Great Ice Field isn't far. Go east to find the entrance to a cavern, which is guarded by a burly Anouki. Having heard of Link's success in tracking down the Yook imposter, the guard steps aside so the lad may enter the cavern beyond. Run inside and smash the cavern's pots for hearts and Bombs. Read the nearby stone tablet for a tip you'll soon find helpful: **The Yook are vulnerable when they inhale deeply.** Good to know!

Equip Link's Bombs and exit the cavern, stepping out into the freezing harshness of the Great Ice Field. No wonder the Yook can't stand it here! The entire place is nothing but a frozen wasteland, and its inhabitants have had enough. Seeing an intruder, a nearby Yook stomps toward you with an angry growl. Any chance this could actually just be a harmless Anouki in disguise?

As the tablet in the cavern hinted, the Yook are only vulnerable while **inhaling deeply**. Keep away from this first one until it starts sucking air in preparation for an attack. The moment you see the Yook start to inhale, quickly toss a Bomb into its mouth. The Yook swallows the explosive, coming down with a nasty case of Bomb belly. Rush forward with Link's sword while the monster is stunned and finish it off with a fast barrage!

Yook

Threat Meter
▮▮▮▯▯▯

Speed: Slow

Attack Power: 1/2 heart (club); 1 heart (breath attack)

Defense Power: 1 Bomb to stun; 5 hits to defeat

Yook are members of a dangerous tribe of creatures that live in the Isle of Frost's eastern wastelands. Having suffered years of oppression at the hands of a rival tribe, the Yook are incredibly mean-spirited and quick to attack anything that steps foot on their turf. Their favorite method of harassment involves inhaling deeply and then roaring out a huge cone of frost, effectively turning their harsh environment against their enemies. Link can exploit this attack by tossing Bombs into a Yook's open mouth. It's the only way to close their yappers!

Move across the ice field, using Bombs and blade to eliminate each Yook that roars in your direction. You can see lots of chests and things along the high outside ledges, but these are all out of reach at the moment. Note them down as you work at eliminating the Yook from the Great Ice Field.

Use the many pots and bomb flowers in the ice field to help you overcome the Yook guardians.

CAUTION

Don't touch the freezing icicles to the north or Link becomes frozen for a moment and suffers damage! Keep away from icicles like these.

Wipe out all six Yook guardians in the ice field to banish the wall of freezing icicles to the north. Now you can reach the temple! You still have one last obstacle to clear, however: The Yook imposter that was posing as Aroo! This guy looks big and mean, but he's actually no different than any other Yook. Get some distance and stuff his big mouth with a Bomb, then finish him off with cold steel!

Task 3: Enter & Clear the Temple of Ice

You've fought your way through freezing wind and bitter Yook, and you've finally reached the temple doors. Any place called the Temple of Ice surely won't be very pleasant, but it's got to be better than this frigid field! Best hurry inside and find that pure metal.

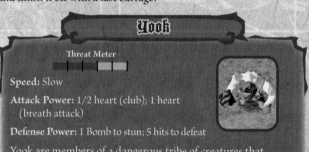

Temple of Ice

Temple of Ice: 1F

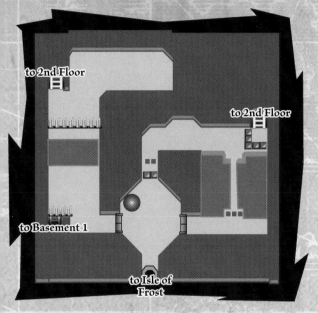

to 2nd Floor

to 2nd Floor

to Basement 1

to Isle of Frost

Temple of Ice: 3F

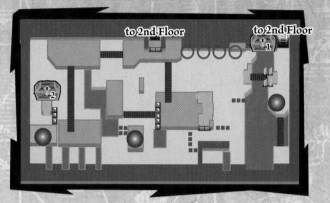

to 2nd Floor

to 2nd Floor

1

2

Temple of Ice: 2F

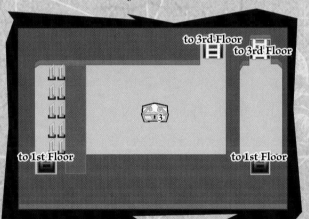

to 3rd Floor

to 3rd Floor

3

to 1st Floor

to 1st Floor

Temple of Ice: B1

to Boss Chamber

to Basement 2

6

to 1st Floor

4

5

Legend

1	Dungeon Chest #1: Big Green Rupee	
2	Dungeon Chest #2: Wisdom Gem #12	
3	Dungeon Chest #3: Grappling Hook	
4	Dungeon Chest #4: Yellow Potion	
5	Dungeon Chest #5: Small Key	
6	Dungeon Chest #6: Wisdom Gem #13	
7	Dungeon Chest #7: Small Key	
8	Dungeon Chest #8: Big Red Rupee	
9	Dungeon Chest #9: Boss Key	
10	Dungeon Chest #10: Heart Container #11	

⬤ Orb   ▪ Floor Switch   ◯ Lever

Temple of Ice: Pure Metal Chamber

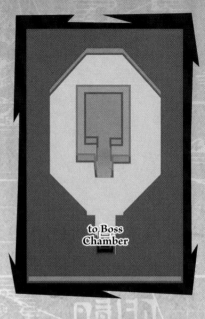

to Boss Chamber

Temple of Ice: B2

7

8

9
to Basement 1

Temple of Ice: Boss Chamber

to Pure Metal Chamber

10

to Basement 1

Dungeon Denizens

Enemies

Green Slime Ice Bubble Ice Keese Rock ChuChu

Boss

Stag Beetle Yook Gleeok, Two-Headed Dragon

Temple of Ice: 1F

Hope you've dressed warmly, because it's not much nicer inside the temple! Break the pots in the entry chamber for hearts if you like, then move to the colored blocks that plug up the north passage. You've got to remove these obstacles and there's only one way to do so: whack the nearby colored orb to lower the red blocks, then cross the blocks and stand right next to the blue ones. From there, hurl Link's Boomerang southward to strike the colored orb, changing it back to red. This lowers the blue blocks and raises the red ones, allowing you to pass but preventing any escape. What a chilling prospect!

Items to Obtain

Azurine Big Green Rupee Big Red Rupee Boss Key Heart Container #11

Grappling Hook Small Keys x3 Wisdom Gem #13 Yellow Potion

1   2   3   4

Task 3:
Enter and Clear the Temple of Ice

Move slowly down the hallway beyond the blocks: A Blue ChuChu leaps up from the ground to ambush you! Snap the ChuChu with the Boomerang to disperse its electrical charge before you attack. Beyond the Blue ChuChu lies a staircase surrounded by red blocks and an extremely narrow footbridge that spans a wide chasm to the south. Ignore the staircase and carefully cross the footbridge just after the pair of spinning blade traps pass by. You can cross in one dash if you time it just right!

Smash the pots if you like and then tap the wooden peg to make Link hop onto it. As Link balances on the peg, ready the Boomerang and hurl it northward, striking a crystal orb on a tall pedestal. Whack! The orb lights up and some nearby icicles melt away.

Whew, made it! Step on the ledge's pressure switch to lower a nearby sealed door. Now you can return to the entry chamber! No need to do so, though. Instead, backtrack to the narrow footbridge and notice some lowered blue blocks at its south end. Stand just north of the blocks—but not in the path of the spinning blade trap—and then ready a Bombchu. Send the Bombchu westward to blast the orb in the entry hall and color it blue, raising the nearby blue blocks but lowering the red ones you passed near the northeast staircase. Cross the footbridge and make for the stairs.

Run northward and then west, crossing the walkway that the icicles had been blocking. This walkway is made of slippery ice, so be careful! When you reach the snowy clearing on the other side, go north to find a small treasure chest on a thin ledge. Open the chest for a **big green Rupee**!

Dungeon Chest #1:
Big Green Rupee

Big Green Rupee
You got a **big green Rupee**! It's worth 100 Rupees!

Temple of Ice: 2F

There's not much to do on your first trip to the temple's tiny second floor! Smash the pair of pots for items if you like, and then proceed up the north steps to reach the next floor above.

Levers & Beetles

Four levers line the north wall of the floor. You'll obviously be using these later, so remember where they are!

Temple of Ice: 3F

Now *this* floor has a bit more going on. Be careful when crossing the ice around here: it's extremely slick and causes Link to slide all about! The effect is more noticeable when Link moves at greater speeds, so you can increase your traction by walking slowly. Go south from the stairs and cross a narrow footbridge to reach a tiny ledge with four pots and a small wooden peg.

Run south past some lowered red blocks and enter a tiny alcove. Break the pots and read the stone tablet for a clue about the levers you just saw: **The one due north of this tablet should be pulled last!** Draw a straight line northward for future reference and then continue exploring the floor.

Be careful when venturing westward: a number of vicious Stag Beetles stomp about around there! These guys are tough for Link to deal with at present because their huge metal masks repel all blows. It's best simply to avoid them for now, although you can try to knock them into pits if you like. Fortunately, Link's shield is enough to repel a Stag Beetle's charging attacks—even when it isn't being strengthened by Neri!

Stag Beetle

Threat Meter

Speed: Normal

Attack Power: 1/2 heart (contact)

Defense Power: Grappling Hook to weaken; 1 hit to defeat

These bugs mean business! Stag Beetles are incredibly tenacious, relentlessly pursuing their quarry. They attack simply by rushing forward and poking their foe with their sharp horns! Link is ill-equipped to deal with Stag Beetles until he acquires a handy new item that allows him to combat them on even terms.

Leap across the short gaps near the floor's southwest corner to find a stone tablet tucked away in the corner. The tablet advises you to **pull the lever on the far left** first. Now you know when to pull two of the levers!

The final stone tablet stands at the floor's northeast corner. Read it to learn that you must **pull the one in front of the tongue second**. Now you can determine the exact order! Return to the levers and pull them in the following sequence:

1. Pull the **far west** (left) lever first.
2. Pull the **far east** (right) lever second.
3. Pull the **middle east** (second from the right) lever third.
4. Pull the **middle west** (second from the left) lever fourth.

Success! A door opens to the south, granting you access to the floor's network of higher ledges and walkways. Climb the stairs and knock the Stag Beetle off the ledge above. Equip the Boomerang and carefully cross the icy north walkway.

Two new yet familiar enemies await you on the far ledge: an Ice Bubble and an Ice Keese! These floating baddies are very much like their fiery cousins, except they'll each freeze Link in a block of ice if they manage to touch him! Combat Ice Bubbles and Ice Keese just as you do the flaming varieties: Keep away and Boomerang them from afar to knock Ice Bubbles to the floor and defeat Keese outright. When the Ice Bubbles are down, hurry to pulp their vulnerable skulls with Link's powerful blade!

A locked door and a darkened crystal orb are on the icy ledge, but you can't do much with either at the moment. Journey onward to the floor's northwest ledge and dispatch another Ice Bubble and Keese here. Yet another orb stands nearby, but ignore it for the moment. Move south and defeat more frosty monsters to secure the southwest ledge. There's a glowing red orb just to the west: throw a bomb down to activate the orb.

With the blue blocks down, you can reach a small chest on a nearby ledge. Drop to the ground and run up the nearby steps to reach the chest, then flip its lid to claim a sparkly **Wisdom Gem**. Score!

Dungeon Chest #2:
Wisdom Gem #12

Wisdom Gem #12
You got a **Wisdom Gem!** Collect these items and use them to power up the Wisdom Spirit.

Task 3:
Enter and Clear the Temple of Ice

Return to the east side of the floor and climb the stairs to return to the upper ledges and walkways. You've lowered the blue blocks and can now run west to reach the central ledge, where a stone table stands. The tablet instructs you to **stand on the nearby blue tile** and follow a pattern of numbers written upon it: 2, 1, 3, and 4. Whatever could that mean?

Maybe the tablet is trying to tell you how to activate all the orbs you've been noticing on these upper ledges? It's worth a shot! Stand on the nearby blue tile and ready the Boomerang, then trace a flight path that strikes each of the surrounding orbs in the sequence shown by the tablet. Light the orbs in this order:

1. Light the **northeast** orb first.

2. Light the **northwest** orb second.

3. Light the **southwest** orb third.

4. Light the **southeast** orb last.

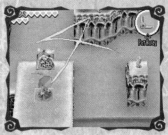

Presto! The orbs all light and a **small key** drops from the ceiling, landing on a nearby platform. No need to leave your spot: Just sit tight and toss the Boomerang over to retrieve the key with ease! There's nothing left to do here, so go to the locked north door, unlock it, and proceed down the stairs beyond.

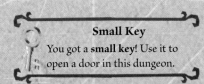

Small Key

You got a **small key**! Use it to open a door in this dungeon.

Temple of Ice: 2F Revisited

Link comes under attack the moment he reaches the second floor: Two fearsome Yook drop from above and quickly close in! Dash away from the fiends as fast as you can and then ready Link's Bombs. Wait for the Yook to inhale, then toss Bombs right into their mouths. Try to keep both of them stunned as you work at dispatching each one in turn.

⟶ TIP ⟵

If you're running low on Bombs, make good use of the bomb flower in the room's southwest corner. Good thing these grow in the cold!

Wipe out the Yook to melt some icicles near the pit to the west and cause a large ornate chest to appear in the middle of the chamber. Bet something good is in there! Open the treasure chest to claim what may be Link's coolest tool: the **Grappling Hook!**

Dungeon Chest #3: Grappling Hook

Grappling Hook

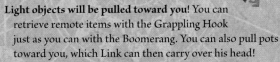

You got the **Grappling Hook**! Now you can tap distant objects to grab onto them (or use it as a weapon)!

Light objects will be pulled toward you! You can retrieve remote items with the Grappling Hook just as you can with the Boomerang. You can also pull pots toward you, which Link can then carry over his head!

You'll be pulled toward heavy objects! Latch onto heavier objects such as wooden pegs, rocks, torches and treasure chests to cause Link to zip toward them, sailing right over pits and chasms!

You can make tightropes: String tightropes between two pegs so you may tiptoe across a void. Link can use his other tools while tiptoeing across the rope! Or use the tightrope you've strung as a giant slingshot to send Link shooting across wide gaps and onto tall ledges!

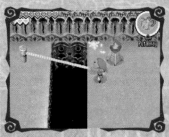

Right on! A new toy! Let's test this baby out. Move to the edge of the west pit and ready the Grappling Hook just as you would any other item (equip it through the Items tab and then ready it by tapping the Item icon or by holding a trigger button). Link begins to twirl the Grappling Hook, eager to toss it at anything you tap! Try tapping the wooden peg across the pit to make Link throw out the rope. The Grappling Hook latches onto the peg and Link is quickly pulled across the pit! How useful! Proceed down the stairs beyond.

Temple of Ice: 1F Revisited

Here you are, back on the temple's first floor. Now you can explore the west half of this area! Be careful, though: More villainous Stag Beetles lurk over here, along with a few hidden Green Slimes. The Green Slimes hang out at the northeast corner, so keep near the stairs and lure the Stag Beetles over to you. Now that you've got the Grappling Hook, you can make short work of Stag Beetles! Try using the Grappling Hook on them and see what happens.

Like the Boomerang, the Grappling Hook is an extremely versatile tool. Use it during combat to stun and disable tough enemies. The Grappling Hook obliterates weaker monsters outright!

The four pots near the stairs all yield hearts. Heal up after the fight!

Clear the area of Stag Beetles and Green Slimes and then have a look at the strange statues along the north wall. The middle statue looks a bit different than the rest: its eyes aren't red and its tongue isn't quite as long as the other two. Let's make that tongue a little longer! Latch onto the middle statue with the Grappling Hook to make Link pull its tongue out. The statue's eyes light up, and a row of icicles to the south dissolves. Cool!

Mosey southward and stand near the pit. Use the Grappling Hook to grab onto the wooden peg to the south and sail across the void. Be ready to fight, though: a final Stag Beetle creeps about over here! Use the Grappling Hook to make short work of the critter, then step on the nearby pressure switch to open the sealed east door. You've now got a clear path back to temple's entrance!

Revisit the entry chamber and notice two tongue statues on the north wall. You couldn't do anything with these guys before, but you sure can now! Yank out each statue's tongue with the Grappling Hook to melt the ice that's blocking the floor's southwest stairs. Nice move! Now dash downstairs to reach the temple's first basement floor.

Temple of Ice: B1

You've thoroughly explored the temple's top three floors. Now let's check out its basement! Use a Bomb to blast through the cracked wall at the foot of the stairs and then proceed north through the hole. A wall of icicles blocks access to the room's tongue statue, but step on a nearby pressure switch. Doing so causes a small treasure chest to appear on a nearby ledge to the east.

Low on Bombs? Return to the first floor and smash the pair of pots near the staircase to stock up.

Drat! The gap between your ledge and the east one is a bit too wide to jump across. Guess you'll just have to get creative! There are no wooden pegs about, but ready the Grappling Hook anyway and toss it at the small chest. The chest is too heavy to pull to him, so instead, Link is yanked across the pit and over to it. Awesome! Open the chest to claim a valuable **Yellow Potion**.

Dungeon Chest #4:
Yellow Potion

Yellow Potion
You got a **Yellow Potion**! Down it to replenish all of Link's hearts!

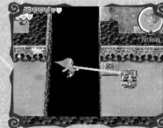

Task 3:
Enter and Clear the Temple of Ice

Step onto the pressure switch near the chest to extend a bridge across the pit. There is no need to head backward at present. Instead, journey east and smash a group of pots in the far corner. Hey, one of the pots was covering a blue tile on the ground! There seems to be no way forward, so try placing a Bomb on the blue floor tile. Blammo! The north wall is blown open, creating a way forward.

Smack the stone statue on the north ledge for a tip: You can **create a tightrope** by **connecting a rope between two pegs**. No way! Let's give this a try. Move to the peg east of the statue and ready the Grappling Hook. Tap the peg, then trace a line eastward to the peg on the next ledge over. Voilà! The Grappling Hook's rope stretches between the two pegs, forming a tightrope.

Tap the wooden peg to make Link hop onto it. From there, simply move eastward across the tightrope. Link uses his catlike reflexes to balance himself perfectly as he tiptoes across! You must make a tightrope here to proceed.

Icicles & Colored Blocks

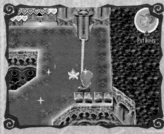

You can't make much progress going south: a row of icicles gets in your way. Move north instead, carefully eliminating the pair of Stag Beetles that skitter on the narrow, icy trail. You may find it easiest to knock these pests into the surrounding abyss! Fight your way to the floor's northeast corner, where you find a locked door and another tongue statue. You have no key, so latch onto the statue's tongue and yank it all the way out. The southern icicles then dissolve away.

Wow, that's one long tongue! Notice how the tongue slowly retracts into the statue. You've got to hurry past those icicles before the tongue retracts all the way into the statue! Move south as quickly as you can, being careful not to slip off the icy trail. Don't stop moving until you reach the floor's southeast corner!

That was close! The icicles reappear when the tongue finishes winding back in, but that's okay because you've already gotten past them. Grab onto the stone block in the southeast corner and pull it southward to get it out of your way. Dash around the block and run north to find a pressure switch tucked away in a narrow alcove. Step onto the switch to extend a footbridge across the west pit.

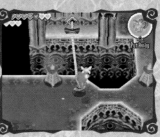

Nice job! Now you can freely move about the area without having to bother with those southern icicles. Cross the footbridge and stand near the burning torch beyond. Whip out the Grappling Hook and aim north at a bright red lever sticking out from a nearby wall. The lever's completely out of reach, but that's no problem for a hero with a Grappling Hook! Use the Grappling Hook to grasp the lever from afar and pull it. This reveals a small treasure chest back near the moveable stone block.

Cross the footbridge and open the chest to claim a **small key**. Excellent! Now you can open the locked northeast door. Do so and then open the small chest in the chamber beyond for a special prize: another glittering **Wisdom Gem**!

Dungeon Chest #5: Small Key

Dungeon Chest #6: Wisdom Gem #13

Small Key
You got a **small key**! Use it to open a door in this dungeon.

Wisdom Gem #13
You got a **Wisdom Gem**! Collect these items and use them to power up the Wisdom Spirit.

Here's another good reason to explore this northeast chamber: a glowing red orb stands here! Step just outside the room and hurl Link's Boomerang through the doorway and into the orb, whacking the crystal to color it blue. This lowers some red blocks to the west and raises the blue ones in the chamber's doorway. You can't reenter the room anymore, but at least you can move forward!

Ominous Tightrope Challenge

Return to the stone statue on the ledge near the floor's center. This time, use the Grappling Hook to stretch a tightrope between the two pegs to the west of the statue. Tap the nearest peg to make Link hop onto it, then start tiptoeing across the rope.

When you reach the midway point, switch to the Boomerang and trace a wide circle around the area, targeting four crystal orbs to the north. Whack the orbs to light all four and melt the icicle patch to the north. Great! Now switch to the Bow and fire an arrow northward into an eye crest on the wall. Thwack! The eye reddens and the icicles you noticed in the floor's southwest chamber quickly melt away.

You're almost out of here! Continue crossing the tightrope to reach the west ledge. Hey, there's another one of those strange blue tiles on the ground near the south wall! Plant a Bomb on the tile to blow a hole through the south wall, granting you fast access back to the floor's southwest stairs.

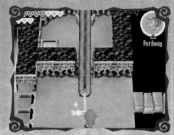

Now comes the fun part! Return to the small chamber near the stairs and then use Link's Grappling Hook to latch onto the tongue statue that the icicles had previously been blocking. Pull the long tongue all the way out until you manage to open a sealed door at the far north end of the floor. Heads up! This tongue slowly winds back into the statue, just like the previous one. The sealed door slams shut when the tongue fully retracts!

Rush to the north end of the room before the tongue retracts and the sealed door closes. Cross the east footbridge and dash north through the hole you blew in the wall near the small chest. From the ledge beyond, ready the Grappling Hook and latch onto a remote northwest peg that was previously surrounded by raised red blocks. The blocks are down now, so sail over to the peg without delay.

Use the Grappling Hook again to reach the ice-covered northwest ledge, and then again to reach the next ledge ahead. Just keep latching onto those wooden pegs as you zip from one bit of floor to the next. Move as quickly as you can until you finally manage to dash through the north door before it closes.

Good hustle! You're now standing right near the Boss Key block, but you've no Boss Key with which to lower it. Guess you've got more dungeon-delving to do! Smash the pots near the Boss Key block for hearts and then run down the nearby stairs to reach the temple's lowest basement floor.

Temple of Ice: B2

This place is huge! Not to worry: This is the final basement floor. Just find that Boss Key!

A sealed door blocks the east passage, so go west from the stairs and wipe out the roving Stag Beetle. A small raised platform is over here, but a patch of icicles prevents you from exploring it. Smash the pots in the corner for hearts and items and then go north, using the Grappling Hook to grab onto a nearby torch and cross the northern pit.

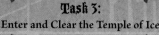

Task 3:
Enter and Clear the Temple of Ice

You can't reach the red Rupee on the narrow northern ledge, so ignore it for the moment. Equip the Bombs and then proceed east into a narrow chamber. Heads up! A wall rises behind Link as he enters the room, and a huge Yook drops in from above to attack! Green Slimes are about as well, so run around to avoid the Yook and eliminate the Slimes first. Then feed the furry monster a Bomb when it starts sucking in air. Clear the room of baddies to melt the northern icicles and reveal a wooden peg.

TIP

Use the bomb flower in the room's southeast corner if your supply of Bombs is running low.

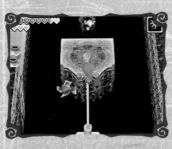

Nice swordsmanship! You're now able to stretch a tightrope between the two pegs to the north. Do so and then carefully tiptoe across the chasm just after the nearby spinning blade trap makes a pass. Balance on the far peg as you toss out Link's Boomerang to beat down a few Ice Keese fluttering about.

Connect another tightrope between the middle peg and the next one to the north, then tiptoe across to reach the far northwest ledge. Hey, there's a stone statue over here! Whack the statue for a clue on what you must do next: **Use the Grappling Hook in a new and creative way**. What's that supposed to mean?

Grappling Hook Antics

A quick search around shows there's no obvious way to cross over to the narrow west ledge. To get there, you must stretch a tightrope between the two pegs on this ledge, then move around to the rope's west side. Walk Link into the rope to make him stretch it back, then release to send him flying westward as if flung from a giant slingshot!

Now *that's* how you cross a pit! Run south and use the Grappling Hook to quickly eliminate the Ice Bubble floating around over here. Smash the collection of pots in the corner for items, then approach the cluster of darkened orbs atop the nearby steps. You know what to do! Stand in the center of the orbs and unleash a spin attack to light them all up at once.

Presto! A huge treasure chest appears on the floor's southwest platform and a sealed door opens near the southern stairs. Place a Bomb against the south wall near the orbs to blast through and reach the narrow ledge with the red Rupee. Dash south to collect the Rupee, then use the Grappling Hook to cross the south pit and return to the floor's southwest corner.

You can't reach the big treasure chest as the southwest platform is still being blocked by icicles. Go east instead, moving past the southern stairs and through the door you've just opened. Explore the odd region beyond, ripping through a couple of Stag Beetles in the area.

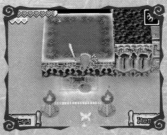

Looks like you're trapped! There's a locked door to the east and a sealed door right nearby, but you're unable to open either one at present. Tricky! To proceed, stretch a tightrope between the two burning torches near the locked door. Use the rope as a rubber band to spring up onto the raised north platform. Neat! Now use the Grappling Hook to move from one platform to the next, using torches as anchors.

Grappling Hook along to the northernmost raised platform and then ready the Bow. An eye crest decorates the north wall! Free an arrow into the eye to redden it and lower the nearby sealed door. Now you can continue exploring northward!

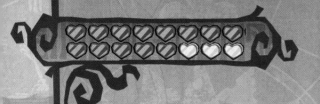

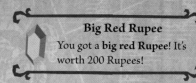

Drop to the ground, smash the nearby pots, and then move north through the door you've just opened. You encounter a strange sight in the northern chamber: Two eye crests stick out from the north wall, but the eyes shut whenever Link faces them. How are you supposed to shoot them? With a bit more Grappling Hook creativity!

Clearing the northeast chamber not only nets you a big red Rupee, it also lowers the nearby sealed door. Now you can explore the floor's southeast corner! There you find a small patch of icicles and a tall plateau covered in wooden pegs. Time for a bit of climbing! Use the Grappling Hook to cross the pit to the west of the plateau, then quickly batter the Ice Bubble that bounces about the narrow southern ledge.

Jump to the narrow center platform and then stretch a tightrope between the two nearby pegs. Stand north of the tightrope and then fire arrows into it. With a bit of careful aiming, you can bounce arrows off the tightrope and into the eye crests while they're open! Redden both eyes to reveal a small treasure chest on the west ledge. Sneaky! Open the chest to claim a **small key**.

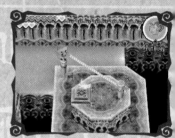

When the ledge is Bubble-free, your next task is to scale the plateau. You can't reach any of the wooden pegs with the Grappling Hook from ground level, so tap the southern ledge's wooden peg to make Link hop onto it. Now you've got enough height to target the plateau's lowest peg! Sail over to the peg, then repeat this process until you reach the top of the rise. Step on the pressure switch you find on top to dissolve the nearby icicle patch and open a new way forward!

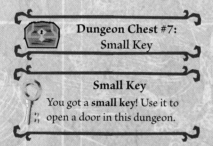

Acquiring the Boss Key

With small key in hand, backtrack south, stepping on a pressure switch to extend a footbridge leading back toward the locked east door. Tap the door to open it, equip Link's Bombs and then enter the chamber beyond. Look out. Link becomes trapped inside this room, and must battle a burly Yook and two Ice Keese to reclaim his freedom! Keep a distance and eliminate these threats with Bombs and fancy swordplay to reveal a chest in the room's center. Inside you find a **big red Rupee**. Very nice!

You're almost finished! Drop off the north end of the plateau and then walk down the passage that the icicles were blocking. The walkway is icy and narrow, so watch your step! You eventually reach a small alcove that sports a few pots, a pressure switch, and a Stag Beetle. Use the Grappling Hook to help you splatter the bug, and then step onto the pressure switch to melt the icicles near the chest platform to the west.

Super job! Return to the floor's southwest corner and open up that big ol' treasure chest to claim the **Boss Key** at last. Your path is now clear: Carry the key upstairs and then use it to sink the Boss Key block you noticed before. Smash the many pots in the small room beyond for hearts and items, and tap the stone tablet to reveal the blue warp light. When you're ready to face the final showdown, proceed up the nearby stairs.

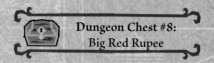

Dungeon Chest #9:
Boss Key

Boss Key
You've found the **Boss Key**!
It's a huge, heavy key.

Gleeok, Two-Headed Dragon

Threat Meter

Speed: Immobile

Attack Power: 1 heart (fireball); 1 1/2 heart (snowball); 1 heart (bite); 1 heart (tidal wave)

Defense Power: Grappling Hook to weaken; multiple hits to defeat!

Link hears the sound of rushing water as he enters the temple's final chamber. Without warning, a massive two-headed dragon emerges from the flowing river ahead! Twin roars echo through the frigid cavern and the epic struggle begins.

At the start of the fight, Gleeok's two heads simply take turns attacking. They always shake for a moment just before spitting out a dangerous projectile: Fireballs come from the red head (left), while Snowballs fly out from the blue one (right). Being struck by either projectile deals a full heart's worth of damage to Link, so keep well away from them!

TIP

Gleeok's fireballs and snowballs don't track Link, so simply move to one side to avoid them.

CAUTION

Link becomes frozen by the blue head's snowballs and suffers and additional half a heart's worth of damage when he's forced to break free. Keep away from those balls!

...continued

Four sturdy pegs stand about the ledge. These pegs are the young hero's keys to survival! Gleeok is too huge and remote to harm directly at first, so you've got to get creative. Keep near the sealed south door and wait for one of the heads to start wiggling, indicating that it's about to attack. Quickly ready the Grappling Hook and stretch a tightrope between two of the pegs to defend yourself from Gleeok's projectile attacks!

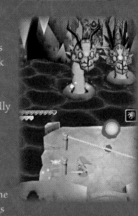

Your tightrope bounces Gleeok's fireballs and snowballs back toward the monster. Work at striking the red head with snowballs and the blue head with fireballs! You must carefully angle the tightrope in order to bounce the balls back properly. Stretch it between the **upper right and lower left** pegs to reflect Gleeok's snowballs back at the red head, and between the **upper left and lower right** pegs to bounce fireballs back at the blue head.

NOTE

Striking a head with its own projectile has no effect on the monster.

Gleeok quickly becomes wise to your tricks and doesn't let you keep a tightrope stretched for long. Shortly after you string up a rope, one of the heads moves forward to bite it apart. There's nothing you can do against this, so simply keep Link near the south wall to avoid being bitten.

TIP

Try to stretch your tightropes just as one of the heads begins to wiggle. This gives you the best chance at reflecting the attack back at the opposite head!

...continued

Gleeok also loses patience from time to time and decides to send a huge wave of freezing water crashing toward you. Both heads sink beneath the surface just prior to this tidal wave attack. The moment you see Gleeok dive, quickly tap one of the two rear pegs to make Link hop onto it. The water rushes past harmlessly, but don't get too comfortable: you still need to dodge any chunks of ice that come floating your way!

 TIP

Wait for the ice chunks to draw near, then hop off the peg and wade to one side to avoid them. (You can also attack and destroy ice chunks with the sword.)

Reflect three fireballs into the blue head and three snowballs into the red head to smash apart both of Gleeok's masks. The battle changes once both dragon heads have been revealed: Gleeok rushes forward and quickly bites off the two northern pegs! Afterward, the dragon takes turns inhaling deeply with one of its heads and then expelling a wide cone of fire or frost at you. Run to avoid this attack if you can!

Gleeok's breath attacks are brutal, so its best not to let him power them up. Each time one of the heads lowers and starts sucking in air, notice that its tongue sticks out a bit. How convenient! Use the Grappling Hook to anchor the tongue to the nearest peg and drag the head to the ground.

...continued

Wham! Gleeok's head comes crashing down onto the cold, hard ground. Immediately rush forward and unleash a series of lightning-fast sword strikes while the head's down. Take that, monster!

Keep avoiding Gleeok's tidal wave attack as you yank its heads to the ground in turns. Punish both heads with numerous blows until Gleeok has had enough. The day is yours!

Dusted Dragon

Having no answer for Link's incredible Grappling Hook ingenuity, Gleeok finally falls under the young hero's blade. The dragon's twin heads explode into thick clouds of pure sand, which then fly directly into Link's hourglass. Two more minutes' of worth of sand have been added to the magical timepiece!

Task 4:
Return & Speak with the Chief

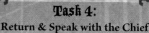

Magnificent effort! You've braved this frigid temple's traps, solved its tricky puzzles, and beaten an incredibly powerful fiend. Your reward materializes in the center of the chamber: a giant treasure chest that holds another **Heart Container**! Collect this precious gift, then cross the walkway that appears and proceed up the north stairs beyond.

Dungeon Chest #10: Heart Container #11

Heart Container #11

You got a **Heart Container**! Your heart meter has been increased by one heart!

Link enters a small chamber filled with soft light. There's the pure metal, just sitting on the tall pedestal ahead! Grab the **Azurine** from its resting place to obtain the Anouki tribe's pure metal at last. Fantastic work!

Azurine

You got the **Azurine**! It's the second pure metal you need to make the Phantom Sword!

Task 4: Return & Speak with the Chief

The True Aroo

Stepping outside, Link is buffeted by the Great Ice Field's bitter winds. He's greeted by an Anouki, who stands right nearby. It's Aroo! The coated creature thanks Link for sniffing out his imitator, and says he finally managed to escape the temple. The Yook had been holding him hostage inside, but they abandoned their posts when Link stormed the structure. What luck!

Returning to the Island Chief's house, Link finds the head of the Anouki tribe in high spirits. The chief is happy to hear of Link's success in the Temple of Ice and wishes the boy luck in his quest. The Azurine is yours!

You've done everything you need to do around here, but there's lots of extra activities to do as well! Check the Missing Links section for complete details on all the optional tasks you can do now that you've found the Grappling Hook. When you're ready to move on with the main story, your next stop is Mercay Island for another return trip into the Temple of the Ocean King!

Missing Links

Now that you have the Grappling Hook, a vast array of optional tasks has opened up to you. There's so many goodies to find at this point, it's tough to know where to begin! Since you're already hanging out at the Isle of Frost, let's start right here. Loads of neat discoveries await you on this tiny isle!

Looting the Great Ice Field

You don't have to go far to find fortune on the Isle of Frost! After exiting the temple, hop onto the peg near Aroo and then toss the Grappling Hook at another nearby peg that stands atop the tall west ledge. Hop onto that peg so you may reach the next one above, and continue zipping upward until you reach the highest plateau.

...continued

Run south until you come to another peg. This one's a marker: Stop here and toss your Grappling Hook east across the gap to latch it onto a distant peg to reach the east edge of the island. Head south from there to find a small chest sitting on a side ledge. You'll come back to this one in a moment! Leave it for now.

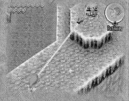

Continue south until you spy another small chest sitting atop a slightly taller plateau. To get the goods, you must hop onto the peg to the south, then latch onto the elevated chest with the Grappling Hook to fly over to it. Nice one! Pop the chest's lid to pad your wallet with a **big green Rupee**!

Overworld Chest #29:
Big Green Rupee

Big Green Rupee
You got a **big green Rupee**! It's worth 100 Rupees!

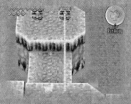

Drop off the plateau and use the nearby peg to reach the higher one to the west. Run to the next peg and hop onto it, then toss Link's Grappling Hook north to grab hold of one of two nearby treasure chests. Score! Open both chests to claim a **red Rupee** from each, then Grappling Hook the peg to return to the main pathway.

Overworld Chest #30:
Red Rupee

Overworld Chest #31:
Red Rupee

...continued

Red Rupee
You got a **red Rupee**! It's worth 20 Rupees!

Red Rupee
You got a **red Rupee**! It's worth 20 Rupees!

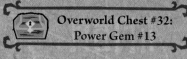

You haven't forgotten about that chest on the side ledge, have you? Backtrack there and drop down to the side ledge to reach the chest. Flip the chest's lid to claim a shimmering **Power Gem**!

Overworld Chest #32:
Power Gem #13

Power Gem #13
You got a **Power Gem**! Collect these items and use them to power up the Power Spirit.

Raiding the Estates

You've finished pillaging the Great Ice Field. Now let's raid the Anoukis half of the island! Pass through the central cavern to return to Anouki territory, then dash north to reach the Anouki Estates. Use your newfound Grappling Hook to explore the two tiny islets to the west. Latch onto the southwest isle's peg and then dig at the center patch of snow to unearth a long lost **treasure map** (or take the bridge from the estates to the islet with the treasure map)!

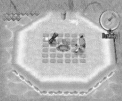

Treasure Map #17
You got a **treasure map**! It reveals the location of a sunken treasure on the Great Sea.

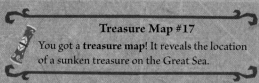

Next, Grappling Hook the northwest isle's peg to sail over there. Hey, look: a stone statue! Smack the statue to learn that the Old Wayfarer has **buried** something valuable just outside his hut at Bannan Island. Interesting! You'll have to pay the Wayfarer a visit sometime soon.

Tasks
Complete!

...continued

You're not done yet! Use the Grappling Hook to visit the tiny isle that lies just southeast of the estates. Again, dig in the center patch of snow to uncover a vast amount of wealth in the form of a big gold Rupee. Nice!

Big Gold Rupee

You got a **big gold Rupee**! It's worth 300 Rupees!

One More Chest

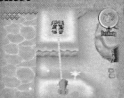

There's just one last thing for you to collect from this chilly island. Travel south to return to the main Anouki village, then spy a small treasure chest on a high ledge at the west end of town. You can finally reach this chest now that you've got the Grappling Hook! Climb the steps to the south to reach a neighboring ledge, then toss the Grappling Hook north. Zip over to the treasure chest and pop its lid to claim a glimmering **Wisdom Gem**!

Overworld Chest #33: Wisdom Gem #14

Wisdom Gem #14

You got a **Wisdom Gem**! Collect these items and use them to power up the Wisdom Spirit.

Thanks from Aroo

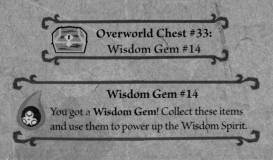

Aroo isn't shy about expressing thanks to Link for saving him from those awful Yook. He soon mails his savior a letter containing lots of kind words, along with a very special present: another shiny Wisdom Gem! See? It pays to help people out!

Wisdom Gem #15

You got a **Wisdom Gem**! Collect these items and use them to power up the Wisdom Spirit.

Quick Trip to Harrow

Now that you've finished the Temple of Ice, head back to Harrow Island! Remember those two treasure maps? Go pick those up now! Simply pay the stone statue the 50 Rupee cover charge, then hop into the sandpit and start digging away. Keep trying until your Shovel manages to uncover two new maps!

NOTE

You can claim a total of four maps from Harrow Island, but only two of them are obtainable right now. The other two become available for discovery only after you have the fourth and final sea chart from the Temple of the Ocean King.

Treasure Map #18

You got a **treasure map**! It reveals the location of a sunken treasure on the Great Sea.

Treasure Map #19

You got a **treasure map**! It reveals the location of a sunken treasure on the Great Sea.

Chest at Goron Island

Your next destination is Goron Island. With the aid of the Grappling Hook, you can now reach that treasure chest sitting atop one of the Goron homes! To get there, visit the young Goron who had been frightened by the Yellow ChuChus on the central ridge before. While standing near the Goron, aim southwest with the Grappling Hook and then latch onto a large rock on the neighboring ledge.

Whee! Link zips over to the rock. You're now standing atop the Goron home. Walk south a few paces to locate that previously out-of-reach treasure chest and kick it open to claim a valuable prize: a shimmering **Courage Gem**!

Overworld Chest #34: Courage Gem #12

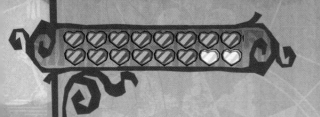

CAUTION

Hitting a wall head-on is the worst thing that can happen, as Gongoron bounces backward and must clear his head for a moment before he can continue the race. If you see a collision on the horizon, try to hit the wall at an angle so that Gongoron sideswipes off it instead.

Make a sharp turn when you reach the island's northwest corner and then rush south down another long straight, smashing through three more gems. As you near the far wall, make a sharp U-turn and aim to roll into the nearby pair of speed arrows that face northward. This sends you zipping through two more gems; aim to roll into the next pair of arrows ahead, which face southward. This causes you to quickly change directions and speed south, crashing through another two gems. Keep rolling south down the steps beyond.

Make a tight turn at the foot of the steps and start rolling westward. Smash through one gem and keep going west until you reach the edge of the island. Don't hit that wall! Make a sharp turn and roll south, breaking two more gems as you dash for the trio of speed arrows at the island's southwest corner. Roll right into the arrows to start flying eastward, smashing apart four more gems as you bomb down the long straight that follows.

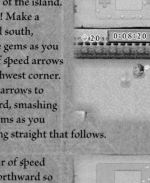

Roll past the pair of speed arrows that face northward so you can shatter the lone gem at the island's far southeast corner. Quickly double back to the speed arrows after breaking the gem and then use the arrows to sprint northward, crashing straight through another two gems. Roll right up the steps beyond, making a sharp right turn to avoid the wall at the top. Cross another pair of speed arrows that face eastward to zip through another gem.

Courage Gem #12

You got a **Courage Gem!** Collect these items and use them to power up the Courage Spirit.

Goron Game

You've only one stop left to make here in the southeast quadrant: Dee Ess Island, where the Goron Game is finally open for business! Speak with the large Goron at the island's lower pit to learn the rules: For just **50 Rupees**, you can participate in an exciting race that takes you all about the island! You get to play as Gongoron and must roll along the race course as fast as you can. As you roll, you must also shatter 30 gems to open the final path to the finish! How fast can you get there?

The Goron operator says the current record time is 35 seconds and hints that you'll get something nice if you can do better. Let's give it a try! Pay the 50 Rupees to start the game. You begin at the far north end of the island and must roll all around the isle as Gongoron, smashing through every gem you see along the way. Start rolling westward as fast as you can, breaking the first three gems on the initial straightaway.

NOTE

The gems are all shown on your map screen. Use this to help pinpoint their locations.

While speeding down the initial straight, try rolling across the speed arrows on the ground. These give you a short burst of velocity, helping to improve your overall time. Try to roll across each speed arrow you see, but be careful not to go so fast that you lose control!

Tasks
Complete!

...continued

The final series of gems are all clustered together and they each move about. Roll around and smash them all as quickly as possible. Break this last group of gems to lower the nearby gate, which allows you to reach the final leg of the course! Hurry through the gate to reach the island's northern pit.

The final stretch is nothing but short straights and tight corners that twirl inward, leading toward the center of the pit. Use the speed arrows to make good time through the straights and be sure you don't hit the walls when rounding the corners that follow. Keep circling around until you finally reach the finish!

It will most likely take you a few tries to set the new record, so don't give up! A familiarity with the course layout certainly helps and you'll see improvement each time you race. Finish with less than 35 seconds on the clock to win a fabulous prize: another **Bombchu Bag**! You're now at maximum Bombchu capacity!

Bombchu Bag #2

You got another **Bombchu Bag**! Now you can carry 10 more Bombchus, for a new maximum of 30. You couldn't possibly carry more!

You don't have to be a racing ace to come out on top at the Goron Game. There's a wide spread of consolation prizes to be won as well! Here's what you might win based on your finish time:

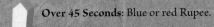

Over 45 Seconds: Blue or red Rupee.

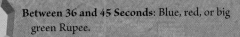

Between 36 and 45 Seconds: Blue, red, or big green Rupee.

...continued

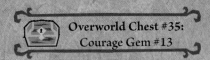

35 Seconds: You have a chance of either a random ship part, a random treasure, or a big red Rupee after winning the Bombchu Bag.

Under 35 Seconds: Bombchu Bag #2 (first win); random ship part (each consecutive win).

Random

Isle of Ember: Courage Gem #13

Remember that treasure chest you noticed sitting on the tiny isle at the Isle of Ember's northern tip? You're finally able to reach it! Use the Grappling Hook to latch onto the chest and sail over to it. Open the chest to claim another sparkly **Courage Gem**! Pocket the goods and then latch onto the east torch to return to the mainland.

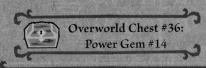

Overworld Chest #35: Courage Gem #13

Courage Gem #13

You got a **Courage Gem**! Collect these items and use them to power up the Courage Spirit.

More Stuff at Molida

Three important items await discovery at Molida Island! First, enter the central cavern near Romanos's house. Leap across the row of tall square pillars that stretches eastward across the water, stop on the last pillar, and then hurl the Grappling Hook eastward to latch onto the small treasure chest on a remote ledge. Pop the chest's lid for a sparkly **Power Gem**!

Overworld Chest #36: Power Gem #14

Power Gem #14

You got a **Power Gem**! Collect these items and use them to power up the Power Spirit.

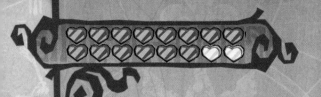

After claiming the Power Gem, drop from the ledge and loop through the cavern, climbing the northwest stairs to reach a grassy outdoor meadow. Sprint eastward and then south, arriving at the ledge that overlooks Romanos's house. From here, hurl the Grappling Hook eastward, grabbing onto a barrel that sits on a tiny isle to the east. Smash the barrel against the nearby stone tablet to release a Cucco, then pick up the Cucco and leap eastward off the ledge, using the Cucco to glide over to the tiny eastern isle. Continue using the Cucco to traverse the isles, stopping at one that features a large tree. Whip out the Shovel and dig in front of that tree to find a long-forgotten **treasure map**!

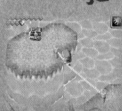

Treasure Map #20

 You got a **treasure map**! It reveals the location of a sunken treasure on the Great Sea.

That's not all there is to find here! Go to the island's northern tip using the Old Wayfarer's secret underground passage as you did once before. Go all the way to the Temple of Courage and then stretch a tightrope between the two pegs to the west of the structure. Tiptoe across the rope to reach a tiny isle, where a treasure chest awaits. Pop that box open to claim another lovely **Courage Gem**!

Overworld Chest #37: Courage Gem #14

Courage Gem #14

You got a **Courage Gem**! Collect these items and use them to power up the Courage Spirit.

Spirit Island: Power Gem #15

Another prize awaits you at Spirit Island! Although you can't power up any of your spirit fairies at present, you can finally explore the eastern half of the isle. Grappling Hook the small peg to get over there, then carefully move north. A hoard of Octoroks fires at you from the north: Use Link's shield to block their rocks and the Grappling Hook to dispatch the monsters from range.

Cross the northern ledges to reach the far east side of the isle. Beware: A Like Like roams about over here! And it's not alone. A new breed of enemy hides close nearby. Can you see it? It's disguised as a nearby **green Rupee**! This monster is called a Rupee Like, and it just loves snacking on Link's Rupees! Combat Rupee Likes just as you do normal Like Likes: Throw Bombs at them from afar when they start to inhale, then finish them off with cold steel!

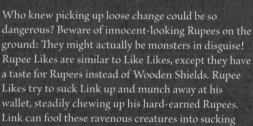

Rupee Like

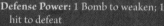
Threat Meter

Speed: Slow

Attack Power: 1/2 heart (devour); Rupees lost over time

Defense Power: 1 Bomb to weaken; 1 hit to defeat

Who knew picking up loose change could be so dangerous? Beware of innocent-looking Rupees on the ground: They might actually be monsters in disguise! Rupee Likes are similar to Like Likes, except they have a taste for Rupees instead of Wooden Shields. Rupee Likes try to suck Link up and munch away at his wallet, steadily chewing up his hard-earned Rupees. Link can fool these ravenous creatures into sucking down Bombs—a great way to upset their stomachs and make them vulnerable to his blade!

Battling past these villainous creatures earns you a great reward. Fight your way to the chest on the highest platform to add another **Power Gem** to your collection. Nice work!

Prima Official Game Guide

1

2

3

4

Tasks
Complete!

...continued

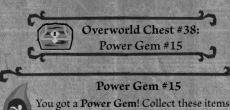

Overworld Chest #38:
Power Gem #15

Power Gem #15

You got a **Power Gem**! Collect these items and use them to power up the Power Spirit.

Back at Bannan

Warp to the northwest quadrant and set a course for Bannan Island. More treasure awaits discovery! Begin your search by Grappling Hooking over to the chest on the tiny southern isle near the pier. Flip the chest's lid to claim yet another gleaming **Power Gem!**

Overworld Chest #39:
Power Gem #16

Power Gem #16

You got a **Power Gem**! Collect these items and use them to power up the Power Spirit.

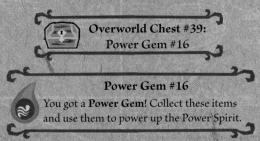

Head for the Old Wayfarer's hut next. Pop in and say hello if you like, then recall what the stone statue told you back at the Isle of Frost: The Wayfarer has buried something valuable near his hut! Dig in front of the wooden sign right near hut to uncover a hidden **treasure map!**

Treasure Map #21

You got a **treasure map**! It reveals the location of a sunken treasure on the Great Sea.

More cool stuff is waiting to be claimed on the island's east side. Head through the central cavern as if you were going to visit Salvatore and his Cannon Game. Armed with the Grappling Hook, you're now able to reach the little isles to the north! Run a tightrope between the two pegs near Salvatore to reach the first isle, where two chests sit on some sand. Open both chests to claim a big green Rupee from one and a glistening **Courage Gem** from the other!

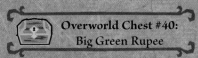

Overworld Chest #40:
Big Green Rupee

...continued

Overworld Chest #41:
Courage Gem #15

Big Green Rupee

You got a **big green Rupee**! It's worth 100 Rupees!

Courage Gem #2

You got a **Courage Gem**! Collect these items and use them to power up the Courage Spirit.

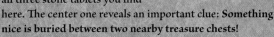

But wait, there's more! Stretch another tightrope between the two pegs to the north. This time, use the rope as a slingshot to catapult Link to the neighboring isle to the west. Nice! Now read all three stone tablets you find here. The center one reveals an important clue: **Something nice is buried between two nearby treasure chests!**

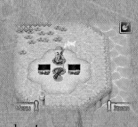

Why, you've just seen a pair of treasure chests! Zip back across the water and return to them. Dig at the sand right between the two chests to unearth another one of the Wayfarer's buried **treasure maps**. That guy hides stuff everywhere!

Treasure Map #22

You got a **treasure map**! It reveals the location of a sunken treasure on the Great Sea.

Last Stop: Uncharted Island

Avast! Only one more treasure awaits your discovery for the time being. Drop anchor at the Uncharted Island and enter the central cavern. Pay a visit to the Golden Chief if you like; it's been a while! Afterward, use the Grappling Hook to run a tightrope between two wooden pegs near the cavern's entrance. Tiptoe across to reach a tiny ledge and open the chest you find there for one more **Courage Gem**. Your collection is growing so fast!

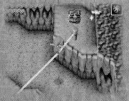

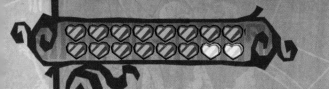

...continued

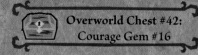

Overworld Chest #42: Courage Gem #16

Courage Gem #16

You got a **Courage Gem**! Collect these items and use them to power up the Courage Spirit.

Sunken Treasures 17–19, 21 & 22

Though you've found six new maps since your last salvage outing, you're only able to haul up five sunken treasures at this time. Why, you ask? There's no way to reach the treasure that map #20 points to—it lies in the as-yet inaccessible waters to the east of Bannan Island! You must approach sunken treasure #20 from the Great Sea's northeast quadrant, which you can't do until you've found the fourth and final sea chart. Not to worry: We'll remind you about it when the time comes!

...continued

	Contents	Bonus Rupees	Location
	Sunken Treasure Chests		
17	Ship Part	Green (9)	NWQ; NE of Isle of Gust
18	Ship Part	Green (5); Blue (1); Red (1)	SEQ; NW of Goron Island
19	Ship Part	Green (5); Red (1)	SEQ; West of Goron Island
21	Ship Part	Green (5); Blue (1); Red (1)	SWQ; NW of Molida Island
22	Ship Part	Green (21)	SEQ; South of Harrow Island

Tasks
Complete!

Contents

New Horizons: Overview

Having thoroughly explored the entirety of the southeast quadrant of the sea, Link and friends still find themselves lacking one of the pure metals they need to reforge the mighty Phantom Sword. With no place else to turn, the group decides another rummage through the Temple of the Ocean King is in order. There's one last sea chart inside that dreary place, and it's high time they found it!

A Link to the Present

Max 21:00   Max 50   Max 30   Max 30

Lvl 1   Lvl 1 Lvl 1   x16   x16   x15

x22

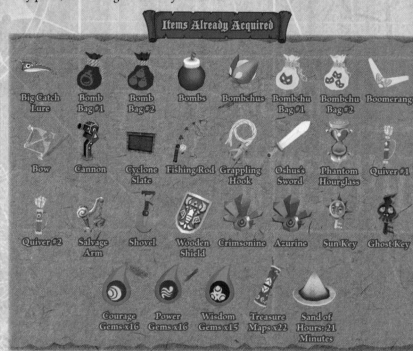

Items Already Acquired

Big Catch Lure	Bomb Bag #1	Bomb Bag #2	Bombs	Bombchus	Bombchu Bag #1	Bombchu Bag #2	Boomerang
Bow	Cannon	Cyclone Slate	Fishing Rod	Grappling Hook	Oshus's Sword	Phantom Hourglass	Quiver #1
Quiver #2	Salvage Arm	Shovel	Wooden Shield	Crimsonine	Azurine	Sun Key	Ghost Key
Courage Gems x16	Power Gems x16	Wisdom Gems x15	Treasure Maps x22	Sand of Hours: 21 Minutes			

Task 1: Obtain the Final Sea Chart

Back for More

Ready to make another sweep through the Temple of the Ocean King? This time you've got to reach the lowest floors in your search for the fourth and final sea chart. Armed with Bombchus and the Grappling Hook, you're now able to claim goodies from many of the floors you've already visited. We'll guide you in getting each valuable prize as you descend to the temple's lowest depths.

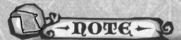

> **NOTE**
>
> Not interested in treasure hunting? Use the yellow light in the temple's entry hall to warp directly to the Sacred Crest chamber, skipping past the first six basement floors. This removes the same amount of time from the Phantom Hourglass as it took you to reach the Sacred Crest chamber on your last trip through the Temple of the Ocean King.

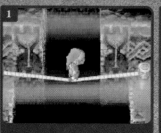

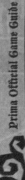

Temple of the Ocean King: Fifth Visit

Temple of the Ocean King: B1

to Basement 2

to Entrance

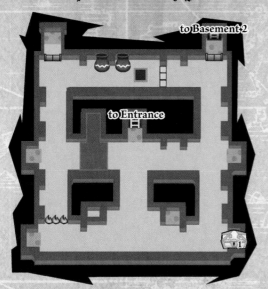

Temple of the Ocean King: B2

to Basement 1

to Basement 3

Temple of the Ocean King: B3

to Checkpoint Chamber

to Checkpoint Chamber

to Basement 2

Temple of the Ocean King: Checkpoint Chamber

to Basement 4

to Basement 3

to Basement 3

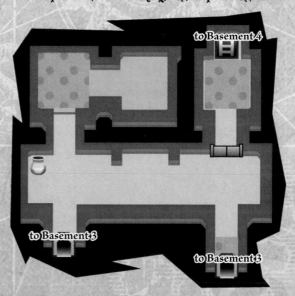

Legend

 Dungeon Chest #1: Courage Gem #17
 Dungeon Chest #2: Wisdom Gem #16
 Dungeon Chest #3: Force Gem
 Dungeon Chest #4: Force Gem
 Dungeon Chest #5: Force Gem

 Dungeon Chest #6: Treasure Map #23
 Dungeon Chest #7: Red Potion
 Dungeon Chest #8: Power Gem #17
 Dungeon Chest #9: Round Crystal
 Dungeon Chest #10: Triangle Crystal

 Dungeon Chest #11: Ship Part
 Dungeon Chest #12: Big Green Rupee
 Dungeon Chest #13: Big Green Rupee
 Dungeon Chest #14: Big Green Rupee
 Dungeon Chest #15: Force Gem

 Dungeon Chest #16: Ship Part
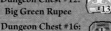 Dungeon Chest #17: Force Gem
 Dungeon Chest #18: Sea Chart #4

Bomb Wall   Orb   Floor Switch   Lever   Red Jar   Yellow Jar

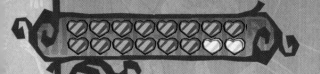

Temple of the Ocean King: Sacred Crest Chamber

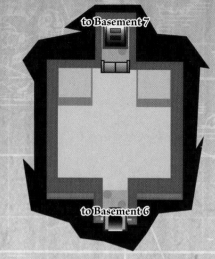

to Basement 7

to Basement 6

Temple of the Ocean King: B4

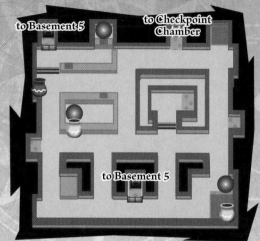

to Basement 5

to Checkpoint Chamber

to Basement 5

Temple of the Ocean King: B5

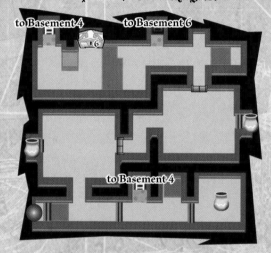

to Basement 4

to Basement 6

to Basement 4

Temple of the Ocean King: B7

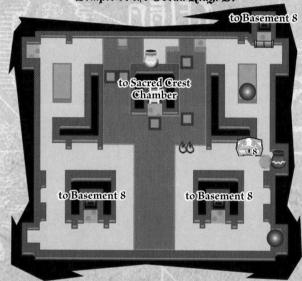

to Basement 8

to Sacred Crest Chamber

to Basement 8

to Basement 8

Temple of the Ocean King: B6

to Basement 5

to Sacred Crest Chamber

Temple of the Ocean King: B8

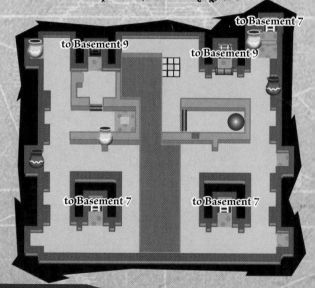

to Basement 7

to Basement 9

to Basement 9

to Basement 7

to Basement 7

Task 1:
Obtain the Final Sea Chart

Temple of the Ocean King: B9

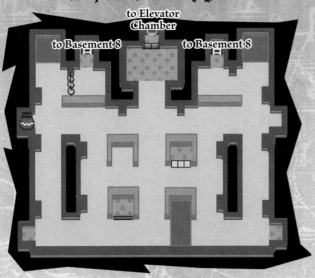

Temple of the Ocean King: B11

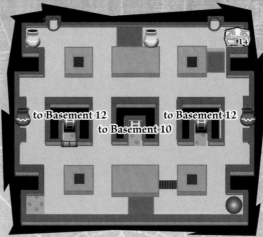

Temple of the Ocean King: Elevator Chamber

Temple of the Ocean King: B12

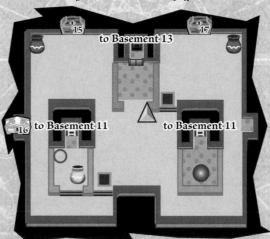

Temple of the Ocean King: B10

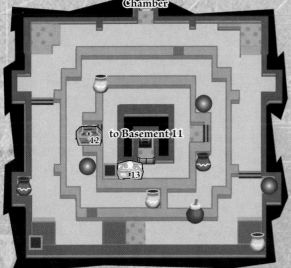

Temple of the Ocean King: B13

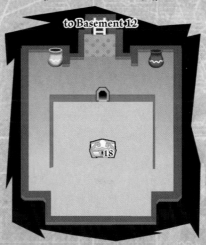

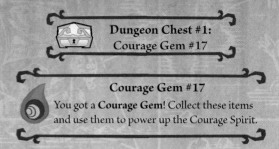
Courage Gem #17

You got a **Courage Gem**! Collect these items and use them to power up the Courage Spirit.

Items to Obtain

Big Green Rupees x3

Courage Gem #17

Force Gems x6

Power Gem #17

Red Potion

Round Crystal

Sea Chart #4

Random Ship Part

Small Keys x4

Square Crystal

Treasure Map #23

Triangle Crystal

Wisdom Gem #16

Dungeon Denizens

Enemies

Phantom

Phantom Eye

Wizzrobe

Temple of the Ocean King: B2

Proceed through the second basement floor as normal, bombing open the south wall to gain fast access to the small key chamber. Then use the nearby orb to swap the colored blocks and quickly reach the central locked door. Don't head downstairs just yet, though. Instead, dash east and bomb your way through the north wall to reach the northeast safe zone.

Smash the yellow pot at the safe zone for a 30-second time bonus, then ready a Bombchu. Send the critter through the tiny hole in the north wall and then into a darkened crystal orb in the chamber beyond.

⟶ TIP ⟵

Wait for the spike pin in the chamber to roll westward before releasing the Bombchu.

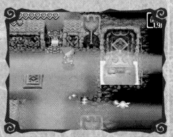

Ka-pow! The Bombchu lights the orb and a huge treasure chest appears at the far east safe zone. Cross the central corridor and sprint to the chest. Open it to add another **Wisdom Gem** to your stash!

Temple of the Ocean King: B1

It doesn't take long to claim your first prize! Upon reaching the temple's first basement floor, go west from the entry safe zone and use the Grappling Hook to run a tightrope between two wooden pegs near a pit. Hop onto the peg and cross the rope, firing an arrow northward at the halfway point to strike an eye crest on the wall.

Poof! A large treasure chest appears in the floor's southeast corner. Dash to that safe zone and open the chest for a sparkly **Courage Gem**! Afterward, proceed through the floor as normal, blasting the bomb blocks up north to help speed things along.

Dungeon Chest #2:
Wisdom Gem #16

Wisdom Gem #16

You got a **Wisdom Gem**! Collect these items and use them to power up the Wisdom Spirit.

1 2 3 4

Task 1:
Obtain the Final Sea Chart

Temple of the Ocean King: B3

On this floor, there's no need to go hunting after those Force Gems anymore. Now that you have the Grappling Hook, you can take a massive shortcut and quickly reach the Checkpoint Chamber! When no Phantoms are about, simply proceed to the pair of torches along the north wall at the northwest corner of the floor. Run a tightrope between the torches and then use it like a slingshot to bound up onto the high northwest ledge. Now simply dash through the doorway to reach the Checkpoint Chamber and continue on to the next basement floor!

→TIP←

Nab the small key from the patrolling Phantom before taking this shortcut. You can use it to help you breeze through a lower floor!

Temple of the Ocean King: B4 & B5

Begin the fourth basement floor just as you did last time: Move east from the entry safe zone and then fire an arrow into the eye crest at the floor's northwest corner. This disables all gust jars on the floor! Now return to the entry safe zone and start sending Bombchus out to destroy all Phantom Eyes within range.

Next, send Bombchus through the small holes in the north and south walls. Blast the crystal orb in the southern chamber to lower the spikes near the **small key**. Bombchu the orb in the northern chamber to drop the northwest spikes. Collect the small key, then use it to open the northwest door and descend the stairs beyond.

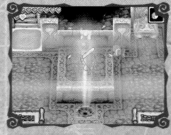

Terrific! You've finally made it to the fifth basement floor's northwest corner. Now you can finally get to that huge treasure chest! Shovel up the loose soil to uncover a gust geyser, then fly up to the ledge above. Smack the orb up there to shut off the gust jar to the east. Now Drop down and open the chest in safety! Claim another valuable **treasure map**.

→TIP←

After opening the chest, reactivate the gust jar and use it to sail across the east pit. This shortcut lets you skip most of the fifth basement floor! Before heading downstairs, remember to whack the northeast orb to reveal that Red Potion treasure chest.

Dungeon Chest #4:
Treasure Map #23

Treasure Map #23
You got a **treasure map**! It reveals the location of a sunken treasure on the Great Sea.

Temple of the Ocean King: B6

There's little new to see and do on this floor. Make your way to the big red door and trace the sacred crest on it as you did before—the same triangular crest Zauz showed you. The door opens wide, allowing you to proceed to the next basement floor.

Temple of the Ocean King: B7–B9

No need to go circling around this floor just to get to its eastern side: Your Grappling Hook provides a fantastic shortcut. From the entry safe zone, step onto the moving platform that draws near and ride up to the floor's northern end. Instead of stepping off

to the west, throw the Grappling Hook eastward and latch onto the nearby treasure chest. Perfect! You've zipped over to the **round crystal** chest at the floor's east side.

→TIP←

If you acquired the small key from the Phantom at B3 before taking the Grappling Hook shortcut, you can use it to open B7's locked northeast door and quickly reach B8 via the staircase beyond. This little shortcut puts you near a yellow pot with some bonus time!

Ignore the round crystal for the time being and hop onto the nearby wooden peg. Toss the Grappling Hook southeast from this vantage, striking a crystal orb on a tall nearby platform to light it. Presto! A giant treasure chest appears to the south.

The chest disappears after a few moments, so you've got to be quick! Wait to activate the orb until the patrolling Phantom is in the south, then light it and sprint over to the chest. Pop the chest's lid to claim another wondrous **Power Gem**!

Dungeon Chest #8:
Power Gem #17

Power Gem #17
 You got a **Power Gem**! Collect these items and use them to power up the Power Spirit.

Return for the round crystal and then carry it south while you make for the southeast stairs. Go down to the eighth basement floor and then ready a Bombchu. Send the Bombchu rolling north, through small hole in a nearby wall and into a crystal orb in the chamber beyond. Blammo! The orb lights up and the sealed northeast door opens. Carry the round crystal north as you make for the northeast stairs.

The ninth basement floor is very much as it was before. Dispatch those sneaky Wizzrobes before they chop away at your hourglass sand and bounce an arrow into the southeast eye crest to reach to a pressure switch that controls a trapdoor. Dunk the patrolling Phantom to claim his **square crystal**, and then place the crystal into the northwest pedestal to lower the nearby flames. Now you can retrieve the **triangle crystal** from the chest near the northwest stairs!

TIP

Don't miss the chest at the southwest safe zone! Like the Red Potion chest on B5, this one always reappears each time you visit the Ocean King's temple.

Bring all three shaped crystals to the large northern safe zone, one at a time. Remember the secret to activating the Elevator Chamber? You must place the crystals in this order:

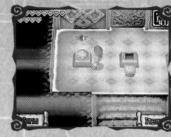

Place the **square crystal** on the central platform.

Place the **round crystal** on the west platform.

Place the **triangle crystal** on the east platform.

The sealed north door then opens to the Elevator Chamber. Step through and hang out for a moment as the elevator takes you down. When the room stops rumbling, exit the Elevator Chamber through the same door to find yourself standing at the temple's tenth basement floor!

NOTE

You'll probably want a good ten minutes' worth of sand in the hourglass at this point. If you have significantly less, consider returning to the surface and blazing through those first nine basement floors again.

Temple of the Ocean King: B10

At last! You've finally reached a new basement floor of the temple. A look at your map shows the area to be a giant mazelike chamber. Two gold Phantoms patrol the outermost halls and three Phantom Eyes float about the inner corridors. Start sending Bombchus southward from the entry safe zone, rolling them through the small hole in the nearby wall and into the two nearest Phantom Eyes to destroy them both. Blast the crystal near the east Phantom Eye as well to light it and lower some spikes to the west.

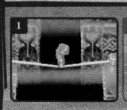

Task 1:
Obtain the Final Sea Chart

CAUTION

Gold Phantoms are the most dangerous type. Although they move quite slowly, every gold Phantom on the floor warps right next to Link whenever he's detected. Don't stray from safe zones when gold Phantoms are about!

Dash east when the Phantoms aren't about, using the Grappling Hook to cross some nearby pegs and reach the elevated northeast safe zone. Hey, there's a huge boulder up here! Wait until the nearby Phantom starts lumbering down the east corridor, then tap the boulder to roll it down the steps and into the Phantom. Crash! The monster is defeated and the boulder rolls off into a pit.

Now cross to the chamber's northwest side to find another giant boulder. Roll this one as well to smoosh the Phantom in the west corridor. The Phantom drops a **small key**! Hurry southward and collect the key, then smash a nearby red pot to create a tiny puddle of safe zone.

NOTE

When both Phantoms are defeated, a small treasure chest appears near the middle of the maze. You'll get to it soon enough!

Small Key
You got a **small key**! Use it to open a door in this dungeon.

Breaching the Maze

While standing on the safe zone puddle, send a Bombchu rolling through a hole in a nearby wall. Roll the Bombchu directly northward through the hole and into a crystal orb beyond. Boom! The orb lights up, lowering some spikes near a safe zone to the east.

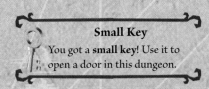

Next, sprint east and use the Grappling Hook to cross a pit, landing at the floor's southern safe zone. Examine the wall just east of the safe zone and notice that one spot looks a bit funny. It's a false wall! Plant a Bomb there to blast a hole right through to the central corridors at last.

TIP

Use the Grappling Hook or Boomerang to snag a 15-second time bonus from the yellow pot in the floor's southeast corner.

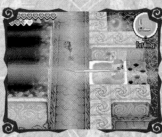

Run through the opening you've just created and duck into the nearest safe zone. You're now within range of the final lingering Phantom Eye. Stun it with the Boomerang and then finish it off with Link's blade. When all Phantom Eyes are defeated, a giant treasure chest pops into view—but it's out of reach, sitting atop a high wall near the southern stairs! You'll have to find some way to get up there.

Circle around the maze's innermost corridor and step on the far pressure plate to lower some spikes that block the way to a nearby safe zone. Move to the safe zone to finally reach the chest you revealed after defeating the gold Phantoms! Open the chest to become one **big green Rupee** richer.

Dungeon Chest #12:
Big Green Rupee

Big Green Rupee
You got a **big green Rupee**! It's worth 100 Rupees!

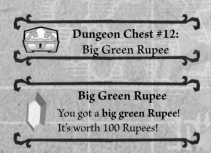

TIP

Low on Bombchus? Use the Boomerang and Link's sword to poke out those Phantom Eyes instead!

TIP

Want to make up for lost time? Dig up a nearby gust geyser and then float to the top of the maze's walls. Spy a yellow pot atop a neighboring wall and smash it with the Grappling Hook or Boomerang for some extra time! Drop down afterward and run south, smashing a yellow pot at the south end of the maze for yet another time bonus.

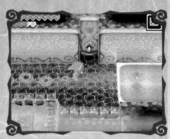

When the Phantom Eyes are no more, avoid the patrolling gold Phantoms as you travel to the floor's northeast corner. Pull the lever on the north wall to extend a footbridge between the two tall ledges close by. This will soon come in handy! Next, skip to the nearby safe zone, which sports the large chest the Phantom Eyes left behind for you. Open the chest to obtain another **big green Rupee**!

Now let's get that giant chest. Work your way out of the maze once more and move to the floor's southern safe zone. Hop onto the peg there and then toss the Grappling Hook northward to latch onto the huge treasure chest! Zip over to the chest and open it for yet another **big green Rupee**. After opening the chest, drop to the ground and unlock the nearby door so you may continue exploring downstairs.

TIP

Don't miss breaking the nearby yellow pot! It contains a 15-second time bonus.

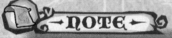

Dungeon Chest #13:
Big Green Rupee

Dungeon Chest #14:
Big Green Rupee

Big Green Rupee
You got a **big green Rupee**!
It's worth 100 Rupees!

Big Green Rupee
You got a **big green Rupee**!
It's worth 100 Rupees!

NOTE

How's your time, hero? You're doing great if you've got more than eight minutes left!

Cross over to the floor's west side next, moving to yank the lever in the northwest corner. This extends yet another footbridge between two tall nearby ledges, which you'll soon find helpful.

Temple of the Ocean King: B11

Your tactics at the start down here are similar to the floor above: Remain on the entry safe zone and use Bombchus to decimate the surrounding Phantom Eyes. Obliterate all four Phantom Eyes on the floor to cause a large treasure chest to appear at the floor's northeast corner!

Return to the northeast corner and dig up a gust geyser from beneath a mound of loose dirt. Quickly ride up to the ledge above. These are the elevated platforms you've been linking with walkways! Use the walkways to navigate the platforms and step on two pressure switches up here.

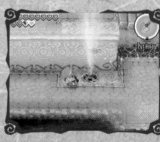

1

2
3

4

Task 1:
Obtain the Final Sea Chart

Now return to the floor's central safe zone. You have two more pressure switches to activate on the tall platforms to the south. From the central safe zone, send a Bombchu rolling to the southeast corner of the floor, right into contact with a darkened orb. As the Bombchu rolls off to light the crystal, dash south from the safe zone and locate a patch of soft earth near the middle raised platform. Dig there to uncork a hidden gust geyser!

Soar upward to reach the high platform. By now, your Bombchu should have lighted the orb, extending a walkway to the neighboring southwest platform. That walkway won't stay there for long, so dash across without delay! Step on the pressure switch you find there, then cross back over and step on a fourth pressure switch atop the tall southeast platform.

After all four pressure switches have been activated, the sealed door blocking the western staircase lowers. You're all finished here; hurry down to the next floor!

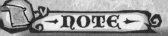

→NOTE←

Got more than five minutes left on the clock? If so, you should have no trouble reaching that sea chart!

Temple of the Ocean King: B12

The twelfth floor is a bit different from the last two. You begin trapped in a southwest chamber. Smash the pots for items and 30 seconds of extra time, then pull the nearby lever to lower the southern spikes. Return to the entry safe zone and send a Bombchu rolling past the disabled trap and around to blow away a Phantom Eye lurking in the nearby hall.

Now that the area is free of sentries, bolt for the floor's northwest corner and snatch up a red pot. Carry the pot east and smash it on the ground halfway between the northwest safe zone and the other large safe zone nearby to make another puddle of safe zone.

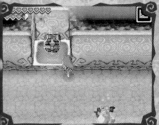

Now, move to the northeast safe zone and open the small chest you find there to obtain a **Force Gem**.

Dungeon Chest #15: Force Gem

Force Gem

You got a **Force Gem**! Use this item to open a door within this temple.

Snatching up this Force Gem causes a Phantom to appear right nearby. This guy's a bit lazy: He just turns in place, looking all around. Wait until he's looking the other way, then quickly carry the Force Gem to the puddle of safe zone you recently made on the floor. Use the puddle as a midway point between here and the large central safe zone to the east.

When no Phantoms are looking, step off the puddle and dash east toward the large central safe zone. Tap one of the three pedestals you find there to place the Force Gem onto it. The pedestal shines brightly and then retracts into the floor. Two more Force Gems must be found!

CAUTION

Placing the first two Force Gems triggers the appearance of two frightening Wizzrobes! These invisible villains appear on your map as scary skull icons. Track the Wizzrobes' movements and quickly defeat each one with well-timed spin attacks when they appear to strike!

The next Force Gem is close by: The patrolling gold Phantom is carrying it! Don't go after the Phantom until you've lured the Wizzrobe toward you and defeated it. Then look to sneak up behind the Phantom and shoot an arrow into its back while it's not looking. Whack! The Phantom falls to its knees and the Force Gem drops to the ground. Grab it quick and hurry back to place it on a pedestal before the Phantom snaps to.

CAUTION

The darker parts of the floor cause Link's footsteps to create lots of sound. Walk when crossing dark sections to quiet Link's footfalls.

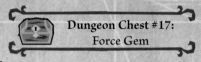
Force Gem

You got a **Force Gem**! Use this item to open a door within this temple.

Placing the second Force Gem on a pedestal triggers the appearance of another Wizzrobe. Eliminate this second and final pest to reveal a hidden treasure chest at the floor's western safe zone! Avoid detection as you venture over to open the chest and claiming a **ship part** from within!

Dungeon Chest #17: Force Gem

Force Gem

You got a **Force Gem**! Use this item to open a door within this temple.

Once again, a Phantom materializes out of thin air after you pop the chest's lid. This one's more active and begins patrolling the area. Wait until he's not looking and then sprint to your safe zone puddle. Run to the eastern safe zone when it's safe to do so, then

carry the Force Gem back around to the large central safe zone.

Dungeon Chest #16: Ship Part

Ship Part

Random

You got a **ship part**! Visit the Shipyard to install it onto Linebeck's ship.

The final Force Gem sits inside a chest at the floor's northeast safe zone. A strip of spikes blocks your way, so you must take the long way around. Send a Bombchu to destroy the roving Phantom Eye to the southeast before making your move. Again, find a red pot in the corner and smash it on the ground between the northeast safe zone and the one about halfway down the floor's eastern wall. Then open the chest at the northeast safe zone to claim the final Force Gem!

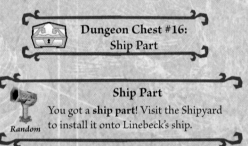

After all three Force Gems have been set onto the pedestals, the large north door opens. Hurry through to reach the final floor!

Temple of the Ocean King: B13

You've made it! This is the thirteenth and final floor of the temple. But beware: The temple's curse is in full effect down here, and time drains from the Phantom Hourglass as you move about! Hurry to the ornate chest at the chamber's center and open it to claim the item you seek: the final **sea chart**!

Dungeon Chest #18: Sea Chart #4

Sea Chart #4

You got the final **sea chart**! This one reveals the northeast quadrant of the Great Sea.

You're all done here! Nabbing the final chart causes a familiar pool of blue light to appear in the chamber's northwest corner. Step into the light to flash back to the Temple's entrance with your prize. Fantastic job! Your next stop is high adventure at the northeast quadrant of the sea.

Missing Links

While traveling to the sea's northeast quadrant, take a moment to make a few special stops. A few easy goodies are within your reach!

Harrow Island: Treasure Maps #24 & #25

Warp to the sea's southeast quadrant and set a course for Harrow Island. Now that you've obtained the final sea chart, you can dig up two new **treasure maps** from the island's sandpit! Pay the 50-Rupee cover charge to dig in the sandpit, then start searching. Keep digging until you come up with those two maps!

Treasure Map #24

You got a **treasure map**! It reveals the location of a sunken treasure on the Great Sea.

Treasure Map #25

You got a **treasure map**! It reveals the location of a sunken treasure on the Great Sea.

Sunken Treasure #23

The treasure map you found on your last trip through the Temple of the Ocean King points to a sunken prize just northwest of the Isle of Frost. Sail there and then plunge your salvage arm into the briny depths for a chance at nabbing a few Rupees—and another minute's worth of sand for the Phantom Hourglass!

Task 2: Explore the Northeast Quadrant

Getting Your Bearings

A whole new section of the sea awaits your discovery now, but first you've got to get there. Warp to the southeast quadrant and then sail northward until you reach the northeastern seas.

First thing's first: new threats await you in these eastern waters! Gyorgs rule the sea up here, and these fast, sharklike predators are tough to handle with your ship's cannon. Try to blast them from the waters if you can, but if that fails, be quick to jump to avoid their attacks!

Gyorg

Threat Meter

Speed: Fast

Attack Power: 1 heart (contact)

Defense Power: 1 hit to defeat

When the fins of these large, sharklike creatures suddenly peek up from the surface, you know you're in trouble! Gyorgs are some of the most dangerous enemies prowling the northeastern sea. They hunt in packs, often speeding past their quarry and then suddenly rounding to attack by means of a head-on collision! Blasting these fast-moving predators with the cannon is difficult—it's usually easier just to wait for a Gyorg to make its attack run, then jump of harm's way before impact!

All attempts at visiting the nearest island prove fruitless: The isle is surrounded by tall rocks, and the only passage through is blocked by a massive cyclone. How rude! Well, there's only one other land mass on the chart. Best set sail for the northeastern island and see what you can find!

Missing Links

Before you rush off to that northeast island, there are a few very profitable ventures you may want to take up. There's more going on in the northeast quadrant than meets the eye!

Last Golden Frog

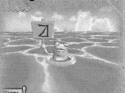

The sixth (and final) golden frog splashes about near the quadrant's southeastern boulders. Blast this golden froggy with the cannon to learn the Cyclone Slate symbol you must trace to warp back to this section of the sea. Now you can quickly return here anytime!

Traveler's Ship

A Traveler's Ship sails about this quadrant's waters, too. Set a course and board the ship to find its cabin filled with monsters! Several Octoroks, a Zora Warrior, and a variety of ChuChus await punishment aboard this vessel. Run about and defeat these fiends, making good use of Link's Grappling Hook and Boomerang to help even the odds.

Safe from the monsters, the ship's captain decides to come out from hiding. The strange man introduces himself as the Man of Smiles and thanks Link for saving him. After you initial chat, speak to him a second time for a reward: Ask to receive something mysterious and you'll be awarded with two great prizes: a treasure map and a very strange item called the Hero's New Clothes!

...continued

Man of Smiles

A peculiar man leading a peculiar life, the Man of Smiles searches the northeastern waters of the sea for high adventure aboard his little Traveler's Ship. Unfortunately, however, adventure ends up finding *him*: A gang of monsters seizes control of his vessel! After being rescued from the beasts by Link, the Man of Smiles becomes forever grateful to the lad. He rewards Link with a special item that starts the boy on a path to unlocking a powerful new ability!

Hero's New Clothes
You got the **Hero's New Clothes**! They're... so light....

Treasure Map #26
You got a **treasure map**! It reveals the location of a sunken treasure on the Great Sea.

Quest for the Great Spin Attack

You've now discovered four separate Traveler's Ships sailing about each quadrant of the sea. After you've visited all four ships, you can complete a short and highly rewarding side quest that leads you all across the ocean! Begin by rescuing the Man of Smiles from the monsters aboard his Traveler's Ship in the northeast quadrant. This nets you the **Hero's New Clothes**, which the Man of Smiles gives to Link as thanks for his rescue. Bring the Hero's New Clothes to the captain of the Traveler's Ship at the northwest quadrant, who fancies himself a **hero**. The self-proclaimed hero is eager to trade you a **Telescope** in exchange for the Hero's New Clothes!

Telescope
You got a **Telescope**! Now you can see at a great distance. No, wait... it's just a Kaleidoscope! Too bad....

Say, wasn't one of those Ho Hos missing something? Warp to the southeast quadrant and plot an intercept course with the Traveler's Ship there. Show the "Telescope" to one of the Ho Hos on board, who quickly notices his name written on the back! The Ho Ho is thrilled to see his old Telescope again and quickly hands Link a reward: a **Guard Notebook** he found during his travels!

 1
 2
 3
 4

Task 2:
Explore the Northeast Quadrant

...continued

Guard Notebook

You got the **Guard Notebook**! Someone lost this dirty leather notebook.

Remember the strange-looking fellow you met aboard the first Traveler's Ship you visited? He mentioned something about a missing notebook! Warp to the southwest quadrant and visit the Traveler's Ship there to finally return the lost Guard Notebook to the ship's captain, Nyave. The man is overjoyed but has little to offer in return. He simply gives Link a sample of some fine adventuring rations: a yummy **Wood Heart**!

Wood Heart

You got a **Wood Heart**! It looks tasty.

You've just done a lot of wayfaring, so why not pay a brief visit to the Old Wayfarer at Bannan Island and see what he thinks? Unfortunately, the Wayfarer isn't around: The mermaid, Joanne, says he left to explore the sea aboard his ship! Warp to the southeast quadrant and notice that two Traveler's Ships are now cruising about. Dock with the Traveler's Ship that sails near the quadrant's northwest waters to catch up with the Old Wayfarer at last.

It looks like the Wayfarer doesn't keep his boat any neater than his hut! No matter. Speak with the man to learn that he's sailing the seas in search of delicious treats for his lovely mermaid, Joanne. Say, perhaps she'd like to try the Wood Heart you got from Nyave? The Old Wayfarer gladly accepts the gift you offer and extends Link his heartfelt thanks. He also hints that he's got something good for Link back at his hut!

A fantastic prize now awaits you at Bannan Island! Warp back to the northwest quadrant and set a course for the isle, but watch out: You are ambushed by a giant sea monster just as you near the dock! This is the exact same type of creature that attacked you long ago when you first tried docking at Molida Island. Keep sailing in a semicircular pattern in front of the monster, firing cannonballs into its large eyeball until you finally sink it. Pull up to the harbor after the beast has fallen.

...continued

The Old Wayfarer is as good as his word. Return to his hut to find him there, waiting alongside Joanne. Open the giant treasure chest the Old Wayfarer has pulled out for you to receive a fantastic reward: the fabled **Swordsman's Scroll**!

Overworld Chest #43: Swordsman's Scroll

Swordsman's Scroll

You got the **Swordsman's Scroll**! Memories of veteran swordsmen flow through it.

Great work! With the Swordsman's Scroll in your possession, you now know how to perform the great spin attack! Simply execute three regular spin attacks as fast as you can to make Link bust into a great spin that's truly something to behold! While spinning like a tornado, you can move Link about to obliterate anything in his path. Take some time to practice on the island's local wildlife!

→ NOTE →

Though incredibly powerful, the great spin attack is also quite dizzying. Link becomes momentarily stunned after performing a great spin, so be careful when you use it!

Prizes from Smiles

You wouldn't have that great spin attack if it wasn't for the Man of Smiles! Why not pay him a visit and thank him? You'll have to wipe out the monsters on his ship again, so be prepared for a fight! After the Man of Smiles appears to thank you, speak with him a second time to receive a cool reward: the **Prize Postcard**!

Prize Postcard

You got the **Prize Postcard**! It has a stamp on it, so put it in a mailbox.

...continued

So what to do with this exciting new gift? It's a postcard, so you've got to mail it! Visit any island and tap its mailbox to mail out the Prize Postcard. Now you'll periodically receive special prizes in the mail, like treasures and ship parts! Cool, huh?

Maze Island

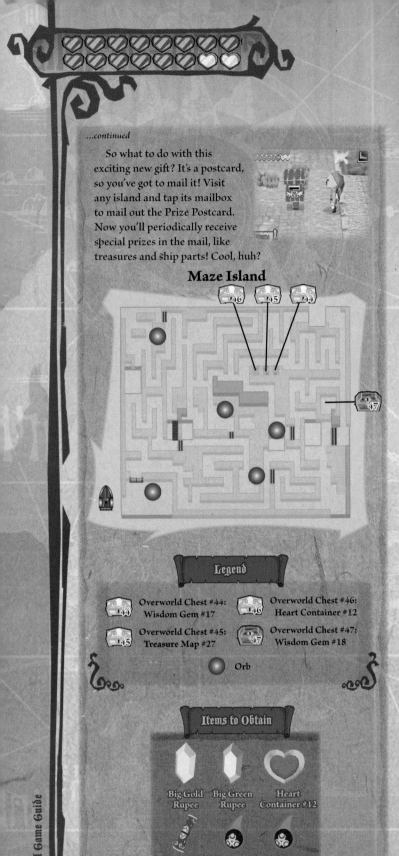

Legend

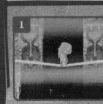

Overworld Chest #44: Wisdom Gem #17

Overworld Chest #46: Heart Container #12

Overworld Chest #45: Treasure Map #27

Overworld Chest #47: Wisdom Gem #18

● Orb

Items to Obtain

Big Gold Rupee · Big Green Rupee · Heart Container #12

Treasure Map #17 · Wisdom Gem #17 · Wisdom Gem #18

Your sea chart shows just two islands within the bounds of the northeast quadrant, but there are actually three. Sail the quadrant's northern waters to discover a tiny island that's not shown on your sea chart! Ciela scribbles in the isle, allowing you to dock there.

Holy cow, this entire island's just one big maze! Smack the stone statue near the pier to learn that you've landed on Maze Island, home of the great Treasure Maze challenge! The rules are simple: pay 20 Rupees to brave the maze and whack a number of stone statues with Link's sword. Smack each statue before time expires to reveal a giant treasure chest near the middle of the maze! Get to that chest before time runs out to claim a very special prize.

The Treasure Maze features three challenge levels: Fantastic prizes can be won at Beginner, Normal, and Expert difficulty! Simply pay the Rupee cover charge to cause a crystal orb to appear nearby. Whack the orb to reveal the locations of each of the stone statues you must seek out within the maze! The entry door then slides away, granting you access to the labyrinth. Hurry inside and smack those statues before time expires!

→TIP←

Take a moment to mark the stone statues on your map or you'll never remember where they stand!

Treasure Maze: Beginner

Your first trip into the maze is the easiest: You only need to whack four statues with Link's sword to reveal the prize chest. Scribble down the statue locations and then dash into the maze.

The maze can be approached in many different ways. Here's what worked best for us on Beginner:

Turn right from the start and dash east along the maze's southernmost corridor. A strip of spikes blocks easy access to the southeast statue, so you must take the long way around. Circle around the passage until you reach the southeast statue, whacking it with Link's sword the moment you get there (or use a bomb if you're in a hurry).

Prima Official Game Guide

260

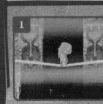   

Task 2: Explore the Northeast Quadrant

Treasure Maps

#	Location	First Chance to Get	Item(s) Required	Notes	Leads To	Got It?
29	Isle of the Dead	After Temple of the Ocean King 5	None	Go through underground passage to reach chest atop "king's eye" ledge.	Sunken Treasure #29: Ship Part	❏
30	Temple of the Ocean King: B10	During Temple of the Ocean King 6	Hammer	Use Hammer on SW-most pressure switch to reveal chest.	Sunken Treasure #30: Ship Part	❏
31	Temple of the Ocean King: B12	During Temple of the Ocean King 6	Hammer	Strike orb at B12 then use Hammer to escape confinement & reach chest.	Sunken Treasure #31: Big Gold Rupee	❏

Sunken Treasure Chests

#	Contents	Bonus Rupees	Location	First Chance to Get	Item(s) Required	Got It?
1	Ship Part	Green (9)	SWQ: SW of Molida Island	After Temple of the Ocean King 3	Salvage Arm; Treasure Map #1	❏
2	Sand of Hours (1 Minute)	Green (12); Red (1); Big Green (1)	SWQ: NE of Mercay Island	After Temple of the Ocean King 3	Salvage Arm; Treasure Map #2	❏
3	Ship Part	Green (12); Big Green (1)	NWQ: SW of Isle of Gust	After Temple of the Ocean King 3	Salvage Arm; Treasure Map #3	❏
4	Sand of Hours (1 Minute)	Green (9)	NWQ: SE of Bannan Isle	After Temple of the Ocean King 5	Salvage Arm; Treasure Map #4	❏
5	Ship Part	Green (5); Red (1); Big Green (1)	SWQ: N of Molida Island	After Temple of the Ocean King 3	Salvage Arm; Treasure Map #5	❏
6	Treasure	Green (12); Big Green (1)	NWQ: W of Bannan Island	After Temple of the Ocean King 3	Salvage Arm; Treasure Map #6	❏
7	Ship Part	Green (5); Red (1)	NWQ: E of Isle of Gust	After Temple of the Ocean King 3	Salvage Arm; Treasure Map #7	❏
8	Ship Part	Green (21)	SWQ: SE of Mercay Island	After Temple of the Ocean King 3	Salvage Arm; Treasure Map #8	❏
9	Sand of Hours (1 Minute)	Green (5); Red (1)	SWQ: W of Cannon Island	After Temple of the Ocean King 3	Salvage Arm; Treasure Map #9	❏
10	Ship Part	Green (5); Blue (1); Red (1)	NWQ: SE of Isle of Gust	After Temple of Courage	Salvage Arm; Treasure Map #10	❏
11	Sand of Hours (1 Minute)	Green (21)	NWQ: N of Isle of Gust	After Temple of the Ocean King 4	Salvage Arm; Treasure Map #11	❏
12	Ship Part	Green (5); Blue (1); Red (1)	SEQ: N of Dee Ess Island	After Temple of the Ocean King 4	Salvage Arm; Treasure Map #12	❏
13	Ship Part	Green (9)	SEQ: E of Harrow Island	After Temple of the Ocean King 4	Salvage Arm; Treasure Map #13	❏
14	Ship Part	Green (8); Big Green (1)	SEQ: NE of Goron Island	After Goron Temple	Salvage Arm; Treasure Map #14	❏
15	Ship Part	Green (5); Red (1)	SEQ: S of Isle of Frost	After Goron Temple	Salvage Arm; Treasure Map #15	❏
16	Ship Part	Green (9)	SWQ: S of Cannon Island	After Goron Temple	Salvage Arm; Treasure Map #16	❏
17	Ship Part	Green (9)	NWQ: NE of Isle of Gust	After Temple of Ice	Salvage Arm; Treasure Map #17	❏
18	Ship Part	Green (5); Blue (1); Red (1)	SEQ: NW of Goron Island	After Temple of Ice	Salvage Arm; Treasure Map #18	❏
19	Ship Part	Green (5); Red (1)	SEQ: W of Goron Island	After Temple of Ice	Salvage Arm; Treasure Map #19	❏
20	Ship Part	Green (21)	NWQ: E of Bannan Isle	After Temple of the Ocean King 5	Salvage Arm; Treasure Map #20	❏
21	Ship Part	Green (5); Blue (1); Red (1)	SWQ: NW of Molida Island	After Temple of Ice	Salvage Arm; Treasure Map #21	❏
22	Ship Part	Green (21)	SEQ: S of Harrow Island	After Temple of Ice	Salvage Arm; Treasure Map #22	❏
23	Sand of Hours (1 Minute)	Green (9)	SEQ: NW of Isle of Frost	After Temple of the Ocean King 5	Salvage Arm; Treasure Map #23	❏
24	Ship Part	Green (5); Red (1)	NEQ: W of Isle of Ruins	After Temple of the Ocean King 5	Salvage Arm; Treasure Map #24	❏
25	Ship Part	Green (9)	NEQ: E of Isle of the Dead	After Temple of the Ocean King 5	Salvage Arm; Treasure Map #25	❏
26	Ship Part	Green (5); Blue (1); Red (1)	NEQ: W of Isle of Ruins	After Temple of the Ocean King 5	Salvage Arm; Treasure Map #26	❏
27	Ship Part	Green (21)	NEQ: E of Maze Island	After Temple of the Ocean King 5	Salvage Arm; Treasure Map #27	❏

Sunken Treasure Chests

#	Contents	Bonus Rupees	Location	First Chance to Get	Item(s) Required	Got It?
28	Treasure	Green (5); Blue (1); Red (1)	NEQ: NW of Isle of Ruins	After Temple of the Ocean King 5	Salvage Arm; Treasure Map #28	❑
29	Ship Part	Green (12); Big Green (1)	NEQ: W of Maze Island	After Temple of the Ocean King 5	Salvage Arm; Treasure Map #29	❑
30	Ship Part	Green (5); Red (1)	NEQ: S of Isle of Ruins	After Mutoh's Temple	Salvage Arm; Treasure Map #30	❑
31	Big Gold Rupee	Green (9)	NEQ: S of Isle of the Dead	After Mutoh's Temple	Salvage Arm; Treasure Map #31	❑

Treasures

Who doesn't love finding **treasure**? No self-respecting adventurer, that's for sure! Discover these little baubles all over the place and sell them to the Treasure Teller at Mercay Island for fast cash. Or, stash the goods inside Freedle's Magic Boxes to share them with friends over Tag Mode!

Treasures

Treasure	Name	Description	Value	Got It?
	Pink Coral	Coral, polished to a shine. It's an object to be admired!	varies	❑
	Pearl Necklace	Pure white pearls, strung together into a stunning necklace.	varies	❑
	Dark Pearl Loop	Rare dark pearls, strung into a jaw-dropping necklace.	varies	❑
	Zora Scale	It is said that a Zora dropped this rare and sparkling scale!	varies	❑
	Goron Amber	This tasty Goron treat is valuable because it contains a bug!	varies	❑
	Ruto Crown	Some say this regal crown was once worn by a Princess of Zora.	varies	❑
	Helmaroc Plume	This flamboyant feather was dropped by a Helmaroc bird.	varies	❑
	Regal Ring	A princely ring handed down among royal generations.	1,500 Rupees (Treasure Teller)	❑

> **NOTE**
>
> The HoHos do not always buy Regal Rings. Sometimes they will want other items and will always pay more than the Treasure Teller.